THE END OF NOWHERE

The End of Nowhere

American Policy Toward Laos
Since 1954

by Charles A. Stevenson

Beacon Press   *Boston*

Copyright © 1972, 1973 by Charles A. Stevenson
Library of Congress catalog card number: 70–179156
International Standard Book Number: 0–8070–0252–6 (casebound)
0–8070–0253–4 (paperback)
First published as a Beacon Paperback in 1973
Beacon Press books are published under the auspices
of the Unitarian Universalist Association
Published simultaneously in Canada by Saunders of Toronto, Ltd.
Printed in the United States of America

9 8 7 6 5 4 3 2 1

Map of Laos by Leo Durling

To My Parents

This is the end of nowhere. We can do anything we want here because Washington doesn't seem to know it exists.

An American official,
Vientiane, Laos, November 1960

LAOS

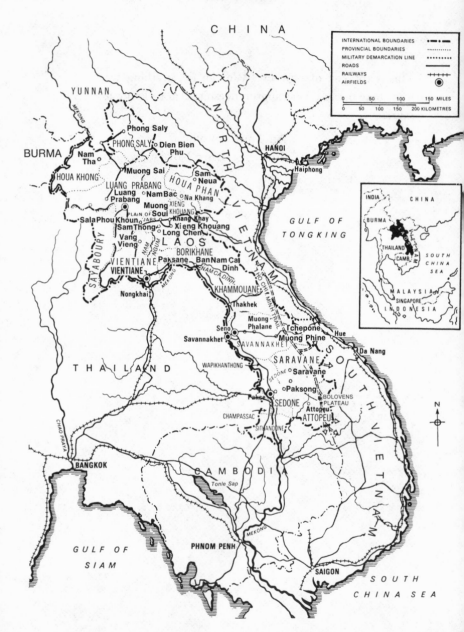

CHINA

YUNNAN

BURMA

Phong Saly

PHONG SALY Dien Bien Phu

Nam Tha

HOUA KHONG Muong Sai

Sam Neua

LUANG PRABANG HOUA PHAN

Luang Prabang NamBac Na Khang

Muong Soui XIENG KHOUANG

Sala Phou Khoun PLAIN OF JARS Khang Khay

SamThong Xieng Khouang

Vang Vieng Long Chen

LAOS

BORIKHANE

Paksane Ban Nam Cai Dinh

VIENTIANE

VIENTIANE NAM CA DINH

Nongkhai KHAMMOUANE

Thakhek

Muong Phalane Tchepone

Seno Muong Phine Hue

Savannakhet SAVANNAKHET

Da Nang

WAPIKHANTHONG SARAVANE

SEDONE Saravane

Paksong

Pakse BOLOVENS PLATEAU

SEDONE Attopeu

CHAMPASSAC ATTOPEU

SITHANDONE

THAILAND

NORTH VIETNAM

SOUTH VIETNAM

GULF OF TONGKING

MELONG

NAM NGUM

HO CHI MINH TRAIL

SEDONE

CHAO PRAYA

BANGKOK

CAMBODIA

Tonle Sap

MEKONG

GULF OF SIAM

PHNOM PENH

SAIGON

SOUTH CHINA SEA

INTERNATIONAL BOUNDARIES
PROVINCIAL BOUNDARIES
MILITARY DEMARCATION LINE
ROADS
RAILWAYS
AIRFIELDS

0 50 100 150 MILES
0 50 100 150 200 KILOMETRES

INDIA CHINA

BURMA

THAILAND SOUTH CHINA SEA

CAMB.

MALAYSIA

SINGAPORE INDONESIA

N

Contents

Acknowledgments

This is a case study of the evolution of American policy toward Laos since 1954. As such, it draws upon the literature of decision-making and the tradition of testing general propositions in specific circumstances. My intellectual debt to Richard Neustadt and to Graham Allison is more than I can express, and probably more than I realize.

Originally a doctoral dissertation for the Government Department of Harvard University, the manuscript has been revised and brought up to date by additional interviews and research. For the opportunity to complete this book while simultaneously maintaining a more than full-time job, I am deeply grateful to Senator Harold Hughes and his staff.

Since most of the details of policy-making are still classified or otherwise closed to scholars, I have had to rely on the public record—in newspapers, memoirs, and congressional hearings—supplemented by interviews with eighty-six participants in policy-making with regard to Laos. Some of the officials interviewed served in Washington, others in Laos; some were at the highest levels of government, others in carefully delineated bureaucratic slots. People from all relevant agencies were interviewed: White House staff; State Department; Pentagon civilians and military officers; Central Intelligence Agency; foreign aid personnel; and the Congress. Many were quite candid. Some, whether candid or not, were reluctant to have all or even part of their remarks attributed by name. They have been cited as Confidential Sources.

Interviews were conducted primarily during the first half of 1969 and the spring of 1971. Part of the cost of travel to New York and Washington was financed by grants from the Harvard Government Department. Interviews were conducted following a rough list of questions on which the subject was expected to have knowledge. At first, no notes were taken during the interviews. But, for greater accuracy and more detail in both questions and answers, extensive notes were taken in most of the interviews. Each subject was provided with a chronology similar to that in the Appendix, which was useful in triggering memories and, on some occasions, in provoking responses. Several officials were kind enough to be interviewed more than once. Obviously, and regrettably, more interviews would have provided more material and possibly answers to my remaining questions.

I am grateful to the many people who saw this manuscript at various stages of its preparation and made important and useful suggestions for trying to improve it. These people include my advisor, Professor Richard Neustadt, Dean Don K. Price, Assistant Professors Samuel Williamson, Doris Kearns, Graham Allison, and John Steinbruner. I am also indebted to Dick Allison and Lee Sigal for penetrating questions and detailed suggestions. For subjecting my ideas to friendly criticism, I want to thank the members of the "Roundtable"—especially Tom Karas, Paul Halpern, and Marty Wishnatsky. Several former officials not only granted interviews but later reviewed the manuscript for accuracy in what they said or knew. These men were Winthrop Brown, William Bundy, Averell Harriman, and J. G. Parsons. Insofar as I have not accepted all of the suggestions made by these various people for corrections or improvements, I stand responsible for the remaining statements and judgments.

Charles A. Stevenson

Washington, D.C.

June 27, 1971

THE END OF NOWHERE

Putting Laos in perspective

Laos was not all that goddamned important.
—CHESTER COOPER, *NSC Staff Member, 1961–67*[1]

Warfare is scarring Laos and killing its people. Hundreds of villages have been destroyed. Perhaps one-fourth of the people have been driven from their homes in over a decade of active conflict. The daily roster of death is as much for this small country as 1,000 per day for the United States.* As part of its contribution to the war, the United States has dropped over a million and a half tons of bombs—nearly three-fourths the total dropped by U.S. planes in World War II and over twice that dropped on North Vietnam. And yet the war goes on.

If the Laotians had their way, the war would probably have ended long ago. But instead of letting a quiet civil war resolve itself, soldiers or agents of at least six nations contributed directly to the conflict. Laos has been the blood-spattered chessboard, and its people the pawns, for the grand strategists in Washington, Peking, Hanoi, Saigon, and Bangkok.

We know little of the thinking and plotting in other capitals, so these pages will concentrate on the picture as seen from Washington and Vientiane. Sometimes Americans initiated actions, sometimes they acted in response to the actions of

---

* These figures are only for the dead on the side of the Royal Laotian Government which since 1968 has averaged about 10 per day. Estimates of deaths in Pathet Lao areas have been at least twice as high. If accurate, these figures mean that the people of Laos have for at least four years suffered combat fatalities at a rate which for the United States would be over 3,000 each day.[2]

1

others. The purpose of this book is not to judge who started what, but rather to explain what U.S. policy makers thought, said, and did.

In fact, the United States has only sketchy knowledge of the "other side" in Laos. Reporters and others who have talked to people in or from Pathet Lao areas say that those people live in caves, in fear and anger over U.S. bombing. They grudgingly pay taxes and perform forced labor for their rulers. Many resent the presence of the North Vietnamese.[3]

About American involvement in Laos, we know much more, despite the efforts to conceal the whole story from the U.S. public. The basic fact is that Americans control most of what happens in areas allegiant to the Vientiane government. The United States provides essential advice, coordination, and supplies for the war. Outside of a few cities, Americans or their agents perform most of the functions of the central government. U.S. funds support the economy and the government.

Costs of this involvement have been high, especially when compared to the political results. Since 1954,* the United States has spent several billions of dollars to carry out its policies in Laos. Official figures show a total of $800 million in economic aid through June 1972, most of this going for budgetary support and the financing of imports. Military aid over the same period totals $1.06 billion. Even these figures do not tell the whole story, for they exclude the cost of U.S. bombing and, until this year, the cost of CIA activities. Nevertheless, proof of the escalating war in Laos is clear from the officially admitted figures that direct military aid is now three times the 1969 level and over ten times that of 1964. In 1971, about 70 percent of both B-52 and fighter-bomber combat sorties in Indochina were directed against Laos, at a cost of $1.05 billion in munitions alone and a total cost of just over $2 billion.[4]

The human costs have been staggering for the Laotians, but not inconsequential for the Americans. Pilots have been

* A chronology of events is included in the Appendix. It provides an overview and sequence of actions which might not always be clear from the narrative.

shot down. Advisors in the field have been killed. From 1964 through mid-1972, over 400 Americans died in the fighting in Laos and nearly 300 men were listed as missing.[5]

Despite these expenditures of men and money, the Royal Laotian Government has maintained only a precarious existence in Vientiane and a tenuous hold on the towns of the Mekong Valley. Dramatic advances during the 1971–72 dry season pushed Pathet Lao control from about two-thirds to over 80 percent of the territory and from one-third to about half the population.

All the antagonists try to deny or conceal their involvement in Laos. The North Vietnamese have never admitted having ground forces within their neighbor's territory, although the number of men involved now is about 80,000. Nor do the Chinese discuss their 20,000 men on road-building crews. The Thai say only that "volunteers" have gone into Laos, despite authoritative reports that 6,000 regular troops are operating across the border. Similarly, the United States denies having men engaged in ground combat operations in Laos. Although the number of Americans reportedly involved with troops, and thus in combat, is fairly small—probably under 200—any at all would be contrary to presidential assurances and congressional legislation.[6]

Secrecy has the advantage of minimizing diplomatic outcries, but it also prevents adequate public awareness of what is happening. Only the American people are in the dark, for the people in Laos know from firsthand experience what the Americans are doing. The North Vietnamese and Pathet Lao broadcast their versions of the truth about U.S. activities, often years before official admissions. Enterprising reporters have filed stories which add to our knowledge but lack definite confirmation from Washington. As a result of partial and unconfirmed evidence, we are not totally sure what to believe.*

For six years the U.S. government claimed that it was conducting armed reconnaissance flights over Laos, when in fact

---

* Although official sources generally refuse to admit certain specific facts, few will take issue with press reports on the extent of U.S. involvement. Some sources went so far as to commend the accuracy of certain journalists, such as T. D. Allman and Henry Kamm.

American pilots and planes flew tactical and strategic bombing missions. Except for one "mistake" early in 1969, admitted by Defense Secretary Melvin Laird, U.S. officials vehemently deny that American combat troops have been sent into Laos, despite testimony to the contrary from participants in such border actions. Laird claimed the right, however, to "hot pursuit" and brief incursions. Revelations of hitherto secret documents in 1971 confirm the U.S. involvement in many covert operations in Laos.[7] [See "Postscript on the Pentagon Papers."]

Although Americans do not directly control military ground operations, they provide guidance and necessary support. Too few U.S. personnel are in Laos for them to operate regularly with small units, other than commando squads. Instead, they serve as caseworkers, traveling to their assigned units to discuss plans and needed U.S. assistance. Although they carry weapons and are occasionally involved in fighting, they see themselves as advisors rather than commanders. Perhaps in fear of embarrassment over the death of Americans leading intelligence and commando teams in the trail area, U.S. personnel were reportedly barred from such operations by early 1971.[8]

Air operations of bombing, troop transport, and supply are vital to the Laotian forces and constitute the most significant part of the U.S. involvement in Laos. Much of this effort is technically civilian, since the CIA has contracted for operations by Air America and Continental Air Services. Strategic bombing, of course, is carried out by U.S. planes based primarily in Thailand. Some of the propeller aircraft officially assigned to the Laotian air force, in fact, are owned and flown by Thai and American pilots.[9] Travel within the country is also generally on U.S.–financed planes.

In addition to this leverage on military operations, the United States has considerable influence on the Laotian economy. At $350 million per year, direct American aid is about ten times the size of the Laotian budget and 75 percent larger than the total gross national product of $202 million. Without this aid to the Laotian armed forces, soldiers would not be paid and would not have replacement parts and weapons. Without the economic aid to finance imports and to back the Laotian currency, the kip, inflation would probably run rampant.[10]

Such extensive assistance necessarily makes Laotian officials dependent on the United States. Military commanders acknowledge their subservience by resisting their own desires to take over from Souvanna Phouma, for they know that the Americans will threaten aid cutoffs in order to preserve the Premier's position, as they have done in the past. Businessmen try to curry favor with the Americans, so that they will receive lucrative contracts. Souvanna himself has tailored his negotiation demands to U.S. policy, as in his reluctance to challenge U.S. military activities in the southern panhandle region of his country.

Whether or not the United States has a commitment to preserve and defend the current Laotian government is open to question. Although U.S. officials categorically deny any such commitment, Souvanna Phouma asserts that the American obligation is firm, if not formal. Years of close involvement and mutual dependence have made Laos a client of the United States, one whose fate cannot be taken lightly. The history of U.S. policy since 1954 illustrates what the Symington Subcommittee concluded when it observed, "It is the day-to-day implementation of policy which frequently, and sometimes almost imperceptibly, provides the building blocks for future commitments."[11]

Why and how has the United States become so deeply involved in Laos? The purpose of this study is to answer that question, both by examining the sequence of decisions since 1954 and by suggesting general propositions about the way American foreign policy is made. It is a troubling question since, as noted at the start of this Introduction, "Laos was not all that goddamned important" even to officials involved in the crises of the Kennedy Administration.

The basis for whatever importance Laos did have was its context in the cold war as an area directly threatened by international communism. Starting from the belief that Moscow, Peking, and, more recently, Hanoi and Havana, are bent on expansion and conquest, particularly in nearby states, U.S. policy makers have tried over the years since World War II to contain such expansion. By treaty commitments, military assistance, and economic aid, the United States has attempted to strengthen local governments against external attacks and internal subversion.

Laos was included in the containment strategy as a first line of defense against China and North Vietnam. Unless those nations could be held in check, the rest of Southeast Asia might fall. Laos was one of President Eisenhower's dominoes, although the one least valuable in terms of raw materials or size of population. Secretary of State John Foster Dulles applied the containment policy to Laos most directly on the day after the end of the 1954 Geneva Conference. He told the Senate Appropriations Committee:

> "Whether this can be stopped at this point, and whether Laos and Cambodia and the southern part of Vietnam, Thailand, Malaya, and Indonesia can be kept out of Communist control depends very much on whether we can build a dike around this present loss. The only thing we have to build that dike with is this [foreign aid] money, at least from the material standpoint. There are some people there who are well disposed, but they are weak and they are feeble, and they cannot stand alone. . . . It will be a domino business, unless we can bolster this situation up."[12]

These attitudes have been, and remain, at the root of American policy toward Laos since 1954. When fighting broke out in the summer of 1959, the State Department called Laos "a front line of the free world," because it was responding to "part of the pattern of Communist bloc aggression. . . ."[13] President Kennedy saw Laos as a cold-war problem and argued, "The security of all Southeast Asia will be endangered if Laos loses its neutral independence. Its own safety runs with the safety of us all. . . ."[14] President Johnson claimed that "The Communist side has been largely responsible for the continuing difficulties and dangers in Laos."[15] He thought it important to show the world that aggression could not succeed in Indochina.[16] President Nixon declared that, since 1954, "this small country has been the victim of persistent subversion, and finally invasion, by the North Vietnamese."[17]

Preventing the "loss" of any territory to a Communist nation has long been a primary U.S. foreign policy objective. Officials knew, from the political backlash following Chiang Kai-shek's loss of power in China, that further such setbacks had to be avoided. Thus, whenever Laos seemed in danger of slipping under Communist control, U.S. policy makers believed that it had to be strengthened and supported.

The Communist threat is a primary reality for officials in Washington. Almost all Communist nations are openly and consistently antagonistic to U.S. policies and interests. The Soviet Union is capable of destroying the United States militarily, and China is increasing its own nuclear arsenal. This overriding fact is applied, by extension, to all areas of international relations. Consequently, Laos is important to the top policy makers only when, and insofar as, its pro-American orientation is endangered.

Military and political survival in Washington both depend on sensitivity to whatever seems to be a Communist threat. Since all officials know this, they are also alert to developments which might weaken U.S. influence. These are the issues which rise to the top for consideration and decision, the ones on which leading policy makers are willing to spend time.

These priorities lead to the neglect of other factors which have a less direct effect on foreign policy. Busy men, concerned about numerous situations in many countries, have little time to consider data other than those immediately and directly influencing another nation's foreign policy. Diplomats in the field may file long reports on economic or social conditions, but these facts receive attention only if they impinge on tariffs, or nationalization, or the prospects for revolution or anti-Americanism.

Since policy makers must be selective in the attention they pay to incoming information, they generally concentrate first on those data which seem most likely to affect them. Anything which seems to involve communism is necessarily a higher priority than an issue which does not. When communism is not at issue, a policy maker will usually give more attention to information which relates to possible changes in international relations than to factors without impact on foreign policy. There were, no doubt, extensive reports from Vientiane to Washington about the maneuvers of the major Laotian families for power within their society, but they were generally not significant for U.S. officials because all of the families were considered pro-American.

Over the course of time, men and women with direct experience in Laos rose to important middle-level roles in the policy machinery in Washington. They were able to bring understanding and perspective which was probably lacking in the early years of U.S. involvement in that distant country. Sometimes they brought their expertise to bear on major decisions, but often they were not included in the high policy councils which debated and decided the crucial issues. If they did not already share Washington's viewpoint of the Communist threat to Laos, they were nevertheless forced to work within that policy context.

The images of Laos held by most high-level American policy makers in the years since 1954 have been remarkably different from the realities observed in Laos by other Americans. In part, these differences stemmed from the natural tendency to see all nations as roughly similar when they have such institutions as kings, premiers, cabinets, parliaments, and armies. Confronted with these familiar concepts, foreign policy officials may have failed to see important similarities with feudal warlords or city hall politics. Washington officials also tended to believe that the Laotians shared America's concerns and enthusiasm for U.S. involvement in Laos. In the early years, before the U.S. presence became so dominant, the consensus in Washington was that Laos was a battleground in the struggle against communism, a small nation struggling to be free from communism and foreign domination. In subsequent years, U.S. officials believed that their involvement in Laos was welcomed by the people and was limited to what the Laotians themselves wanted.

These images of Laos are largely distorted, misleading, and untrue. Many Americans who served in that unknown country knew the truth but were unable to change the dominant views in Washington. American policy toward Laos was consequently built on a foundation of misperception.

Laos is not a nation in the general understanding of that term. As Bernard Fall wrote, "Laos is neither a geographical, nor an ethnic, nor social entity, but merely a political convenience."[18] When the few existing roads are passable, there is still little trade or travel among regions. There are so many different tribal clusters (at least forty-two) and so many major linguistic families (at least five) that a multicolored ethnolinguistic map of Laos resembles a Jackson Pollock painting. Even the boundaries on such a map are fictitious, since mountain tribesmen have always moved without much political interference back and forth across the borders with North Vietnam and Burma. The Mekong River also is a highway rather than a fence, permitting considerable trade with northeast Thailand. Although Laos has never had a thorough census, the population is thought to be nearly 3 million. There is general agreement that nine times as many Lao live in Thailand as in Laos itself.[19]

Laos has adjusted to foreign domination rather than struggling to be free of it. Except for the mountain tribesmen who fought to stay in their home regions, the native armies have been generally ineffective. The Lao had not resisted the French as vigorously as had the Vietnamese, and even in the early years of independence from France, the Laotians were much less sensitive to "colonialism" than the United States assumed. Many of the leaders of the independence movement—and especially Souvanna Phouma—were culturally Frenchified and quite willing to keep French advisors and civil servants in their governments.[20]

Americans became dominant but were reluctant to admit that they might be disliked simply for that reason. Only the Pathet Lao struggled openly against the growth of U.S. influence in Laotian affairs. The Lao accepted it and took advantage of the opportunities it provided for financial enrichment. Even today, despite the enormous suffering which the war has brought to Laos, there is little evidence of willingness for the Americans to leave.

Fear of North Vietnamese conquest, no doubt, makes many Laotians support continued American involvement. In spite of U.S. support, the North Vietnamese still have the admitted capability to capture almost all of Laos whenever they wish. Only the administrative capital of Vientiane and the central towns of Savannakhet and Thakhek have been immune from attack or harassment in recent years.

The reality of the Communist threat has changed greatly since 1954. Until 1960, the Soviet Union lacked diplomatic relations and influence in Laos. The Chinese also remained aloof from the Laotian affairs, in accord with Chou En-lai's pledge of noninterference at the time of the Bandung Conference in 1955. Only the North Vietnamese were much interested or involved in Laos at that time, and they limited their activities to encouragement and some training of the Pathet Lao. At no time before the border clashes in disputed territory at the end of 1958 did the United States have any evidence of foreign Communist troops in Laos.[21] Yet American policy makers talked and acted as if they believed that only the Royal Army and the threat of U.S. nuclear retaliation kept the Chinese and North Vietnamese from marching to the Mekong.

Now the Communist threat is much more real. Although the Soviet Union retreated into the background after 1962, the Chinese have sent men to build roads through northern Laos. Early in 1972 an estimated 30,000 Chinese were in Laos, perhaps one-fourth of them troops to protect the road crews. The North Vietnamese, likewise, have increased their personnel in Laos to over 90,000, about three-fifths of whom are involved in the trail areas leading to South Vietnam and Cambodia.[22]

Whether this threat has grown from aggressive or defensive motives, the prevailing American belief over the years has been that the other side has always initiated escalation of the conflict. The evidence presented in subsequent chapters is much less clear-cut. Throughout the early years of U.S. involvement, Americans focused on the Communist/anti-Communist antagonism, to the neglect of other important facts about Laos.

If the Americans had looked behind the red labels and rhetoric of the Pathet Lao, they would have seen a much different threat to Laos—the threat of regional disintegration and ethnic warfare. Those dangers were just as real as, and probably more important than, that of expansionist communism, but the United States responded only to the problem which touched its cold-war nerve.

Despite the figurehead presence of Prince Souphanouvong and Lao domination of the inner Communist party, the following of the Pathet Lao has come almost entirely from non-Lao minorities. The Pathet Lao have been most successful in creating political and administrative organizations in those areas where the Lao are in the minority, the same places to which the lowlanders never were able effectively to extend their administration. As late as 1959, the Pathet Lao program called only for a return to the local control they had exercised in the two border provinces and for a genuine coalition government at the national level. These were the understandable demands of repressed ethnic minorities.[23]

There are four major ethnic groups in Laos, each distinguished from the others by its language, location, social structure, and method of agriculture. The Lao-Lu or valley Lao live where their name suggests, in the lowlands along the Mekong and its tributaries. The tribal Tai groups, living in the upper valleys, have a feudal, patrilineal social structure, as well as a separate religion based on the worship of ancestral deities. Scattered throughout the country, but distinguished by their darker skin, animist religion, and slash-and-burn agriculture, are the Lao-Theng, or Lao of the mountain sides. This term is political, however, since it implies a unity with other Laotians which does not exist. The common term for these people is the derisive term Kha, or slave. The other major group includes those tribes like the Meo and Yao which live high on the mountains and ridge lines, each well organized and fiercely jealous of the slopes it uses for its slash-and-burn agriculture and for the cultivation of opium. Although reliable statistics do not exist, the population of Laos is probably composed in the following way: Lao-Lu, 40 to 50 percent; tribal Tai, 15 to 25 percent; Lao-Theng (Kha), 30 percent; Meo-Yao, 5 percent. More significant than these overall national figures are the regional ones. Except for Khammouane Province, which borders the southern panhandle of North Vietnam, ethnic Lao are in the minority in all provinces bordering North Vietnam and China.[24]

Lao dominate the government and administration, as well as what there is of a money economy. They form an historical elite, drawn primarily from the provinces of Vientiane, Luang Prabang and Champassak, which has excluded non-Lao from all but token opportunities for educational and social advancement. They have not ruled oppressively, but that may be simply because they have not extended their administration very far or very effectively. With the population so small, less than 3 million people in a country nearly the size of Britain, Laos lacks a land problem—the traditional source of rural discontent. In the years since 1945, however, the Lao have kindled grievances as they have tried to extend and centralize their control.[25]

Governments in Vientiane have had only a vague policy of assimilation for the other ethnic groups. They seem to have acted on the assumption that the minorities would become Lao in language, dress, religion, and so forth. This contrasts sharply with the Pathet Lao, who have consistently appealed to ethnic groups by emphasizing their grievances against the Lao. The Pathet Lao have also allowed tribal languages and schools in areas under their control, while the Royal Government has forbidden publication of such languages and has generally discouraged the organization of minorities. Even during the civil war of 1960–62, the Royal Government never appealed to non-Lao ethnic groups or to the Buddhist priesthood as a group.[26]

Nor has the central government ever been particularly close to the people outside the cities. An opinion survey in 1956 revealed that fewer than half the people queried knew the name of their own country, and only 10 percent knew the name of the Prime Minister or where the King lived. Another survey in 1959 showed that the King, who then had reigned for fifty-six years, was known by name to only about one-third of the people interviewed in Vientiane and the provincial capitals and to less than 20 percent in the villages. Apparently, the only government officials who have much contact with the people are politicians who try to win support through grants of money and projects—and this happens only at election time. The farther one goes from the major towns, the less important are the political struggles in the capital. Robert Shaplen quotes one American official on the mountain people: "They think of their situation solely in terms of their own ridgelines. They know when and where they're likely to be shot at, and that's it."[27]

Although the King has few direct links to the people, he is a symbolic rallying point. The ruler since 1959, Savang Vatthana, has played a careful balancing role, always acting to preserve the royal position in the struggles between various contending factions. While denouncing the Souvanna Phouma government, the Pathet Lao in recent years have still professed allegiance to the King.[28] The monarchy may be the only symbol capable of unifying the many ethnic and political groups within Laos.

One clear proof of the ethnic as well as political nature of the struggle between the Royal Government and the Pathet Lao can be seen in the composition of the contending armies. The Pathet Lao forces reportedly consist primarily of Kha and tribal Tai men native to the regions where they operate. The Lao, by contrast, furnish the Royal Armed Forces with virtually all of its leadership, although they account for only 56 percent of the men. In 1966, 10 percent were Tai and another 10 percent were from other minorities. The Meo were listed at 24 percent, but that figure may be misleading since most Meo forces were organized in a clandestine, CIA-supported army not under the direct chain of command from Vientiane.[29] *

* Ethnic troubles apparently continue to plague the Royal Army. For example, in 1968 these soldiers performed poorly and lost an

Ethnic divisions are only part of the reality of Laos. Also important is the basic peacefulness of the people. Armed forces have always been external creations, financed first by French and later by the Americans. Most U.S. officials with experience in Laos have commented on the reluctance of the Lao to fight or to be diverted from their simple, personal pleasures. The mediocre combat record of Laotian forces (other than the Meos) bears witness to their lack of enthusiasm for war.

These many facts have been available to U.S. policy makers throughout the years of extensive American involvement in Laos, but they do not seem to have altered U.S. policy. Except for the creation of the Meo army, the United States has always supported and worked with the ruling Lao elites. This understandable policy, nevertheless, made it easy for Americans to identify their own interests with preservation of the role and power of those elites.

In reality, about twenty major families dominate the political scene in Laos, and these clans often have deeply rooted antipathies toward each other. For example, the Voravongs, including Phoumi Nosavan, have never forgiven the Sananikones for their presumed involvement in the 1954 assassination of Defense Minister Kou Voravong. Some of these families also have deep regional roots: the Champassaks in the southern province of that name; the Voravongs in Savannakhet; the Sananikones in Vientiane and the vice-regal family of Souvanna Phouma and Souphanouvong in Luang Prabang.[30] These ethnic and factional divisions are the basis of the Laotian political system. All effective political decision-making power rests with about 2,000 people, by one scholar's estimate. The parties which have formed, reformed, merged, disintegrated, and otherwise transmogrified over the years, have tended to be the personal

important outpost in Northern Laos despite advantages in air support, numbers, and artillery. One of the major causes of the defeat, Peter Braestrup reported in the *New York Times*, January 3, 1968, was that two-thirds of the Royal soldiers were from southern Laos. They treated the northern peasants as enemies and got no advance word of Pathet Lao attacks.

organizations of strong leaders rather than groups having special interests or ideological commitments.[31]

Throughout its involvement, the United States has intervened in order to strengthen one faction or another. Americans in Laos at first tried to manipulate these factions for foreign policy results, usually greater hostility toward the Communists and greater subservience to the United States. When the clan approach proved inadequate, the CIA bolstered a group of young elites who saw more to be gained by uniting along generational lines than by dividing along familial ones. Now that warfare is the major U.S. activity in Laos, political factions are less important than military ones, which must be carefully balanced to prevent coups or political disintegration. What other effects the increased U.S. military involvement has had on these factors of the Laotian political system are not known at present.

Top officials in Washington have persisted in their chessboard view of Laos, despite the available evidence of the details of internal developments. These incongruities between American images and Laotian realities are basic to understanding the story that follows, as is the cold-war context from which many of these misperceptions arose.

American policy toward Laos may seem to be a series of mistakes. Looked at in retrospect, that may be a useful lesson. But to the men who had responsibility for that policy, it was a series of difficult choices among generally undesirable alternatives. Before judging those men and their policies on the basis of current hindsight, let us consider their decisions and actions as they saw them.

CHAPTER ONE

Taking up the Frenchman's burden (1954)

We have a clean base there now, without a taint of colonialism. Dienbienphu was a blessing in disguise.
—JOHN FOSTER DULLES[1]

By 1954 the French had lost their seven-year war in Indochina, politically if not militarily. At the Geneva Conference they agreed to a cease-fire, the regrouping of belligerents, and the eventual withdrawal of most of their forces. Departure of the French presaged major political realignments both within Southeast Asia and among the nations concerned with events there. The impending decisions seemed likely to determine the basic policies and power configurations in that area for years to come, as in fact they did.

The United States faced the question of what to do in these new circumstances. American officials were particularly disturbed at what they considered a surrender to the Communists of North Vietnam. Secretary of Defense Charles Wilson said that the Geneva agreements were hardly "something to enthuse about." Secretary of State John Foster Dulles called the partition of Vietnam "a very serious loss." President Dwight D. Eisenhower welcomed the end of bloodshed but admitted that the settlement contained provisions which he did not like. Senate Majority Leader William Knowland of California was much less restrained; he called the agreements "one of the great Communist victories of this decade."[2]

Communism threatened all of Asia, in the opinion of American policy makers. Direct attacks on South Korea had brought substantial American forces back to the mainland in 1950. At the same time the United States had acted to support

16

the French struggle against Ho Chi Minh's insurgents in Indochina. Chiang Kai-shek's troops had regrouped on Taiwan, uncertain whether they would next fight the Chinese Communists on that island or on the mainland. Although a cease-fire prevailed throughout the region in July 1954, few men in Washington expected the Communists to rest content with the territory they then controlled.[3]

Since the Communist threat remained basically unchanged, although temporarily quiescent, American policy makers saw no reason to alter their policy of aiding those who were resisting that threat. As they defined the situation in Indochina, the danger was real and the time for action short. The French were going to pull out; someone had to replace them with money if not with men. The problem set for an interdepartmental Task Force was to recommend "a U.S. policy toward Indochina following the Geneva cease-fire agreements which will preserve the integrity and independence of Laos, Cambodia, and Viet Nam in order that they might form a barrier to further Communist encroachment in Southeast Asia."[4]

The suggestions from this Task Force did not significantly influence the American response to the Geneva settlement, for the basic lines of policy had already been established. There was a general consensus among the leading officials on two specific actions: conclusion of a treaty intended to deter further Communist attacks and assumption of the burden of assistance formerly carried by the French. President Eisenhower later looked back on his policy of aiding the French before the Geneva Conference and wrote: "The decision to give this aid was almost compulsory. The United States had no real alternative unless we were to abandon Southeast Asia."[5] The decisions after Geneva were no less compulsory. In fact, there is no evidence of any suggestions by American officials that the United States abandon its involvement in Indochina. Although policy makers had slightly different perspectives on the issue at hand, they converged on this basic, two-pronged approach.

President Eisenhower viewed Indochina in broad, geopolitical terms. It was a battleground in the struggle against the "encroachment of Communist aggression." The loss of that

area to the Communists, he felt, would have serious and detri-
mental economic, moral, and strategic effects, First, Indochina
supplied important raw materials—in particular, tin, tungsten,
and rubber. Second, a Communist victory would put many
people under "a dictatorship that is inimical to the free world.
. . . Asia, after all, has already lost some 450 million of its
peoples to the Communist dictatorship, and we simply can't
afford greater losses." Third, there was a "falling domino"
principle at work, through which the loss of Indochina would
lead to the disintegration of the Western position and would
threaten the "island defensive chain" of Japan, Formosa, and the
Philippines.[6]

To prevent that sequence of events, the President
favored a concert of European and Asian nations which would
publicly declare its security objectives and its willingness to
fight. Such a declaration, he hoped, might deter actual conflict.
In the spring of 1954 Eisenhower had repeatedly rejected
proposals for intervention without allies in the deteriorating
situation in Indochina. Secretary Dulles also was more interested
in building a security system in Asia than in trying to salvage
the French position there. He was instrumental in persuading
the President to support his efforts to arrange a defense treaty
for Southeast Asia.[7]

Dulles favored an alliance system because he believed
in the deterrent effect of defense pacts. This faith in treaties
underlay his whole foreign policy, not in the naive assumption
that treaties were inviolable but in the strategic calculation that
an American commitment would deter any potential enemy.
The Russians might break their promises, but not the United
States. And America's massive power could defeat any ag-
gressor. Consequently, peace could be preserved by stating U.S.
intentions early and clearly, either by formal treaty or by in-
escapable public statement.[8]

His views of communism were more rigid than the
President's, since he had little faith in the possibility of reaching
lasting agreements with Moscow. Dulles saw the cold war as
fundamentally a moral rather than a political conflict. Although
he displayed great tactical flexibility at times in dealing with the

Soviet Union and other Communist nations, he maintained a consistent and unchanging set of beliefs about Communists and their foreign policy, beliefs which encouraged a suspicious, unyielding, antipathetic approach to those nations.[9]

Since March 1954, Dulles had been working actively to recruit members for a Southeast Asian treaty system. He originally considered united action the best way to bolster the French at Geneva, but he was thwarted by the British, who refused to join discussions until the end of the conference was in sight. Prime Minister Winston Churchill and Foreign Secretary Anthony Eden visited Eisenhower and Dulles at the end of June and agreed to minimal acceptable conditions for an armistice in Indochina as well as to the establishment of a joint study group to recommend ways of organizing collective defense in Southeast Asia. That group reported on July 17, just in time for implementation after Geneva.[10]

On July 21, the day the conference ended, the United States increased its lobbying efforts to get a security treaty. The President announced that discussions were under way. Under-Secretary of State Walter Bedell Smith said, on his departure from Geneva, "We must get that pact." Secretary Dulles said: "The important thing from now on is not to mourn the past but to seize the future opportunity to prevent the loss in Northern Vietnam from leading to the extension of communism throughout Southeast Asia and the Southwest Pacific."[11]

Other officials in the State Department shared Dulles' assessment of the danger in Asia and the proper American response. The Assistant Secretary for the Far East, Walter Robertson, was even more firmly anti-Communist than Dulles. Speaking a month after Geneva, he made this estimate of Soviet and Chinese objectives: "What do the Communists want? The answer is 'the world'—their world, our world, everything." He drew upon his experience in China to justify his support for a defense pact. "Every day since my first intimate contact with the Communists back in 1945 I have had continuing reason to become convinced of one simple truth. That is that the only successful resistance to Communist expansion is strength."[12] Robertson was particularly influential with Dulles on Southeast

Asian and Chinese matters since the Secretary felt less knowledgeable there.[13] American policy toward Laos between 1954 and 1959 was much more the product of Robertson's vigorous anticommunism than of any of the traits or attitudes of Eisenhower or Dulles.

Pentagon officers supported the policy of containment and apparently had no objection to a security treaty. The face of the issue to them, however, was primarily budgetary. Since the United States had begun underwriting the French effort in Indochina in 1950, its share had increased steadily, climbing to 40 percent by the end of 1952 and 78 percent by the time of Geneva. Since 1946 it had spent over $2 billion on military aid for that war. The commitment of these resources was a heavy burden for a Defense Department already forced to revise its strategy in order to cope with severe budget cuts after the Korean War. Any savings that could be made in Indochina would be welcome.[14]

One illustration of the Pentagon's efforts at economizing came in July 1954. As soon as word came through of the initialing of the cease-fire agreements, the Defense Department sent an order to stop all shipments to Indochina. This order had been prepared for several weeks, during which time the United States military advisors in the country had been carefully screening equipment to prevent anything not absolutely necessary from reaching the battle zones in the northern part of the country. The United States hoped to recover almost all of the equipment it had provided to the French Union forces.[15]

The Joint Chiefs of Staff had hoped to withdraw nearly all United States Army units from the Far East by 1957. The State Department objected and compelled a reassessment of the Communist threat to the area. The Chiefs abandoned their long-range plans, but did win a decision to withdraw four of the six American divisions in Korea. President Syngman Rhee consented to the plan during a visit to Washington at the end of July.[16]

The United States moved toward a new defense posture in Asia. There was new emphasis on the Island Chain of Japan, Okinawa, Formosa, and the Philippines rather than the mainland. James Reston detected a "policy of detachment" which was to be achieved by "regrouping U.S. ground forces in carefully selected strategic reserves."[17] This posture satisfied the Chiefs because it saved more money for major weapons programs and because it lessened the chances of another American involvement on the mainland of Asia. The "never again" school held sway in the Army after Korea and had vigorously opposed intervention in Indochina in the spring of 1954. This strategy also coincided with Dulles' theory of deterrence and his desire for a treaty that would leave the United States free to choose the means and place of responding to aggression.[18]

The new military strategy evolved slowly. The political basis for it—the defense treaty—grew much more quickly. The day after the end of the Geneva Conference, word leaked out that at least seven nations were expected to gather in the Philippines early in September to set up the alliance. The British went through the formality of inviting the Colombo nations to participate, but only Pakistan accepted. This settled the question of membership. Initial uncertainty over the legal restrictions imposed by the Geneva agreements faded into a determination that the Associated States could not formally join the alliance, but could be protected by it, much as West Germany had been before its formal admission to NATO in 1955. This protection was extended by a special protocol to the Manila treaty. Malaya, Hong Kong, and the areas to the north were left uncovered by the treaty.[19]

The nature of the obligation was to be less than that of NATO, which required the taking of action, in part because of presumed congressional opposition to anything more definite. The United States and Britain agreed on the formula used in the ANZUS Pact, which required only consultation. Dulles went further at the start of the conference in September and made his strategy clear. He said that the United States did not intend to commit substantial forces to a command structure, relying instead upon "the deterrent of mobile striking power, plus strategically placed reserves." In order to distinguish this new alliance from NATO, Dulles avoided the term SEATO and wanted to substitute Manila Pact, or MANPAC. He further qualified the American relationship to the new security arrangement by adding to its text an "understanding" that the terms "aggression and armed attack" applied only to "Communist aggression," although the United States promised to consult in other cases.[20]

While a treaty system was being established for Southeast Asia as a whole, work continued on a specific policy for Indochina. The nations of that area had been receiving some economic project aid directly, but military assistance had been channeled through the French. The interdepartmental Task Force on Indochina faced the questions of whether to continue military aid, and, if so, through what channels.

There was a general consensus in Washington for avoiding the French at all costs, both because of a fear of the taint of colonialism and because of prior bad experiences with them. President Eisenhower saw colonialism as "the crux of this whole thing." Since 1951 he had been pressuring various French governments to make an unequivocal and public pledge to grant independence to the Associated States of Indochina after military victory. Their reluctance to do so, he concluded, made it difficult for the United States to help the French attain that victory. "We are not trying to help anybody support and maintain colonialism," he told a February 1954 news conference.[21]

Secretary Dulles shared the President's antipathy toward colonialism. He began making his views more evident after the collapse of his effort to get united action before the Geneva Conference. In testimony before the Senate Foreign Relations Committee on June 4, he referred to the problem as "one of the great dilemmas" then facing American foreign policy: ". . . when we support the United Kingdom and France in international matters, international gatherings, then we ourselves acquire a taint of colonialism which is rather galling to us because it is contrary to the instincts and traditions of the American people." Dulles also blamed the French loss of morale after Dien Bien Phu for their willingness to surrender North Vietnam at Geneva. This view echoed his assessment of the virtual collapse of the French political system in early May. An official biographer also concluded that "Dulles believed that French presence in Indochina was a liability—France must not reestablish influence in South Vietnam."[22]

Defense Secretary Wilson also believed that colonialism and its consequences were at the root of the crisis in Indochina. This was the basis of his continued opposition to American intervention during the spring of 1954. He disagreed with the Eisenhower-Dulles emphasis on the Communist nature of the struggle there, seeing that the struggle was not only a fight against communism but also a revolution. "We all thought the civil war aspects could be washed out, and the issue of communism clarified," he said on July 20.[23]

Everyone at the highest levels of the U.S. government opposed the French in Asia. American officials thought that Paris wanted to keep the Associated States as puppets, thereby salvaging France's honor and protecting its commercial interests. They also felt that the French had sold out to the Communists by accepting the partition of Vietnam. United States policy makers concluded that they could do a better job, especially if the French were pushed out of the area.[24]

Strained military relations in the field also made Americans reluctant to continue to channel their assistance through the French. One of the conditions required before the United States would even contemplate intervention in May 1954 had been revision of the command structure to give American forces a role in planning operations and training Vietnamese troops. Meeting stiff French resistance, the Chief of the American MAAG (Military Assistance Advisory Group) proposed ways to circumvent the French by dealing directly with the Associated States. As one step toward dissassociating the United States from the French effort Washington told Paris on July 9 that it would no longer continue its training of Vietnamese troops.[25]

The recommendations made by the interdepartmental Task Force in its report of August 12 reflected the consensus on containment and on replacing the French. The group supported both protection for the Indochinese states by the planned collective defense system and continued military and economic assistance. Following the lead of the Secretary of State, it ruled out formal membership in the alliance for those states but suggested guarantees to them. The Task Force also recommended a new policy of direct aid to the recipient countries, no longer "operating through a French key hole and subject to a French veto."[26] On August 17 the President approved the order to direct all aid to the Associated States rather than through France.

Implementation took place with a vengeance. Especially with regard to Vietnam, Americans maneuvered to strengthen their position. They acted in the context of the French National Assembly's rejection of the European Defense Community Plan at the end of August. The EDC defeat made the United States even less willing to tolerate or support financially French influence in Southeast Asia.

When a French delegation visited Washington at the end of September, it had no trump and had to follow the American lead. Mendes-France even instructed his delegation: "In Southeast Asia it is the American who is the leader of the coalition."[27] The main issue was on Vietnam, where the French agreed, in an unpublished protocol, to support Ngo Dinh Diem. But on the question of financial assistance, the United States promised only to "consider" the French requests. Meanwhile, the Americans made clear their plans to equip and train Vietnamese forces without the use of French intermediaries. As a further slap in the face, the Vietnamese announced, while the talks were going on, that they wanted all French troops withdrawn by March of 1956, far ahead of the French timetable. If this move was not engineered by the Americans, it certainly was not contrary to their own policy.[28]

During talks between Dulles and Mendes-France in November, the United States pushed even harder to supplant the French in Indochina, especially in the training of troops. Dulles resisted Mendes-France's plea for support of larger French and Vietnamese forces on the grounds that they were intended solely for internal security, not for resistance of external aggression, since that latter function was performed by the Manila Pact. This policy became even clearer three weeks later when the United States announced a drastic reduction in monetary support for French and Vietnamese forces.[29]

By the end of 1954 the United States was already actively involved in South Vietnam. Laos, however, remained in the background, where it had been the entire year. Until 1959, Vietnam was the central focus of United States policy in the former Indochinese states. It has remained preeminent since then, except during occasional crises in Laos and Cambodia. The State Department did not even have a separate "country desk" for Laos until the autumn of 1955, so Laotian questions were often juxtaposed and then subordinated to Vietnamese ones.

During the intervention debate in the spring of 1954 Dulles made a distinction between Vietnam and the other two states of Indochina. While all areas of Asia were important, only some were "essential." Laos and Cambodia were not essential, he told his May 11 news conference, because of their remoteness and small populations.[30] Dulles still hoped to preserve the territorial integrity of these states, but he considered them clearly secondary in importance to Vietnam. Consequently, the United States took no active role in discussions on Laos at Geneva.

Laos emerged in a good position from the Geneva Conference because of the lack of importance attached to it relative to Vietnam, rather than through its own diplomatic skill. The Russians and Chinese were willing to let Laos and Cambodia remain independent, undivided states. Chou En-lai persuaded the Vietminh to pull their forces out of Laos and sought to neutralize the area, especially against American bases. He agreed to provisions which disallowed only alliances in conflict with the United Nations Charter—a major concession. Then, at the last minute on July 20, with the agreements on Laos and Cambodia still in a first draft and with the Laotian delegation already asleep for the night, the Cambodian delegate threatened not to sign until his country was permitted freedom to call upon assistance in case its security was endangered. After several hours of frantic discussion Molotov finally granted that exception. Mendes-France then said that what had been granted to Cambodia could not be denied to Laos. After a flush of angry exasperation, Molotov agreed: "All right, Laos too."[31]

The cease-fire agreements provided that the Vietminh forces would evacuate the country within four months, but that the French could retain 3,500 men at two bases, at Vientiane and Seno, and could provide the Lao army with 1,500 French instructors. The Pathet Lao, who had not been accorded delegate status at the conference, were permitted to regroup in the two northern provinces of Sam Neua and Phong Saly pending national elections in 1955. They were promised "special representation in the Royal Administration of the province" in the interim.[32]

Policy makers in Washington viewed the situation in Indochina after Geneva pessimistically. Under-Secretary of State Bedell Smith told a subordinate in September that he expected the ultimate loss of the two northern provinces in which the Pathet Lao had been permitted to regroup. Administrative personnel were reluctant to provide supplies and support to an enlarged mission in Vientiane because they feared that Laos would quickly collapse. The same mood prevailed in November, when Secretary Dulles sent General J. Lawton Collins to study the situation in Vietnam. "Frankly, Collins," Dulles said, "I think our chances of saving the situation there are not more than one in ten."[33]

Commitments clashed with this pessimism in a November 1954 debate on the military aid budget. The issue in August had been whether the Americans would step in for the faltering French and help defend the Associated States against communism; an affirmative response seemed unavoidable. The issue in November, however, was how to pay for the 32,000-man army which the French had built up among the Laotians. Faced with sharply reduced funds for their own forces, the Joint Chiefs of Staff wanted to reduce the budgetary impact of foreign military aid. Laos was only a secondary target in this effort since its program, costing about $40 million, was tiny compared to the $3 billion planned for military-related aid. But some staff members proposed, and the JCS accepted, a paper recommending no force-level objectives for Laos. One bureaucratic argument for that proposal was that the Pentagon would not be able to control the funds it provided because the State Department objected to the establishment of a MAAG as a violation of the Geneva agreements.[34]

The State Department argued that the Communist military threat was much greater than the JCS assumed and that, in any event, it was politically necessary to maintain support for the Laotian army. Those forces were the only arm of the government whose organization was effective and far-reaching. State secured from the mission in Vientiane an estimate that the army could be reduced to 23,650 without jeopardizing U.S. foreign policy objectives. The JCS countered with an estimate that an army of 15,000 would be adequate for internal policing, the only military objective seen for the Laotian soldiers. Asked to reconsider their recommendations in January 1955, the Chiefs replied that their views had not changed and that support of the Laotian army could be justified only if political considerations were overriding. The State Department compromised slightly by agreeing to a reduction in the size of the army to the 23,650 figure.[35]

In practice, the cut never occurred. No one in Laos tried to pressure the army to make a verifiable reduction in its forces. Nor did the U.S. mission ever learn the exact number of men in the army. Except for a few partial inspections, the Americans had no knowledge of the army's size other than the reports from the Laotian generals.[36]

Newly arriving Americans were too busy coping with the problems of adjusting to Laos to worry much about these debates in Washington. Ambassador Charles Yost had arrived in September 1954 and had moved into a home "with no hot water other than that heated in the kitchen and carried upstairs, with no air-conditioners of any kind, with leaking roofs and hordes of rats."[37] On January 1, 1955, the small United States Operations Mission (USOM) in charge of administering the aid program set up both home and office in a tent in a Royal Government pasture in Vientiane.

CHAPTER TWO

Driving the rats from the barn (1955–1959)

> *I am certain there were many things radically wrong with that program. They were corrected . . . but there was never any time that it seemed we would be justified in burning down the barn to kill the rats. I think we have killed the rats and we still have our barn, better than it was when we started.*
> —WALTER S. ROBERTSON *on April 21, 1959*[1]

To those men in the American mission in Vientiane, Laos was a quite different entity from the one which confronted the policy makers in Washington. Initially, the new arrivals faced the difficult problems of setting up shop and getting their programs going. Until 1954 the U.S. diplomatic presence in Laos consisted of a single Foreign Service Officer, who did his own typing. The new men in a rapidly expanding organization had to adjust to a strange country and unforeseen difficulties.

Simple facts of everyday existence often overshadowed the work people had to do. Those facts were primitive conditions, discomfort, disease, and a strange way of life. Men in Washington might also be distracted by personal problems, but they had none of the environmental ones. The director of the CARE operation in Laos from 1954 to 1956 quoted one friend as saying, "There are only two kinds of Americans in Laos—those who have amoebic dysentery, and those who don't know it." He also described the way personal and bureaucratic problems diverted the energies of many people assigned to the mission.

28

The swarms of middle and lower echelon Americans involved in economic aid seemed enmeshed in the endless housekeeping, personnel, and supply problems of their own mission—as were we all to a degree—but the fight for quarters, the difficulties in getting furniture and food and other supplies flown in, the infinity of the reports demanded by Washington, all seemed to take up so much time and strength that there appeared to be little time left in which to get on with the job. Some of the economic missioners whom I met were so preoccupied by the little world in which they lived that at times I doubted they were really in Laos.[2]

These conditions rarely came to the attention of Washington except when the mission asked for more administrative support or for better people. Secretary Dulles was so amazed by the conditions on his visit in 1955 that he ordered funds sent immediately to improve them.

Various personnel problems plagued the American aid program in its first few years. The rapid increase in the size of the mission—from a dozen or so at the end of 1954 to forty-five in the autumn of 1955 to eighty-two in August 1956 to over one hundred in December 1957—severely strained the housing and other facilities, not to mention the bureaucratic shufflings which must accompany such growth. As early as May 1956 an internal study found morale at a low ebb, in part because of the poor living conditions and lack of adequate policy direction. As late as 1958 the Program Evaluation Office (PEO—the group established to administer the military aid program) was at only two-thirds of its authorized strength because of the inability to recruit people for Laos. Nor were the people sent to Laos of the highest calibre. Ambassador Parsons had to obtain transfers for eight men in the PEO who were chronically drunk or had other serious adjustment problems. And an investigator early in 1960 concluded that the military advisors were "the worst collection of misfits I ever saw."[3]

These facts of life in Laos were painfully evident to the Americans in Vientiane. Healthy officials in comfortable Washington could ignore these facts by fitting reports from Laos into their preconceived notions of what the place was like. The men in the field, however, had to live with the primitive conditions, the feudal political system, and the Lao's lethargic approach to the questions of communism and economic development. The newly arrived Americans quickly learned that only a few families influenced governmental policy. Consequently, they began to cultivate these groups.

Washington officials saw Laos primarily in terms of the conflict with international communism. Laos was "a finger pointing into the heart of Southeast Asia," the forward battle area in the struggle to prevent Communist expansion.[4] Americans stationed in the country were also highly sensitive to the problems of Communist influence and control, but they had a more complex picture of the situation, one in which communism was often a lesser reality than divisions based on family, ethnic group, or region. They also faced more immediate problems than any posed by the regroupment of Pathet Lao forces into two northern provinces. Those administering the economic assistance had a full-time job just processing the necessary papers. The Central Intelligence Agency operatives were just beginning to develop their network of agents; they did not start to play a major policy role until well into 1957. The CIA was first, however, in arranging arms deliveries. The top officials of the country team were preoccupied with coordinating the activities of the rapidly expanding staff.

Although there was no immediate threat of Communist expansion, Lao leaders soon recognized that the Americans could be manipulated into giving more support, diplomatic and material, by appropriate references to that danger. Crown Prince Savang, for example, told an American reporter in January 1955: "Laos wants to be on the side of the free world. We want to keep our present alignment. Life here in Laos is not compatible with communism."[5] The Prime Minister since November 1954 was Katay Don Sasorith, who had struggled against the

French and was author of a tract entitled *Laos—Ideal Corner-stone in the Anti-Communist Struggle in Southeast Asia*. He favored close relations with Thailand, a view shared by the Americans who wanted to pull Laos away from French influence.[6] *

What Communist threat there was, was largely symbolic. Allowed by the 1954 agreement to regroup in the provinces of Sam Neua and Phong Saly, the Pathet Lao claimed administrative control of both areas.[7] Success in that claim weakened the central government and strengthened the Pathet Lao bargaining position in the reconciliation talks. In the circumstances prevailing in late summer 1954, neither the Vientiane government nor the International Commission for Supervision and Control (ICC) was able to challenge this assumption of control physically, so they did not do so verbally. The ICC missed one major opportunity by not challenging an agreement reached at Khang Khay on August 30, 1954, which left ambiguous whether the Pathet Lao were to control the whole or part of the two provinces. Because of the Indian representative's desire to avoid an open breach with nonunanimous resolutions, many of the early disputes were avoided or papered over by compromise. Throughout the autumn of 1954 and the whole of 1955 the ICC tried to bring the conflicting parties together, acting more as a negotiating than as a control body. It was not until January 7, 1956, that it passed a resolution (with the Polish delegate abstaining) which firmly declared the right of the

* There is no adequate account of the fall of the Souvanna Phouma government in 1954. The standard books relate Souvanna's resignation on October 20 to the assassination of Defense Minister Kou Voravong one month earlier. Blame for the killing is usually put on the Sananikone family, the political purpose being to remove the cabinet member most strongly in favor of reconciliation with the Pathet Lao. Whether foreigners intrigued to engineer Souvanna's ouster and the naming of Katay, who opposed a coalition government or integration of the armies, remains to be proved. It seems unlikely, however, that the United States played a major role in these events since the CIA was just beginning to set up shop in Laos at the time. The French or Thais seem more likely sources of the trouble.

Vientiane government to establish its administration in the two disputed provinces. By then, however, the Pathet Lao had achieved de facto partition.[8]

The French did not share the American view of the Communist threat. They repeatedly opposed U.S. efforts to push hard against the Pathet Lao because they feared such actions might undermine the Geneva agreements and explode into a new war. They also wanted to preserve their political, economic, and cultural position in Laos against an American takeover.

Even before the Geneva agreements were reached, the French command in Indochina was highly sensitive to American influence, fearing that the United States wanted to replace France in that area. The French and Americans had mirror-image suspicions of one another, both with some justification. Secretary Dulles gave ground for suspicion in March 1955 when he vigorously denied governmental support of efforts by American businessmen to supplant French interests. He did envision, however, a growing United States economic presence "as American interests increase and American business people become more aware of this area, as dollars become more available to government."[9]

Americans in Laos considered replacing the French one of their primary tasks. They had not received orders from Washington to this effect, but they interpreted their mandate as permitting it. Sensing Washington's displeasure at the French capitulation on Indochina and the defeat of EDC, they felt free to ignore, oppose, and undermine the French in Laos.

Vestiges of colonialism had to go, they believed, in order for Laos to be able to resist Communist aggression or subversion. A nation still heavily dependent on its former master was not deemed truly free and independent. Perhaps more significantly, the Americans in Vientiane felt that the French were more interested in preserving their role than in working to resist the Communist threat. The French, therefore, had to be eliminated if Laos was to do its duty in free-world defense.[10]

In practice, the Americans consciously disassociated themselves from the French. They even avoided social contact with them. Bernard Fall told of visiting the home of an American official whose wife, confused by Fall's crew cut and French tropical shorts, asked, "I hope you're not one of those goddamned French?"[11] *

One way to reduce French influence, the men in the United States Embassy concluded, was to link Laos more closely to Thailand. During French rule, all trade had been channeled through Saigon. Just as a matter of economy, it was much easier to transport goods from Bangkok than from the South Vietnamese capital. United States aid programs subsequently encouraged the development of road and rail links from parts of Thailand to the Laotian border. Many officials from southern Laos also preferred closer relations with Thailand; one of the most important was Katay Don Sasorith, Prime Minister from November 1954 until February 1956.

Thailand was highly favored in Washington as well. With Vietnam in danger of falling to communism, American officials wanted to draw a line somewhere. Thailand seemed like the best bet. After a Russian veto in June 1954 of a Thai request for UN border observers to help thwart any aggression, the United States acted to reassure Thailand by granting enough additional aid to double the size of its army. The joint Anglo-American talks preliminary to SEATO reportedly concluded that Indochina was likely to prove indefensible and that Thailand would have to be the next line of defense. The Thais rejected, however, an American effort to establish bases there until their country was "definitely threatened."[12] One of the best ways to defend Thailand was to keep the areas across the Mekong in strong, pro-Western hands.

American efforts to push Laos closer to the Thais and away from the French were not very successful. Never as

* This view has been widely held throughout United States involvement in Laos. As late as 1961, orders to Special Forces requested information on the attitudes of local officials as to whether they were pro-army, pro-American, or pro-French. The Green Berets were also told to "avoid anything that reminds the people of French control." See, "Outline of a Civil Assistance Program," sent with covering letter dated September 22, 1961, reprinted in Donald Robinson (ed.), The Dirty Wars (New York: Delacorte Press, 1968), pp. 232, 236.

antagonistic toward the French as the Vietnamese, Laotian leaders were content to let the French keep their positions in the government, where they were influential advisors. Several thousand French civilians remained in Laos after 1954, thus helping to preserve French cultural preeminence. Not until 1958 did the Americans succeed in putting their own favorites into power.[13]

The French military presence in Laos declined under pressure of the Algerian war. The troops remaining were generally permanent settlers who had taken Laotian wives. They were, consequently, less eager for fighting and usually less able than those called back to France. In spite of a Laotian request for more French troops, the numbers declined. The French never established their second authorized military base in Laos, and the one at Seno never had its full complement of 3,500 men. In 1955 there were 2,500 men. This dropped to 1,173 in 1957 and later to 450. Nor did the French ever fill even half their authorized quota of instructors for the Laotian army. In 1955–56 they had only 670, and this dropped to 400 by 1958.[14]

American military advisors grew frustrated at French lethargy in the face of a perceived Communist threat. They could teach only the use of weapons; they could not accompany troops in the field or teach tactics. Since they could not legally do the job which the French were increasingly reluctant to do, they looked for other means to act. For one thing, the Americans tried to bolster the police forces, which they trained in Thailand to avoid a clear violation of the terms of the Geneva accords. They also sponsored Laotian soldiers at American military training schools.

Simultaneously, the CIA was building up its own separate organization in Laos. Since the Americans had been unable to change the minds of the French or the Laotian leaders regarding the Communist threat, the CIA sought out and groomed for power people who shared its view of the danger. Each part of the American mission thus acted to impose its definition of the situation on the Lao.

Whether these U.S. agents taught the Laotians which levers to press to get more kernels of American aid or whether they learned from their own process of trial and error, the Laotian political and military leaders soon demonstrated that they could play the anti-Communist game for fun and profit.

Although Laos had one of the highest-paid armies in Asia, its military commanders cleverly instituted a pay raise in January 1955 when they were supposedly about to undergo a force reduction. This might have been a way of supporting the same number of soldiers while reducing the paper size of the army. Later testimony before Congress left in doubt the question whether the United States Embassy knew about the increase at the time it occurred. In any event, the American mission quietly acquiesced to this action, as it did to Laotian demands for control over the disbursal of military pay. As a result, the size of the army was never certain. Although the State Department and Pentagon assured Congress that stringent budgetary procedures prevented unauthorized force levels, sources stationed in Laos at the time have admitted that the United States never did know precisely how many soldiers were being supported by the monthly cash grants.[15]

Laotian officials were also able to play on American anti-communism during Secretary Dulles' first and only visit to Laos on February 27, 1955. Some members of the Katay cabinet wanted to send troops to regain control of the two northern provinces and wanted American support in the form of military aid and encouragement. In particular, they wanted air transport and logistical support for their forces. Since the cabinet was not unanimous and the subject was highly sensitive, Dulles met separately with the Crown Prince, the Prime Minister, and other officials.[16]

Dulles had not put much faith either in the Geneva agreements or in the ICC's ability to guarantee them. He saw that partition had been achieved and he wanted to end it. He promised Crown Prince Savang that the United States would aid Laos individually or collectively if it were attacked by the Communists. In return, the Crown Prince assured him of the Laotian government's willingness to fight subversion. Dulles also gave private assurances of American support for a campaign against the Pathet Lao. When the news bubbled out at the diplomatic dinner at the end of his visit, the British and French ministers sent urgent cables to London and Paris, which then instructed their envoys to warn the Laotian government that Britain and France would give Laos no support whatsoever if it encountered difficulties during such a military offensive. This incident effectively killed the plan.[17]

One further agreement to emerge from Dulles' visit was a plan to send Lao officers and men to Thailand to be trained by United States Army officers. This was, of course, a way of taking over that responsibility from the French and circumventing the provisions of the Geneva agreement. Probably under pressure from the French, this was soon reduced to a small training program just for Lao officers and police personnel. These and other efforts to link Laos with Thailand were in keeping with the new Americans posture of strong support for Thailand which had grown out of military analysis in the summer of 1954.[18]

Thereafter, Lao crisis managers confined their activities to winning more U.S. aid and stopped short of allowing foreign military intervention in their defense. When fighting broke out in the contested provinces in July 1955, sources in Vientiane told newsmen that North Vietnamese units and even a few Chinese were accompanying Pathet Lao battalions. Thailand, always more concerned about events in Laos than other members of SEATO, raised the question of intervention. The British still favored working through the ICC; Eisenhower and Dulles were preoccupied with the Big Four summit talks at Geneva. The Laotians themselves said that they resented the Thai suggestion since the Pathet Lao were "an internal affair."[19] Although there were numerous incidents during the subsequent years, none troubled Laotian politics or Laos' self-proclaimed allies abroad until December 1958. Nor did the Royal Army throw its weight around the Laotian political arena until the same time. Its leaders were content to sit back and receive the American largesse.

Most American assistance went to finance the Laotian army. That was considered a good investment because, as Walter Robertson said in 1959, "The army is probably the most important force in the country combatting communism."[20]

Since Laos was seen by Washington only in its cold-war context, anti-communism was the litmus test for American support. There were practical considerations, too. As Ambassador J. Graham Parsons, who held that post from the summer of 1956 until the spring of 1958, later testified: ". . . the Army is virtually the only branch of the Laos government service that had an organization which reached throughout the countryside and which could act as an arm of the Royal Government in remote places."[21]

Little effort went for strengthening the civilian arms of the Royal Government for several reasons. The initial American decision was simply to keep the army in being after the French ended their support. Given limited budgets and a lack of concern for Laos except in terms of containing communism, U.S. planners had few resources and little interest to devote to the country. Since the army received the bulk of the funds, it grew in size and strength, far outstripping the civilian government. There had been no clear choice in 1954 for a military-dominated government in Laos; but that was the chief consequence of the American aid program, one later rationalized by Ambassador Parsons and others.

Economic aid went mainly to projects which had military significance. Various programs were established to train police and civil servants and to help in creating institutions like the national bank. But the bulk of the project assistance, about half of the $18.7 million spent during the 1955–59 period, went for transportation projects to build, improve, or maintain roads and airfields. These projects, of course, had direct military significance, as well as making trade easier and cheaper. By contrast, the agricultural program was quite small during this period, running at 7 percent of the project aid and totaling only $1.3 million during 1955–59. This compares to at least $184 million spent on military budget support during the same period, in a country where about 95 percent of the people are primarily or exclusively farmers.[22]

Both military and economic aid were seen in 1955 as necessary for victories by pro-Western elements in Laos in the elections scheduled for that year. But that objective was not matched by a program carefully balanced for electoral support. Rather, the United States provided aid primarily to the army and for military purposes without regard for political support in the villages or for long-run economic improvement. In fact, a U.S. government official told a congressional committee as late as June 13, 1956, that the aid programs in Laos, Cambodia, and Vietnam were the least stabilized of Asian programs and that "We are still in the process of developing them." The same admission had been made a year earlier by a different official.[23]

Exact amounts of aid given in this first five-year period are almost impossible to determine. Three different sources, all supposedly drawing upon the same information supplied by the foreign aid agency, provide inexplicably differing figures. For example, military budget support for fiscal year 1955 is given as $40.9, $13.4, and $28.2 million and for 1956 is $47.3, $34.9, and $33.7 million. Some of these variations may come from distinctions between obligations and actual expenditures or from changing definitions of what constitutes each category. Even if the published figures could be reconciled, the picture would still be incomplete, for the Central Intelligence Agency spent large sums for its activities in Laos. In fact, the CIA budgeted for some military assistance at the request of the Defense Department, in order to lessen the budget which DOD had to defend before Congress.[24]

The basic trends are consistent. There was a large increase for the first full year of the program, fiscal 1956. Aid dropped somewhat during fiscal 1957 and then was cut sharply for 1958 and then again for 1959. The first large cut coincided with the establishment of a coalition government including the Pathet Lao and the cessation of aid pending agreement on currency reform. The 1959 cut is misleading, however, since each dollar of aid after devaluation in October 1958 could finance more that twice the previous outlay of kip.[25]

As seen from Washington, the aid program in Laos was designed to bolster the army and government rather than to promote economic development or self-sufficiency in defense. When abuses came to light, State Department and foreign aid officials responded by citing political objectives. "This is a program to keep Laos this side of the Bamboo Curtain."[26] The same goal prevailed in Vientiane, where difficulties in administering the aid program took second place to the political objectives until those goals seemed endangered by a coalition government and the abuses had grown distressingly evident.

Although the Pentagon had been reluctant to approve force levels for the Laotian army, in part because of their inability to oversee the use of funds through a regular MAAG (Military Assistance Advisory Group), the need for the equivalent of a MAAG soon became evident. During 1955, the civilian economists in the United States Operations Mission (USOM) had the job of judging requests for equipment. Since they were not trained or experienced in that kind of work, Pentagon officers won approval to establish a Program Evaluation Office (PEO) at the end of the year. They argued the administrative necessity of having some United States military personnel on the scene. In order to avoid overt contravention of the Geneva agreements, the men sent to Laos were all officially retired from the services, at least in the early years. They went about in civilian clothes, but under one PEO director their crew cuts and white shirts, shorts, and socks were so similar as to constitute a uniform.[27]

Despite these subterfuges, the PEO was, in practice, a MAAG. Testimony on the work of the PEO was regularly deleted from congressional hearings "for security reasons" except for one curious slip in 1957, when Laos was included on a list of "countries where MAAG personnel are stationed."[28] The PEO was not established as a full-fledged MAAG, but it gradually evolved into one as it took over more and more of the training responsibilities of the French. Its officers began with police training activities in 1955 and followed those with civic action programs in 1957. The PEO official functions grew from disbursing and budget evaluation to end-use inspection, to weapons training, and, finally, in July 1959, to tactical training and field operations.[29]

While the United States increased its involvement in Laotian affairs, the Royal Government and Pathet Lao moved haltingly toward a reconciliation. There is no evidence that American pressure altered the speed or direction of this movement before 1957, but it did become an important force in the domestic politics of Laos. In the first few years the Americans were still learning their way around; if anyone provided a guiding hand, it was likely to have been the French.

The Geneva agreements had called for a unified, independent state in Laos, and the Royal Government had promised the complete integration of all factions in the government and the political system. Disagreements over the technicalities of these arrangements, which reflected more profound differences among the factions, brought delays. The major problem throughout 1955 was preparing for the elections scheduled that year. In order to allow time for a political settlement between the Royal Government and the Pathet Lao, the elections were postponed from August until December. But even direct talks between Prime Minister Katay and Pathet Lao leader Prince Souphanouvong in October failed to resolve the differences. The government demanded immediate control over the two northern provinces; the Pathet Lao demanded joint election supervisory committees and postponement of changes in the status of the contested provinces until after the elections. As a result of this impasse, the Pathet Lao boycotted the elections, which were held only in the remaining ten provinces. Katay's party won twenty-one of the thirty-nine seats at stake.[30]

After a six-week political crisis following the post-election resignation of the Katay government, Prince Souvanna Phouma was named Prime Minister. He pledged: "No effort shall be spared so that the negotiations with the adverse party be crowned by the loyal reconciliation longed for by all."[31] By early August 1956 Souvanna had reached agreements in principle with a Pathet Lao delegation headed by his half-brother, Prince Souphanouvong, on the need for a cease-fire in the disputed areas, a foreign policy of neutrality, and the political rights of the Pathet Lao. The Prime Minister then reactivated Washington's concern by making a two-week trip to Peking and Hanoi.

This trip was the turning point for many people in

Washington—proof that Souvanna would knuckle under to the Asian Communist leaders. American officials tried hard to prevent the trip by repeated warnings of the dangers of getting too close to the Communists. Coming so soon after the agreement with Souphanouvong, the journey was symbolic confirmation that Souvanna meant to work with the devil.[32]

In fact, the visit was part of Souvanna's effort to prove his neutrality and willingness to achieve reconciliation with the Pathet Lao, and the results were fairly innocuous. The Laotians secured Chinese reaffirmation of Chou En-lai's promises at the Bandung Conference not to intervene in Laotian affairs. In return, the Lao delegation agreed to forbid the installation of American bases or the entry of American military advisors into Laos. They refused, however, to permit the establishment of a Chinese consulate-general in Vientiane or to accept Chinese economic aid. Nor did they accept the North Vienamese request to exchange diplomatic missions similar to that which Laos had in Saigon. Nevertheless, the American reaction was to press even harder against a coalition.[33]

Opposition to a coalition government in Laos was a basic feature of American policy during the Eisenhower administration. Politically, the Republicans could not tolerate the "loss" of further territory to Communist domination, especially not after their virulent criticism of the Truman administration for the "loss" of China. Apparently, everyone dealing with Laos during those years feared that the Pathet Lao would dominate and then completely take over any coalition. One official credited Walter Lippmann with the best expression of this belief: "In any political marriage, the Communists are always the male."[34]

- The roots of this fear go back to the 1948 coup in Czechoslovakia. That event seems to have produced or confirmed the belief in the minds of the men who later dealt with Laos that coalitions with the Communists were dangerous and unworkable. Walter Robertson expressed the consensus among U.S. policy makers in 1959: "We very much feared when they took the Communists into the Government that the same thing would happen to Laos as happened to Czechoslovakia. We very much feared the Communist coalition would bring the Communists dangerously into the country."[35]

American officials seemed to believe that the Pathet Lao need not and should not participate in the government of Laos in any way. They riveted their attention not to the problems of building a viable economic and political system throughout the country but, rather, to the areas controlled by the Pathet Lao. Both Royal Laotian and United States officials seemed obsessed with the two "lost" provinces, often to the relative disregard of the other ten.

For instance, the first air drops in a large famine relief program in September 1955 went into Phong Saly province. One of the few village aid projects in the early years operated in Xieng Khouang near the border of Sam Neua. Although a breakdown of aid projects by province is unavailable for the 1950s, one State Department source remembers being criticized by Laotians and Americans for his suggestion at the time that too much attention and aid were being devoted to Phong Saly and Sam Neua.[36]

The hope of extirpating the Pathet Lao with a strong anti-communist force posed a dilemma for United States policy makers. In order to obtain congressional financing and support, they had to emphasize Laos' vital, strategic position in Southeast Asia. But those arguments were turned back on them when they threatened to suspend aid in order to prevent a coalition. Lao leaders occasionally cited congressional testimony on the importance of Laos when the United States Ambassador warned that a coalition would not find favor in Washington.[37]

Aid suspension was not a credible threat at first. If Laos were considered vital because of its strategic position, it would be foolish to "burn down the barn to kill the rats." The perceived risks to overall American policy in the area far outweighed the gains from opposition to a coalition alone. Only when the abuses in Laos jeopardized the whole foreign aid program did those risks seem justifiable.

Events in the autumn of 1956 made aid suspension a much more tolerable risk. The mixed political and military committees, set up by Souvanna Phouma and Souphanouvong in August, reached agreements at the end of October. The political committee went even further than Souvanna had been willing to go in the summer and agreed to the establishment of diplomatic relations with consenting neighbors and to the acceptance of aid given unconditionally by any nation.[38] To U.S. officials, this looked like an opportunity for Soviet and Chinese aid missions and for subversive embassies run by Peking and Hanoi.

American aid officials soon had a pretext for disciplining the Laotian government when they discovered that four import licenses totaling about $14 million in goods had been issued by the Laotians without the requisite U.S. approval. To prevent corruption and to have some control over Laotian trade, Americans had demanded such approval since 1955. In light of growing evidence of aid abuses, this discovery seemed to require strong action. After much agonizing over the possible effects of such an action, embassy and Washington officials agreed to suspend aid in December 1956 until the United States received assurances that regular procedures, including American agreement on import licenses, would be followed in the future. Administration witnesses later cited this act as proof of their determination to end abuses in the aid program even at the risk of pushing Laos closer to the Communists.[39] The aid was resumed after a month; its suspension had not had a significant impact on the Laotian economy or politics.

Lacking much leverage with its aid program or its embassy's importunings, the United States increased its direct, but covert, intervention in Laotian political affairs. Although Ambassador Parsons claims that, except for the aid program, the United States limited its intervention in internal affairs to open persuasion,[40] the testimony of other people in Laos at the same time reveals a wide range of U.S. activities.

"The CIA was the arm of policy implementation under Parsons," one source says. The Agency's staff in Laos had been expanded and its intelligence network fairly well established by 1957. It was, consequently, the best source of information and leverage on Laotian politics. The CIA had its own special perspective on the situation, however, one occasioned by its rivalry not with other Americans but with the French. Agency operatives had no rivals within the embassy because they were the most effective at getting jobs done; they also had access to funds for special and emergency operations. The PEO had not yet assumed a training role in Laos and was largely divorced from policy discussions. Ambassador Parsons also mistrusted and did not get along well with the PEO director during 1956–58, General Rothwell Brown. The USOM was preoccupied with the mounting difficulties of administering the aid programs. Only the Foreign Service Officers worked with the CIA on policy, and they were partly dependent on the Agency for intelligence and covert operations. The primary competition for the CIA in Laos was the French Deuxieme Bureau and the network of Frenchmen who were high officials in the Royal Government bureaucracy. It is not surprising, therefore, that the CIA was the most vigorous opponent of Lao whom it considered under French influence or control.[41]

Souvanna Phouma was one such leader, for he was considered hopelessly pro-French as well as dangerously naïve about the Pathet Lao. Souvanna persisted in denying that the Pathet Lao were under foreign control and in saying that no Lao could be a Communist. Although there was disagreement between the Ambassador and some of the junior officials over the extent of North Vietnamese control over the Pathet Lao, Parson's view, strongly supported by Walter Robertson and others in Washington, was that the Pathet Lao were Communists and posed a significant threat to Laos.[42]

Former Premier Katay Don Sasorith was the embassy's choice to replace Souvanna. Katay's anti-Communist credentials were still impeccable in spite of his willingness to negotiate with the Pathet Lao in 1955. After all, the talks had eventually broken down. Katay visited the United States in January 1957 and returned to Laos to launch a violent propaganda campaign against the Pathet Lao. The United States Embassy, on the heels of its temporary aid-suspension the month before, made thinly veiled threats to stop aid altogether if the Pathet Lao were brought into the government and administration. One journalist close to the Pathet Lao claims that Americans went to every member of the National Assembly and warned them of dire consequences if the Pathet Lao were allowed into the government. Even a pro-American Lao admits that the United States made these threats and implies that Katay had strong American backing for his crusade. Katay did not succeed in forcing Souvanna from office, but he did mobilize more rightists against a coalition. Souvanna's government modified its position by demanding that integration of Pathet Lao troops precede rather than follow the establishment of a coalition.[43]

Souvanna Phouma must have felt threatened by this campaign, for he asked Britain, France, and the United States for a declaration of support for his government and its policy. The tripartite note sent in reply on April 24 gave the support, but linked it to "firmness" in resisting the "extraneous conditions" which the Pathet Lao sought to achieve. American diplomatic sources cited as such conditions the establishment of a coalition government including the Pathet Lao, acceptance of diplomatic missions, and the adoption of a policy of neutralism. Agreement to these conditions "would have given the Communists their most significant gains in Southeast Asia since the partition of Indochina," they reportedly said.[44]

Shortly after this note, on May 11, Souvanna was defeated in the National Assembly on votes supporting his approach to the negotiations. The votes were ambiguous, however, since the assembly had unanimously approved the August 1956 agreements with the Pathet Lao. But Souvanna resigned immediately, thus starting a governmental crisis which continued until August 25. Katay tried and failed twice to form a government. He differed from Souvanna primarily in urging a harder line in the negotiations. An old leftist and neutralist, Bong Souvannavong, also tried and failed. In the end, Souvanna Phouma succeeded in forming a new government, but only after using the trick of limiting his cabinet to half the former size to gain additional votes. (Cabinet members were not allowed to vote on their own investiture.)[45]

American officials viewed Souvanna's return as a serious setback for the West. They were reportedly willing to accept amnesty for the Pathet Lao and individual participation in

politics, but not as an established party.[46] The British shared the
American concern over a coalition, but had not been so vigorous in opposition. The French, by contrast, were active on behalf of Souvanna Phouma, who was regarded as pro-French
(since he had studied in France and his wife was partly French
in ancestry). Most French activity was not directed from Paris
but came from French advisors to the Lao government. They
were much less concerned about the consequences of a coalition government since they expected to retain their influence.[47]

Souvanna resumed talks with the Pathet Lao and
worked out arrangements for a coalition by early November. On
November 18, Prince Souphanouvong symbolically returned the
two provinces to the Crown Prince and joined the new coalition
government as Minister of Reconstruction and Planning. There
was one other Pathet Lao member of the cabinet, as Minister of
Religion and Fine Arts. Elections were to be held the following
May for twenty seats to be added to the National Assembly.

In retrospect, it appears that domestic and foreign opposition to a coalition did succeed in stimulating provisions in the
final coalition agreements which fell short of original Pathet
Lao demands and which inhibited any Pathet Lao attempt to
dominate the new government. Only two Pathet Lao representatives were put into the cabinet, and in relatively insignificant
posts. The 1957 agreements reversed the sequence stipulated a
year before on the return of the two provinces so that the return preceded the coalition government. In practice, the events
were almost simultaneous. Instead of specific pledges to accept
Chinese and North Vietnamese diplomatic missions and Chinese
and Soviet aid, Souvanna merely promised to improve relations
with Laos' neighbors and to accept any aid that did not conflict with the country's sovereignty. But neither nation offered
aid and no Communist nation established a diplomatic mission
until the Soviet Union did in October 1960 following the Kong-
Le coup. The 1957 agreements also declared the "de facto dis-
appearance" of the Fighting Units of the Pathet Lao with their
integration into the Royal Army. Only 1,500 (of a force then
estimated to be about 6,000) troops were to be integrated; the
rest would return to civilian life. And all war material was to

be handed over to the Royal Government. The unanimous vote of approval given to the new coalition government on November 19 demonstrated the general satisfaction with these arrangements on the part of many politicians who had been suspicious earlier.[48]

Only the United States voiced its opposition to the coalition. State Department officials conceded that the agreement was a reversal for United States policy, but their official statement referred only to the principle of coalition and not to specific provisions of the Laotian settlement.

> The reunification of Laos under conditions that would guarantee its sovereignty and independence would be highly desirable. The United States feels, however, that a coalition with the Communists is a dangerous line of conduct, for the history of similar coalitions elsewhere in the world reveals that they end tragically in penetration and seizure of the country by the Communists. Consequently, the evolution of the situation in Laos is a source of serious concern to the United States, which is observing very closely the situation in that country.[49]

Assistant Secretary Robertson reportedly feared that the coalition could prove "dangerously contagious." But Secretary Dulles was more cautious and hopeful. "Let's watch it. It might work," he said.[50]

The State Department reconsidered its policy toward Laos in the weeks after the coalition and many people thought that the United States would have to pull out of the country. The conclusion was, however, that termination of aid would be tantamount to abandoning Laos to the Communists. In order to make the best of a bad situation, the people in the embassy in Vientiane came up with a plan to help anti-communist forces win the elections the following May. Such a victory, they hoped, would enable the next prime minister to exclude Pathet Lao representatives from the cabinet.[51]

That plan, named Operation Booster Shot, was a village-aid program designed to counter the criticisms that American assistance until that time had been concentrated in the cities and had brought little benefit to the masses of people in the countryside. As one CIA operative explained the thinking in the embassy, "We thought that politics is politics the world over, so we tried to transplant Tammany."[52]

The United States spent over $3 million on more than ninety projects, including well-digging, small irrigation and flood-control dams, construction of hospitals and repair of schools and temples, repair of roads and airfields, and airdropping 1,300 tons of food, medical, and other supplies. These were all high-visibility projects, calculated to have psychological appeal rather than long-range economic benefits. Bernard Fall reported that many pro-government candidates were given lines of credit for cash or merchandise to use in making gifts to village heads or individual villagers.[53]

Horace Smith, the new United States Ambassador in March 1958, concluded that Booster Shot "has had a greater impact on Laos than any other aid program which the United States has undertaken in this area to date."[54] The aid did not produce an electoral victory for the anti-communists, however, and its impact may have been to weaken those very groups. Rather than working through the Laotian government and politicians and letting them take the credit for the projects, United States personnel were flamboyant and aggressive in carrying out their tasks. The U.S. Air Force, for example, was highly visible, in spite of the initial plans calling for unmarked planes. Some civil action programs were intended to be implemented through the Royal Army. But Laotian reluctance and lethargy permitted American eagerness to take over and dominate the program. In Ambassador Smith's enthusiasm to see concrete results from the crash project, he gave the various groups in his country team a free rein which he never succeeded in pulling taut.[55]

Even before the elections, however, the concern in Washington shifted from the dangers of a Communist takeover of power in Laos to the dangers of publicity and congressional criticism about the aid program there. The minor abuses and lack of controls which had been overlooked because of the sense of urgency in implementing the program had mushroomed into problems of scandalous proportions.

A *Wall Street Journal* article on April 9, 1958, first directed public attention to the spectacle of the American aid program in Laos. It discussed some of the projects which had had problems and gave examples of the many luxuries flooding into Laos on the commodity import program. It criticized the lack of any real economic development despite the $100 million expended up to that time. The author also quoted one American official as saying: "One trouble is that in 1955 we started to throw in anything just to impress the Laos government, and now we're stuck with a bunch of assorted, unrelated projects but no real program."[56]

There had been storm warnings, to be sure, but harried administrators were as reluctant to heed them as happy picnickers. Senator Mansfield, reporting on his 1955 visit to Laos, complained that the American mission was too large and its programs too expensive. He also criticized the high cost of supporting a Lao soldier, which, at about $1,000 per man per year, was the highest of any country in Asia. The administration responded that it was merely continuing what the French had done, but it failed to note that much of that burden had been financed by the United States during actual hostilities.[57]

Further criticism of the high cost and large size of the Lao army was made in 1956 by Clement Johnston, chairman of the board of the U.S. Chamber of Commerce, who studied the foreign aid programs in Southeast Asia at the request of the Senate Foreign Relations Committee. He recommended reductions in both the size of the army and its pay. He cited an administrative laxity which was repeatedly denied but in fact never corrected for several years. "At least we think that the army is good, but we are forced to take it on faith since we have no means of checking the numbers, the whereabouts, or the efficiency of the great bulk of the troops." Johnston was also the first to point to the artificially high exchange rate and the resulting smuggling, which he called "a danger signal that should not be ignored."[58]

Another warning had come from within the executive branch in May 1956. This was the so-called Sessions Report, which gave the findings of an International Cooperation Administration–State–Defense study group on foreign aid programs in Southeast Asia. It criticized both the administration and the feasibility of the program in Laos. The report said that morale was low and that the USOM lacked adequate direction. Noting the limited absorptive capacity of the Laotian economy, it recommended reductions at first in imports and ultimately in the Lao army.[59]

Why were these warnings ignored in Washington? The simplest explanation is that no one considered the problems his responsibility. ICA officials were in perpetual trouble with Congress over the foreign aid budget and wanted to avoid any hints of scandal; meanwhile, they saw that the bulk of the aid went to pay the army and, thus, was the Defense Department's responsibility. The Pentagon, which continued to approve aid to the Laotian army because of political considerations important to the State Department, was content to see that army in being and increasingly anti-communist. The Far East Bureau of the State Department was constrained by its own cold-war definition of the situation. As long as Laos was preserved for the free world, corruption and waste were acceptable annoyances. The CIA, of course, faced no sanctions if the abuses were disclosed; in fact, corruption probably made its job easier.

Men in the embassy in Vientiane saw the abuses and realized the potential for public scandal. They asked Washington for support in pressuring the Lao for reforms, but they were ignored. In the early autumn of 1956 Ambassador Graham Parsons, newly arrived at the end of July, and the head of the USOM, Carter de Paul, came to the conclusion that the kip had to be devalued. The Laotian government was strongly opposed to such a move, in part because of the memory of the rapid inflation which followed the 1953 devaluation relative to the French franc, to which the kip was then tied. Washington officials were also reluctant to press for a devaluation at that time. The ambassador persisted, even to the point of assembling a sheaf of seventeen documents on the currency problem which had evoked no effective action from Washington. He presented these to Under-Secretary Christian Herter when both men met in Saigon in the spring of 1957. Only then did Washington begin to take steps to help orchestrate a devaluation, which did not finally occur until a year and a half later. By then, Parsons had returned to the United States and was able to push for more action from his position as Deputy Assistant Secretary for the Far East.[60]

Nothing stirred Washington to strong action on aid abuses until newspaper publicity brought the Congress and budgetary considerations into play. Even the General Accounting Office (GAO), whose raison d'être seems to be to find any examples—significant or petty—of possible government waste or mismanagement for congressmen to use to justify their budget cuts, was slow to make its findings available. GAO had investigated aid programs in Vietnam and Korea in the autumn of 1956 and had appended a brief discussion of the programs in Laos and Cambodia based entirely on Washington records. The draft was not submitted to ICA until the summer of 1957, and comments not returned until January 1958. ICA, of course, was in no hurry to have Congress see the report. GAO began to sniff paydirt after the coalition government was formed, and, in December 1957, decided to send a special team to Vientiane for a field survey. The investigation did not take place until March 1958, but its report was released at the end of April without having first received comments by ICA. One GAO official even admitted that the report was released quickly in order to ride the crest of the wave of publicity about Laos prompted by the April 9 article in the *Wall Street Journal*.[61]

Congressmen viewed the reports about Laos not in terms of communism but, rather, in terms of the foreign aid program. Those who were against that program seized on the examples of poor administration. Those who favored it warned the ICA and State Department officials that these were the kinds of problems which had to be avoided or corrected if the program were to continue to receive support. The end result was that every official connected with foreign aid knew that he had to prevent such scandals from occurring or from reaching public view. They acted to correct the abuses in Laos not because of a judgment that the situation was intolerable in itself but, rather, because knowledge of it was jeopardizing the entire foreign aid program.

Almost every committee handling the foreign aid program devoted two or three days to hearings on Laos in 1958. By July, Senator Everett Dirksen could say that when the congressional conference committee met to resolve differences on the foreign aid bill, "there is going to be a rough go and Laos has become a symbol."[62] In 1959 Congressman Porter Hardy's Government Operations Subcommitee held nineteen days of hearings just on Laos, with testimony running to almost 1,000 pages. It is from these post hoc analyses and justifications that most of the published information on Laos comes, since discussion of Laos in earlier years was almost entirely deleted for security reasons.

While the Congress focused its attention on the specific examples of unsuccessful projects and the seemingly needless luxuries imported with aid-generated funds (dozens of "sleek Cadillacs, Buicks, and Fords," "4½ tons of feather dusters," "73 tons of sporting goods, fishing tackle, and thermos jugs," and so forth),[63] it overlooked many of the causes of these abuses. These causes were to be found not simply in bad judgment or Laotian venality but also, and perhaps more basically, in the way the U.S. mission was organized to implement the aid program and the special circumstances of the Laotian economy.

The causes of these problems are clear when one examines the operational stresses on the U.S. mission. The abuses which horrified congressmen later discovered resulted largely from the nature of the organization established to implement the aid program and the slowness with which it adjusted to the conditions in Laos. Rigid application of standard procedures and inflexibility in the face of difficulties are inherent in bureaucracies. The corrections which the embassy then tried to make often foundered on the obstinacy of the Laotian government, whose sovereignty, survival, or personal profits seemed threatened by the proposed reforms. Those concerns are probably inherent in all governments.

United States aid was given to Laos in a crash program which operated under primitive conditions. The officials who began work in the tent in the pasture in Vientiane on January 1, 1955, had been hastily assembled. Although the President had decided in mid-August to rechannel aid to Indochina directly through the governments of the Associated States, the ICA did not decide to set up separate missions until November 14. It was apparently not until December that the three-man mission was also given the responsibility of administering the payment of troops in the Lao army. On January 1 it faced the immediate task of keeping the army in being and developing programs and organizations for future activities.[64]

Conditions were unfavorable for the usual kind of program to support an army. Laos lacked the customary array of financial and marketing institutions which could be used to import goods to absorb the currency given as troop salaries. Normally the United States would institute a commodity-import program, through which the central bank would generate counterpart funds with local currency deposited by importers to pay their foreign exchange costs. But the Lao economy was only superficially monetized, and imported relatively little. There were no banks in Laos. There were no experienced importers because foreign trade had been handled through Saigon. Government officials lacked administrative skills for the new situation, not to mention established procedures and even forms to process.

Faced with the urgency of paying the army, the United States began a cash-grant program and helped to establish a national bank to handle it. The embassy would then deposit a check drawn on a New York bank in the dollar equivalent of the kip required to support the army. The bank would then issue the kip, holding the dollars as backing. Lao army officers would pay their men, who could then buy goods from importers. These kip would return to the bank when importers used them to buy dollars to finance their transactions. Since this whole process would take weeks or months, it was deemed necessary to provide regular cash grants to support immediate payments to the army.[65]

During the first few months the American mission was fully occupied just meeting regular deadlines and helping to organize the institutions and procedures to carry out its program. There was little opportunity to examine the requests for assistance, both because of a lack of time and a lack of expertise in judging military requirements. The Chief of the ICA Mission admitted later to Congress that "The economic aid we recommended was simply the dollar value of the military budget requirement translated at 35 [kip to the dollar]."[66] These initial difficulties must have continued for some time, since administration witnesses admitted as late as June 1956 that the overall program for Laos was still being developed.

Although an American sat with the Import-Export Commission from its creation, the United States did not get formal agreement to controls over its aid until July 1955. An agreement then stipulated that the dollars were to be ". . . used only as agreed upon between our two Governments." The controls were de facto veto power on import license requests and general guidelines on what kinds of commodities would be permitted. These guidelines were the standard for all commodity import programs and, for the most part, prohibited obvious luxuries such as liquor, jewelry, and expensive automobiles. As a further check, the United States, in November 1955, contracted with a private accounting firm to verify the prices shown on the import license applications.[67]

These controls proved inadequate for the inexperienced but wily businessmen of Laos. Some managed to win approval for imports without going through the official commission. Others would get the necessary approvals but would never import the goods, selling them instead in Bangkok or elsewhere. This diversion was easy because, for nearly all of the first three years of the aid program, it was impossible to obtain through-bills of lading to Laos. As a result, actual imports were only about one-third of the total licensed. There were additional incentives to avoid actual importation because of the difficulties in selling too many goods in Laos and because of the profits to be made outside the country. The United States was supporting the kip at thirty-five to the dollar, although the free market rate in Bangkok and Hong Kong was up to 110 by 1957. Since an importer had to pay only thirty-five kip for each dollar of goods for which he had a license, he could—and many did—make huge profits by selling the goods elsewhere and then reconverting his earnings into two or three times the number of kip initially invested.[68]

Under these circumstances, the record of abuses and irregularities began to pile up. Not only were Laotians able to circumvent the various procedures established to control the effects of the aid program, but several Americans associated with the program performed highly questionable, if not illegal, acts. One official accepted $13,000 in bribes from a construction company in return for his help in securing contracts and overlooking deficiencies in its performance. Several officials went to work for private contractors soon after participating in decisions to award them contracts in Laos. One director of the USOM sold his apparently inoperable 1947 Cadillac at a highly inflated price to the head of a construction company, who soon thereafter dismantled the car and hid it in an abandoned well.[69]

These examples illustrate the climate of corruption in Laos, both among the profiteering businessmen and within the U.S. mission. They are also further evidence of the personnel problems faced by the embassy. While some men were lured by profits, others were lured by the prospects of notoriety. Haynes Miller, an end-use auditor of foreign aid funds, was forced to resign from his position in 1957 after he made repeated complaints about fraud and corruption in the program. He returned to the United States, gave his evidence to several investigative groups, and wrote an article about aid to Laos. Although a congressional committee later charged that he had been "railroaded" out of Laos because he was "close to discovering" proof of more corruption and inadequate performance by U.S. contractors, the evidence from Ambassador Parsons is that Miller had had serious adjustment problems. Miller was ostracized by his fellow workers at least because of his personality, though possibly also because he threatened their job security.[70]

In view of the mounting and indefensible criticisms, the State Department fell back on its political justification for the aid program. "Since we are financing a program of security, not the economy of Laos, we cannot discontinue aid to Laos because of economic considerations."[71] Yet, this is precisely what happened—once before, once after, and once even at the very moment that the State Department submitted the quoted statement to Congress in March 1958.

Two flaws had become apparent in the economic aid program—abuses in the import system and overvaluation of the kip. The latter was a major cause of the former because of the temptations generated by the chance of exchange profiteering. The unrealistic exchange rate also meant that the foreign aid budget was higher than it had to be to finance the same programs. As detailed earlier, the embassy began pressing for devaluation late in 1956. It seized upon the discovery of import license irregularities to win Washington's approval for a suspension of aid for thirty days, during which time the Lao again promised to get American agreement to all import licenses.

In implementing this and subsequent aid stoppages, however, the United States left most of the teeth out of its action. Project aid continued since it lacked the water-tap quality of cash grants. Although the grants stopped or were delayed, Washington agreed to let the army be paid anyway. The State Department considered the army too important for the defense of Southeast Asia against communism to let its strength be jeopardized for the sake of ICA's control procedures. Over time, payment with unsupported kip could have produced a severely disrupting inflation, but for the fact that the central bank had managed to accumulate large gold reserves which it was able to use to back its kip and finance imports. The cash-grant system had, thus, created a situation which destroyed the efficacy of any controls which the United States deemed necessary. As if this were not enough, the embassy tried to make amends by resuming aid after thirty days and paying more than the amount which had been held back.[72]

During 1957 Washington kept open its option of suspending aid by requiring monthly approval of the aid disbursements. When further import-licensing irregularities became known in the summer of 1957, the embassy demanded firmer assurances from the Lao government. Although this demand came at a time of governmental instability—the cabinet crisis followed by the establishment of the coalition—the Laotians used these circumstances as an argument against further infringements on their sovereignty through tighter controls. It was not until November that Laos agreed to issue import licenses, and then only if they had the countersignature of an American official.[73]

Sovereignty was a delicate issue in all of these negotiations for stricter controls. The United States had argued for the principle of complete independence from France but then, for reasons of good management and accountability to Congress, demanded procuratorial controls. Moreover, these demands were made solely to prevent abuses which might stir public criticism of the aid program, without regard for their effect on the Laotian political scene. They may even have run counter to American anti-communist objectives in Laos, since sovereignty and the aid program were major issues in the 1958 elections, in which leftist forces won over half the seats at stake.

Currency reforms were debated in Washington throughout 1957, but with no clear agreement on what should be done.[74] There was also disagreement within the embassy in Vientiane. Most discussions came down to a split between economists and politically sensitive administrators and diplomats. The economists favored rapid devaluation and free convertibility with the dollar. The others, fearing massive capital flights, higher aid levels to support the kip, and loss of congressionally desired controls over imports, argued for continued controls. They also argued that the timing had to be carefully chosen to avoid disastrous political consequences in Laos.

Ambassador Parsons was called to Washington for consultations in the autumn of 1957. A fundamental review of policy took place, prompted primarily by the agreement on a coalition government including the Pathet Lao. The basic decision at that time was to try to bolster the anti-communist forces in Laos with Operation Booster Shot. At the same time, however,

Parsons was able to win approval for economic aid reform demands. Washington officials were then much more willing to use aid levers to get political and economic changes.

The new American demands were for a USOM countersignature to all import licenses and devaluation at the earliest possible time. It was also decided to hire an economist from the International Monetary Fund for a special study mission to obtain recommendations for implementing the devaluation. Going outside the United States government for such advice served at least two purposes: it evaded the bureaucratic wranglings which had inhibited discussions until then and it gave an "objective" international imprimatur to the changes which the United States wanted the Lao government to make.

Except for the import licensing procedure, the Lao government resisted these changes. Prime Minister Souvanna Phouma paid an unofficial visit to Washington in January 1958 to explain his reasons, although American officials thought that he was coming to negotiate an agreement. The Premier said that no changes could be made before the May elections without risking a severe dislocation of the price structure and consequent benefits to the Pathet Lao. He did agree in principle to devaluation and left his Finance Minister to work out details.[75]

When these subsequent discussions dragged on without agreement, the United States decided to apply more pressure. It suspended aid in February and March until the Laotian government agreed in writing to put all dollars received into a blocked account pending devaluation. This prevented the issuance of import licenses at the 35:1 ratio. The new American ambassador, Horace Smith, showed his determination to act shortly before he left for his post in March 1958 when he told the IMF economist, "I'm going to run this through. Will you help me?"[76]

Before those economic reforms could be achieved, they took on an even greater importance because of the publicity about aid abuses in April. The old defense that Laos was still anti-communist was no longer credible, both because of the coalition with the Pathet Lao and because of the 1958 election results. In the May 4 balloting for twenty-one additional seats in the National Assembly, the Pathet Lao and their sympathizers won thirteen. They succeeded because the opposition votes were fragmented among the four traditional parties, who nominated eighty-four candidates for the twenty-one positions. It was not surprising, therefore, that the Pathet Lao could win so handily with only 32 percent of the overall vote. But the results nevertheless deeply shocked Washington, where confident predictions of a pro-Western victory were still being made on May 7, when results were incomplete.[77] This setback, coupled with the scandal in the aid program, seriously threatened both American policy in Laos and the entire foreign aid budget.

Loss of the election by pro-American candidates changed the definition of the situation by Washington officials. ICA recognized the increased urgency of doing something quickly to appear to stop aid abuses. The fact that most of the scandalous examples had occurred a year or two before was irrelevant; what mattered was a public display of administrative attacks on waste. The Far East Bureau in the State Department had been caught indulging in falsely optimistic predictions; it, too, had to make a show of action. The Pentagon and CIA went along with the decision for more drastic action because they also won the right to continue their efforts to put the anti-communist forces into power. By offering their plans at a time of policy review, they were able to obtain a broader mandate for action. Careful timing thus enabled the clandestine forces to change the face of the issue from an aid question to a broader political one.

Under these circumstances, Washington officials agreed to take their most drastic action thus far—to stop aid entirely until the kip was devalued. This was done on June 30, 1958. At the same time, the CIA launched a series of political maneuvers, examined in detail in the next part of this chapter, designed to rally anti-communist forces in Laos. These actions were on separate, though related, tracks. Contrary to the opinion of most writers that the United States cut off aid to force Souvanna Phouma from office and replace him with a strong anti-communist, the evidence is strong that American aid would have been suspended no matter who was Premier.[78] The impetus to take any action was the growing scandal over the aid program. The American groups in Laos which used this opportunity to work against Souvanna acted without close supervision from Washington and without regard for economic reforms.

Souvanna's government fell in July. Aid was not resumed until nearly two months after the formation of the Phoui Sananikone government in August, and then only after the devaluation of the kip. If achievement of a pro-Western government had been the primary objective of stopping aid, payments could have been resumed, at least in a token way, as soon as that government took office. Not to do so clearly risked undermining the new cabinet by lending proof to the Pathet Lao charges of loss of sovereignty to the Americans.

Although the political objectives were important, they had been pushed into the background by the immediate problem of salvaging the aid program. The United States had tolerated eight months of a coalition government with the loss only of pride. Laos was not in immediate danger of jumping behind the Bamboo Curtain. But the aid program in the Congress, where Senator Dirksen had called Laos a symbol in the fight for appropriations, was in immediate danger because of Laos. Unless the abuses were ended by devaluation, the whole Laotian program might be terminated.

The plan finally accepted by the Laotian government on October 10 combined features suggested by the economists and the diplomats. It instituted free convertibility for the kip at eighty to the dollar and eliminated import licensing and most money transfers. The United States shifted to a regular commodity import program through which it, rather than the Lao government, decided on the articles and procedures for financing. It was bound to support the kip exchange rates, however, through occasional direct grants to replenish exchange reserves in times of need. The agreement also entailed some civil service, police, and education reforms.[79]

From Washington it appeared that the aid suspension had been successful in forcing the currency reforms. But, in the field, the story was slightly different. Although Washington had forbidden the expenditure of defense support funds, the military mission, at the suggestion of CINCPAC (Commander in Chief, Pacific Forces) authorized money for the Laotian troops through a contract designated for "transportation."[80] This circumvention of official policy, apparently without the knowledge or approval of anyone in Washington, was not the last time that subordinates took Laos policy into their own hands. It was only another example of what was becoming a major feature of that policy—separate operations run by separate parts of the country team for disparate objectives.

The American Embassy in Vientiane was deeply split over which groups to support and in what ways. The division was more than an intellectual disagreement on policy, however, since it revealed the same cleavages as those over personalities and organizations.

Normally an embassy follows standard procedures and a predictable division of responsibility. In Laos, as elsewhere, each organization with the embassy developed its own friends and clients in the host country. The men in the PEO, for example, worked with the Royal Army officers and, naturally, became protective of them and their interests in meetings of the U.S. country team. Aid officials worked with their counterparts in the Laotian government and with American contractors. The CIA was active on a wide scale, particularly in the army and civilian groups, both political and social. The Foreign Service Officers, including the Ambassador, worked most closely and frequently with the top officials of the Lao government and with the Foreign Ministry. Their ties to political groups which were out of power were minimal.

Special circumstances in 1958 and 1959 made the embassy in Vientiane more fragmented than usual.[81] Horace Smith had arrived as Ambassador in March 1958. His previous assignment was in Manila, where he had been Acting Ambassador for nine months. That position had brought him into close and friendly contact with U.S. military officers. He saw eye-to-eye with the staff at CINCPAC and assumed that he would have no trouble with the PEO in Laos. His relations with the CIA, however, were bad from the start.

Henry Hecksher was the CIA Station Chief in Laos.

He had assumed that post in the summer of 1957, replacing Milton Clark, whose energies had gone primarily toward setting up the Agency's staff and intelligence network. Hecksher was considered arrogant and resourceful. His men had been active in policy discussions and implementation under Ambassador Parsons; they expected to continue to play a major role under Smith.

Smith, however, did not get along with Hecksher. The new ambassador was affable, but had trouble getting his embassy under control. Hecksher considered him inexperienced and tried to run CIA operations with as little ambassadorial interference as possible. Since the two men disagreed over which faction to support, their actions worked at cross-purposes.

Washington officials permitted these conflicts to go unresolved for several reasons. One was simply the lack of reliable information from Laos. Smith did not tell Washington about many of his suspicions concerning CIA activities because, given Hecksher's evasiveness and denials, he lacked proof that the Station Chief was not cooperating. Hecksher reported to his superiors, William Colby and Desmond Fitzgerald, who themselves favored an active CIA role in Laos. Another reason for inaction in Washington was a lack of confidence in Smith. Several of his superiors doubted his abilities and ultimately an attempt was made to replace him. That idea was rejected partly on the grounds that it would be bad publicity for an already notorious situation.

No one in Washington felt the need to act to resolve the conflict in the field. CIA was satisfied because it was able to act unhindered in Laos. Officials in the Far East Bureau of the State Department sympathized with the CIA's anti-communism and did not disapprove of the 1958 operations, insofar as they knew of them. Now Deputy Assistant Secretary Parsons brought firsthand knowledge of Laos to the Bureau. Since he had worked well with the CIA during his ambassadorship, he was tolerant of its activities. When evidence of the rift in the country team had become unmistakably clear, the CIA had achieved a virtual coup d'etat in Vientiane. Confidence, or lack of it, in Smith no longer mattered. His subordinates on the country team could make end runs to Washington with impunity.

Smith was successfully isolated from his CIA staff and from the Lao. He spent much of his time in the company of his interpreter, both for discussions with the Lao and for translations of some documents. Since he was optimistic and trusting at first, he did not learn until it was too late that some of his subordinates were working behind his back.

On assuming his post, Smith had two major objectives: to get economic reforms and to improve relations with the French in Laos. The first goal has already been discussed; the second was Smith's own, for which he secured Dulles' and Robertson's blessings shortly before going to Vientiane.

Better relations with the French may have seemed an unobjectionable goal to the men in Washington, but it was anathema to the Americans in Laos, particularly the CIA. They had contributed, of course, to the Franco-American estrangement, but for what they thought were reasons of policy. Smith's determination to cooperate with the French would have brought him into profound conflict with the CIA even if Hecksher had been more submissive. By working with the French, he came to see their perspective on Laos and especially their reasons for favoring Souvanna Phouma. The CIA, having been trying for at least a year to bring anti-French, anti-communist, and pro-American forces to power, vigorously opposed this apparent reversal of policy.

Even before the 1958 elections, new political divisions were becoming evident in Laos.[82] A group of younger people, primarily though not exclusively in Vientiane, had grown up in the Junior Chamber of Commerce. These people were re-formist, anti-communist, and, most significantly, united across the traditional clan and party lines. They supported one of their fellows in a losing fight for one of the seats in the 1958 elections. After those elections, they decided to form a new political group, the Committee for the Defense of National Interests (CDNI). At the same time, Souvanna Phouma brought together the parties of Phoui Sananikone and Katay Don Sasorith into the

Rally of the Laotian People (RLP), thus belatedly uniting the factions which had fought each other in the elections.

The Young Ones (*les Jeunes*), as the CDNI members were called, were at first more interested in programs than personal political power. But the CIA people in the American Embassy saw them as a new elite force and were impressed with their anti-communism. Through advice and assistance they helped the CDNI to play an active role in the maneuverings to form a new government. Souvanna Phouma also supported the movement at first, seeing in it the kind of broadly based support which would keep the older politicians from fractionating.

A generational as well as organizational split developed within the American Embassy over the question of support for the Young Ones. Ambassador Smith worked with, knew, and thus tended to favor the older, established politicians. But many of the younger members of the staff preferred greater support for the Young Ones, both because of the friendships and appreciation for their political skills they had developed while working with them and because of their sympathy with the reforms which they sought. This gap widened over time and led to the virtual estrangement of the Ambassador from the CIA members of the embassy. Other younger Americans supported the CIA position, but only those not directly in the Foreign Service line of command and efficiency reports were able to act independently of, or contrary to, the Ambassador.

The question of support for a new government brought these divisions into the open. Tradition called for Souvanna Phouma to resign after elections and then be given the first opportunity to form a new cabinet. Souvanna had maneuvered himself into a strong position through the establishment of the RLP and through an offer to the CDNI of some minor cabinet posts, despite the parliamentary tradition that reserved such positions for members of the National Assembly.

But powerful forces were lining up against him. The older Lao politicians could always be counted on to act in their own interests regardless of any formal alliance such as the RLP. The CDNI members were urged by their American supporters to hold out for a more prominent role than Souvanna had offered. In any case, they had some reasons to distrust Souvanna because of his closeness to his half brother and hence to the Pathet Lao, and they blamed him for the defeats in the elections. Even a French advisor to Souvanna gave some discreet encouragement to the CDNI.

Ambassador Smith supported Souvanna, but the younger people in the embassy, led by the CIA, worked behind his back to oppose Souvanna and promote the CDNI. They had tacit support from Washington, since Deputy Assistant Secretary Parsons and others in the Far East Bureau distrusted Souvanna. In addition to fearing his presumed naïveté about Communists, these Washington officials now blamed Souvanna for the leftist election victory; they thought he had reneged on a promise to reduce the number of anti-communist candidates. In these circumstances, the Far East Bureau overruled Smith's objections to support for the CDNI and decided to support the CDNI demand for a place in the new cabinet.

Encouraged by Washington and free of effective control by the Ambassador, U.S. officials in Laos intervened directly in the political maneuvering. There is no corroboration for the charge made by a journalist sympathetic to the Pathet Lao that the United States paid $100,000 for each National Assembly vote against Souvanna,[83] but there is also no doubt that many Americans made quite clear their opposition to his continuation as Prime Minister. One U.S. source admits that CIA agents were "counting their votes and stagemanaging the whole affair."[84]

The very fact that aid had been suspended as of July 1 made consideration of American wishes imperative. The aid stoppage also gave additional leverage to the CIA effort to get the CDNI a place in the new cabinet. With or without direct bribes, the CIA had demonstrated by its many activities that it had resources and influence in the embassy. The Americans who favored the established politicians had less visibility and much less that they could do for their friends. Those Lao who wanted to increase their power, wealth, and influence were more likely to be attracted to the CIA's position than to that of the Ambassador.

Souvanna tried to retain his position by offers to the CDNI, but they were rejected. He declared Laos' obligations under the 1954 Geneva agreements "fully accomplished" and thereby forced the ICC to adjourn sine die on July 20. Three days later, however, he lost a crucial confidence vote on the issue of monetary reform and resigned.[85] The aid suspension and American opposition were too much to overcome. Souvanna tried to form a new cabinet, but without CDNI participation the Americans would not support him. Since the CIA had Washington's approval of CDNI membership in the cabinet and since its agents had persuaded the CDNI to oppose Souvanna, the former Premier was checkmated.

On August 18, Phoui Sananikone succeeded in forming a government by a narrow margin. He reluctantly agreed—under pressure from the Crown Prince as well as some Americans—to include four CDNI members in his cabinet, as ministers of Foreign Affairs; Finance and Economic Affairs; Justice; and Information, Youth and Sports. He also announced that his primary objective was "the struggle without fail against the implantation of the Communist ideology in Laos," a goal seconded by his Vice Premier, Katay Don Sasorith, who said that "Our number-one enemy is communism."[86]

Phoui soon demonstrated his anti-communism very clearly by moving closer to Thailand, raising the diplomatic mission in Saigon to embassy status, and establishing official relations with the Nationalist Chinese on Taiwan. These actions, plus the subsequent permission given the Americans to send military instructors for the army, were later cited by Souvanna Phouma as the "fundamental errors" by which Laos, under American pressure, turned away from a policy of neutrality.[87]

Although the cabinet was united in its anti-communism, it was divided by suspicion and distrust. The political arrangement was aptly called a "marriage of convenience."[88] Gradually the Young Ones were shunted into the background, their counsel unasked or unheeded, their power diminished. The United States took no direct action to bolster them because it had found another group to support—the Young Ones in the Army.

Devaluation of the kip in October opened the way for

an altered but increased American role in Laos. The country team developed a plan which got enthusiastic support in Washington. It provided for new and accelerated programs in administration, public works, village improvement, health, information, and agricultural improvement, all selected for their psychological impact on the Laotians. The plan differed from earlier aid programs in its increased reliance on the army for implementation through civic action projects. One administration witness told a congressional committee that the Royal Army "is the only instrument of government which could serve out in the villages as a symbol of the present pro-free world government." He added that the new plan included funds for improving the supply system for the army and for training "selected junior officers and NCO's" in the United States.[89]

Although these training operations were circumventions of the Geneva agreements, the United States was moving toward full assumption of training through an agreement with the French, who had progressively reduced their contingents in Laos. The new head of the PEO, sent to Laos on a study mission in October 1958 although he did not assume command until the following February, was John A. Heintges, a highly regarded general, who did not retire but was officially put on civilian status and had his name dropped from the army's list of officers. For the first time, the Pentagon took an active interest and role in Laos. Backed by Ambassador Smith, the energetic Heintges secured an agreement with the French to take over more of the training of troops within Laos, through the subterfuge of having American officers ostensibly subordinate to French commanders. The United States also increased its military aid by nearly 40 percent, a figure which understates the relative increase because of the devaluation of the kip.[90] *

These steps served to strengthen the political position of

* The Pentagon's new interest in Laos seems to have been part of a general shift of attention and resources to the Far East in the months after the 1958 crisis in the Straits of Taiwan. One example of this was the establishment of a staff on Okinawa (Task Force 116) to plan for contingencies of U.S. intervention in Asia. For more on this group, see Chapter Three.

the army and to bring it more closely under American control. Before the 1958 elections the Laotian Army had resisted American efforts to run a big civic action program because of a power struggle with the Vientiane politicians. Now richer and more confident, it started the projects enthusiastically. The Americans paid particular attention to a young Colonel, Phoumi Nosavan, who had just returned from the French École Supérieure de Guerre. He had risen under the tutelage of his cousin and former Defense Minister, Kou Voravong (who was assassinated in 1954), and remained close to another cousin, Marshal Sarit, who had just taken power in Thailand. With American military and CIA support, he had become so powerful that Phoui Sananikone made him Secretary of State for Defense when he reorganized his cabinet in January 1959. Americans who worked with him were convinced that he did not seek political power, but just wanted to be boss of the army. That was sufficient for American support, however, since the United States was most interested in his vigorous anti-communism.[91]

While the army grew stronger, Phoui Sananikone grew weaker. The CDNI half of his cabinet grew restless. There were rumors of a coup. In order not to appear complicit with such an event, Ambassador Smith was ordered to take a two-week "vacation" outside of the country. Whether or not American military and CIA men were actively promoting an army takeover is uncertain. They clearly preferred Phoumi Nosavan to Phoui Sananikone, but they may have unleashed uncontrollable forces in their enthusiasm for the young officers in the army. Officials in Washington were reluctant to take sides in a dispute between two anti-communist factions. The situation remained as before, with the CIA active for its clients and the State Department unwilling to support its ambassador. Perhaps nothing could have been done earlier unless State and CIA had been forced to choose between the factions and then replace either Smith or Hecksher. In the absence of such a decision, Hecksher was free to strengthen Phoumi. One should note that Hecksher was only one of several CIA operatives in Asia in the late 1950s who ran their own political shows largely independent of any effective control from Washington.[92]

Faced with the threat of an army coup, Phoui Sananikone devised a clever political move, perhaps with some urging from other members of the American mission. He seized upon some mid-December border incidents in a remote area near the Vietnamese demilitarized zone as proof of an increased Communist threat and as a pretext for asking for special emergency powers for one year. The source of the provocation is ambiguous, however, since the first Laotian patrol to be fired upon was moving into an area which had once been governed as a part of Vietnam and in which no Laos military post had ever been established. In arguing that the incident served merely as a pretext for political maneuvering, Hugh Toye cites this evidence and draws the striking parallel to Thailand, where Marshal Sarit had used the Communist threat to assume full powers less than three months before.[93]

Phoui's move succeeded in getting emergency powers, but he was then thwarted by the CDNI. The Prime Minister had promised to offer some cabinet seats to the older RLP politicians, a move which would have upset the careful 4-4 balance between RLP and CDNI members. The Young Ones objected and threatened to resign. They may have threatened other things as well, for Phoui ended up eliminating the other three RLP members from his cabinet, which then consisted of Phoui and seven CDNI members, three of them military officers.[94]

To gain support for emergency powers, Phoui had promised the army a $1 million pay raise. This had been requested in late November and approved by the U.S. country team in early December. With a budget submission deadline upon them, the embassy decided to include the request as an addition to its already prepared program. CINCPAC approved the pay raise in mid-December, but said that the funds had to come from the original budget. Embassy officials told the Laotians of the approval and of the conditions, but were either misunderstood or ignored, for the announcement of the pay increase was made on January 5. The State Department shocked the country team by sending a cable absolutely forbidding the increase. The cable arrived on January 7, only three days before the first payment was to be made. The shock came in part because Washington had never overruled a CINCPAC budget submission before. This time, former Ambassador Parsons strongly opposed the increase on the grounds that the army was already too highly paid. The embassy responded with a defense of the increase, pointing to the danger to troop morale if the promised increase were not granted and also citing the Communist threat. Five days later the State Department acquiesced to the increase because of the commitments already made.[95] This was further evidence of the ability of the Lao to manipulate the United States Embassy by alleging a crisis, as they had done in 1955, and another instance, like those involving the CIA, when Washington submitted to a fait accompli in the field.

As the power of the army had increased during the autumn of 1958, so had its anti-communism. The Pathet Lao claimed that the Phoui government launched a savage repression against Pathet Lao cadres in the northern provinces, killing all that they could find. Members of the Neo Lao Hak Xat party were allegedly killed, including some who were Royal Government administrators. Whether or not killing took place, a CDNI member of the cabinet did admit that the government's policy was "vigilant, active, determined. Under its aegis, Communist sympathizers and long-time fellow travelers of the Pathet Lao were dismissed from government service."[96]

The purge continued quietly in the early months of 1959. The army wrestled with the still unresolved problem of integrating the two Pathet Lao battalions (totaling about 1,500 men) which remained encamped at Xieng-Ngeun in Luang Prabang province and on the Plaine des Jarres. The major point of dispute was whether the Pathet Lao would be able to keep their high ratio of officers once they were integrated. In April the Royal Government finally agreed to the proposed number of officers, but held out the possibility of a renege through the device of requiring officers to pass examinations appropriate to their rank. At the last minute, the Pathet Lao battalions refused to go through with the integration on May 11. The following day Prince Souphanouvong and other NLHX leaders were put under house arrest in Vientiane. At the same time the Royal Army encircled the two battalions. On May 17, after further political arrests, and the expiration of an ultimatum to the battalions, Souphanouvong asked the soldiers to accept integration. Although the Prince's action probably had little to do with the ultimate outcome, the Xieng-Ngeun battalion capitulated on May 18. That night, however, the battalion on the Plaine des Jarres melted through its cordon and headed toward the North Vietnamese border. That the Pathet Lao did so with 700 men, their families, chickens, pigs, weapons, and household articles is testimony to the military skill which the Royal Army was to display in many subsequent encounters with the Pathet Lao.[97]

Although the Pathet Lao made suggestions for reconciliation, the Phoui government rejected them. It was both shocked at the escape of the battalion and seemingly carried away by the momentum of its struggle. On May 25 it declared that the Pathet Lao had committed an act of open rebellion, leaving only a military solution possible. The American government gave strong verbal support to the Royal Government's position on May 29.[98] The stage was set for the first serious military crisis in Laos since France's Indochina war, a crisis made possible by the American policy of building a strong army which imposed an intransigent anti-communist policy on a weak and divided political system. John Foster Dulles' "dike" against Communism had been built and was waiting for the flood.

CHAPTER THREE

Building a military bastion (1959–1960)

*. . . I suppose you could sum up the performance of
the last year and a half by saying that we have created a little
order out of the chaos in the military situation in Laos. This
program we are embarked on now needs a lot of time. . . .*
　　　　—ADMIRAL HARRY D. FELT, *CINCPAC, on March 8, 1960*[1]

The Pathet Lao attacks on Royal Government positions
in the summer of 1959 were serious, not in themselves, but in
their effects on Laotian politics. They undermined the sense of
security and stability which the Royal Government had tried
to achieve. They also revealed the fundamental inability of the
Lao army to stand and fight and win, in spite of over $200
million in American aid. U.S. newspapers treated the attacks as
a major crisis, thereby stimulating a high-level policy review in
Washington. Subsequent American policy, however, reflected
the divisions within the embassy at Vientiane which had emerged
over a year before. Military groups came to dominate both the
Royal Government and U.S. policy toward Laos.

Driven from the government a year before, the Pathet
Lao had continued to spread their cadres throughout the country, especially in the mountainous border regions and among
the various tribes derisively called Kha (slaves) by the Lao.
They had much greater political success than the Royal Laotian
Government's civic action teams, which often lost local support
by their chicken- and daughter-stealing. Once established, the
Pathet Lao then acted to guarantee village allegiance by selective assassination.[2]

Many of the Pathet Lao teams were trained in North
Vietnam, China, and the Soviet Union, although Bernard Fall
put the number of men involved at only 200.[3] Even such a small

number could have a tremendous impact among the isolated, ethnocentric communities of Laos. Neither was direct outside assistance very great in absolute terms, nor was it necessary. A soldier could not carry much through the mountains and jungle. Any political organizer would ultimately need to win the support of the people with whom he was working. The most important service provided by the North Vietnamese was sanctuary in case of trouble, although they also at times provided training and leadership for some operations.

Although the United States later claimed that the 1959 fighting was an attempt by "Communist-led forces . . . to impose their will over the Kingdom [of Laos] and its small army,"[4] the only political demands which the Pathet Lao made were for a restoration of the coalition government of 1957–58. The initiation of the hostilities should be attributed to the Phoui Sananikone government, as it was in a Rand Corporation study a year later.[5]

Once fighting broke out in mid-July, however, the Royal Government felt severely threatened. Mere rumors of advancing North Vietnamese troops were sufficient to drive Royal Government troops fleeing in terror; they had a similar effect on politicians in Vientiane, who asked the United States for assistance in meeting the threat.

Conflicting intelligence reports prevented the United States Embassy, and later Washington, from taking prompt action. "We were slow to become convinced of North Vietnamese participation," one embassy source has said. The CIA, with a good network among the Meo tribes, did not become worried about the situation until clashes at the end of August threatened the Plaine des Jarres. Meanwhile, the Americans in Laos seemed content with the new agreement, signed July 23, which called for U.S. military advisors to begin training Lao combat troops. By early August, over one hundred additional advisors had arrived in Laos to instruct in the use and maintenance of equipment. The French remained in nominal but ineffective command and were still the only advisors who could accompany the Lao on tactical operations. Since this new arrangement had been under negotiation for several months, it hardly satisfied the Royal Government's request for emergency aid.[6]

Until the embassy in Vientiane transmitted a greater sense of urgency, policy makers in Washington concerned themselves with more pressing matters than the penetration of remote Sam Neua province. President Eisenhower's major problem was what to do about the steel strike which started on July 15 and was to last 116 days before the Taft-Hartley Act was invoked. He also was preparing for a trip to Europe and a visit to the United States by Soviet Premier Khrushchev. Secretary Herter spent three weeks in Geneva from mid-July until early August in talks with the foreign ministers of France, Britain, and the Soviet Union. The main topics were Berlin and general European security matters, but Herter did raise the issue of Laos with Soviet Foreign Minister Gromyko, who disavowed any Soviet role in the crisis and put all the blame on the United States. One week after the Geneva talks ended, Herter left Washington again for an Organization of American States meeting in Chile, August 11–20. Six days after his return, he left for Europe with the President. Thus, the man in operational charge of policy toward Laos during most of the summer crisis was the new Assistant Secretary of State for the Far East, J. Graham Parsons.[7]

Parsons had moved up from his post as Deputy Assistant Secretary on July 1, succeeding Walter Robertson. The new man tried consciously to change the operating style of his Bureau from saber-rattling to a nonprovocative handling of crises. When the Royal Laotian Government cried "invasion" on August 1, the State Department's response was decidedly low-key.[8] An official statement issued the same day sharply criticized the regimes in China and North Vietnam for their unceasing intrigue and agitation, but it was hedged with doubts about the current situation in Laos. "With this new outbreak of fighting it *may be* that the Communist imperialists in the Far East are seeking to provoke a serious crisis." (Emphasis supplied.) A notable omission was the word "support." The statement instead used "respects" in sentences on the Laotian will to remain independent and to follow a policy of neutrality. Nor did the United States promise additional aid. The statement's conclusion left no doubt as to the hesitation and lack of urgency with which the United States viewed the situation. "It therefore views with concern what *may be* a deliberate effort of insurgent elements, *apparently* backed by Communists from outside, to provoke a crisis in Laos. . . ." (Emphasis again supplied.)⁹

    Not satisfied with the American response to its request for assistance, the Royal Laotian Government decided to take the matter to the United Nations. Both the French and the Americans in Vientiane urged this step—the French because they wanted to keep the crisis limited and the Americans because they opposed direct U.S. intervention and preferred a multilateral approach. On August 4 the Royal Government declared a state of emergency in five provinces and sent a message to United Nations Secretary-General Dag Hammarskjøld accusing North Vietnam of having sent arms and provisions to the Pathet Lao. The following day the British government proposed sending UN observers to Laos. Later in the month, however, when the Prime Minister's brother, Ngon Sananikone, made a special trip to the United Nations, he requested only the suggestion of procedures to achieve a peaceful settlement. In other words, he did not charge North Vietnamese aggression or ask for UN troops.¹⁰

    While the United States Embassy reacted calmly to the events of late July and early August, officials in Washington expressed "serious concern" that international communism was on the march again. Although he had died the previous May, John Foster Dulles' ideas lived on in the State Department, where men showed an amazing readiness to perceive Moscow's involvement in the trouble in Laos. In briefings on August 5 and 11, press officers implicated the Soviet Union in what they saw as the prelude to a new Communist military offensive in Southeast Asia. The "proof" of Soviet instigation of the crisis was a recent visit by two North Vietnamese officials to Moscow. Since the United States Embassy had given no support to these allegations, one must attribute them to the State Department's conditioned response of viewing with alarm any hints of Communist activity.[11]

The American news media were conditioned in the same way and were always ready to depict the Laotian troubles in terms of the global struggle with communism. Although there was little military activity in Laos during the rest of August, that fact did not stop the "war." The first headlines attracted journalists to the scene of the purported action. Once there, they needed something to report. This the Laotians provided by relaying sketchy radio messages from remote areas and by stating rumors as irrefutable facts. Any hint of North Vietnamese participation was particularly welcomed since it fit the popular conception of "aggression," which is always a bigger story than a mere civil war. Bernard Fall, who was there at the time, admirably documented the misinformation, the exaggerations, and the poor analysis which reporters filed from Laos during August and September.[12]

As these reports were received and printed, the crisis took on a life of its own. In Washington and other world capitals, leaders were forced to deal with Laos because it was a "hot" issue, although the heat was greater in the public press than in intelligence reports. Public attention was enough to force spokesmen to have to decide what to say to the inevitable questions about the situation. And these answers could not contradict the published reports unless new information were released.

But the information was not available. The United States could neither confirm nor deny reports of a Communist invasion because it was uncertain of the facts and heavily dependent on information from the Royal Lao Army. There were no American eyewitnesses to the events in Sam Neua, no military advisors yet stationed with the troops in the troubled area. Nor had any decisions been made on the Laotian request for assistance. When a *New York Times* reporter arrived in Vientiane looking for a story, the embassy decided to announce the agreement reached several weeks before on a joint Franco-American training program for the army. In that way, the

United States appeared to be doing something in response to the crisis.[13]

That announcement then prompted charges by the Chinese that the United States was intervening in Laos. The State Department denied that it was establishing any bases in Laos or that it was sending troops there.[14] It did not mention that the new U.S. training program involved the dispatch of 110 more enlisted men to work in the PEO. The Soviet Union added its charges on August 17, blaming the Royal Government for violating the Geneva and Vientiane agreements (the latter established the coalition and political settlement) and for flooding the country with American servicemen who directed various war preparations. The State Department responded two days later with a denial of those charges, another implication that the Soviet Union was behind the trouble, and a hope that some way could be found to "tranquilize the situation."[15]

One major factor inhibiting the American response to the crisis was the fear of jeopardizing the forthcoming visit to the United States of Soviet Premier Khrushchev. Even if the military situation were more serious and North Vietnamese participation in the fighting clearly proved, it seems unlikely that the United States would have threatened to use, much less have used, its own forces in Laos. President Eisenhower had consistently shied away from such bellicosity since 1954 and would do so again a year later in Laos. He promised to talk to Khrushchev about Laos during their meetings. But when the two leaders met in September, the President was still so reluctant to introduce a discordant note into the discussions that he avoided the topic of Laos entirely.[16]

Laos policy was handled at the middle levels of government during most of August. President Eisenhower did not even see the plan worked out between the State and Defense Departments until the day before he left on his two-week trip to Europe to confer with NATO allies about his forthcoming talks with Khrushchev. The President told his news conference on August 25 that he had just learned of the Laotian request for assistance, which he characterized as "some help to reinforce their police forces and the units they keep for internal order."

Although he said the request was under "urgent study," he strongly denied that there was any evidence of "a Communist invasion."[17]

Why the decision for increased aid to expand the Royal Army was not made until August 25 is a mystery. Despite persistent reports of incidents, there was no major military drive until August 31. The earlier clashes had ended by the start of August and had produced only the agreement on an emergency military training program. The Royal Government continued to announce attacks and probably renewed its request for United States aid, but American intelligence sources could discount the need for an immediate response. What prompted a decision just before the President left for Europe?

One possible explanation is that the bureaucracy took until then to devise its plan and win the necessary approval. No person involved in the planning, however, remembers any particular disagreement on increasing aid. Nor does this explanation account for the timing of the decision. Something must have happened just before the President's departure to raise Laos above the threshold of significance for top policy makers and to make them give the events there urgent consideration. Bernard Fall, who was in Laos at the time, attributed the crisis atmosphere to alarming but false press reports.[18]

The event causing the greatest concern in Vientiane and Washington between August 5 and 31 was the reported fall of Ban Pak Cadinh on August 23. This small police and army post, about seventy miles from the capital, was on the only road linking Vientiane with the south. Its loss could have been seen as a very serious threat. If Pathet Lao forces had captured the town, they would have made their first penetration to the Mekong, thereby menacing Thailand as well as the integrity of Laos. Since Washington officials have no clear memory of the sequence of events, one can only suppose that this was the incident that triggered emergency discussion on aid to Laos.

But the truth of the matter is, as Bernard Fall documented, that a bridge had been washed out by heavy rains. There was no attack on Ban Pak Cadinh except by the forces of nature. The Laotian government failed to list any such attack the following month in its list of incidents submitted to the United Nations observer team. The whole incident had mushroomed from speculation over the interruption in the supply of fresh vegetables to the capital.[19]

Whatever triggered the American decision, the response fell far below Laotian expectations. Secretary Herter, appearing before the Senate Foreign Relations Committee on August 24, called the situation "very dangerous" but recommended only UN observers. He did not even tell the senators of the plans to increase aid, either because he forgot or because no decision was then about to be made. The official announcement was not made until two days later. Its wording was much sharper than the August 1 statement, for it declared that the United States "strongly supports the determination of the Royal Lao Government to resist Communist efforts to undermine the security and stability of Laos." The American government promised increased assistance to permit "temporary emergency increases" in the army and local police forces: the army from 25,000 to 29,000 and the militia from 16,000 to 20,000. The aid was to be limited, however, to small arms, tents, jeeps, and so forth; no tanks, artillery, or modern weapons were included. The first shipment to arrive, on August 31, consisted only of 2,640 pairs of jungle boots.[20]

That same day the Pathet Lao forces launched a series of attacks at several points in Sam Neua and began moving toward the capital city of the province. Direct contact with Royal Lao forces was at a minimum, usually only mortar fire or sightings of figures in the fog. The Royal Government claimed then and later that Vietminh (North Vietnamese) troops participated in these attacks, but the United Nations observer team found no direct evidence of their participation, only the testimony of villagers that the Pathet Lao had received support from across the border. The Information Minister at the time, Sisouk na Champassak, wrote afterward that the attacks were made by the "Lao-Viets—whom one might conveniently call just Viets, in this case." But these people, even if they were associated with the Pathet Lao, were the same fierce, independent Black Tai tribesmen who had long occupied the mountains straddling the border.[21]

These attacks, magnified to the world by the reports of the many journalists in Laos at the time, prompted reconsideration of the American position. The Royal Government felt sufficiently threatened to declare a nationwide state of emergency and to change its request to the United Nations from mere observers to a UN force. American policy makers studied the matter and decided to support only an observer team.

President Eisenhower had already made his opposition to intervention clear. In discussions with British Prime Minister Harold Macmillan on August 29, he agreed to the British proposal to get United Nations observers sent to Laos "at least to determine the accuracy of our suspicion that the aggressors—the Pathet Lao units—were Communists."[22] The President had doubts about the evidence; he was reluctant to become militarily involved in Southeast Asia, particularly at a time when he was hoping to improve relations with the Soviet Union. And no one was arguing strongly for intervention.

The State Department was no more interested in intervention than the President. Throughout the summer of 1959 it responded to Laotian requests for assistance with ritual reaffirmations of support, but little else. The aid increase it announced on August 25 was specifically labeled temporary. At no time did the Department threaten American intervention as a last resort, as Secretary Dulles would likely have done.

But Herter was no Dulles, and the Department under him was less assertive and less influential with the President than before Dulles' resignation and death the previous spring. Nor was Herter particularly concerned about or interested in Asia, especially when he had just faced a crisis over Khrushchev's six-month ultimatum on Berlin and expected more in the future. Herter saw Laos as a place where the United States could work more closely with its allies in Asia, particularly France. Ambassador Smith had been trying to improve relations with the French in Laos since his arrival in 1958.[23]

No one further down the State Department's chain of

command advocated direct military intervention. Assistant Secretary Parsons agreed with the country team's unanimous recommendation for money and equipment, but n'ot men. He also had firsthand experience with Laos, which made him skeptical of some of the reports from the Royal Army. From his broader regional perspective, Laos was also secondary to Vietnam. He likened Laos to the important but peripheral Shenandoah Valley while Vietnam was Northern Virginia.[24]

The Central Intelligence Agency continued its operations as before. It had a fairly accurate picture of the events in Laos and saw no need for direct intervention. It did increase its logistical support to the Royal Army in mid-August, however, by chartering transport planes belonging to Air America. This airlift was conducted more for its political than for its military effects. Since the Agency was supporting the army in the domestic political arena, it is understandable that it would want to demonstrate its ability to support its clients.[25]

Military opinion was divided and circumspectly given. Some officers were more willing to threaten or risk intervention than others. Yet none were outright advocates of such action because the President's opposition was too clear. In good military fashion, they proclaimed America's capability to extend its force into Laos and quietly took steps to prepare better for that contingency. Admiral Arleigh Burke, three-term Chief of Naval Operations, suggested that the navy "might" be called into the Laotian crisis on August 17, only to have his speculation officially denied a short time later. The Commander of the Seventh Fleet, Vice Admiral Frederick N. Kivette, said on August 21 that the situation in Laos was a diplomatic and political one but that his fleet was always ready for anything. The head of the Tactical Air Command said on September 4 that the United States could send fighters and fighter-bombers to Laos within thirty-five hours of a decision to do so.[26]

Officers at CINCPAC headquarters seemed to be the most vigorous advocates of aggressive action. One source in Laos has said that CINCPAC favored putting in both American troops and firepower. The CINCPAC Staff Director, however, has denied that anyone favored more than increased supplies.

What is clear is that the navy was ready for action and not averse to threatening aerial intervention.[27]

Military readiness for possible intervention had been significantly increased earlier in the summer of 1959 with the establishment of Task Force 116 on Okinawa. It grew out of concern over the trend of events in Asia, notably the 1958 Taiwan Straits crisis and the 1959 Chinese attacks on Tibet and later India, as well as the situation in Laos. Initially there was a small nucleus staff on Okinawa which made contingency plans for operations in Southeast Asia and was ready, with supplemental staff, to implement them if so ordered. Forces earmarked for possible operations were scattered throughout the Pacific—army paratroops and marines in Okinawa, air force units in the Philippines, transport planes in Japan. This group was not readied for action in 1959, but it was put on alert several times after the coup of August 1960 and in 1962 deployed marines into Thailand.[28]

Arguments against intervention proved decisive, even among the military. Laos was a landlocked country, with poor logistical facilities and often impenetrable weather. The navy could not be very effective from so far away. The air force was unwilling to get involved unless it could do strategic bombing. And the army was still dominated by the "never again" school, which strongly opposed getting involved again in a land war in Asia. The Laos matter also arose at a time when the Pentagon was debating conventional as against guerrilla war training. The traditionalists won that debate, thus making intervention in a guerrilla situation even less likely. The only decision which the military apparently got was an order to the Seventh Fleet to make a show of force in Southeast Asian waters.[29]

On September 4, 1959, Laos appealed to the United Nations for an emergency force to repel an invasion by North Vietnam. This appeal prompted a reconsideration of American policy. The foregoing analysis suggests why no basic change emerged. The fight for U.S. intervention had been lost; a consensus remained for increased aid and a multilateral search for a solution. U.S. officials felt compelled to give diplomatic support to Laos even as they were denying it military support. The State Department issued a formal statement on September 5 which upheld the Laotian claim of Communist intervention—not on the basis of foreign troops, but on the much more tenuous grounds of "supplies and military weapons that could be provided only from Communist territory," Communist propaganda about U.S. activities, and the coincidence of the fighting with a visit by Ho Chi Minh to Moscow and Peking. The statement supported the call for UN assistance but implied that actual forces might not be necessary.[30]

Since the Americans were unwilling to act alone in Laos, they had to support the British and French in their reluctance to do more than throw the matter into the United Nations. Both European nations were dubious of many of the claims by the Royal Lao Government and wanted UN observers to establish the facts in the case. They sponsored a resolution calling for observers, which was calculated to avoid a Soviet veto. The Soviet delegate cast the only vote against the resolution, but the Council President ruled that it was not a veto since the proposal was procedural rather than substantive.

Eight days later the UN observers arrived in Vientiane. Although their investigations were hampered for a while by lack of access to the areas of conflict, they eventually visited them and discovered no evidence to establish clearly North Vietnamese participation in the fighting. The Royal Government claimed as early as September 7 that all non-native forces had been withdrawn from the country, but they stuck by their charge that the attacks were instigated and supported by the North Vietnamese. Although the UN team did not reach the same conclusions as the United States, its dispatch did serve to defuse an explosive situation.[31]

One effect of the UN action was that Secretary-General Hammarskjøld took a renewed personal interest in Laos. He had visited the country the previous March and in November paid a second visit, this time leaving behind a personal representative to study the Laotian economy. This representative could also provide an otherwise unobtainable UN "presence" in the country in case of future trouble. Evidently Hammarskjøld planned to rechannel enough UN assistance to Laos to free it from its dependence on the United States and, therefore, bolster its proclaimed policy of neutrality. Throughout 1959 Hammarskjøld tried to increase the UN role in Laos. He even told Secretary Herter that the CIA was active in roiling the waters and in manufacturing evidence of Communist activity.[32]

The summer crisis had important effects in Laos as well. Most significantly, it undermined the position of Phoui Sananikone, who had tried and failed to win UN assistance and who then made an abortive trip to the United States to appeal directly to the UN. Struck by illness and second thoughts while in Washington, he never went to the United Nations. But his actions, and his increasingly precarious health, further eroded his support among the army and the Young Ones. Meanwhile, the United States decided to push ahead its plans to strengthen the Lao Army and to intensify American training and support for it. These actions gave self-confidence to the army leaders whose opposition to Phoui Sananikone was already growing.[33]

The showdown came in December.[34] Both RLP and CDNI factions blamed each other for the unsuccessful results of the appeal to the United Nations. The RLP demanded a reduction in CDNI strength in the cabinet. Whether because of political or personal disagreements, Phoui decided to shift CDNI Foreign Minister Khamphan Panya to another cabinet post. The CDNI took this as evidence of an intention to weaken the government's anti-communist orientation, along with the earlier postponement in October of the start of a trial of Pathet Lao leaders, who had been under arrest since the previous May. Phoui may also have planned to negotiate with the Pathet Lao before the elections scheduled for the following April.

At this point the CIA entered the picture without the knowledge or approval of the Ambassador. Long closely tied to the CDNI, the Agency men in Laos convinced the CDNI cabinet members to stand united in opposition to the transfer of the Foreign Minister. Faced with a united front, Phoui ousted all CDNI members on December 16 and hastily formed a cabinet of RLP members. At the same time, he hinted that Laos would move toward a foreign policy of more effective neutrality.

Encouraged by the CIA to resist these moves, the army demanded the government's resignation and surrounded Phoui's house on December 25, first with police, two days later with three armored cars, and two days after that with two light tanks. On December 29 Phoui lost his strongest political ally when Katay Don Sasorith died of an embolism. The next day Phoui offered his resignation to the King (who had acceded to the throne on October 29) at the same time that the King was declaring an end to the Prime Minister's government. That night troops occupied communications centers, the airport, the power plant, and the national bank to secure their victory.[35]

The American Embassy was deeply divided over its response to the political crisis.[36] As in 1958, the Ambassador, supported by the British and French envoys, favored the older politicians while the CIA station chief wanted to strengthen the Young Ones, especially those in the army. For several months both CIA and the PEO had been building up General Phoumi Nosavan as a future strong man in Laos. Phoumi was not only intensely anti-communist and pro-American, but he had close ties to his cousin, Marshal Sarit of Thailand. By supporting Phoumi, the CIA operatives in Laos thought that they could forestall another coalition and establish an effective anti-Communist government.

Ambassador Smith wanted to support Phoui Sananikone, but he was outmaneuvered by Henry Hecksher. The CIA station chief had frequently acted on his own, often, Smith suspected, without telling the Ambassador. Earlier in 1959 Smith took his complaints to CIA Director Allen Dulles, who ordered his station chief to be more open with the Ambassador. Smith and Hecksher had become so estranged from each other that the Ambassador demanded his subordinate's transfer. Since Washington had little confidence in Smith, it was slow to comply. The CIA agreed only to reassign Hecksher at the end of a normal tour of duty, rather than leaving him in place. And the Agency transferred him to northeast Thailand, from where he could still direct some operations in Laos.

Since there was so much intriguing behind his back, Smith had difficulty controlling his country team. A few weeks after the coup he confided to a reporter, "I often feel I'm swimming upstream and losing way."[37] Hecksher was relatively free to act as he saw fit because he had the support of his own superiors in Washington. He did not tell them about everything he was doing, but no one else reported on him since the Ambassador himself was often left in ignorance.

The PEO was also independent. General Heintges was energetic and had strong support in CINCPAC and in the Pentagon. He and Smith pushed through the increased training program over State Department opposition and then acted in the summer of 1959 to secure his position by establishing separate communication channels to Hawaii and Washington. Although the ostensible purpose of the system was to facilitate work with field training groups, the new channels permitted him to deal with Washington without the knowledge of the Ambassador.

Washington reflected the divisions in Vientiane. The State Department generally supported its Ambassador and, hence, Phoui Sananikone, but not very enthusiastically It preferred not to have to choose between anti-communists. Since no one in State remembers a decision to support the Christmas coup, the Pentagon and CIA may have agreed on their plan without consulting State. Or that choice may have been made at CINCPAC, which had long vigorously backed Phoumi. In any event, the military mission in Laos was ordered to work with the CIA. At least one American was so close to the Laotian army leaders that he was told of the intended coup the day before it occurred. Both the CIA and the military hoped that General Phoumi would emerge as the head of the Laotian government.[38]

Once the coup took place, the State Department was stirred to action. Assistant Secretary Parsons and others opposed Phoumi Nosavan's becoming Prime Minister because of the militarist image it would give the government. They also doubted Phoumi's political skills. They were able to prevail over the CIA and Pentagon because of a clever move by the United States Ambassador. Faced with the coup, Smith rallied the British and French ambassadors, to whom Phoumi was also an anathema. Perhaps because he feared that his move would be weakened if he were identified as the instigator, he apparently arranged for the British, French, and Australian representatives to come to him and request that he join them in going to the King.[39] This action changed the face of the issue in Washington. No longer was the question which man, Phoumi or Phoui, was the better anti-communist; now it was whether Phoumi was worth the cost in antagonizing America's allies.

The King was caught in the middle, sympathetic to General Phoumi's anti-communism but disturbed at the military coup. He stood aloof from the generals for the first few days in January while they tried to bolster their case and work out arrangements with government officials in other parts of the country. On January 4 he received the four Western diplomatic representatives, who expressed their concern and urged the King not to name a military man, especially General Phoumi, to head the new government. The same day he also received a cable from Secretary-General Hammarskjøld, then in the Congo, apparently urging the same thing. The King decided to name a government responsible only to himself, since the assembly had been prorogued by the army, and empowered only to prepare the forthcoming elections. He either suggested, or had suggested to him, the names of two old, respected politicians, Prince Boun Oum of Champassak and Kou Abhay. The latter became Premier on January 7 in a government dominated by General Phoumi Nosavan.[40]

Although the election result most feared by the pro-Western groups was a repeat of the Pathet Lao victory in 1958, the major battle was between the RLP and the CDNI. The Pathet Lao never had a chance. The government openly revised the rules to double the election deposit required of candidates, to increase the educational requirements so as to exclude automatically more than half the Pathet Lao leaders, and to gerrymander districts "to break up Pathet Lao zones of influence and prevent the movement from forming highly compact groups."[41] Shortly before the elections the army began a series of operations in areas of southern Laos known to be sympathetic to the Pathet Lao. They "meted out discipline" to individuals and sometimes whole villages, which they set afire. General Phoumi led a vigorous propaganda campaign and the CIA gave extensive financial assistance. Although the RLP and CDNI could not agree on the division of candidates, such an alliance was not necessary. The overwhelming results would have surprised even the most adept American big-city machine politician or the election officials of some rural county in the South. One CDNI leader, commenting on the charges of election rigging, said blandly that "the truth sometimes appears impossible to be true."[42]

Once again the major Western ambassadors went to the King and pleaded with him not to appoint General Phoumi as Prime Minister, despite the fact that the CDNI, now reformed as a political party, the Paxasangkhom (PSK), controlled thirty-two of the fifty-nine seats in the assembly to the RLP's twenty-seven. The King acceded and appointed a former RLP member, Tiao Somsanith, who had formed a close alliance with Phoumi before the election. The new cabinet consisted almost entirely (eleven of fourteen positions) of PSK members.[43]

What had the United States accomplished in Laos by the summer of 1960? It had spent $300 million during the previous six years. With token exceptions of aid to education, public health, and agriculture, this money had gone primarily to support an army not very reliably estimated to be 29,000 and a village militia of 20,000. A side effect had been widespread profiteering and corruption by well-placed Lao officials. The army's support was necessary for the survival of any government, not least because the army was the major instrument of government administration in remote areas. And the survival of the army depended on the continuation of American aid, which had assisted the rise to power of strongly anti-Communist and pro-American offers. This chain of dependency guaranteed that the Laotian government would avoid a coalition with the Pathet Lao, would align itself closely to the United States, Thailand, and South Vietnam, and would oppose pro-Communist elements both politically and militarily. The ICA summarized the results of its aid with customary self-congratulation in the spring of 1960: "That Laos has remained free is attributable largely to U.S. aid."[44]

That conclusion shows the continued prevalence of a cold-war perspective on Laos. Americans in Washington and Vientiane still believed that international communism threatened Laos and could be resisted only by building up the army. The gradually increasing efforts in education and agriculture were too little and too late.

By 1960 the Pathet Lao had extended their control throughout the areas which they nominally held and even beyond. Bernard Fall quoted a "friendly Asian military observer" who visited some of these remote areas in the spring of 1960: "The Pathet Lao in hundreds of villages had almost reached the stage of political organization that enabled the Viet-Minh to defeat the French in Viet Nam."[45] An American reporter, writing in January of the same year, had concluded: "If free elections were held today in Laos, every qualified observer, including the American Embassy, concedes this hermit kingdom of Southeast Asia would go Communist in a landslide."[46] Four months later, of course, pro-American candidates won a carefully managed election.

American hopes rested on the army, but how reliable was it? Admiral Felt testified predictably in March 1960 that he had no doubts about the reliability of the regular forces. But the previous summer a French advisor had discovered that at least four of the twelve battalion commanders he was training were openly sympathetic to the Pathet Lao. The army was also inept at guard duty and ineffective in battle. In May 1959 it had permitted one Pathet Lao battalion to escape, though surrounded. A year later the Pathet Lao leaders had escaped from prison, this time with their guards. The 29,000-man army had been unable to defeat either the 1,500 Pathet Lao regular soldiers or their more numerous guerrilla cadres. In spite of the optimism at CINCPAC and in Washington, the PEO director in Laos admitted, "We have yet to give this country a fighting army."[47]

Newspaper articles, critical of the aid program,

prompted the Pentagon and State Department to send a special budgetary survey mission to Laos early in 1960. The investigators discovered that the Royal Laotian Army was in worse shape than the military reports had indicated. The weapons were often too heavy for the small Lao soldiers; some of the men were armed with rifles which would not fire. Many units were dependent on ground transportation which bad weather and poor roads often rendered unusable. The mission concluded that the United States should not expand its aid effort, but in fact should phase out its assistance, turning whatever tasks remained over to Filipinos.[48] *

This report met an icy reception at CINCPAC and the Pentagon. Officers there resented criticism of the programs they had defended so vociferously. They also still believed that Communists were ready to take over Laos and all of Southeast Asia. ICA likewise defended its multimillion dollar aid programs by reference to the Communist threat. Only the State Department was sympathetic to the report, perhaps because it was becoming more critical of reliance on the Laotian army for political as well as military roles. The head of the mission was called to see Secretary Herter, who complimented him on the report but said: "You realize, of course, nobody will do a damn thing about it. There are too many vested interests."[49] And so there were.

Laos was relatively quiet after the elections in May 1960. The Pathet Lao did not attack and the politicians did not conspire. The gloomy reports of the winter had given way to much brighter assessments in the summer. One National Security Council staff member visited Laos in July and August and wrote a glowing and optimistic report about the American effort there. He mailed his report from Vientiane on the evening of August 8. That same evening a CIA case officer visited

---

* Filipino military technicians had been sent to Laos after 1958 as a less conspicuous substitute for Americans. They handled supply depots and repair facilities. The French accepted this subterfuge because they were told that the Filipinos were necessary to prevent the equipment from being wasted. (Confidential Source.)

his friend Captain Kong-Le, a young officer trained at the United States Army's Ranger School in the Philippines who had been apolitical most of his career. The CIA man stayed with Kong-Le until about midnight; he left without any inkling as to what would happen three hours later.[50] The Americans thought that Laos had become a quiet, peaceful bulwark against a Communist advance in Southeast Asia. But they had not reckoned with Captain Kong-Le.

CHAPTER FOUR

Coordinating chaos (1960)

By the time a message to the field had been composed in Washington, it had ceased to be an operational order and had become a philosophical essay.
JAMES DOUGLAS, *Under-Secretary of Defense*[1]

In the early hours of August 9, 1960, the Second Lao Paratroop Battalion spread throughout Vientiane, seizing government offices, communications centers, and the power station. Soldiers set up roadblocks around the city and parked jeeps on the airport runway to prevent any landings. A few hours later the battalion commander, Captain Kong-Le, broadcast an appeal over the captured radio for an end to fraternal bloodshed and governmental corruption and for the return to a foreign policy of genuine neutrality. The main thrust of his argument was toward these points, but he was also critical of the United States. "It is the Americans who have bought government officials and army commanders, and cause war and dissension in our country."[2]

Little blood was shed in the coup. The only casualties were two guards at the home of the Army Chief of Staff. There was no effective opposition because of the absence of most of the Cabinet from Vientiane. They had flown to Luang Prabang the day before the coup to confer with the King on the arrangements for the long-delayed cremation of his father, who had died the previous October but whose embalmed body awaited a sandalwood tree large enough to contain it in a sitting position for the final rites. The Cabinet, though saved from house arrest, was unable to participate in the political maneuvering of the next few days. During their absence the forces were released which thwarted subsequent attempts at reconciliation.

Two years would pass before all major political factions would reassemble in Vientiane under a single government.

American analyses of Kong-Le's motives and political sympathies were almost as numerous as the authors of them. Ambassador Winthrop Brown, who had arrived in Vientiane only a month before the coup, considered the short, twenty-six-year-old officer a sincere nationalist, who was angry at the way he and his men had been treated and was disgusted at the conspicuous waste evident in Vientiane.[3] The embassy knew that the troops had cause for dissatisfaction, for General Phoumi Nosavan had informed them four days before the coup that he had not paid his troops for two months. Phoumi said that the money had gone "for other purposes."[4]

Most of the Americans in Vientiane thought that Kong-Le was acting on his own—a junior officer rising in anger against the generals. They believed he was deeply troubled by the continued civil bloodletting and wanted the various national groups reconciled. "I have fought for many years and have killed many men," he said, "but I have never seen a foreigner die."[5] Embassy personnel shared many of the captain's criticisms of the aid program and did not think that he would turn against the United States. They could point to his quick suppression of the anti-American shouts and placards which blossomed the day after the coup.[6]

Opinion in Washington was divided over Kong-Le. The CIA, whose people had worked most closely with the young officer, had a benign view. They saw him as a lone wolf, friendly to Americans and hostile to the Communists. Military officials who hoped to work through General Phoumi in fighting the Pathet Lao more vigorously saw their plans threatened by the coup, if not entirely upset. Pointing to Kong-Le's call for neutrality and criticism of the United States, these Pentagon officials demanded that Kong-Le be opposed and replaced. The same view prevailed at the highest echelons of the State Department, where officials feared that Kong-Le might be another Castro. Faced with the reports of the coup leader's anti-American statements, they chose to discount the CIA analysis and treat the young captain with the skepticism they wished they had shown toward the Cuban leader.[7]

Washington's initial decision was to seek the removal of Kong-Le. This would have been a likely response even if the coup leader had not criticized the American aid program in Laos because of the vested U.S. interest in the status quo. The United States, like most nations, has always found it easier to deal with an established government than with insurgents. The Somsanith government's anti-communism was certain, while Kong-Le's was doubtful. And the leaders of the army financed over the previous six years by $300 million were unwilling to tolerate this upstart.

Cables to Vientiane called for the expeditious removal of the coup leader, but gave no specific orders for implementation. The embassy had no sure way to achieve this result other than by assassination, which was morally distasteful as well as difficult to arrange quickly or without appearing to implicate the United States. Political intrigue was limited by the absence of the major government figures from the capital. Nor was the embassy as concerned about the long-range consequences of the coup as Washington. It was willing to wait and see what the Laotians might work out.[8]

While the Americans waited, Kong-Le tried to form a new government. The Somsanith Cabinet would neither resign nor return from Luang Prabang. The young captain formed a forty-man Provisional Executive Committee to govern the country until a new administration could be formed. It consisted of army officers, politicians, and administrators, both leftists and known anti-Communists, who had all declared themselves in sympathy with the coup. Kong-Le then turned to the politicians who were in Vientiane—the leftist Quinim Pholsena, Prince Souvanna Phouma, and Prince Boun Oum. Quinim advised him to go to Souvanna, but the Prince, who had disavowed the use of his name in connection with the forty-man committee, wanted the captain to go through the formalities of National Assembly votes in order to set up a new government. Boun Oum reportedly refused to head a new government as well.[9]

After three days of missions to and from Luang Prabang, the Somsanith government agreed to resign on conditions which the coup supporters found excessive. Kong-Le, ignoring those conditions, demanded the removal of the government. Souvanna Phouma agreed to convene the National Assembly, of which he was the President, on August 13. Forty-one members attended and voted unanimously a motion of no confidence in the Somsanith government. They acted, however, in an atmosphere of disorder and intimidation. Thousands of people—in a town of only 70,000—marched through the streets and surrounded the National Assembly, which had already been encircled by paratroops. Zealous young people, many of whom had been political prisoners before Kong-Le's general amnesty, stirred the crowds to frenzy with their marching and shouting. They had organized a society of Lao youth soon after the coup and were a powerful agitational prop to the new leaders. Their anti-American slogans lent support to those who feared that Kong-Le was working in tandem with the Communists. Led by the young people, the crowd stormed the assembly building. It was quieted only by the appearance of Souvanna Phouma, who announced the assembly's vote of no confidence in the Somsanith government.[10]

The King received a deputation from the assembly the following day. Tiao Somsanith decided to resign in order to avoid bloodshed, despite urgings to the contrary from some of his cabinet, especially General Phoumi. Upon receiving the resignation, the King nominated Souvanna Phouma to form a new government. This was done during the next two days, and on August 17 Kong-Le formally transferred power to Souvanna and declared his coup at an end. The new cabinet excluded the CDNI members and others who had held posts in the Somsanith government, thus further provoking General Phoumi.[11]

Angry at the coup, which followed the same plan which he had prepared for his own seizure of power,[12] General Phoumi flew from Luang Prabang to his headquarters at Savannakhet and formed a committee against the coup on August 15. He was in a strong position not only because he controlled most of the supplies of the Lao Army, which had been channeled into the southern part of Laos for security reasons, but also because he had the support of the commanders of four of the country's five military regions. (The only exception was the fifth region, headquartered in Vientiane.) He obtained this support primarily because he promised to pay the salaries of all who joined him, a promise dependent on continued assistance from the Americans assigned to work with him.[13]

The U.S. officials in Savannakhet believed that their orders were to do everything possible to help Phoumi. In the absence of a firm decision from Washington to stop supporting and advising the Royal Army, they were free to use their initiative and their resources. On August 12 skillful propaganda broadcasts began from "Savannakhet Radio." This new station, using an American-supplied transmitter, fulminated against the coup and tried to rally support to Phoumi. The General began moving troops south from Luang Prabang and North from his own headquarters; he also sent some of his intelligence officers into the capital to carry out sabotage and terror raids. On August 16 one of Phoumi's transport planes flew over Vientiane, dropping leaflets denouncing Kong-Le and heralding a military drive on the capital. "Don't believe in Kong-Le," the leaflets said. "He's fooling you about neutrality. He's bringing the Communists in. Just wait and your old government will return."[14]

Souvanna Phouma now headed a legitimate, recognized government. The United States was compelled to deal with him, in spite of American doubts as to his orientation to the Pathet Lao. Ambassador Brown had developed good relations with him during his own first few weeks in Laos and neither feared nor distrusted his leadership. But officials in Washington disagreed with Brown's assessment. They were still apprehensive about Kong-Le and eager for his removal, or at least his eclipse. They were unwilling to accept the complete loss of authority by the CDNI elements whom the United States had so strongly supported. They would accept Souvanna only if he would drop Kong-Le and bring CDNI members into the Government. When these conditions were presented to Souvanna, he rejected them outright. But he must have seen the writing on the wall, for he did initiate efforts at reconciliation soon afterward.[15]

More than American pressure drove Souvanna toward a coalition with Phoumi. Thailand had been ready to intervene with paratroops soon after the coup. Sarit told a visiting American official, "In dealing with coups, you don't wait for the dust to settle." Four days after the coup, Washington sent urgent cables to Saigon and Bangkok, telling the embassies to try to cool down Diem and Sarit. At the time, the State Department feared trouble with the Chinese if outside troops intervened in Laos.[16] Thwarted from direct intervention, the Thais nevertheless took other actions to influence events in Laos. They closed the supply line at the Nong Khai ferry across from Vientiane, thereby depriving the capital of foreign goods, especially POL supplies and many foodstuffs. They also gave various forms of assistance to Phoumi, while keeping open his supply line, through which came American military aid. On August 20, shortly before Souvanna took his first steps toward reconciliation with Phoumi, word circulated in Vientiane that Phoumi's forces had captured Paksane, a town eighty miles southeast of Vientiane, after having been conveyed through Thailand. Sarit also provided Phoumi with some troops and artillery which proved quite helpful in his subsequent attack on Vientiane.[17]

On August 23, Souvanna flew to Savannakhet, where he conferred with Phoumi. The two men agreed to convoke the National Assembly at Luang Prabang, away from the turmoil of the capital, and to form a coalition government. Six days later, meetings began at the royal capital in a foreboding atmosphere. "This is our last chance," Souvanna said. "If we cannot come to an agreement, civil war will certainly follow."[18]

The coalition government formed on August 31 continued the exclusion of the Pathet Lao and included at least five pro-American ministers in its membership of fourteen. There were also at least two CDNI ministers. Souvanna Phouma was Prime Minister and held several other portfolios. Phoumi Nosavan was Vice Premier and in charge of the Ministry of Interior. The general's brother-in-law was Minister of Communications and Public Works. Conservative General Ouane was in operational charge of the Defense Ministry. Quinim Pholsena was transferred from Interior to Information. The American Embassy was quite pleased with this result and recommended strong support for the new government. General Phoumi, however, decided not to stay in the cabinet. Thinking he had American support, he launched his own counterrevolution.[19]

Instead of returning to Vientiane with the other officials of the new cabinet, Phoumi flew to Savannakhet shortly after agreeing to the coalition. Several factors may have prompted this sudden change of mind. One was Kong-Le's reluctance to have Phoumi in the cabinet, an attitude made known in a Vientiane radio broadcast on the afternoon of August 31. Hearing of this and of a reported threat to his life should he go to Vientiane, Phoumi went first to his own headquarters. Souvanna removed these obstacles to Phoumi's participation in the government that same evening. Soon after arriving in the administrative capital the Premier went to Kong-Le and persuaded the coup leader to recant his views publicly the next day. Souvanna also offered to let Phoumi bring a battalion of his own men to the capital for protection. Even if caution had been his primary reason for avoiding Vientiane on September 1, he soon had other reasons for staying out of the cabinet. Once in Savannakhet, he was urged by many of his advisors, including American military and CIA personnel, to hold out for the Defense Ministry. That advice matched Phoumi's own ambitions, so he readily accepted it.[20]

The Americans around Phoumi thought that the most important aspect of U.S. policy toward Laos was the creation of a strong, anti-communist army. They had demonstrated their opposition to the Kong-Le coup by immediately helping Phoumi to plan an attack on the capital. Although they were under the nominal control of the Ambassador and Washington, they were free to give advice and to make contingency plans. They may not even have told their superiors what they were doing. Phoumi shared their anticommunism and knew that they supplied his army. He had no incentive to reject their advice.[21]

Phoumi thought he had American support and knew

that three of the five commanders of military regions were with him all the way. The only exceptions were the garrisons at Luang Prabang and Vientiane. (The former switched sides when the King approved the new government; the latter remained under the control of Kong-Le.) Phoumi made a quick trip to Bangkok and received further encouragement to fight back from his cousin, Marshal Sarit, who had said publicly: "When any southeast Asian country becomes more neutralist, it becomes more Communist."[22] Souvanna confirmed whatever suspicions these men may have had about the new Laotian government's drift toward communism when, on September 2, he called for peace negotiations with the Pathet Lao. Phoumi decided to fight the August 31 coalition government. On September 5 he reestablished his countercoup committee; five days later he proclaimed a new revolutionary group nominally headed by Prince Boun Oum of Champassak, head of one of the three major political dynasties in Laos, the one whose power rested in the southern provinces. The civil war was on.[23]

Washington's picture of the events in Laos was fuzzy. Without clear and reliable evidence of what was happening, officials were reluctant to make firm decisions for or against the contending factions. No one wanted to support the coup, but no one wished to act in uncertainty and confusion. The easiest route was to let Ambassador Brown try to work something out that would reconcile the non-communist groups. At the same time, however, no one was willing to force Phoumi to accept the new situation. Consequently, each American group in Laos had a license to bolster its client. The end result of this hesitation and indecision was a loss of control over policy from Washington and the loss of effectiveness in Laos.

One should remember that policy toward Laos was not a high priority item in the last few months of 1960. The presidential campaign absorbed domestic attention, while Cuba and the Congo dominated the international news. The question of Laos was raised at President Eisenhower's news conference only twice—the day after the coup and a week later. On August 10 the President said that he was still "trying to get some real

details" on the situation, thus brushing aside a question on re-
appraising our policy. A week later, he said, "Laos is a very
confused situation." He said that the administration was following developments and would "take any kind of action that seems
to be indicated."[24] In other words, we were waiting and watching; nobody was very upset.

Within the bureaucracy, however, the policy debate
continued. But little of it reached the surface of public awareness. In fact, the only formal American comment on Laos
between the President's August 17 news conference and the
recognition of the Boun Oum regime in mid-December was a
strangely worded statement isssued on September 10. That statement made two statements of fact: that, "according to broadcasts," a revolution had started in Laos; and that Americans
were not in danger. The only other paragraph in the statement
went as follows:

> The United States has in the past consistently
> supported duly constituted governments of Laos in
> their efforts to maintain the independence and integrity
> of Laos against Communist encroachment from with-
> out or within. It would regret a situation in which vio-
> lence destroyed unity thereby increasing the danger of
> such encroachment. The United States has no desire to
> intervene in the internal affairs of Laos. It has consis-
> tently adhered to and supported the policy that their
> affairs should be settled by peaceful means by the Lao
> themselves. It would, however, be immediately con-
> cerned by the efforts of any other outside power, or the
> agents thereof, to take advantage of the disturbed con-
> ditions prevailing and to intervene directly or indi-
> rectly.[25]

There are several curious features in this statement.
First, there is no declaration of support for or opposition to
either the Royal Government or the self-proclaimed revolutionaries. The juxtaposition of the fact of the establishment of
the revolutionary committee with a declared policy of anti-

communism might imply tacit support. But it could also be read as a compromise between those groups which wanted to support Phoumi and those which still thought they might work with the government of Souvanna. The qualification that the United States had "in the past" supported the "duly constituted" government implied that such support might not now exist. The remainder of that sentence seems to impose a condition for receiving such support: a policy against "Communist encroachment." Since Souvanna was trying to reach a settlement with the Pathet Lao, this statement was a warning to him to break off his talks.

Another aspect of the statement is noteworthy. The disavowal of any desire to intervene in Laos is coupled with a warning against others who might also consider intervention— presumably China, the Soviet Union, and North Vietnam. But the support for a settlement "by peaceful means by the Lao themselves" seems to be an addition by those policy makers who opposed military action by Phoumi against Souvanna.

Put together, these statements suggest that Washington could find agreement only on a policy of temporizing. Policy makers could not agree on which faction to support, in spite of the technical legality of Souvanna Phouma's regime and the self-professed revolutionary status of Boun Oum. They repeated the usual disavowal of intervention and warned others against the same. Their only standard of judging between factions was the principle of Communist encroachment. They left open the possibility of supporting whichever group seemed least likely to bring in Communists, whether indigenous or foreign. And two months later they cast their lot with the most anti-communist group.

"A tug of war was going on in Washington over Laos policy," a highly placed source has declared. The September 10 statement was indeed a compromise in which anti-communism was the only unifying principle. Each agency concerned with Laos had its own information from the field and its own perspective for interpreting it. When policy makers disagreed, they bargained and compromised. For several weeks they were unable to agree to oust Souvanna or fully to endorse Phoumi. Their indecision gave their subordinates in Laos a relatively free hand to act according to their own preferences.[26]

The State Department had cables from Ambassador Brown and an unusually united country team. Brown had tried since the coup to reconcile Souvanna and Phoumi and, thus, was a vigorous supporter of the August 31 settlement. He thought that it was the best solution under the circumstances, especially since it excluded the Pathet Lao while uniting the centrist and rightist forces.[27]

Assistant Secretary Parsons was inclined to support Brown's actions and recommendations. As a former Ambassador in Vientiane himself, he had detailed knowledge of the personalities involved (other than Kong-Le) and sympathy for Brown's position. Moreover, he and Brown had been close friends ever since they were classmates at Yale. Parsons distrusted Souvanna because of the Premier's naive attitude about Communists, but he favored the coalition between Souvanna and Phoumi.[28]

Higher in the State Department, however, the distrust of Souvanna was even greater. The officials most actively involved in Laos matters were Secretary Herter and Under Secretary Livingston Merchant. Both were suspicious of Souvanna's relationship with his half-brother and with the Pathet Lao. They both also believed that Kong-Le was violently anti-American and close to the Communists, despite the CIA evaluation that the young captain was only a sincere neutralist. In these views they were close to the prevailing opinion in the Pentagon and CIA. They disagreed, however, on Phoumi Nosavan and Boun Oum because they doubted that the General and the Prince had the political skills to run an effective anti-communist government. Herter, Merchant, and other officials in the State Department also suspected that Phoumi's army might bungle an armed attempt to overthrow Souvanna's government.[29]

The Pentagon had no doubts about what should be done. Aggravated by the State Department's indecision, high-ranking civilian and military officials in the Defense Department all wanted to give full American support to General Phoumi

Nosavan. They doubted that Souvanna's government would survive or would be able to resist the Communists. They knew that Phoumi was ready and eager to move north and take Vientiane. All that he lacked was a green light from Washington. "We didn't know enough about the people in Laos," Admiral Arleigh Burke (Chief of Naval Operations, 1955–61) admitted. "But once we had settled on someone to support, I believed that, as long as he was supporting us, we should support him all the way through."[30] The Joint Chiefs, Defense Secretary Gates, and other officials in the Pentagon all believed that the United States should put its money on Phoumi and then give him free rein.[31]

Reports to Washington from CINCPAC and from the military mission in Laos buttressed the Pentagon's stance. U.S. officials cabled their doubts about Souvanna, fears about Kong-Le, and faith in Phoumi. In contrast to Souvanna, one officer recalls, the General "seemed to be against corruption, and showed promise of being able to establish a government which would show some initiative and, hopefully, could work constructively toward rolling back the advance of Communist encroachment."[32] Another officer concluded by September that "The Communists had proven to us beyond a doubt that a political solution was useless and that a military solution was our only hope."[33]

The CIA also backed Phoumi, but with less fervor. In contrast to Pentagon officials, CIA men supported the August 31 government because they thought that Phoumi would dominate it. They agreed with the prevailing view of Souvanna as a "weak reed," but they also doubted Phoumi's military capabilities. The CIA conclusion in Washington was that Phoumi led a "bloated army" which was not very good in a fight. Although this assessment proved correct, it was not widely accepted at the time.[34]

In Laos the CIA played a much larger policy role than in Washington. Although Agency officials like Richard Bissell, Deputy Director for Plans (1959–62), maintain that their operatives in the field very strictly followed orders and reported their actions to the Station Chief in Vientiane (Gordon Jorgensen), the evidence from other sources is contradictory. These officials say that the Agency men in the field were quite zealous in bolstering Phoumi and in urging him to move against Souvanna. They had separate communication channels to Washington and, thus, could have bypassed even the Station Chief. They reported not to Bissell, but to his subordinates, Colby and Fitzgerald, who had long favored Phoumi. With so few controls on their activities, they were free to act with impunity and even to go beyond their instructions.[35]

Washington officials were unable to coordinate the emerging chaos in Laos because they lacked a consensus and a shared perspective on the situation there. Each agency had its own information, its own clients, and its own preferred solution. There was overwhelming support for Phoumi Nosavan, but not for any specific plan to return him to power. There was also the traditional reluctance to go contrary to the recommendations of the Ambassador on the scene. Normally, in such situations the matter would have gone to the President for resolution. But in the waning months of the Eisenhower Administration, Secretaries Herter and Gates consciously tried to avoid bothering the President for decisions. When they did raise issues involving Laos, Eisenhower responded with maxims which did little to resolve the basic conflicts. One participant remembers that, at different times, the President said: "I don't want the U.S. image involved in favoring one side," and, "As long as it doesn't look as if we're backing down, go ahead."[36]

With indecision in Washington encouraging independent action in Laos, American policy there grew more tangled during September. One of the most important decisions early in the month was to try to replace Souvanna Phouma. The embassy was instructed to find a substitute who was pro-Western and had a broad political base. Ambassador Brown, who favored continued support for Souvanna, said he had no ideas and asked for suggestions. After some further discussions in Washington, State recommended Phoui Sananikone, the Premier who was eclipsed by Phoumi Nosavan and the CDNI during 1958 and 1959. Brown responded by pointing out Phoui's drawbacks: Phoumi hated him; Souvanna disliked him; the King would not support him; and, he no longer had a political base.[37]

Already in September Brown was angering Pentagon officials by his support for Souvanna and his resistance to Washington's directives to try to replace the Prince. The Ambassador sincerely believed that the only viable solution for Laos was a coalition of centrist and rightist elements, and so he argued the impossibility of arranging the kind of pro-American government demanded by Washington. He was encouraged in this stance, at first, by evidence of some support in the policy debates. On one occasion, Brown received a joint State-Defense cable ordering him to tell Souvanna that the United States could not support the Premier's government but would welcome him as Laotian Ambassador to Washington. A few hours later, Brown received a cable from Parsons suggesting that the Ambassador not comply with the directive because the Assistant Secretary was trying to work out a different solution.[38]

Parsons later joined his superiors in working for Souvanna's ouster, but only after the Premier had turned in desperation to the Soviet Union for help. Although Souvanna himself, and consequently many other commentators, have blamed Parsons for the failure of American policy in Laos—Souvanna called him "the most reprehensible and nefarious of men"[39]—the available evidence suggests that the Assistant Secretary fought a lonely battle in Washington for the embassy's recommendations. He ultimately lost because of the forces arrayed against Souvanna and against the spectre of Communist gains in Laos. His major victory was only to keep open the option of accepting the August 31 settlement until Washington swung its support fully behind Phoumi in November.

That was a Pyrrhic victory, however, because the fact of indecision between Souvanna and Phoumi enabled the General's supporters to strengthen him vis-à-vis the government. Although some State Department officials wanted a coalition of conservative and neutralist forces, they were unwilling to force Phoumi to join it. Throughout September the CIA and military advisors continued to aid Phoumi and his forces. Since Thailand had closed supply routes to Vientiane, they channeled all aid through Savannakhet, including that designated for the dissident forces in the north. They even helped Phoumi prepare plans for his eventual march on Vientiane.[40] Whether or not they encouraged him to try to seize power, they certainly did nothing to stop him.

Phoumi obliged his supporters by keeping alive the Communist threat. On September 16 he claimed that six battalions from North Vietnam had crossed into Sam Neua. A few days later commanding officers in the area denied the presence of any foreign troops, but the headlines went to the first report. On September 18 Vientiane was shelled from the Thai side of the Mekong. Kong-Le's forces finally counterattacked on September 22, routing a much larger force of Phoumi's troops near Paksane.[41] This was only the first of several ignominious military reversals for the well-financed troops of the revolutionary General.

As the threat of military action grew, the United States military took its standard precautionary steps. The navy sent a task force with 1,400 marines into the South China Sea in what were described as "standby actions" in view of the events in Laos. The threat which prompted these actions, officials said, was that the Pathet Lao might take over the two northern provinces. No one asked for or was given an explanation of the utility of such naval power in an area so distant from the sea.[42]

The inevitable conclusion is that this was just a show of force and a demonstration of naval readiness. (One official at CINCPAC said that this carrier attack force, numbered seventy-seven, often started steaming toward a trouble spot even without orders, which usually followed shortly.)[43]

While the soldiers prepared for war, the diplomats continued to try to negotiate a peace. American Embassy officials traveled between the capital and Savannakhet, trying to persuade Phoumi to make contact with Souvanna's government. But Phoumi, continually reinforced with American supplies and advised to hold out for a better offer, rejected these pleas. Americans also went to Luang Prabang to try to get the King to take some unifying action, but met with a similar lack of success. Although he did offer to conduct meetings between the antagonists, he assiduously avoided angering either side.[44]

The King was in a delicate position. His family's traditional rivals for power were the dynasties in Vientiane and the south now headed by Souvanna Phouma and Boun Oum. He wanted to do nothing that might jeopardize his position and that of the monarchy. So he bent with the wind. At first he called the coup just an internal quarrel between army officers. When Somsanith resigned, he called on Souvanna to form a new government. But when Phoumi refused to deliver the formal investiture papers which had been brought from Vientiane for the King to sign, the King seemed relieved and made no special efforts to support the new government. He later presided over the establishment of the August 31 coalition but never criticized Phoumi for failing to stay with it. The United States tried several times to work through the King to pressure the contending factions, but he remained aloof.

As September ended, the different strands of American policy were obviously tangled. The military assistance to Phoumi strengthened him against the established government rather than the Pathet Lao. But his men were easily defeated by Kong-Le's forces in the few skirmishes which took place. As viewed from Washington, the effort to replace Souvanna Phouma was being undermined by the reluctant, foot-dragging civilians in the embassy. Nothing seemed to be working out as planned or ordered.

Washington reacted to this confusion by pulling in the reins and looking at a map. The first decision was to stop its aid to Laos. General Williston B. Palmer, head of the military assistance program, announced a slowdown in aid on September 24. "We must wait for the situation to clear before we know what United States aid policy will be." A few days later, on October 1, he called the Laotian situation "confused" and said that the suspension of aid was decided "because we have not been sure who is responsible for anything."[45] In fact, the cash grant aid had been suspended at the time of the coup and military aid was not formally stopped until October 7. General Palmer had announced the arms policy prematurely.[46] But the sense of confusion was widely felt in Washington, where it prompted a new effort to untangle policy.

The final straw, which broke the resistance to a reexamination of official policy, was Souvanna's opening to the left—both domestically and internationally. The Prime Minister had pleaded with American officials for assistance in overcoming the Thai blockade of the capital. The embassy asked Washington for supplies of food and fuel, but was rejected. Many U.S. officials doubted that Souvanna would carry out his threat to seek help from the U.S.S.R. They thought that their own understanding and fear of communism would be shared by a leader isolated in his blockaded capital. With nowhere else to turn for help, Souvanna announced on September 30 that he was taking steps to establish diplomatic relations with the Soviet Union. Four days later he announced that he would start talks immediately with representatives of the Pathet Lao aimed at bringing them back into the national community.[47]

These were the very actions which American policy had consistently tried to prevent over the previous six years. Few people in Washington had accepted the embassy's argument that a denial of aid to Souvanna would force him to turn to the Communists. Now it was too late.

Alarmed at the trend of events in Laos, in particular Souvanna's decision to accept a Soviet embassy, Defense Secretary Gates persuaded Under Secretary Dillon, his next-door neighbor and Acting Secretary in Herter's absence, to send a mission to Laos to straighten things out. The mission consisted of Parsons, Assistant Secretary of Defense for International Security Affairs John Irwin, and Vice Admiral Herbert Riley, the staff director at CINCPAC. Parsons and Irwin left Washington on October 8, after one day's notice; Riley joined the group in Hawaii.

The purpose of the mission was viewed differently by various participants in the decision. One State Department official thought it was to bring unity out of the confusion of policy in Laos. Another thought that it was to lessen the "chasm" between State and Defense in Washington. This official also agreed with a Defense Department official, who said that the purpose was to get an agreed set of facts for future decisions, particularly on Souvanna's relations with Kong-Le and the Pathet Lao. Still another Defense official thought that the mission was to do something—to implement the presumed decision to support Phoumi as against Souvanna.[48]

Parsons says that his directive was to bring unity to American policy while, at the same time, maintaining the effectiveness of the Laotian army. Irwin remembers only that he was to determine the amount of support which could be given to Phoumi. Riley says that the group was to discover whether the existing government had the determination to resist the Pathet Lao.[49] Although memories can be faulty after so many years, it is significant that these recollections coincide with the known position of each member's department at the time. They also are consistent with the actions each took during the mission.

State's desire for a unified policy sprang from much more than a sense of tidiness. The divergent actions by different American agencies in Laos, despite the general consensus among the country team in Vientiane, were becoming counterproductive. Only a clear policy imposed from above could prevent each group from adhering to its established position and supporting its client against other factions. There was uncertainty in Washington because the information relayed from Laos was viewed skeptically. "It was always distorted," one official complained. "I couldn't get good information from anybody."[50] Better information was an important objective of the mission.

Much more important than information was the general problem of power. Throughout Asia at the time State and Defense struggled for control over American policy. The diplomats wanted to utilize their skills and lessen military influence. The soldiers believed that the danger of war in the area was still quite real and that they had to bolster the various national armies. By giving military aid, they also became more influential than the diplomats with their meager economic programs.[51] Laos was one arena for this tug-of-war.

The Defense Department's interest in the amount of support which could go to Phoumi has already been explained at length. Anti-communism was all that mattered to the Pentagon. With the tacit acquiescence evidenced in the September 10 statement, the military officers in Laos continued to act as if the policy decision had already been made to support Phoumi's rebellion. Officials in Washington and Hawaii did nothing to weaken that assumption. CINCPAC's special role in these matters was an outgrowth not only of its operational responsibility for administering military aid but also for its persistent hawkishness about Asia. One official has commented that CINCPAC always put "an extra zip" into recommendations from the field for opposing the Communists.[52]

When the Parsons mission arrived in Vientiane on October 12, the members went into immediate talks with Souvanna Phouma. Parsons did most of the talking. He spelled out the major requirements for American support. First, Souvanna would have to end his talks with the Pathet Lao about a new coalition government. Second, he would have to resume discussions with Phoumi and agree to a major CDNI role in the cabinet. Third, he should move his government and the national treasury away from the turmoil of Vientiane to Luang Prabang, where the King's influence would be stronger. Fourth, he would have to clip the wings of Kong-Le, who was acting behind his back in distributing U.S. military aid to members of the Pathet Lao. Souvanna firmly rejected all the demands, but later was persuaded to try to restrain Kong-Le.[53]

These conditions, which had been worked out in Washington after Parson's departure and then had been cabled to Vientiane, represented the lowest common denominator of American policies, with no changes to account for developments since August. Rejection of negotiations with the Pathet Lao had been a basic feature of American policy toward Laos since 1954. It seemed particularly necessary in 1960 because Souvanna was seen as too weak to resist dangerous concessions to the Pathet Lao. Support for a predominant CDNI role in the cabinet went back to the summer of 1958. The gimmick of moving the capital to Luang Prabang served two purposes: to put the government closer to the King, in the hope that he would take a more active and pro-American role, and to make it possible for Phoumi and Souvanna to work under the same roof since the General feared for his own safety in Vientiane. Opposition to Kong-Le was based both on his uncertain sympathies and his recent actions, which seemed to favor the Pathet Lao.

Souvanna, too, was consistent in striving for national unity, with both the Pathet Lao and Phoumi. He still believed that an accommodation could be worked out which kept Laos free from internal or external Communist domination. He was angered at the American interference in his country's affairs, especially since it seemed to be so one-sided—and against the legitimate government. "My political position has not changed since 1956," he said. "The United States is free to make its choice and if U.S. aid is not continued, the Lao Government will get it someplace else."[54]

Faced with this impasse, Parsons and Brown looked for another solution. They wanted to resume aid to Souvanna in order to prevent his dependence on the Soviet Union. But they knew that they could not get agreement from Washington on a change in policy unless Souvanna accepted some of their conditions. Brown, especially, wanted concessions from the Premier to buy time and avoid an immediate clearcut choice between Souvanna and Phoumi. Since the event which triggered the suspension of military aid to the neutralists was the report that Kong-Le was distributing it to the Pathet Lao, Souvanna's agreement to restrain the young Captain could be used to justify a resumption of aid. This was done a few days later when Souvanna put Kong-Le under two weeks' house arrest for having led a major demonstration to welcome the new Soviet Ambassador. There was also the hope that Souvanna would be able to work something out with Phoumi before the end of the monsoons in November permitted large-scale military actions. The two diplomats reasoned that Washington could not really object to a continuation of the existing two-pronged policy of aid to both Vientiane and Savannakhet.[55]

Brown went to Souvanna on October 17 and got his agreement to a continuation of existing American policy. Aid would go to both camps. Souvanna demanded that the equipment to Phoumi not be used against his government or Kong-Le's forces. Brown gave his assurances. The Prime Minister also asked for a reinsurance provision in this gentlemen's agreement: that, while equipment continued to be delivered to Savannakhet (the only arrangement that Thailand would allow), Vientiane be given the cash-grant assistance to pay all the armed forces. In this way, Souvanna would have some leverage on Phoumi to prevent his violation of the understanding. Brown supported this, but was reversed in Washington. The fear in the capital was that Souvanna would abuse his stranglehold on Phoumi. Since the leading officials of Defense and State distrusted Souvanna much more than Phoumi, they denied him the only weapon which could have guaranteed a coalition of conservative and neutralist forces.[56] Cash-grant aid went to both factions, but the military aid went only to Phoumi.

These agreements made Parsons more hopeful about the future course of events in Laos. Staying over a few days in Bangkok, he drafted his report to Washington, recommending continued support for both sides under the conditions which Brown had offered to Souvanna. Parsons felt that the Premier would now have time to mobilize support for his government.[57]

Admiral Riley was shocked by this report. He was also angry at the fact that Parsons had not consulted with him or Irwin about it. Parsons seemed to view his position as leader of the mission, while Riley thought the three men were coequal. Riley drafted a separate report, which Irwin found closer to his own views. The differences were vast. Riley saw Souvanna as an "accommodator" who lacked moral principles. In contrast to Parsons, he had great confidence in Boun Oum and Phoumi and in their determination to resist communism. He particularly objected to what he considered Parsons' support for a "collaborationist government" including the Pathet Lao. He wanted the United States to throw its weight firmly behind Phoumi.[58]

Rather than bringing unity to American policy, the split report only widened the chasm. The mission had also projected the basic divisions in Washington into Laos, where it became clear that the United States was backing two horses in a race only one could win. This occurred when Irwin and Riley traveled to see Phoumi in Savannakhet. Parsons made excuses for not going, but the real reasons were his antipathy toward

Phoumi and his sense of the impropriety of dealing both with an established, recognized government and its self-professed rebels.[59]

Some people have charged that Irwin and Riley "gave Phoumi the green light to march on Vientiane."[60] Neither Irwin nor Riley remembers any such orders or even mild encouragement. But the effect of their visit was certainly to reinforce Phoumi's resistance to a settlement with Souvanna—a result more of what they did not say than what they did. In particular, they did not press Phoumi to negotiate with Souvanna or threaten him with reduced aid if he did not. One American source close to Phoumi has said that, in his view, the purpose of the mission to Laos was "to find out what Phoumi needed or if in fact he would be capable of retaking Vientiane." The same source, who had been urging strong support for Phoumi, admitted that the effect of the mission was to free his own hand. "I couldn't get to first base until the Parson-Irwin mission."[61]

While Washington adopted what seemed to be an even-handed policy, the men in the field acted to strengthen only Phoumi. Military aid continued to pour into Savannakhet, despite Phoumi's reluctance to forward that part which was destined for Kong-Le's forces. Transports of the CIA-controlled Air America carried supplies from Bangkok and thence out to Phoumi's forces in the field. The United States supported several clandestine radio stations which broadcast propaganda against the established government. Two hundred Lao paratroops whom the United States had been training in Thailand were turned over to Phoumi, despite a promise to Souvanna that it would not be done.[62] The State Department was not notified until the troops had been redeployed. The diplomats in Vientiane had no comparable leverage.

American agents were at work in other parts of Laos as well. In mid-October they won the allegiance of Meo tribesmen in the region bordering North Vietnam by promising to supply military equipment and Special Forces cadres. At the same time others were rallying officers in Luang Prabang to Phoumi's side. The garrison mutinied on November 11 and swung its support to the anti-communists.[63]

Events in Laos soon enabled supporters of Phoumi in Washington to win a clear decision against Souvanna and for their man. Still checked by the Thai blockade, Vientiane exhausted its fuel supplies on October 25. Two days later, Souvanna announced that he would be "very happy" to accept Soviet offers of assistance. In early November he made special visits to Pathet Lao areas to try to advance an agreement with them. These actions, which were cited as proof of Souvanna's Communist sympathies, destroyed any remaining hopes among Washington officials that Souvanna could be trusted to resist Communist encroachment.[64]

After the Parsons-Irwin mission, Washington "reached a state of agreed disenchantment with Souvanna Phouma," according to one highly placed source.[65] Arthur Schlesinger put the matter more bluntly, if less accurately: "In late October, a few days before the American elections, State and Defense agreed that Souvanna must go, though they disagreed on how this should be accomplished."[66] In spite of Brown's continuing support for Souvanna, the consensus in Washington was that he had moved too close to the Communists. There never had been strong defenders of the Laotian Premier in the American capital, but a firm decision to replace him was not made until Thursday, November 10, just two days after the 1960 elections.[67]

That decision was easier in November than it would have been in August or September because of the efforts to bolster Phoumi in the meantime. The General not only had the allegiance of all military commanders except those in Vientiane, but he also had the determination, the equipment, and the American advice to move north and overthrow the government. This was the only remaining decision which Washington could make, for it had foreclosed the possibility of working through Souvanna when it denied his request for aid and continued to strengthen Phoumi in case Souvanna should prove unacceptable. The open options of September and October had been turned by Phoumi's American supporters into an inevitable choice in November.

Except for twinges of guilt over the prospect of aiding

a revolution against a government which the United States ostensibly supported, Washington officials thought that the decision was a safe one. They were pleased that they had secured Souvanna's approval of continued aid to Phoumi's forces, for that seemed to legalize the U.S. effort. In spite of Brown's arguments against Phoui Sananikone, they still believed that the former Premier could be returned to power now that Souvanna's government was isolated. In secret testimony to the Congress on November 14, one official said that there were two problems which had to be resolved in the approaching, very delicate crisis to replace Souvanna. One was how to bring about the change without the loss of Vientiane. The other was how to achieve the result primarily by political means so as to minimize the risks of intervention by other powers.[68]

The first public indication of the American decision against Souvanna on November 10 came when the Premier ordered the recapture of Luang Prabang on November 14. The State Department responded sharply, saying that "such an open use of force would further exacerbate the situation. It would lead to further divisions and might facilitate additional Communist gains."[69] At the same time, however, Washington officials began hinting of the sharply increased possibility of an open civil war. They seemed to be using these implied threats as a way of forcing a bloodless political realignment in Vientiane, since they reportedly feared that a civil war would lead to Communist domination of the country. Someone in Washington leaked word on November 19 that the United States had cautioned General Phoumi against a military effort to overthrow Souvanna. In the American capital, officials were hopeful that political pressure would be sufficient.[70]

Souvanna had no reason to succumb to the United States because he had already been denied most of the help which the Americans could have given. He was fighting for his political survival and had nowhere to turn but to the Pathet Lao. His willingness to establish a neutralist rather than Communist government is shown both by his political dealings in November and by the fact that he delayed requesting Soviet assistance until American opposition to his government was unmistakably clear.

On November 16 Souvanna denounced the U.S. assistance to Phoumi as illegal. The same day, the cabinet decided to establish "good neighbor relations" with China and to send good will missions there and to Hanoi. Two days later, Souvanna concluded an agreement with the Pathet Lao on a coalition government. He tried to keep alive the possibility of a tripartite cabinet, for his agreement with Souphanouvong called for such a coalition. There was a crucial proviso, however, excepting military officers. Phoumi would have to be excluded from the government, although his followers would not.[71]

The United States Embassy now made a final effort to prevent open civil war. It protested strongly when Phoumi abortively started his march north on November 23. Since this attack surprised but did not displease Washington officials, who claim not to have encouraged it,[72] one should surmise that Phoumi acted largely from ambition which had been increased by the individual but not official support of his United States advisors. As long as Phoumi received American aid, he was impervious to the embassy's protests.

The embassy pressed its argument more strongly when Phoumi, now armed with artillery (some of which was supplied by Thailand, which also provided some Thai troops) and advised by Americans, successfully struck at some of Kong-Le's forces on November 29. Ambassador Brown requested U.S. air support for Kong-Le. When that idea was rejected, he demanded an immediate halt in aid to Phoumi. He argued that Phoumi had broken his promise not to use his equipment against the neutralists and, thus, had negated the assurances which Brown had given to the established, recognized government of Souvanna Phouma.[73]

Military aid to Phoumi's forces was reportedly halted on November 30, but the Royal Government was not told of this action until December 6, following a protest by Souvanna. This decision, one State Department official recalls, was made not because of Phoumi's violation of his understanding with the Americans not to use troops against the Royal Government but, rather, out of fear that the Soviet Union would take the matter to the United Nations. Realizing that the evidence of U.S. complicity in the attack was strong, State wanted a defense against the charge. The UN argument was much more persuasive than one which assumed a moral obligation to a government which the Americans had subsequently decided to overthrow.[74]

This decision deeply angered the Pentagon. Military and civilian officials alike considered this action terribly wrong, for it removed support at the time that Phoumi supposedly needed it most—and for the least acceptable reasons. They viewed this as only the latest in a series of intolerable actions by Brown to delay or prevent implementation of what they considered official policy to be.[75] They realized and objected to the fact that Brown preferred Souvanna and continued to work in his behalf.

Brown risked his career by using the administrative weapons at his disposal. The Ambassador admits that he did receive cables from Washington that were obvious compromises, sometimes with contradictory instructions. He would ask for clarifications, thereby reopening debates which had been theoretically settled. On several occasions the Pentagon took the drastic step of complaining directly to the State Department, demanding immediate and unambiguous cables to Brown to start supporting Phoumi in certain specified ways. Secretary Herter responded bitterly, "I think I know how to instruct my ambassadors."[76]

Another of Brown's actions which particularly angered the Pentagon was his successful protest against communications between Washington and the American advisor assigned to Phoumi which were never relayed to either Brown or his PEO chief, General Heintges. Brown threatened to resign if the situation were not changed; it was.[77]

These bureaucratic victories were not enough, however, for Phoumi had sufficient support to continue his attacks on Kong-Le's forces. Nor did policy directives from Washington prevent the Americans closest to Phoumi from encouraging him to resist U.S. pressures to work with Souvanna or to halt his offensive. Even the suspension of aid was only partially effective. Just after the PEO had refused a request for funds from

Phoumi, an embassy worker observed a CIA operative entering the General's office, cash in hand.[78] Policy control and coordination had been lost in the chaos of divergent interests.

Once Phoumi moved north, the dominoes fell quickly. The emergency Soviet airlift, begun on December 4, was too little and too late. On December 8, forces loyal to Phoumi occupied Vientiane, only to be forced to withdraw the following day. With Phoumi's troops approaching the capital, Souvanna flew to Phnom Penh, leaving General Southone in charge. On December 12 Phoumi called thirty-eight members of the National Assembly together in Savannakhet and had them pass a motion of no confidence in Souvanna's now exiled government. The King consented on the following day and nominated Boun Oum to form a provisional government. On December 15 the United States announced its full support of the new anti-Communist government in Laos. Overnight, the news reports from Laos switched labels: Phoumi's forces became the "Royal Government troops" and Kong-Le's became the "pro-Communist rebels." With Kong-Le's retreat from Vientiane on December 16, after three days of bloody fighting which left 500 casualties, the town in a shambles, and even a large part of the American Embassy destroyed by fire, a new situation emerged. Attention shifted from the question of who would rule Laos to the one of who might intervene there.[79]

Increased Soviet activity in Laos seemed to pose a threat to the newly established government. Until Souvanna's flight to Cambodia, the Russians had been winning favors at little risk or cost to themselves. They were at last able to set up a diplomatic mission in Vientiane and had begun gaining good will with their airlift of food and fuel, which started on December 4. This cost them little, but, once active, it forced them to support their new friends. Although the Soviet Union had shown little interest in Southeast Asia before, the growing rift with China compelled the Russians to try to preserve good relations with Communist parties in the area—especially in North Vietnam. In view of direct American support of one group of counter-revolutionaries, they could not stand idly by.[80]

On December 13 the U.S.S.R., condemned "the United

States intervention in the internal affairs of Laos" and warned that the "Soviet Government cannot ignore the threat to peace and security in Southeast Asia" arising from it. The Soviet note also charged that the United States had violated the Geneva agreements by supplying new and modern weapons, as well as American advisors, to the rebel troops.[81] When the United States responded four days later, after the fall of Vientiane, it turned the argument back on the Russians by charging that they were now supplying rebel forces. The American note said that the introduction of new weapons and supplies had always been approved by the legal government of Laos. It concluded by placing "the responsibility for the current strife in Laos where that responsibility properly belongs—squarely upon the U.S.S.R. and its agents."[82] *

    This exercise in war by press-release was only the surface manifestation of a much more serious antagonism. Since the United States had acted to drop Souvanna Phouma because of his turn to the Communists for support, it was, of course, deeply suspicious of any Soviet activity in Laos. The airlift made all Laos questions psychologically more important. In fact, the transport planes were not strategically very significant because most military equipment traveled overland from North Vietnam. The primitive airfields in northern Laos could not handle planes capable of lifting major pieces of equipment such as heavy artillery and armored vehicles. But the airlift was strong evidence of Soviet interest in Laos. The Soviet delegate to the 1961–62 Geneva Conference told Averell Harriman that, except for the Second World War, the airlift to Laos had been the highest priority Soviet supply operation since the 1917 revolution. On January 3, 1961, the State Department revealed

---

* One wonders why the Soviet note was not sent until December 13—four days *after* Souvanna Phouma had gone to Cambodia, thereby leaving the Phoumist forces in de facto control. Souvanna had made similar complaints as early as November 16 and a major protest on December 5. Is it possible that policy makers in the Kremlin did not want to risk committing themselves, however indirectly, to the defense of a faltering government which they were not prepared to save? Or was the policy bureaucracy caught flat-footed by the speed of Phoumi's attack?

that between December 15 and January 2 Russian and North
Vietnamese aircraft had flown 184 sorties to Kong-Le and
Pathet Lao forces. This was a major operation.[83]

Washington was concerned about the airlift from its
start, but there was disagreement over the proper U.S. response.
Some Americans in Laos offered to destroy the landing strip at
Vientiane and to assassinate Kong-Le. But these ideas were
rejected by the country team. President Eisenhower was urged
to approve a further intervention by proxy by Thailand even
before the fall of Vientiane. On December 13—after Souvanna
had fled to Thailand but before Phoumi had captured Vientiane
—the President approved the use of Thai and American transport and reconnaissance aircraft, deferring a decision on more
active involvement. Whether or not Eisenhower followed Laos
closely before this time is unclear, but his memoirs suggest that,
by early December, he and his advisors were all waiting and
hoping for Phoumi to win.[84]

Events in Laos forced the next American decision—
whether or not to intervene with U.S. forces. Kong-Le had
retreated north from Vientiane on the road toward Luang
Prabang. He continued to receive Soviet aid, though it now had
to be parachuted to him because of the unavailability of sufficiently long runways. Out of necessity, if not politics, Kong-Le
established a working relationship with the Pathet Lao, who,
for the first time, gave him significant assistance. They helped
him drive the rightist forces from Sala Phou Khoun, the town
at the strategic junction of the road from Vientiane to Luang
Prabang and the one leading across the Plaine des Jarres. Then,
on December 31, he captured the vital airport complex on the
Plaine, thereby permitting direct, unhindered logistical support
to northern Laos.[85]

Stung by these defeats, the new government in Vientiane announced what it later admitted was only a cry of "wolf"
—the alleged invasion of Laos by seven North Vietnamese
battalions. The announcement was linked to a plea for assistance
from SEATO and was intended to bolster the morale of
Phoumi's troops. It may well have had just the opposite effect,

however, for many of the soldiers became less willing to hold on to positions which might be threatened by the dreaded Vietminh. Xieng Khouang, for example, fell easily to the Pathet Lao on December 31. Overseas, it had the intended effect, for it prompted new American support for Laos.[86]

President Eisenhower, who had been following Kong-Le's movements on the map, was particularly disturbed at Phoumi's deteriorating military position. He saw that capture of the Plaine des Jarres would allow the Pathet Lao to cut Laos in half, severing the royal capital at Luang Prabang from the rest of the conservative-held areas. On December 31 the President held a special conference on Laos. The main question at that time was one of intelligence: what was really happening? The Deputy Director of the CIA and JCS Chairman General Lyman Lemnitzer reported on troop movements, but they could not confirm the presence of North Vietnamese or Chinese troops. The President thought that the United States might have "another Lebanon" on its hands, but he declined to take overt counteractions until he had indisputable proof of foreign Communist intervention. He decided on precautionary military moves—redeploying forces nearer to the area—and on renewed diplomatic efforts to win support for the American position.[87]

The situation was urgent for U.S. policy makers because of Phoumi's defeats, the Soviet airlift, and the suspicions of large-scale intervention by North Vietnam. The crisis was much greater than earlier ones involving Laos because the use of American troops was a live option. The enemy was North Vietnam. Many military men wanted to strike directly at what they considered the source of the trouble. Because of the urgency of the situation, U.S. officials seemed to give only lip-service to diplomacy while preparing for military action. No action was taken, however, before substantial opposition developed, both overseas and within the U.S. government.

Diplomatic efforts were important because allied support was still a precondition for military action in Asia. But such support did not seem to be forthcoming. The French, always dubious of the American ability to prevail where they had been driven out and angry at the increasing U.S. influence in the area, opposed the Boun Oum–Phoumi Nosavan government as unviable. They thought that only a truly neutralist government, headed by Francophile Souvanna Phouma, could survive. The British also doubted that a rightist government could last. And, in their role as cochairmen of the Geneva Conference, they were anxious to preserve adherence to those agreements and to the principle of negotiation rather than intervention.[88]

Two basic proposals emerged from the international community in order to halt the war in Laos and prevent a more serious East-West confrontation. On December 15 Prime Minister Nehru proposed the reconvening of the ICC. (Until that time India had given diplomatic support to Souvanna and blamed both Communists and anti-Communists for sending arms into the country.) On December 23 the Soviet Union supported the ICC as a mechanism—it had vigorously but unsuccessfully opposed its adjournment sine die in July 1958—and also called for a renewal of the Geneva Conference to discuss the situation. Prince Sihanouk of Cambodia proposed a larger, fourteen-nation conference on January 1, the plan which was eventually adopted. He wanted in attendance the nations which had been at Geneva in 1954 plus the members of the ICC plus the nations which bordered Laos. This proposal was an outgrowth of the Prince's earlier plan, presented to the United Nations the previous September, for neutralizing Laos and Cambodia with international guarantees.[89]

Both proposals were rejected by the Eisenhower Administration. The ICC had been considered hopelessly ineffective because of the veto power exerted by the Polish member and the obstructive tactics of the Pathet Lao which hampered investigations in their areas. The United States was willing to accept only an ICC fact-finding mission under UN rather than Geneva Conference auspices, and only on condition that it deal with Boun Oum as the legitimate head of government. Even the Canadian government was reluctant to have the ICC reconstituted unless it could be given broader powers and procedures to prevent ineffectiveness. The large international conference was rejected on the grounds that it would be a Communist propaganda sounding board and would be unable to agree on concrete and acceptable measures.[90]

Pressed by the British, who had recognized the Boun Oum government but wanted a more broadly based regime and a reconstituted ICC, President Eisenhower agreed to Prime Minister Harold Macmillan's December 30 suggestions to try to induce Souvanna Phouma to resign and Boun Oum to get formal parliamentary approval for his government. Souvanna refused to resign because he was assured of Communist and neutralist support, even while in exile. The new Laotian government was reluctant because its leaders considered themselves revolutionaries, but they eventually went through the formalities.[91]

Although America's European allies opposed risking direct military involvement in Laos, its Asian allies pressed for it. Thailand, the Philippines, and even Pakistan wanted the United States to take strong action. On December 15 the Thai Ambassador to the Philippines called on SEATO to prepare troops for possible movement into Laos on twenty-four hours' notice. The Philippines government reportedly readied such a military contingent. Thailand, which had long supported Phoumi Nosavan, both diplomatically and (covertly) militarily, was also ready to intervene. At a SEATO military advisors meeting in November, the Thais had demanded a change in the unanimity rule of the SEATO Treaty to free nations to take actions if they wished to. Australia and New Zealand agreed with the British proposals for the renewed ICC.[92]

Faced with these conflicting demands from its allies, the United States felt compelled to give lipservice to the diplomatic track by not rejecting the principle of a negotiated settlement and to keep open the military track by making at least a show of force. Other events also pushed military questions to the forefront. Some military men urged the President to allow the shooting down of Soviet planes airlifting supplies to the Kong-Le/Pathet Lao forces. This proposal became a live option after the December 27 incident in which an American observation plane was fired on by a Soviet aircraft involved in the supply mission.[93]

The escalation ladder built into American military contingency plans had at least four rungs. The lowest was the existing policy of increased material support to Phoumi's army and ostentatious naval deployment in the South China Sea. One step higher was the provision of air support—to bomb enemy installations and to interdict air and ground supply lines. The third rung was the use of American ground troops. Initially, General Lemnitzer told the President, the plans called for U.S. forces to occupy Vientiane and Luang Prabang, leaving the fighting in the countryside up to the Laotians. But since American intervention risked prompting intervention by at least North Vietnam, if not China or the Soviet Union, the fourth rung added plans for up to 40,000 U.S. troops to be put in to various strategic points in Laos and for military actions against North Vietnam.[94]

What the President favored is unclear. In his memoirs he recounted a December 31 statement of a very militant position: "We cannot let Laos fall to the Communists even if we have to fight—with our allies or without them."[95] He said essentially the same thing to John F. Kennedy the day before the inauguration, though he called unilateral intervention "our last desperate hope."[96] But other sources in a position to know say that the President opposed intervention on political and military grounds. He did not want to commit the incoming administration to such a risky policy for which they could then blame his administration. He also recognized the huge logistical problems involved in fighting in a landlocked, jungle country. One official remembers Eisenhower as saying in December: "I came into office because of Korea. I'm not going to fight another Korea. This place is even worse than Korea. So I won't approve the use of airplanes or anything until I'm convinced we'll be successful."[97]

None of the civilian policy makers was eager for intervention. Their concern about Laos lessened as the evidence of North Vietnamese participation failed to accumulate. In the

Defense Department, the civilian officials lost their urgency about Laos and became more aware of the difficulties of putting in troops. State Department officials were basically opposed to risking a war in the face of strong diplomatic opposition. In particular, they feared that intervention would put an unbearable strain on NATO. CIA officials took the position that the use of American ground troops would raise "a considerable likelihood of Chinese intervention."[98]

Nor were the Joint Chiefs agreed on a policy of intervention. General Lemnitzer was apparently for it, at least under some circumstances. But General Decker, Chief of Staff of the Army, stated the widespread army opposition to getting bogged down in another land war in Asia. Admiral Burke, as in 1959, was ready to support intervention if necessary for Phoumi's forces to win. Air Force General White, apparently supported by some of the other chiefs, preferred a policy of air strikes, and against North Vietnam rather than in Laos. The military planners reasoned that North Vietnam was the source of the trouble because of its support for the Pathet Lao and wanted to strike at the source.[99]

The civilians were reluctant to escalate the war so rapidly by striking at North Vietnam, especially with the danger of Chinese intervention. The military also admitted that mere tactical air support was not likely to prove decisive against small units moving through the mountains and jungles. Since President Eisenhower was reluctant to act unless he could be assured of victory, this step, too, was ruled out.[100]

Agreement could be found only for increased military aid and a show of force, so that is what the United States provided. Six AT-6 airplanes were sent to Laos, each equipped with two 30-calibre machine guns and capable of firing 2.36-inch rockets and dropping small bombs. The United States also sent in about 400 special forces personnel to form White Star Mobile Training Teams, which lived in the jungles and helped organize guerrilla activities. These teams first organized the Meo tribes along the Laotian border in North Vietnam into an effective, anti-communist force. Task Force 116 on Okinawa went on alert and added supplemental staff officers to prepare for field operations. On January 2 the Pentagon ordered two aircraft carriers and their auxiliary ships to head toward the Indochinese coastal waters. Thirty C-130 transports were shifted from the United States to Clark Field in the Philippines, ready for landing or air-dropping troops or equipment into Southeast Asia. Pentagon officials were reported to believe that these steps would have a quieting effect on the fighting in Laos.[101]

Suddenly, however, the United States began to back away from military involvement in Laos. The reasons remain obscure. As late as January 3, unnamed but official spokesmen in Washington were telling reporters that the United States had "hard evidence" of participation of substantial numbers of foreign Communist troops on the side of Kong-Le and the Pathet Lao. They also said that it would be unthinkable for the United States to turn its back on its commitments to Laos if help were requested. Intervention could not be ruled out.[102]

By January 5, word had leaked that the United States was now exploring the idea of some form of international conference to stabilize the crisis and disengage Laos from the cold war. Officials said they hoped to get a guarantee of Laotian neutrality and a more broadly based government, including right- and left-wing elements. The same news article, by a reporter close to administration officials, credited the shift in policy to pressure from American allies.[103]

Four main factors forced this retreat to diplomacy. British and French pressure was probably decisive in changing the minds of the men in the State Department, who generally believed that Europe was more important than Laos. Reluctance of the army to get involved in another ground war in Asia weakened the arguments of the more pugnacious members of the Joint Chiefs. Lack of a commitment from the incoming administration to any particular course in Laos made President Eisenhower especially unwilling to embark on military operations. And all policy makers were disturbed at the lack of firm evidence of the participation of the North Vietnamese, but for different reasons. Some were angry at having been duped by the Laotian claims; others believed those claims on faith and were angry that many would not.

Even Thailand backed away from bellicosity. When Laos requested a SEATO observation team to determine the extent of foreign Communist intervention, only Thailand and the United States supported the proposal. When the emergency SEATO Council meeting adjourned in Bangkok on January 4 without having taken action, its Secretary-General, Pote Sarasin, told reporters that there was no definite information, no proof, that foreign Communist troops had actually invaded Laos, as charged by the Boun Oum government.[104]

With further escalation prevented by allied resistance and domestic reluctance, the U.S. policy machine concentrated its efforts on the diplomatic track. It signaled its shift of policy both in background news briefings and a major statement on January 7. That statement repeated many of the points in earlier declarations, arguing the legality of all American aid and blaming the Soviet Union for the continued warfare. But the tone was defensive. There were no warnings to the Communists, as in the U.S. statement on December 31. Instead there was a simple three-point outline of future policy.

> The United States believes that it can best contribute to a solution of the Laos problem:
> —First, by attempting to further international recognition and understanding of the true nature of Communist intentions and action in Laos;
> —Second, by the United States itself continuing clearly to show that it has no intention and no desire to establish a Western military position in Laos;
> —Third, by joining with other free nations to support and maintain the independence of Laos through whatever measures seem most promising.[105]

The first point meant that the United States would continue to blame the Communists, but omitted any intention to oppose the current assistance by force. The second point was a simple denial of Communist charges that the United States planned to build up forces in Laos which might threaten North Vietnam or China. Although such a denial was consistent with earlier official declarations of U.S. policy, it was a change from the policy implicit in the extensive support given to the army over the years and to Phoumi in his struggles against the neutralists. The third point resurrected the principle which had prevented more forceful action in 1954—no intervention without allies—and invited the nations demanding negotiations to try to arrange something. One should note, however, that the United States had not abandoned its hope that Laos would remain pro-Western: the statement called for measures to maintain Laotian "independence" but said nothing about "neutrality."

Thus, even before the end of the Eisenhower Administration, American policy toward Laos had begun to shift toward the policy which the Kennedy Administration eventually adopted. The handwriting on the wall clearly said that America had upset the agreed balance of power in Southeast Asia and that its military approach had been found wanting. When the outgoing President briefed the incoming one on January 19, he admitted that it was the most dangerous "mess" he was passing on to his successor. He repeated his belief that the fall of Laos would lead to the fall of Southeast Asia and urged unilateral intervention as a last resort.[106] The new President was in basic agreement with Eisenhower's analysis and policy, but he decided to reconsider Laos policy from top to bottom.

CHAPTER FIVE

Backing away from the brink (1961)

> *Thank God the Bay of Pigs happened when it did.
> Otherwise we'd be in Laos by now—and that would be a
> hundred times worse.*
> —JOHN F. KENNEDY[1]

The new President entered his office with a determination to keep Laos, as well as other parts of the world, from moving into the Communist orbit. He had not committed himself to any specific policy, but he had frequently cited Laos during the campaign as an example of the failure of the Eisenhower Administration's foreign policy. His most specific criticism was that American aid had strengthened the military forces rather than the civilian economy. His overarching argument, however, was that a stronger America and better leadership could turn back the Communist tide.[2]

Before he could translate that determination into an operational policy he had to cope with the problems of organizing a new administration. He had to appoint people to fill existing positions in the executive agencies and in the White House staff. These people were often strangers to one another and to the expectations, difficulties, and powers inherent in their new positions. Somehow they had to be ready to start exercising their responsibilities as soon as the inauguration ceremony ended on January 20.

Those who were to handle policy toward Laos were well briefed and in position by January 20. Both the Secretary and Under Secretary of State, Dean Rusk and Chester Bowles, had had experience with Asia during the Truman Administration, the former as Assistant Secretary for the Far East and the latter as Ambassador to India. The current Assistant Secretary, J.

Graham Parsons, was kept on temporarily until a replacement could be named. In the Pentagon were the same members of the Joint Chiefs of Staff as under Eisenhower and a new Secretary of Defense, Robert McNamara. Paul Nitze, who had headed State's Policy Planning Staff toward the end of the Truman Administration, was in charge of the Pentagon's foreign policy analysis and liaison with the State Department. His Deputy Assistant Secretary for International Security Affairs (ISA) was William Bundy, brother to McGeorge and former CIA official with some experience with Asian matters. In the White House, McGeorge Bundy was Special Assistant to the President for National Security Affairs; his deputy, Walt Rostow, had already demonstrated a concern about Asia.

Laos was the most urgent foreign policy problem facing the new administration. It was not, however, the most important. Cuba aroused the greatest public concern. Relations with the Soviet Union, especially over Berlin, affected the long-run chances for world peace and for the preservation of America's primary interests in Europe. Laos required immediate decisions, but they were usually tactical rather than strategic. Laos was never a first magnitude problem like the outbreak of the Korean War or the discovery of medium range missiles in Cuba. In these first few months of the Kennedy Administration it was occasionally a second magnitude problem, absorbing the attention of the leading policy makers for a few days. But most of the time Laos was a third magnitude problem, handled at the middle levels of the policy bureaucracy with reference to the guidelines established at the top. The process followed to reach decisions on Laos served as both the baptism of fire for the new policy makers and the vulcanization of the Kennedy foreign policy team.

Every new President seems to think that he has an almost infinite range of choice among policies. Every new administration in recent American history has reexamined many of its predecessor's basic attitudes and actions, changing some and keeping some. John F. Kennedy was no exception. He wanted to correct the errors he saw in the Eisenhower Administration and launch some initiatives of his own. On both points,

Laos was peripheral. Overemphasis on the local army may have been a mistake, but that aspect of policy was irreversible in the short run. New actions were needed in Laos to avert a slide toward a serious confrontation with the Soviet Union and China. But the real challenges to the New Frontier were not in Laos itself, for Laos was only the first hurdle on the path toward settlement of more deeply rooted problems like Berlin and nuclear armaments.

The circumstances facing people new to the policy process encourage this open-minded approach to existing policies. The problems they confront are new to them—if not intellectually, at least politically. Rhetorical criticism of past mistakes in an election campaign must be discarded and the major issue faced: where do we go from here?[3] The way into the problem is secondary to the way out. And the problem in Laos was to establish some stable, tolerable situation.

Laos illustrated this tendency for people new to a problem to ignore what happened prior to their involvement. The definition of the situation given by the holdovers from the Eisenhower Administration was that of a Communist threat to capture all of Laos. They pointed to the large Soviet airlift and to the success of Kong-Le's troops, in contrast to Phoumi Nosavan's retreats. The men new to office did not try to change that definition; they accepted the analysis of the people from whom they had to learn about their jobs. If Laos had received greater public attention during the autumn of 1960, if it had been an issue in the election campaign, the newcomers might have formed their own opinions about the situation. As things were, they were slow to see the wisdom and the possibility of a neutral, non-Communist Laos.

John Kennedy refused to associate himself with any of the decisions of the Eisenhower Administration in its final weeks. Nor did Dean Rusk participate in those decisions, although he was offered the opportunity. The incoming officials did try, however, to become familiar with the major problems they would face. Rusk named a trusted aide, George McGhee, to pay special attention to the two major foreign policy issues at the time—Laos and Cuba. Paul Nitze, representing Defense, began working with Parsons and others on Laos matters even before the inauguration.[4]

The first decision to face the new President was what attitude to take toward the British proposal delivered to the Soviet Union on January 21. The note repeated an earlier call for reactivation of the ICC but circumvented the problem of who headed the legitimate government in Laos by suggesting that the commission be accredited to the King. Although the note had been prepared in consultation with American officials by January 20, its delivery was delayed until Kennedy had seen and approved it. He gave his approval, but he also set in motion a thorough reexamination of policy toward Laos.[5]

On January 23 the new administration held its first full-dress conference on foreign policy. In the light of subsequent events, it is interesting to note that this meeting, in addition to discussing the military situation in Laos, heard a presentation of a new counterinsurgency plan for Vietnam. Thus, from the very start of the administration, Laos and Vietnam were considered together. The same middle level officials met to make plans for both countries. The decisions on one were carefully related to the decisions on the other.[6]

At this time Kennedy formalized his task force system by setting up interagency coordinating groups to investigate various major foreign policy issues, including Vietnam, Laos, Cuba, and Berlin. They were instructed to review policy, develop courses of action, and manage crisis scenarios. In contrast to the formal National Security Council system of the Eisenhower years, which was largely eliminated soon after Kennedy took office, the task forces operated somewhat outside of the normal bureaucratic chains. They also reported directly to the President.[7] The members of the Laos Task Force were Assistant Secretary Parsons, his Deputy John Steeves, Paul Nitze, men from CIA and the Joint Staff, Walt Rostow, representing the White House, and some lower echelon State Department officials.[8]

These men were generally predisposed to take a hard, anti-communist line in Laos. Parsons and Steeves brought to the meetings of the task force their detailed knowledge, distrust of

Souvanna, and support for strong action. Steeves argued, for example, that the United States must prevent the loss of Laos, since that would be "the first step toward the elimination of American free access to Asia."[9] Walt Rostow carried the prestige and influence of the White House staff as he urged firm opposition to the Communists. These three men were willing to support military intervention "if necessary"; no one else on the task force was ready to rule out that response.[10] Their mandate was to make recommendations and develop alternatives. They might have been considered derelict if they had not proposed some military options. And no one thought that the President who spoke so favorably of vigor would approve inaction while pro-Communists took over Laos.

Before this group could complete a review of policy, the President had to answer questions at his news conferences. And those answers both forced him to make preliminary decisions and signaled the task force which direction he wanted them to go. His instinct seemed to be to try for a diplomatic rather than military resolution of the problem. At his first news conference on January 25, for example, the President said that the United States was seeking to establish an "independent, peaceful, uncommitted country" in Laos.[11] Though his answer was brief, his addition of the adjective "uncommitted" suggested a change in the stated Eisenhower policy of favoring a pro-Western government. Whether or not Kennedy intended to signal a modification in policy, such a statement could not help but encourage those arguing for a neutralized Laos. They were few and isolated at first, but their numbers grew with the evidence of the difficulties of taking military action.

Among those favoring neutralization was apparently the embassy in Vientiane. "Observers" there told a reporter for the *Christian Science Monitor* soon after Kennedy's inauguration that America's choice was no longer between a neutralist or a pro-Western Laos, but "between neutralism and a shaky pro-Western regime fighting an indecisive and strength-draining battle against well-supplied Communist forces." This same article reported that Phoumi's attack on the Plaine des Jarres had bogged down, in part because of the reluctance of his soldiers to fight.[12] Such reports strengthened those people in Washington who wanted to disengage from Laos.

Perhaps because of these reports from Vientiane, which must have conflicted with the optimism of the people advising Phoumi, the President called Ambassador Brown home for consultation. He saw the Ambassador on February 3, asked penetrating questions, and seemed to indicate a desire for some form of neutralization of the country.[13] News reports of the meeting gave no such hints, however. They suggested that the United States still favored a nonaligned Laos with pro-Western leanings and still opposed any inclusion of Pathet Lao members in the cabinet.[14]

Policy makers remained divided. Those favoring a diplomatic approach got the first chance to try their policy. This was in line with the President's own hopes. Moreover, military planners were still at work, while the diplomats had readied a new plan. They wanted to avoid both a large international conference and a reactivation of the ICC. The new administration accepted the old one's judgment that the conference would be only a propaganda forum which would do little of substance. The same was true regarding the ICC, which could be easily hampered by the Polish member's veto. The new plan called instead for a tripartite fact-finding mission consisting of neutral Southeast Asian states: Cambodia, Burma, and Malaya. After preparing this proposal, the United States persuaded the King to offer it. Since the King had been relatively immobile during the previous months, always acting to preserve the Royal House, this declaration was all the more remarkable.

The actual wording of the King's statement on February 19 was designed for the widest possible appeal. Some of Souvanna Phouma's ideas were deliberately incorporated into the text. There was no denunciation of any other nation specifically or by clear implication. The King declared friendship for all countries and declared Laos' continued policy of "true neutrality." He went even further than previous Laotian statements, not to mention American ones, when he said: "Within the framework of this neutrality, Laos will not have on its territory either foreign forces or military bases."[15] This provision, Washington sources admitted a few days later, could result in the withdrawal of all Western military advisors and forces from Laos. Such a withdrawal, however, would be conditioned on guarantees of Laotian neutrality and independence and a subsequent request from the Lao government.[16]

Diplomacy moved slowly, as the new administration realized. If either side could gain by delaying, it would do so. And, in Laos, the initiative seemed to rest with the neutralist and Pathet Lao forces, who had secured the Plaine des Jarres and were threatening to sever the road linking Luang Prabang with Vientiane. These events threatened to nullify whatever might be achieved at a conference. Recognizing these facts, the Kennedy Administration also developed policies along a second track—the military one.

If the President were inclined to favor a military solution to the problems in Laos, he was soon disenchanted with the prospects. His military aide has written that he showed "stunned amazement" on learning that if only 10,000 men were sent into Southeast Asia, there would be practically no strategic reserve left for any other contingencies.[17] Nor could those troops be deployed with the speed necessary to counter any large-scale intervention by the Chinese. A military exercise in 1960 had demonstrated the weaknesses in U.S. airlift capability, for it took fifteen days to deploy 21,000 troops (roughly a division) and 11,000 tons of equipment from bases in the United States and in Puerto Rico.[18]

Kennedy responded quickly to these deficiencies. Addressing the Congress on January 30, he called for immediate action to increase airlift capability and accelerate the missile program. With crises boiling in Cuba, the Congo, and Laos, the President declared that improved mobility "will enable us to meet any deliberate effort to avoid or divert our forces by starting limited wars in widely scattered parts of the world."[19]

These military facts of life pushed Kennedy away from the option of direct intervention. No crisis could be successfully handled with such inadequate mobility and such a paucity of conventional forces. Neither the army nor the Marine Corps was eager for action in Laos, because of the rough terrain, logistical problems, and the likelihood of heavy casualties from disease. Air power was still considered indecisive in Laos and too dangerous elsewhere. And none of the chiefs wanted to start on the escalation ladder unless they could be assured the President would go to the top if necessary to prevail.[20]

Basic American strategy was to protect the Mekong Valley. The United States could tolerate Pathet Lao domination of the Annamite Chain, but not a situation which threatened its staunchest Southeast Asian ally across a 500-mile river border. Infiltration through Laos into South Vietnam was minimal at this time, and the South Vietnamese were thought capable of handling it. Thus, Laos was important primarily for the defense of Thailand, and, if Prince Sihanouk wanted it, Cambodia. Within Laos itself, therefore, the main concern was control of the lowlands and especially the one North-South road, route 13, which linked Luang Prabang and Pakse and the towns in between. Control of the Plaine des Jarres, which was invariably called "strategic," was important because it gave the Pathet Lao unhindered access to supplies in North Vietnam and made easier an attack on the road between the two capitals of Laos.

No one high in the U.S. government was willing passively to accept a complete Communist takeover of Laos. Policy debates focused on the alternatives—whether they were neutralization versus communization, or a pro-American government versus a pro-Communist one. The Joint Chiefs of Staff, as one would expect, strongly favored active material support for Phoumi Nosavan and public demonstrations of U.S. determination to oppose further Communist advances. Although the Chiefs disagreed on the desirability of direct intervention, they shared a faith in the efficacy of shows of force. They also believed that if intervention became necessary, the military should not be restricted on its use of weapons or targets. If the Chinese or North Vietnamese were directly involved in the fighting, for example, the U.S. officers wanted to be able to strike directly at the source of the trouble. Even Army Chief of Staff, George H. Decker, who otherwise argued against intervention, wanted full freedom of action. He said: "If we commit troops, we should be prepared to go all the way so as not to get bogged down in an endless war."[21]

Many steps short of direct intervention were available and acceptable to most civilian and military policy makers in the first weeks of the Kennedy Administration. Already the United States had increased its military assistance, both equipment and advisors. The alert to Task Force 116 on Okinawa and the naval show of force in the South China Sea, which had occurred in December, could be repeated. The next level of escalation would be putting troops into Thailand. These forces could either help in the defense of Thailand or lend assistance across the Mekong in the form of air support or troop transport. The members of the Laos task force in Washington eventually developed a seventeen-step escalation ladder, depending on various contingencies of Pathet Lao control.

In late January 1961 there was still some optimism in the Pentagon that General Phoumi's troops would show a worthwhile return on America's $350 million investment. JCS Chairman, General Lyman Lemnitzer, briefed the new National Security Council about an offensive planned by the Royal Army to drive the opposing forces away from route 13 and far onto the Plaine des Jarres. Ambassador Brown later argued with Lemnitzer over whether the Lao would ever develop a good army, but the General's optimism seemed to prevail in Washington. Phoumi launched his attack and soon bogged down. When Lemnitzer reported to the NSC a few weeks later, Phoumi's forces had moved only about twenty miles. American hopes, like the Royal Army on which they had been placed, were soon under heavy attack.[22]

Phoumi's failure to make significant headway weakened the influence of those in Washington who favored military action. The issues were debated in a long NSC meeting on February 8. The newcomers were generally more skeptical of military moves than their more experienced colleagues, but no one wanted to appear weak in the face of a Communist threat.[23] The President was able to defer consideration of military action

pending the results of Phoumi's offensives and the diplomatic
efforts being pursued by the British. The Task Force had more
time to prepare its report because the situation in Laos was not
critical at the moment. The meeting reached a general consensus
on several diplomatic steps which would be taken in order to get
some kind of settlement. The first was the appeal by the King
to Burma, Cambodia, and Malaya. Next would be a request
to SEATO for diplomatic and material support—but not troops.
If these failed, the administration planned to refer the problem
to the United Nations. Only after exhausting these possibilities
would Kennedy consider an international conference, and then
only on the condition that there be a cease-fire and an end to
the flow of supplies from the Communist countries.[24]

Two points should be noted in this diplomatic strategy.
One is the implicit condition that any group dealing with Laos
would have to recognize and, therefore, bolster the legitimacy
of the Boun Oum government. This was, of course, the major
stumbling block for the three neutral nations, the European
members of SEATO, and the United Nations. Secondly, this
was the first formulation of the conditions governing American
acceptance of an international conference on Laos. The United
States wanted to avoid having the conference pressured by
shifting military positions. This was a conscious reaction against
the two years of negotiations and fighting before the armistice
in the Korean War. Ceasefire conditions would also have
strengthened the pro-American forces, since the United States
had no intention of ceasing its own supplies to Phoumi's forces,
which were considered legitimate under the Geneva agreements.

After the King's proposal on February 19, the United
States sought to line up other nations behind it. Official com-
muniqués following talks between the President and the Prime
Ministers of Australia and New Zealand "welcomed" the King's
proposal. Kennedy appealed to Prince Sihanouk to accept membership on the tripartite investigating group. But it was too late.
The Soviet Union and Britain, cochairmen of the 1954 Geneva
Conference, were moving toward agreement on a new international conference, along the lines originally suggested by Sihanouk. The Cambodian leader joined with Burma in rejecting

the Laotian King's proposal on the grounds that it would involve recognition of the Boun Oum government. Other Communist nations also criticized the plan.[25]

In Laos, however, Souvanna Phouma was encouraged by the King's statement. He flew from Phnom Penh to confer with Pathet Lao leaders in Xieng Khouang province. He also sent emissaries to Vientiane to sound out Phoumi and Boun Oum about the possibilities of reconciliation. Both lines got bites. Souvanna was royally treated by "his" cabinet and military forces on the Plaine des Jarres, where he and Souphanouvong declared their solidarity. Soon after he returned to Phnom Penh, Phoumi Nosavan visited him, an amazing act of deference for the man who had last seen him just after the agreement on the August 31 coalition government.* The two men conferred on March 9 and 10 and then issued a joint statement calling for an end to foreign interference in Laos and a policy of strict neutrality. They also agreed on the tripartite commission accredited to the King. These formulas came from the King's statement, but Phoumi went further. He agreed to further discussions on the formation of a provisional government including both rightists and pro-Communists which would organize general elections in Laos.[26] Perhaps Phoumi had seen the handwriting on the wall and knew that his troops had been found wanting.

Washington was growing impatient with the lack of progress on the diplomatic front and Phoumi's unsuccessful offensive. Around the time of the King's statement, after a temporary halt in the Soviet airlift—by now considered the result of bad weather rather than a signal to Washington—the Communists resumed supplying at least fifty tons of material each day. Those men in the government who distrusted Souvanna pointed to his visit to the Pathet Lao as proof that he had

* Why Phoumi changed his mind and agreed to visit Souvanna is a mystery. There is no evidence of U.S. pressure, although it may have been exerted. One can conjecture that Phoumi may have wanted to appear conciliatory for United States consumption or that he may have wanted to forestall Souvanna's return to a wholly Pathet Lao government-in-exile.

sided with the Communists. When James Wilde reported seeing "a massive Communist arms buildup" at Phongsavan, including the latest artillery and some armor,[27] American officials responded with hints that they would be forced to reconsider their policy. Unless the situation improved within two or three weeks, they warned, the Communist forces might be so well positioned and so well supplied as to be unbeatable. And the United States might have to take a much stronger stand.[28]

Kennedy decided to warn the Communists directly of his concern over the trend of events. He sent a message to the Chinese through their Ambassador in Warsaw, where the two countries held intermittent exchanges of propaganda. He sent a letter to Indian Prime Minister Nehru by way of Averell Harriman, his roving Ambassador. He told Ambassador Llewellyn Thompson to deliver his letter personally to Premier Khrushchev, which was done on March 9. All messages made the same basic points. The President expressed his determination not to abandon Laos, even if it meant intervention by American forces. The United States was willing, however, to agree to measures to guarantee a truly neutral Laos, such as a revived ICC. But no agreements could be reached until the Soviet airlift stopped and a cease-fire had been achieved. And time was running out.[29]

Most American pressure went on the Soviet Union. In part, this was simply because Moscow was the only direct link between Washington and Peking, Hanoi, and Khang Khay (the Pathet Lao headquarters). As one U.S. policy maker said, "The Russians were our instruments of civilized leverage in the Communist world."[30] They were also important because their airlift enabled the Kong-Le and Pathet Lao forces to continue fighting. China's role was peripheral. And North Vietnam was seen as dependent on Soviet aid, even if it disagreed with a policy of accommodation and neutralization.[31]

Nor did the Russians seem particularly eager to confront the Americans in Laos. They had vacillated in their support of Asian revolutionaries over the years. Khrushchev himself never showed much interest in Southeast Asia. American analysts of Russian and Chinese policy at this time concluded that the

Soviet Union was interested in negotiations. Until Phoumi's countercoup, the Russians had enjoyed making some gains at the expense of the Americans without much risk to themselves. Phoumi's return, however, directly threatened their newly achieved position and raised in some minds the credibility of their professed support to "wars of national liberation." American analysts concluded that the massive arms buildup in early 1961 was intended merely to prevent Phoumi from "turning back the clock."[32]

This analysis by intelligence specialists was rejected by the officials in the Far East Bureau of the State Department, who believed that the Soviet Union wanted to drive the United States out of Asia. As later in the case of Vietnam, these officials rejected the argument that the problem in Laos was an internal, factional struggle for power and claimed instead that there was aggression from outside. They saw that the neutralist and pro-Communist forces had the capability of moving to the Mekong and believed that these armies restrained themselves only because of the implicit American threat to intervene.[33]

A less parochial judgment, borne out by subsequent developments, was that the Soviet Union was quite willing to put Laos on the shelf and get on with more important issues like Berlin and disarmament. As Premier Khrushchev told Ambassador Thompson, "Why take risks over Laos? It will fall into our laps like a ripe apple."[34]

The Pathet Lao soldiers had less patience than Khrushchev, for they began their harvest early. One reason may have been to gain as much as possible before any imposed settlement. Another may have been to forestall any agreement between Souvanna and Phoumi, who were about to meet. On March 9 neutralist and Pathet Lao forces counterattacked Phoumi's forces at the key road junction town of Sala Phou Khoun. By March 11 they had captured the town, severed the road link between Luang Prabang and Vientiane, and were driving south. Many of Phoumi's troops panicked and fled into the mountains. Later in the month Pathet Lao units attacked in other areas of the country as well as the north, thereby proving their strength and demonstrating Phoumi's weaknesses.[35]

In this atmosphere of crisis and military defeat, the Kennedy Administration moved closer to a decision on intervention. While the diplomatic track was being tried with the King's appeal, the Laos Task Force had concentrated on possible actions in case the military situation deteriorated. Its members were much more willing to favor the use of American force than the President and his senior advisors. Perhaps this stance resulted from the persuasiveness of committed and knowledgeable militants like Steeves and Rostow. Perhaps it was the inevitable result of its mandate to develop courses of action and crisis scenarios instead of simply reiterating hopes about diplomatic agreement. Whatever the cause, the report of the Task Force was practical and detailed. It recommended increased military aid and precautionary military moves which could serve at least as a show of force and, if necessary, as the first steps on a seventeen-rung escalation ladder to full-scale intervention.

On March 9, the same day that the new series of attacks began, the President met with his foreign policy advisors to discuss the Task Force report. The general feeling was that something would have to happen on the diplomatic front within two to three weeks or else intervention might be necessary. Although some of the President's advisors were reluctant to support direct intervention in Laos, none opposed increased aid and a demonstration of strength. The President remained concerned about the fighting ability of Phoumi's troops, however, and tried to encourage him to send his best officers away from headquarters and into the field. He decided to continue to move on both diplomatic and military tracks by approving only increased equipment and training technicians while awaiting the results of Phoumi's meeting with Souvanna and Ambassador Thompson's with Khrushchev.[36]

As the situation worsened in the following days, the President began moving up the escalation ladder. Secretary Rusk made one last effort to convince Soviet Foreign Minister Gromyko of the seriousness with which the United States viewed the crisis in a meeting on March 19. But Gromyko merely repeated the well-known Soviet position, offering no hope for either a quick cease-fire or the end to the Soviet airlift.[37]

Failing to get an encouraging response from the Russians, U.S. policy makers took up the pending business of the Task Force report on escalatory steps. On March 20 and 21 the President met again with his advisors. The issue now seemed to be a test of wills with the Soviet Union in which the new administration dared not flinch from its opposition to Communist advances in Laos. The Russians were behind the trouble, Washington officials reasoned—or at least could stop it by ending their airlift. The United States had to back its determination with a show of force. Walt Rostow argued for the movement of some troops to the Mekong Valley—initially Thailand, but ready to move across the river if necessary. The Joint Chiefs predicted that such action would prompt massive North Vietnamese intervention. The only way to prevail, they argued, was for the President to send in at least 60,000 troops and to promise that they would be supported even to the point of nuclear war with China. Arguing the necessity of such a large commitment, especially in view of the necessary reduction of U.S. strength elsewhere, made it more likely that Kennedy would reject intervention.[38]

Both plans seemed unnecessary at the moment. The President was becoming more strongly opposed to a military action in defense of the Lao Army. He had sounded out congressional leaders and found little or no interest in direct intervention. Many of his advisors were also losing their taste for war in a distant, primitive, landlocked country. Secretary McNamara wanted some kind of overall plan, not just day-to-day decisions. Secretary Rusk was enigmatic. The Joint Chiefs themselves were trying to have the best of both worlds by opposing the intervention which the President was most likely to accept and favoring a situation where they had a blank check.[39]

Unwilling to take major military measures without another attempt at diplomacy, Kennedy chose a show of force and steps preliminary to intervention along with a public appeal to the Soviet Union. The troop alerts kept open his option to use force later, but the President was hoping to avert that decision. The American diplomatic strategy operated on several fronts. Secretary Rusk, soon to leave for a SEATO meeting in Bangkok, was to try to rally that alliance behind a defense of Laos, if necessary. Other U.S. diplomats were supposed to try to convince neutral nations that America was sincere in wanting a neutral Laos. And the United States would maintain contact with the Soviet Union in the hope of convincing the Russians of the President's determination to prevent Laos from falling to the Communists.[40]

Neutralization was gaining in favor among Kennedy's foreign policy advisors. Under Secretary of State Chester Bowles and roving Ambassador Averell Harriman were early converts both to that concept and to Souvanna Phouma as the man to bring it about. What they and the President meant by neutralization remained unclear, since no one at that time favored the inclusion of the Pathet Lao in a coalition government. But the term seemed to have widespread political appeal and was, consequently, emphasized. Its use also tended to undermine arguments for military intervention, since such action would have to be made against self-professed neutralists as well as pro-Communists.[41]

The American diplomatic plan remained unchanged. The United States still insisted on a cease-fire and an end to the airlift before a conference could take place. It would accept an ICC, but only with carefully defined obligations. In line with the new evidence of reconciliation among the factions in Laos, it called for leaving the settlement of internal problems to the Laotians. There were no alternatives for the Soviet Union other than acceptance or the risk of stronger United States military measures.[42]

To maximize the impact of these decisions and to dramatize his concern, Kennedy decided to announce his policy at his news conference that week. He delayed the conference for a day in order to finish preparing his statement, added live television coverage, and changed the time from late afternoon to

the dinner hour. He had Vice President Johnson arrange a brief-
ing on the situation for congressional leaders and approved a
strong statement by Johnson warning that the United States
would not meekly permit Laos to be "gobbled up." All of these
steps heightened public interest in his statement. He also took
the unique step of having maps prepared to illustrate his remarks. They showed the rapid increase in areas under Pathet
Lao control.[43]

On March 23 the President strode before the assembled
newsmen and television cameras in the State Department Audi-
torium. He was a few minutes late because he had continued to
revise the statement on Laos up to the last minute. McGeorge
Bundy and Soviet expert Charles Bohlen had done most of the
drafting of the statement, coordinating various suggestions from
other persons. At first Kennedy objected to the strong wording
and asked that it be toned down. He did not want to be too
belligerent to the Soviet Union. In the end, the statement was a
compromise because Kennedy wanted to threaten to follow the
military track when, in fact, he strongly preferred the diplomatic one. While most of his advisors thought that his verbal
bellicosity was just a bluff, some had to be placated with "fighting words."[44]

Kennedy emphasized the dangerous situation created by
the rapid advances of the Communist forces and the continuing
Soviet airlift, which had amounted to over 1,000 sorties in the
previous one hundred days. He blamed the "present grave problem" on the increase in outside support—both the airlift and
the provision of North Vietnamese technicians. In addition to
this pessimistic description, the President offered something old,
something new, and something borrowed. He supported "con-
structive negotiations" among the Laotian leaders and among
other nations concerned with the problem, based on the British
proposal sent to Moscow that day. He repeated his insistence on
a "neutral and independent Laos," but added, somewhat in-
congruously, that American support for the Boun Oum government was "aimed entirely and exclusively at that result." The
new element was Kennedy's dropping of one of the precondi-

tions for a conference, the requirement for an end to the Soviet airlift. The President called only for a cease-fire, but he did so in strong terms.

> If these attacks do not stop, those who support a truly neutral Laos will have to consider their response. . . . The security of Southeast Asia will be endangered if Laos loses its neutral independence. . . . I know that every American will want his country to honor its obligations. . . .

The only loophole in the American position was the suggestion that allied advice might temper U.S. actions. "Our response will be made in close cooperation with our allies and the wishes of the Laotian Government."[45]

Although the President had refused to threaten or even to announce military actions, word leaked out that the United States was alerting its forces for possible action in Laos. The same military plans used in December were followed again, but this time they posed a more credible threat because the President had dramatized the situation and because he did not have only three weeks left in office. Three aircraft carriers moved toward Laos with 1,400 marines. Long-range troop and cargo transport planes flew from the continental United States to the Philippines. About 150 marines were dispatched to Udorn, Thailand, to service fourteen additional helicopters being given to the Royal Lao Army. On Okinawa, Task Force 116 was alerted and its staffs brought up to operational size. Command was transferred from a marine General to a higher ranking army General. Two thousand marines in Japan were pulled away from a movie which they were assisting in filming. American diplomats sounded out SEATO allies about the possibility of providing troop contingents under the existing Plan Five. In all, about 4,000 troops were ready for battle in Laos—not enough to carry out the intervention plans, but, hopefully, enough to force a change in the diplomatic stalemate.[46]

The Soviet response was not long in coming. The day after the President's Thursday news conference, Soviet Foreign Minister Gromyko requested a meeting with Kennedy, saying that he had a message from Premier Khrushchev. The meeting was set for the following Monday. Meanwhile, Kennedy had received a message from British Prime Minister Harold Macmillan which suggested a reluctance to support the United States militarily in Laos. Since Macmillan was visiting Caribbean nations at the time, before coming to Washington in early April, Kennedy requested an urgent meeting at Key West, Florida, on Sunday, March 26. At that meeting, Macmillan argued against military intervention, but reluctantly agreed, if necessary, to support it both diplomatically and with a brigade of troops stationed in Malaya. The actual agreement contained calculated ambiguity; the British would help, if necessary, but that was not seen as very likely.[47]

Gromyko's meeting the next day with Kennedy was heralded by a leading article in *Pravda* which indicated that the Soviet Union was prepared to accept the British proposal to stop the fighting under certain conditions. But it warned against an expansion of the conflict by the United States or SEATO and required an American commitment to attend an international conference after the cease-fire. When the President and Foreign Minister met, Kennedy did most of the talking, much of it while the two men sat alone on a bench in the Rose Garden. Repeating and emphasizing the points made in his statement, Kennedy stressed the danger of war through miscalculation. He wanted to make clear his determination to prevent a Communist takeover by force in Laos. Gromyko seemed more serious about finding an accommodation than in his March 19 meeting with Rusk. Kennedy came away from the meeting hopeful that something could be worked out.[48]

Although American officials viewed the Laos crisis as a test of will with the Soviet Union, they wanted to defuse the situation without intervention. Laos was a low-priority matter which had been thrust to the forefront by external events. No one believed that a solution in Laos, by itself, could aid in the resolution of other, more important, foreign policy problems. On the contrary, Laos was a stumbling block on the road toward those other issues. Intervention there, as President Johnson was to learn to his dismay when he had intervened in

Vietnam, would detour or prevent a whole range of other foreign policy initiatives. This important attitude among high level policy makers was revealed in a background news conference given in late March, apparently by McGeorge Bundy. Richard Rovere, reporting the interview, said that the administration feared that if it had to intervene in Laos, it would have to abandon—probably for the duration of its term in office—most of the diplomatic initiatives which it had planned in many areas. Given congressional opposition to direct intervention, it also feared that intervention might lead to domestic political disaster. No matter how persuasively the President might argue that intervention was the only alternative to appeasement, the Republicans would raise the "Democrats cause wars" argument and would win.[49]

The SEATO meeting in Bangkok March 27–29 gave further indications of the reluctance of most American allies to support stronger action in Laos. Only Thailand, Pakistan, and the Philippines were willing to pledge troops for an intervention. The French were adamantly opposed under any circumstances. The final communiqué was a much-softened declaration of "grave concern" and the hope that "a united, independent and sovereign Laos"—(note the absence of the term "neutral")—could be achieved through negotiations. If those efforts failed, the SEATO members declared their intention "to take whatever action may be appropriate in the circumstances." Disturbed at this compromise wording, the administration sent a private warning to the Soviet Union using much blunter terms.[50]

On April 1 the Soviet Union replied encouragingly to the British note of March 23. It expressed a willingness to join with Britain in appealing for a cease-fire and implied that that appeal could precede the convening of an international conference. The only discordant note was the reiteration of Soviet support for Souvanna Phouma's government. Averell Harriman and others were beginning to lobby for Souvanna, but no one was willing to drop support of the existing Boun Oum government without negotiations and guarantees. President Kennedy responded immediately with a statement calling the Soviet note "a useful next step."[51] The President was also reportedly encouraged by reports from Ambassador Thompson, who quoted Khrushchev as having said, "If we all keep our heads and do nothing provocative, we can find a way out of our problems in Laos."[52]

The Russians then faced the difficult task of bringing their fellow Communists into line. Their only leverage was in their supplies of military equipment, but they were no more willing to stop aiding their clients than were the Americans. The Pathet Lao, flush with their continuing victories over the Phoumist forces, were unwilling to stop. They may even have launched their offensives on Sala Phou Khoun in March and on Tha Thom and Vang Vieng in April without Moscow's knowledge or approval. The North Vietnamese were no more eager for a cease-fire. And the Chinese had regularly denounced all proposals for accommodations with the capitalists. On April 4 the Russians appealed to Hanoi, in a statement broadcast only in Vietnamese, to accept a cease-fire as a means of creating a favorable atmosphere for negotiations.[53]

Since the Russians, by themselves, could not secure a cease-fire, it took Souvanna Phouma to get the others to accept a conference.* Arriving in Moscow on April 16, he went to confer with Khrushchev at his Black Sea resort. He persuaded the Soviet Premier to bring Souphanouvong to Moscow for discussions. These resulted in a joint communiqué stating that "at present real conditions exist to normalize the situation in Laos." It listed a cease-fire, the fourteen-nation conference, and the reactivation of the ICC as "prime measures." On April 22 the two princes flew to China to meet with Chen Yi, Chou En-lai, and Mao Tse-tung.[54] These meetings apparently secured the necessary agreements, for, on April 24, the Soviet Union joined

* None of the memoirs by policy makers or persons interviewed by the author credited Souvanna with bringing the Communists to Geneva. In a misperception quite common to government officials, they all believed that their own country's statements and actions sufficed to convince the other side of the firmness of U.S. policy. (See Robert Jervis, "Hypotheses on Misperception," *World Politics*, Vol. XX (April, 1968), p. 476, for a brief discussion of this phenomenon.)

Britain in calling for the "prime measures" listed in the Soviet-Lao communiqué. The following day the two princes, now in Hanoi, conferred with North Vietnamese leaders. Souphanouvong declared his willingness to accept a cease-fire because "our troops and people are in the position of a victor." Souvanna Phouma reportedly reached "identical views" with North Vietnam on how to settle the Laotian crisis.[55] After a few more days of diplomatic exchanges, and three days out for the long-delayed cremation ceremony for King Sisavong Vong, Hanoi radio broadcast a cease-fire order on May 2 to take effect the following morning.[56]

The United States grew increasingly restive and concerned while the Communists were being brought together. The Pathet Lao offensives in early April had succeeded dramatically, notably with the fall of Vang Vieng on April 24. That victory removed the last major defensive position of the Royal Government north of Vientiane. The fear in Washington in April was that the capital would fall within a few weeks unless a cease-fire could be arranged.[57]

Fate then intervened to put the new administration and all of its foreign policies in a new and polluted environment. The abortive Bay of Pigs invasion of Cuba shook public and congressional confidence in Kennedy and the President's confidence in his advisors. Congressional leaders in both parties became more reluctant than ever to support military action in Laos. The President himself told Arthur Krock that he could write that Kennedy had "lost confidence" in the Joint Chiefs. No longer would he accept their easy assurances on matters of operational feasibility; no longer would he leave details unquestioned. As one official described the situation, "The Bay of Pigs let the air out of the balloon."[58]

On the day after the invasion collapsed, the President ordered the PEO officers to don their military uniforms and constitute themselves as a formal Military Assistance Advisory Group (MAAG). The prohibition against this in the 1954 Geneva agreements no longer seemed important. In practice, the change meant little, for it only made day-to-day operations simpler. But it did have a psychological effect of demonstrating the American presence at a time when pro-American Laotians were beginning to doubt the U.S. commitment against a Communist victory there. General A. J. Boyle, Commander of the MAAG, announced that American military advisors would go to the front lines if necessary, but they would not fight. In retrospect, the major function of the change was to create an excuse for the poor showing of the Laotian Army until then. Administration witnesses later testified that Phoumi's defeats had been due to the fact that the Americans had not really been in charge of training until April 1961.[59]

A week later, on April 27, with the Pathet Lao offensive still in full swing despite the Anglo-Soviet call for a cease-fire, the President met again with his foreign policy advisors and then with congressional leaders. Rostow, speaking for the Laos Task Force, again recommended a limited commitment of troops to Thailand. This time he had the backing of Averell Harriman, who, at the time, was attending the cremation ceremonies in Laos. Harriman wanted something to negotiate with at Geneva. Troops in Thailand would also lessen the perceived threat to Laos and to the rest of Southeast Asia, since they could act as a deterrent to renewed fighting. The Joint Chiefs objected to the plan, but each in his own way. In the wake of the Bay of Pigs they were reluctant to guarantee its success unless they had an almost unlimited commitment of troops and weapons. Initial plans for intervention called for a limit of 40,000 troops. That figure had been raised to 60,000 by the end of March and was up to 140,000 by the end of April. Nor were the Generals yet willing to accept intervention without an advance promise to allow use of tactical nuclear weapons. General Lemnitzer said: "If we are given the right to use nuclear weapons, we can guarantee victory." (The President later observed, "Since he couldn't think of any further escalation, he would have to promise us victory.")[60]

Faced with differing recommendations from his military advisors, the President accepted the Vice President's suggestion that they put their separate views in writing. He then moved to the meeting with congressional leaders. Admiral Burke addressed the group, arguing for a firm stand in Laos even at the risk of war. When the President asked others for their advice, only the Vice President supported Burke's statement. It was clear that Congress had no stomach for further military adventures.[61]

Two days later the NSC met again. Renewed fighting in Laos had brought a request for U.S. air intervention, but that matter got sidetracked by the widespread disagreement over what to do. This time there were eight different papers from the Pentagon—one each from the Secretary, the service Secretaries, and the four major members of the Joint Chiefs of Staff. The President was appalled at the confusion and ordered the men to reconcile their differences at least so as to present him with fewer alternatives. Two hours after the meeting adjourned at 8:00 P.M., the disagreeing officers met with McNamara and worked out a compromise formula. Immediate action was postponed. The Chiefs alerted CINCPAC, however, to be ready to launch air strikes against North Vietnam and southern China and to be ready to deploy two 5,000-man combat brigades, one to northeast Thailand and the other to Danang, South Vietnam. They cautioned that no firm decision had been made for such action. In the meantime, all contending factions in Laos agreed to a cease-fire.[62]

Divergent opinions among the chiefs strengthened Kennedy's skepticism about a military action in Laos or even Thailand. General Decker had warned about the problems of disease and resupply. His opposition, in itself, made others hesitate about forcing the Army to intervene. Attorney General Robert Kennedy added another reason for caution: "If even the Marines don't want to go in. . . ."[63] Generals Lemnitzer and White had stressed the need to be able to use nuclear weapons as a last resort. Admiral Burke had been hawkish all along. When the President asked more probing questions, he discovered the extent of disagreement and the difficulties with some of the operations. For example, he learned that there were only two airstrips usable for an intervention on the Plaine des Jarres, and those only in good weather. An attack from nearby Pathet Lao areas would short-circuit the operation. Armed with these doubts about his own military advice as well as about the

fighting ability of Phoumi Nosavan's forces, the President refused to take any further steps up the escalation ladder. Unwilling to go "all the way" in military actions, Kennedy put his
hopes on a diplomatic settlement at Geneva.[64]

At the same time, however, Kennedy approved the
start of covert operations against the North Vietnamese, both
in Laos and in their homeland. The President and his advisors
felt that they had to stand firm and draw the line in South Vietnam if they were going to back away from the brink of war
in Laos. On May 11, 1961, he agreed to infiltration of agents
into North Vietnam for sabotage and harassment, as well as
sending special South Vietnamese forces into southeastern Laos
on intelligence and harassment missions. He approved the use
of U.S. advisors "if necessary" in attacks near Tchepone.[65]

Secretary Rusk headed the initial delegation to the
Geneva Conference, but Averell Harriman had been named
chief negotiator since he would be remaining for the duration
of the talks. Harriman was chosen not simply because of his
prestige and long experience, but also as a signal to the Soviet
Union of the seriousness and sincerity with which the United
States approved the talks.[66] Originally scheduled to begin on
May 12, the conference did not actually meet until May 16.
There were several reasons for the delay. The United States
insisted on a cease-fire, which the ICC did not verify until May
12. The United States was also still trying to work out a common front with Britain and Canada. There were doubts as to
which governments would attend. South Vietnam and Thailand
at first refused to come, as did the Boun Oum government representative when Pathet Lao and neutralist delegates were
seated. The United States had objected to seating three Laotian
groups, but, finally, relented under the pressure of the other
delegations.[67]

Once the conference actually began, the whole American policy process for Laos began to switch to the diplomatic
track. Military preparations and considerations were shunted
aside. Discussions centered on negotiating positions and cables
to Geneva rather than the details of military plans. The Pentagon felt sufficiently relieved to order the dissolution of the

augmented staff of Task Force 116. Most of the officers were transferred to other posts, leaving the planning staff at its precrisis level.[68] The foreign policy machinery turned to other problems, like a prisoner exchange with Cuba and a response to the assassination of General Trujillo in the Dominican Republic. The President turned to the domestic problems of pushing his legislation through to Congress and reacting to the start of "freedom rides" in the South.

A few days after the start of the Geneva Conference, Kennedy and Khrushchev announced that they planned to meet in Vienna on June 3 and 4. These meetings were strained and unproductive, focusing mainly on the intractable problems of Berlin and nuclear armaments. The only agreement to emerge was the one on Laos. Their joint communiqué

> . . . reaffirmed their support of a neutral and indepen-
> dent Laos under a government chosen by the Laotians
> themselves, and of international agreements for insuring
> that neutrality and independence, and in this connection
> they have recognized the importance of an effective
> ceasefire.[69]

Khrushchev agreed that Laos was not worth a war between the superpowers, so the path seemed open to a settlement.[70]

After that meeting with the Soviet leader, Kennedy touched Laos matters only occasionally until May 1962. Nor did Secretary Rusk involve himself actively in the day-to-day policy questions. Harriman took most of the initiative, although his superiors read and commented on his cables. The Secretary and President had other problems to face, and were probably glad to push aside the problem which had absorbed so much time and energy since January. Both men also had high regard for the man now handling the conference and other aspects of policy toward Laos. Kennedy had given Harriman his instructions and was willing to let him take it from there. In a moment of doubt in June 1961, the President phoned Harriman in Geneva to make his instructions perfectly clear. "Did you understand? I want a negotiated settlement in Laos. I don't want to put troops in."[71] With that mandate, Harriman took charge.

CHAPTER SIX

Putting the three-headed elephant together (1961–1962)

It's your problem. Work it out.
—JOHN F. KENNEDY *to Averell Harriman*[1]

Almost anything can happen in Laos.
—AVERELL HARRIMAN[2]

The Geneva Conference on Laos was likely to be long and difficult. The Chinese delegates had taken six-month leases on their villas, and previous experience at Panmunjom had shown that they were quite willing to wait until they got an agreement to their liking. President Kennedy wanted the American delegation headed by someone with skill and international stature who would not have to neglect other important duties in Washington. That man was named Averell Harriman.

Harriman occupied an undefined role in the new administration. Considered too old (at sixty-nine) for a major policy position, he became a "roving Ambassador" for the President. Rusk intended to send him to international conferences in his place, since he criticized the frequent traveling of John Foster Dulles. But in March he set the precedent of attending the SEATO Conference. When CENTO and NATO meetings came in April and May, he felt compelled to attend them as well. He attended the opening sessions of the Geneva Conference, then turned the delegation over to Harriman.

While delivering a letter from the President to Prime Minister Nehru in March, Harriman arranged—at his own initiative—a meeting with Souvanna Phouma, who was then visiting New Delhi as part of a world tour to build up support for his Khang Khay government. Souvanna impressed Harriman

with his determination to establish a genuine coalition government, which would save Laos from communism and yet be
truly neutral. Harriman also had a high regard for Ambassador
Brown's judgment in favor of Souvanna since he had brought
Brown to London as a member of his staff during 1941–42. On
March 29, while the world awaited proof of Soviet willingness
to get a cease-fire in Laos, Harriman reported on his talks to the
President. Souvanna considers himself the "man of the hour"
in Laos, Harriman said, and "is a factor that has to be dealt
with." Whether he should be Prime Minister or not, "he certainly should be in any government."[3]

During April, Harriman sided with those on the Laos
Task Force who wanted to put troops at least into Thailand.
He believed that the American negotiating position was weak
and needed bolstering. Intelligence estimates predicted the fall
of Vientiane within a few weeks unless there was a cease-fire
because the pro-American forces were rapidly retreating
throughout the country.[4] The Anglo-Soviet call for a cease-fire
and an international conference on April 24 eased the situation
temporarily.

Told by Rusk on April 28 that the President wanted
him to head the Geneva delegation, Harriman decided to visit
the troubled areas for himself. He arrived in Laos at the time
of the cremation ceremonies for the former King. He spoke
with the King and members of the Royal Government and
later saw Souvanna Phouma briefly at the Phnom Penh airport.
Discussions with these people and with American and other
western diplomats influenced him to consider the possibilities
for an agreement on a coalition government and genuine
neutrality.[5]

Opinion within the American government moved much
more slowly to the same conclusions. The Kennedy appointees
had come around to the idea of neutralization (as opposed to a
victory by pro-Western elements) by the time the conference
started. Career military officers—in Laos and in the Pentagon—
still held out for victory, or at least the prospect of intervention
if the Pathet Lao tried to extend their holdings on the ground.
Officials in the Far Eastern Bureau of the State Department

continued their opposition to a coalition government in principle and to Souvanna Phouma as Prime Minister. Harriman and other New Frontiersmen derisively labeled them "Walter Robertson's boys." In order to get the kind of settlement the President wanted, Harriman would have to bring these dissident forces into line.

First he had to get control of his delegation at Geneva. Rusk had arrived from the NATO meeting in Oslo with 126 people to staff the delegation. Harriman, who always preferred small staffs, was appalled. At his first opportunity, he cut the delegation by two-thirds. He also decided that he wanted a young Foreign Service Officer as his deputy instead of the hawkish, hard-line anti-communist John Steeves, who had been Deputy Assistant Secretary for the Far East since 1959. Steeves was convinced that Souvanna Phouma was a Communist and had tried repeatedly in the autumn of 1960 to bring him under Phoumi Nosavan's influence. When the new administration came to power, Steeves continued to argue for strong action in Laos. He finally "acquiesced" to the decision against intervention at that time. Much more in sympathy with the Kennedy policy was William Sullivan, who, early in 1961, had tried to persuade Parsons and Steeves of a confederal solution for Laos, based on de facto regional control. Harriman wanted Sullivan as his deputy, despite cries of alarm from status-conscious bureaucrats. "The others will accept anyone I name as my deputy," Harriman replied. He was prepared to send home U.S. officials who were unwilling to accept Sullivan's status.[6]

Coordination was difficult, both in Geneva and with Washington. In addition to the plenary sessions the Conference subdivided into two drafting committees to work on the declaration of neutrality and the enforcement protocol. Reports and recommendations had to be prepared for Harriman's approval each morning, then negotiated with Washington during the afternoon and evening. The Pentagon communicated with its own people in Geneva, making additional comments and recommendations, which were often uncoordinated with the State Department.[7]

The Far Eastern Bureau of State resisted many of the

provisions to which Harriman wanted to agree. They acted both out of policy disagreement and out of concern for their own bureaucratic standing. Steeves continued in day-to-day charge of Laos matters in Washington, but he was convinced that Harriman was agreeing to almost everything the chief Soviet delegate proposed. After receiving one cable from Harriman, Steeves snapped, "I suppose the next one will be signed Pushkin."[8] The Assistant Secretary, Walter McConaughy, was another hard-liner, who had faithfully carried out policies of Dulles and Robertson in Asia. He could never seem to understand that Harriman was his superior, although not in his chain of command. Harriman reported only to Rusk and Kennedy. The Far East Bureau served only to coordinate papers, not to make decisions on Laos.[9]

After gaining control over his delegation, Harriman next faced the problem of bringing American policy into line in support of Souvanna Phouma. This was a harder task. Not only did the State Department have residual distrust of the Laotian Prince, but its diplomats were still officially accredited to the opposition government of Boun Oum and Phoumi Nosavan. The Pentagon was also still giving supplies and advice to General Phoumi. Both groups were reluctant to undermine the rightists' position by giving open backing to Souvanna.

The dilemma was real. If the pro-Communist forces decided to withdraw from the Geneva Conference, they might achieve a quick and decisive victory on the battlefield in Laos. Only Phoumi's forces stood in the way. Since the President was determined to resist such a Communist takeover, he had to keep those forces viable. At the same time, the United States had to prove to the other nations at Geneva and to the contending Laotian factions that it would not stand in the way of a neutralist government. It had to make it appear that it had a fallback position in case the conference did not reach a satisfactory agreement. In fact, there was only a phantom option. But this fact could not be made known outside the highest councils of government. Other officials had to—and did—act as if the option of supporting a pro-Western government were open.

Souvanna made Harriman's job (and that of the conference) easier by bringing the contending factions together. Tripartite truce talks began in Laos on May 11, at the small village of Ban Namone in between the royal and administrative capitals. The meetings tried to verify the cease-fire and request ICC investigation of alleged violations. There was rarely agreement, especially since the Pathet Lao vetoed investigations in their areas of control. Nevertheless, these meetings set the precedent for tripartite talks and a tripartite settlement. Although the United States, strongly supported by Thailand and South Vietnam, had pressed for only two Laotian delegations at Geneva, the other delegations cited Ban Namone and insisted on three. The United States relented.[10]

With the encouragement of the major powers, the three princes met in Zurich on June 19 to discuss the matter of a government of national union. On June 22 they issued a joint communiqué which repeated most of the policy principles agreed upon in 1956 and 1957. In discussing "immediate tasks," however, the statement called for a Government of National Union to attend the Geneva Conference and then implement the cease-fire and other provisions adopted by the conference. The provisional government, also tripartite in form, was to govern during elections for a new National Assembly. The princes bypassed the existing National Assembly (chosen in the rigged elections of 1960) by calling upon the King to form the provisional government directly. This was only agreement in principle. The details were to be worked out in subsequent meetings.[11]

One immediate result of the Zurich talks was the agreement of the Boun Oum group to participate in the Geneva Conference. Another was that the principles set forth in the communiqué became candidates for inclusion in the documents being drafted by the conference. Less visible was the boost which the talks gave to those Americans who were arguing for the support of Souvanna Phouma as Prime Minister. Those who considered Souvanna a Communist had to answer the questions of why he had a separate delegation from the Pathet Lao, how he could get Boun Oum to agree unless he did indeed offer a middle ground. Souvanna was clearly in the middle, as was no other Laotian politician of much stature. He was the obvious, if not the inevitable, choice for Prime Minister.

Phoumi Nosavan was the chief obstacle to Souvanna's becoming Prime Minister. Boun Oum was content to retire from the political scene, as he did after the settlement was reached in 1962. But Phoumi, with his American-supplied and -advised army, had to be placated, brought around, given the word that the United States wanted both a coalition government and Souvanna. The General argued, and may well have believed, that the United States was selling his country to the Communists at Geneva.[12]

Invited to Washington for conferences, Phoumi arrived at the end of June. Pentagon officials said that he had been asked to come in order to tell U.S. officials of his eagerness to resist the Pathet Lao. State Department officials said that he had come to see just how far the United States was willing to back him. In meetings on June 29 and 30 he got conflicting signals. McGeorge Bundy and Walt Rostow made him aware of the official American position when he visited the White House. Another official who dealt with Phoumi on several occasions during this period said, "Our major problem was to get Phoumi and his people to accept the facts of life that a military solution was impossible and that a negotiated settlement was the only possible solution."[13] At the Pentagon, however, he was treated as a hero. He had always received strong backing from the Joint Chiefs, though not from DOD civilians. This time he presented large-scale, optimistic plans to push the opposing forces from the Plaine des Jarres, for which he needed increased assistance. He also showed a willingness to work for any government in Laos that would show aggressiveness against the Communists. The Pentagon officers not only applauded his anticommunism but also agreed to increase his army to 60,000. Whether this was an attempt to placate him or not, he acted as if he had the full support of the entire U.S. government. The increased aid reinforced his resistance to a coalition.[14]

Why did American policy makers present such differing faces to the General from Laos? Some readers might suspect that the military officials were deliberately trying to under-mine Presidential policy. But some high military officers have a different explanation. They say they just had not gotten the word to drop Phoumi. They also complain that Kennedy, having abolished the regularized procedures of Eisenhower's National Security Council system, "operated out of his shirt pocket." He told only certain people what he had decided; others were informed haphazardly. He never followed chan-nels. Admiral Burke complains: "The administration threw away policies and left the Joint Chiefs in doubt as to what policy was. The Chiefs just continued to follow the existing policies—like supporting Phoumi—until ordered differently."[15]

For the reasons explained earlier, Kennedy could not issue such an order. The U.S. negotiating position at Geneva required continued support of Phoumi until an effective settle-ment had been reached. Any clear signal to the Chiefs to stop giving aid and encouragement to Phoumi was likely to provoke among them the same kind of outrage which the Laotian General had shown to Harriman. And in the absence of such an order, the Chiefs were free to continue the policies which in their judgment were correct.

All the civilians could—and did—do, was to leak word of their support for a neutral, coalition government. A Wash-ington *Post* diplomatic reporter called the newly revealed steps "forward retreats" on Laos. He said that the administration had decided to stop relying on the SEATO "umbrella" and, instead, seek a truly neutral government safeguarded by ICC inspection. It had also decided to drop its opposition to having Pathet Lao members in the cabinet, so long as the key positions (Prime Minister, Defense, Interior) were in non-Communist hands.[16] The administration had tried to make these points clear to Phoumi, but it could not go further at that time.

Harriman had the assurance he needed, however, to commit the United States to support of Souvanna as Prime Minister. He met with French and British diplomats in Paris in July to tell them of the new American position. Both Euro-pean nations had, of course, long favored Souvanna. The new consensus permitted closer coordination in Geneva and Vientiane. Until that "green light" from Harriman, Ambassador Brown had not been able to work closely with the British and French diplomats in Laos in their efforts to force the contending factions into meetings and agreements.[17]

Progress on other issues at Geneva came slowly.[18] For the first two months there were general speeches in plenary sessions. Delegations hurled charges and countercharges. The only substantive progress came from the presentation of different proposed drafts for conference agreement. Harriman grew impatient and suggested on June 15 that the conference move into restricted sessions, attended only by one delegate and one advisor from each nation at Geneva. Such a procedure, he hoped, would lessen posturing and encourage bargaining. Another month passed before the rest of the conferees agreed to the change.[19]

Maintaining the cease-fire was the most difficult problem in the early weeks of the conference. The United States was determined not to negotiate under the pressure of shifting military fortunes. On June 6, with the Pathet Lao on the verge of capturing the Meo stronghold of Padong, Harriman announced: "We are not prepared to engage in discussion . . . until the pre-conditions established for convening this convention have been met."[20] The United States was also angry because Royal Laotian requests that the ICC investigate the situation had been rejected by the Pathet Lao. For four days the conference did not meet. Eventually the cochairmen were able to bring the delegations back to the conference table.[21] An intermittent cease-fire continued throughout the summer and early autumn.

The three princes' communiqué from Zurich gave a substantial boost to the conference. Their agreement set guidelines for common ground between the Western and Communist positions. Another major obstacle vanished when Harriman succeeded in gaining U.S. government support for Souvanna Phouma. On July 20 the conference moved into restricted sessions.

Regularized procedures took control of the conference,

largely isolating it from outside events. The restricted sessions were held almost daily until mid-September. The cochairmen prepared a systematic schedule of questions for discussion. These were debated seriatim. When general substantive agreement was reached on an item, it was referred to one of the drafting committees for final wording. Further negotiations continued there when necessary. Beginning in September, the cochairmen took the matters on which there had been disagreement and negotiated with specific delegations to work out differences. These negotiations, too, became almost routinized. In order to prevent anger on the part of the less involved nations, the major participants met secretly under the guise of cocktail parties or teas. There were several sets of meetings: bilateral, US-UK-USSR, those three plus the Chinese; those four plus the French; those five plus the Canadians or Indians.[22]

Negotiations also took place outside of Geneva. Drafts and recommended negotiating positions were cabled back to Washington daily, where further discussions took place. Often Thai and Canadian diplomats came by the State Department in late afternoon to urge certain positions on the U.S. delegation. But since their communications with Geneva were more rapid than the Americans' (which had to be routed through the embassy at Paris), they often were talking about matters of which Washington was still ignorant.[23]

Harriman flew to Washington whenever he anticipated some kind of trouble with a part of the U.S. government. These trips enabled him to keep his negotiating mandate and to prevent dissidents from undermining his achievements. The problem was more acute in the first few months of the conference, when McConaughy was still Assistant Secretary, than later when Harriman was in the direct chain of command.[24]

On most major issues, the conference agreed to provisions in between Western and Communist drafts. Sometimes the compromises were achieved by trading clauses, at other times by ambiguity or vagueness. An important proposal by the South Vietnamese delegation called upon members of the conference not to use or permit the use of the territory or resources of Laos for interference in or aggression against other countries.

This wording sought to prevent North Vietnamese use of Laos as a corridor for infiltrating men and equipment into South Vietnam. The Communist nations agreed to this provision only on condition that there be a reciprocal commitment by the conferees not to interfere in Laotian internal affairs.[25]

Another important provision was the statement of the role of the cochairmen, the Soviet Union and Britain. Initially the U.S.S.R. proposed that the ICC should act "under the general guidance and supervision of the two Co-chairmen." Since this implied a veto over ICC activities, the Western nations insisted on different wording. The final protocol also included a sentence which vaguely defined what was more explicitly but secretly agreed between Soviet delegate Pushkin and British delegate MacDonald. "The Co-Chairmen shall exercise supervision over the observance of this Protocol and the Declaration on the Neutrality of Laos."[26]

The United States went to Geneva with a draft filled with specific obligations for the signatories and strong powers for the ICC. Even some of the American participants considered the provisions overly detailed and politically insensitive.[27] Since the draft had been worked out in the still hard-line atmosphere of the Far East Bureau and in consultation with the hawkish officers in the Pentagon, it made no concessions to apparent Communist demands. Nor was it ever presented at Geneva. But the U.S. delegation had to fight many bitter battles to win agreement for deviations from this initial position.[28]

Central to the agreement was the operation of the ICC. The conference members diverged furthest on this question. The Americans and French wanted to establish ICC fixed and mobile inspection teams which would have a free and unrestricted access to all parts of Laos. The Soviet Union proposed only "suitable groups," set up in agreement with the Laotian government, for the sole purpose of supervising and controlling the withdrawal of foreign forces. The final document left the initiative with the ICC, but kept its mandate vague. There was a clear compromise on the question of voting. Unanimity was required for decisions and recommendations on major questions. But the Commission could initiate and carry out an investigation by majority vote. The final protocol also permitted dissents in reports.[29] In sum, the ICC envisioned in the Geneva agreements was weak. It could be only as powerful as the major signatories would agree to let it be.

The question of SEATO troubled the conference until the last minute. The Communist bloc wanted a specific condemnation of the alliance, which the Western nations, of course, resisted. Since the Zurich communiqué had declared that a unified government would not "recognize the protection of any alliance or military coalition" without mentioning SEATO by name, the United States held out for similar wording. In the final days of the conference Souvanna Phouma resolved the deadlock by including a specific reference to SEATO in his new government's declaration of neutrality, which was incorporated into the final declaration by the conference.[30]

From the American viewpoint, the two most important features of the projected settlement were the "corridor" provision (forbidding use of Laotian territory to interfere in any other country) and the "Pushkin agreement." The latter was an explicit understanding between Britain and the Soviet Union (through their chief delegate, Georgi Pushkin) that each cochairman would insure compliance of the nations in its bloc. In other words, Britain promised to keep the United States in line and the Soviet Union promised the same regarding China, North Vietnam, and the Pathet Lao. Agreement on the corridor provision came fairly easily. It was also part of the final documents.

The Pushkin agreement was never made public. President Kennedy considered it a crucial part of the settlement on Laos because it made explicit the understandings he thought he had reached at Vienna and in subsequent correspondence with Khrushchev. Although the Soviet Union had shown little interest in Southeast Asia, the agreement guaranteed that it would stay at least enough involved to prevent the Chinese and North Vietnamese from stirring up more trouble. The first hints that the U.S.S.R. was willing to give such a guarantee came in August 1961. Harriman and Malcolm MacDonald (the chief British delegate) then continued to press for an explicit understanding in the following months. In September, Kennedy himself denied Khrushchev another summit meeting on the then volatile Berlin situation until he had shown some good faith on Laos.[31]

    Deadlock continued in Laos throughout the summer. The three princes had not met since Zurich and the King had not yet proclaimed a coalition government. On July 30 the National Assembly formally amended the constitution to permit the King to name such a government. Souvanna Phouma met with Boun Oum on the following day to try to hasten the process. But the rightist balked, refusing to grant Souphanouvong a major role in the coalition. Soviet Ambassador Abramov made a special visit to the King in August to try to impress on him the need for a coalition including the Pathet Lao leaders.[32] Harriman then decided to try to work something out with Souvanna.

    On September 14 he met the Laotian Prince in Rangoon for several days of talks on the composition of a coalition cabinet. The United States wanted the Pathet Lao in the cabinet, but not in the sensitive posts of Defense and Interior. The best that Harriman hoped for was an agreement to give one of those posts to a neutralist, the other to Phoumi. He argued for that division of portfolios in September, but later accepted Souvanna's plan for two carefully selected neutralists in the two key positions. The most important result of the Rangoon meeting was that it convinced Souvanna that he had American support. Thus strengthened, he set out to bring the left and right together.[33]

    Harriman, too, traveled throughout Southeast Asia after Rangoon with the same purpose. He went to New Delhi, Saigon, and Vientiane. He tried to impress the importance of a coalition on the King, Boun Oum, and Phoumi. But the only tangible result of his visit was an increased willingness to resume tripartite talks. On September 27 the three princes announced an agreement to meet again at Ban Hin Heup on October 6.

    After two days of meetings, they announced their agreement on a coalition government headed by Souvanna

Phouma. Of the sixteen cabinet positions, eight would go to neutralists and four each to the factions headed by Boun Oum and Souphanouvong. Boun Oum accepted the principle of a coalition under Souvanna but not this division of portfolios. Nor did he agree to Souphanouvong's suggested compromise of giving both Defense and Interior to Souvanna. Undaunted, the neutralist Prince flew to Luang Prabang, where on October 19 the King gave him a mandate to form a new government.[34]

For two months Souvanna tried unsuccessfully to arrange another meeting for the three princes in order to work out their differences. Boun Oum repeatedly objected or found reasons for delay. He must have found some encouragement from some Americans in Laos, for the *New York Times* quoted "observers" in Vientiane as believing that the Ban Hin Neup agreements pushed Laos closer to the Communist bloc.[35] In early October General Phoumi met with MAAG Chief General Boyle and CINCPAC Admiral Felt and no doubt learned that some elements within the U.S. government still supported him vigorously. Admiral Felt made a public speech recommending a peaceful solution in Laos but warning that, if such a solution could not be found, U.S. and SEATO forces were always ready to come to the aid of Laos.[36]

A few weeks later, as the monsoon season ended, Phoumi launched a series of "probing actions" deep into Pathet Lao territory. Ostensibly in response to Pathet Lao attacks, the new offensives went far behind the poorly defined but nonetheless real cease-fire line. One American official who dealt regularly with Phoumi considered the General's actions to be counteroffensives against Communist military expansion. He says: "There was considerable evidence that the Pathet Lao were not abiding by the ceasefire and were infiltrating and consolidating into new areas." But he also admits that within the country team the offensives "were controversial to say the least."[37] A British military officer in Laos during 1960–62 has a different viewpoint. Hugh Toye writes that the probes went into "areas where his opponents could be expected to be sensitive and where probes would provoke military reactions which could be used as excuses for delay on the political front." Toye also cites examples of false claims by Phoumi of North Vietnamese invasions.[38]

While Phoumi was launching his new offensives, with tacit or explicit support from some Americans, some officials in the State Department decided to instruct Ambassador Brown to tell Phoumi to hold out for the two key cabinet positions of Defense and Interior. Harriman did not learn of these instructions until later, but officials within the State Department protested sharply. They also got the Pentagon to warn American military advisors in Laos against publicly criticizing U.S. policy there. In spite of the progress at Geneva, some officers reportedly had been saying that the United States should stop talking and start fighting. This further evidence of the lack of firm control over Laos policy strengthened the President's determination to replace the Assistant Secretary, Walter McConaughy. When he reshuffled the State Department over Thanksgiving weekend, he put Harriman in charge of the Far East Bureau.[39]

The cease-fire had broken down. Agreement among the princes was all the more urgent. At Geneva the delegates had ironed out most of their disagreements. Several delegations urged the various Laotian factions to get together quickly. The U.S. delegation issued a statement saying, "The conference cannot finish its business until the princes finish theirs."[40] On December 14 the princes met on the Plaine des Jarres but failed to reach an agreement on the distribution of cabinet posts. Two weeks later they tried again—and failed. Boun Oum charged that Souvanna had given "no proof of genuine neutrality" and that, consequently, the Defense and Interior ministries should go to the rightists. Souphanouvong then left Vientiane, claiming that Boun Oum had reneged on his agreements at Zurich and Ban Hin Heup and had "no intention of finding a peaceful solution to the Laotian problem." He also blamed Boun Oum's attitude on behind the scenes pressure from the U.S. military.[41] The patiently achieved settlement had come unstuck.

Harriman convinced his superiors that drastic action was necessary to bring Phoumi into line. Although he did not favor suspending military assistance, he did hope that a halt in economic aid would bring the Boun Oum government around to a settlement. The United States did not deposit its regular $4 million monthly check in the Lao government's account in January 1962. Squeezed by the aid suspension, Lao banks stopped selling foreign currency on January 4. The Royal Government complained publicly about the aid suspension, probably in hopes of bringing about a reversal. On January 6 it imposed price controls on all goods. On January 10 Boun Oum agreed to meet with the other princes in Geneva despite his doubts about the possibility of a settlement. Two days later the U.S. government announced its intention to resume aid immediately.[42]

Four days before the princes met on January 19 Harriman tried to force one point of agreement by announcing that he and the Soviet delegate both favored giving the Defense and Interior ministries to neutralists. Souvanna Phouma reported agreement on the division of cabinet posts, but Boun Oum was reported to be holding out on the two key ministries.[43] A confused optimism lasted only a few days, when it was shattered by new fighting in Laos.

Nam Tha was the target, a small village about fifteen miles from the Chinese border, important to Phoumi because of its airfield. After repelling Phoumi's drive toward Muong Sai, the Pathet Lao went beyond the previous cease-fire line and moved close enough to Nam Tha to mortar the airfield. If they could close the field, they could prevent air attacks which had been launched from there over Pathet Lao territory and reinforcements for renewed ground attacks. The Royal Army commanders saw the situation differently. They thought that the attack was a deliberate attempt to inflict a decisive defeat on their forces, one which would drive them from northern Laos and give the Chinese and North Vietnamese an unimpeded corridor across the country.[44]

Against American advice, Phoumi decided to reinforce Nam Tha. He disregarded warnings that such action would provoke both the Pathet Lao and the Chinese. He also disputed the analyses which compared Nam Tha's terrain to that around Dien Bien Phu. By the end of January 1962, Phoumi had moved 5,000 men to Nam Tha, including important elements of his artillery. When mortaring started on February 1, Boun Oum used the attack as a pretext for rejecting another meeting on a coalition government. Phoumi continued to build up his forces and sent them on probes into Pathet Lao territory. Hugh Toye notes that the siege of Nam Tha tapered off after the first few weeks. "It was not until further provocative sallies from Nam Tha had resulted in an actual clash that they resumed mortaring."[45]

Once again Harriman urged sanctions against Phoumi. The February aid payment was not made. Convinced that the CIA was behind Phoumi's reinforcement of Nam Tha, Harriman also obtained the transfer of Jack Hazey, the CIA man closest to Phoumi. Others in Vientiane doubted that Hazey was acting contrary to orders, but Harriman won out. Information subsequently came out that Hazey and other CIA operatives, without authorization from Washington, had continued to counsel Phoumi against agreeing to a coalition government. It was also reported that the CIA counteracted the aid suspension by supplying its own funds to Phoumi's forces.[46]

The decision to pressure Phoumi in this way did not come easily in Washington. Although the chief policy makers were agreed on the desirability of a neutral government headed by Souvanna Phouma, they wanted to avoid the impression of being defeated militarily by the Communists. The sanctions imposed affected only the cash grants to pay the army; military equipment continued to be provided. Intelligence reports from Laos, if they were not deliberately misleading on Communist intentions and participation by the North Vietnamese and Chinese, at least were ambiguous enough to permit fears similar to Phoumi's. Secretary Rusk told Harriman to do all he felt comfortable in doing to bring Phoumi around. The President was more skeptical. He was concerned about the deterioration of the kip following the January aid suspension (the Royal Government just printed new bank notes to pay its army) and about the publicity which that act had provoked. Senator Goldwater, for example, had sharply criticized American policy on January 19. Harriman reportedly told the President that he would take responsibility for the outcome. In that way Kennedy could fire him if things went sour.[47]

Ambassadors in Vientiane came into the act in February. They conferred and then selected some of their group to approach the different Laotian factions. The British and Soviet ambassadors, for example, went to the Plaine des Jarres on February 5 to try to convince Souvanna and Souphanouvong to halt their attacks on Nam Tha. Boun Oum then rebuffed Souvanna's calls for another tripartite meeting. On February 18 Souvanna met with the American, Soviet, British, and French ambassadors and reported "wide agreement" on the way to solve the problems. On the same day he conferred with the King and Phoumi. The next day a temporary ceasefire occurred at Nam Tha.[48]

Thailand then became the stumbling block to an agreement. After warning that the fall of Nam Tha would give the Chinese an easy land corridor into his country, Marshal Sarit moved Thai troops to the northern border with Laos on February 13. His government had opposed a coalition government all along, not least because Phoumi was his cousin. As late as January 11, 1962, when the American position on a coalition was well known, the Thai Defense Ministry charged that U.S. policy would "expedite the Communist takeover of Laos."[49] The Nam Tha situation seemed to pose a new and more serious threat, although the Thais had also cautioned Phoumi against reinforcing the outpost so heavily. From Bangkok's perspective, its troop deployment was a reasonable, precautionary response. It also strengthened Phoumi's hand and put the United States on notice that it had to pay attention to its most faithful Southeast Asian ally.[50]

Attorney General Robert Kennedy was touring Asia at that time and visited Bangkok a week after the troops moved north. Sarit made Kennedy aware of his concern and sought assurances of what the United States would do if Thailand's security were endangered. The Attorney General must have relayed Sarit's statements, for, at the end of February, the United States invited Foreign Minister Thanat Khoman to Washington for consultations.[51]

Washington officials knew that Sarit's help would be useful if not necessary to bring Phoumi into line. They knew that Thai leaders were skeptical about the Geneva Conference and deeply suspicious about a coalition government. They also knew of Thailand's doubts about SEATO's effectiveness in view of British and French reluctance to stand up against pro-Communists in Southeast Asia. They concluded that the United States had to give Thailand some explicit assurances that it would not let a coalition and neutralist government in Laos be the first domino to fall and threaten Thai security. On basic strategy the two countries were in agreement. The United States did not want a hostile government in the Mekong Valley; Thailand wanted to defend itself outside its own borders. After six days of talks, Secretary Rusk and Foreign Minister Thanat reaffirmed their mutual interests and declared "full agreement" on the need for "a free, independent, and truly neutral Laos." Their joint statement also made explicit a principle which the United States had held implicitly since Dulles' 1955 visit to Vientiane: that its SEATO obligation was individual as well as collective. In other words, the United States would defend Thailand if the latter were attacked by Communists, even if Britain and France were reluctant.[52]

The Rusk-Thanat agreement smoothed the way for a change in policy by Sarit, but it did not force it. Phoumi had been in Bangkok while Thanat was in Washington. He returned to Vientiane on March 7, fortified in his belief that he should continue to hold out for both Defense and Interior positions. On March 18 he escalated the propaganda war with an unsubstantiated charge that Chinese and North Vietnamese troops had renewed the attack on Nam Tha. Even the continued suspension of American aid did not seem to budge him.[53]

William Sullivan and Michael Forrestal, who had been liaison man with Harriman for the NSC staff since January, were in Laos at the time, trying to get Phoumi's agreement to a coalition. Aware of their failure, they cabled for help from Harriman, who was in the Philippines at a SEATO meeting. Going first to Bangkok, Harriman met with Sarit and spelled out American policy in clear and unambiguous terms. He asked the Thai Premier to join him in meeting with Phoumi. When Phoumi refused to come to Bangkok, Harriman and Sarit went to the border town of Nong Khai.[54]

There Sarit spoke quietly, urging Phoumi to accept a coalition. The General began to outline the reasons for his refusal. But Harriman interruped and said flatly that he had to accept the coalition. American troops would not come to Laos and die for him, Harriman declared. The only alternative to a neutral Laos was a Communist one. His point made, Harriman then went to Vientiane to confer with the King and other officials.[55]

Following those talks, Harriman spoke with amazing frankness to reporters. He said that all thirteen nations at Geneva agreed that Souvanna Phouma should be Prime Minister; Phoumi was the only one delaying a final settlement. He doubted that there could be a viable government if either Defense or Interior was in the hands of a leftist or rightist. Noting the continued suspension of economic aid, he implied that military aid would also be stopped if there were no agreement soon. "We do not have to support a government who does not follow the United States' polices."[56]

Phoumi and Boun Oum continued to hold out for at least one of the key ministries. The King, angered at the suspension of assistance, tried to go over Harriman's head with a direct letter to President Kennedy. The letter questioned the wisdom of a coalition government and expressed a fear of a Communist takeover. The President's reply was stalled for two weeks by bureaucratic disagreement over what to say. Some officials feared that an explicit statement of U.S. policy would encourage the Communists by revealing America's intention to disengage from Laos. They thought that the Communists would begin to place more emphasis on military means, where the Royal Government had proved notably ineffective. Higher officials disregarded these fears. On April 23 the President's reply was sent, telling the King that the United States did not intend to intervene militarily and reaffirming American support for Souvanna Phouma.[57]

Pathet Lao attacks on Nam Tha intensified in late

April, leading to the capture of a key ridge on the twenty-fourth. The next day, Boun Oum and Phoumi traveled to Bangkok to try to regain Thai support. Despite its doubts about American policy, the Sarit government refused further support in accordance with its pledge to Harriman. Thai officials did not pressure the Laotians, but neither did they renege on their promise. Disappointed, but not deterred, Phoumi and Boun Oum continued to Malaya, Formosa, South Korea, and South Vietnam in search of support. Meanwhile, the situation at Nam Tha grew desperate for Phoumi's forces.[58]

On May 2 the Pathet Lao forces moved closer to Nam Tha. The next day they captured Muong Sing, the last Royal Government airfield in northern Laos, through which Phoumi had been reinforcing his troops. A Defense Ministry spokesman charged that Muong Sing had fallen to a massive attack including Chinese troops. The local Laotian commander used that allegation, plus an intensification of mortaring, as a pretext (or a reason, if he actually believed the reports about the Chinese) for abandoning Nam Tha on May 6. There was no direct attack by the Pathet Lao, only the possibility of one. And the Royal Lao troops did not stop at the nearest outpost, but pushed on to Ban Houei Sai on the Thai border and then across the Mekong. In spite of this ignominious retreat, the American White Star Team Leader attached to the forces at Nam Tha found one reason for encouragement. He reportedly cabled to his superiors: "The morale of my battalion is substantially better than in our last engagement. The last time, they dropped their weapons and ran. This time, they took their weapons with them."[59]

The fall of Nam Tha galvanized the Kennedy Administration. But Washington reacted as much to the symbolism of that encounter as to its reality. The truth was that the Royal Lao Army had been tested again and found wanting. The MAAG chief in Laos reportedly cabled some of his superiors that the Lao troops were worthless. A White Star patrol back toward Nam Tha discovered Pathet Lao guerrillas, but no Chinese or North Vietnamese. Nor was there any evidence of a move toward the Mekong, the contingency most frightening to the Americans and the Thais.[60]

Symbolically, however, Nam Tha was a flagrant challenge to the ceasefire and to American hopes for a negotiated withdrawal from Laos. It also made credible the threat to Thailand, which asked for new assurances. Some U.S. policy makers believed that strong action was necessary. They argued that it would clarify the limits of American tolerance—no Communist military takeover. It would also reassure Thailand and forestall any military initiative by Sarit. Roger Hilsman had raised some of these issues even before the fall of Nam Tha. In its aftermath, this became the State Department consensus.[61]

On May 10 the National Security Council met to consider the proposals presented by Hilsman and Harriman. They recommended diplomatic moves to inform Britain, India, and the Soviet Union of the U.S. position and military moves including a naval show of force and the deployment of some troops to Thailand. In essence, it was the same plan considered and rejected almost exactly one year before. The policy debate also took almost exactly the same form as the previous year. President Kennedy was skeptical. At his news conference the day before he said that the United States had only two choices: restoring the ceasefire through political negotiations or introducing American forces. And he said he preferred the former. He also expressed privately his fear that it would be difficult to find an occasion to withdraw troops once they were put into Thailand.[62]

The Joint Chiefs repeated their arguments against intervention unless they could use sufficient force to meet any reaction by the other side. They were also more concerned about Thailand than Laos itself. Their only counterproposals were for reversing our opposition to Phoumi and for instituting a crash program of assistance to his army. They favored the diplomatic protests and the naval show of force.[63]

Kennedy made the minimal decision on which both groups could agree—starting a naval task force toward the South China Sea. (Ambassadorial talks had already begun in Moscow and Washington.) He also deferred a decision on further action for two days, by which time Secretaries Rusk and McNamara and JCS Chairman General Lemnitzer were due back from

Asia. Meanwhile, he sent CIA Director John McCone and White House staffer Michael Forrestal to brief General Eisenhower.[64]

Harriman and Hilsman, fearing that the naval action would be too weak an action by itself, appealed to the President to cancel the order for fleet movement until more fundamental decisions could be made. At first Kennedy agreed. But within an hour he reversed himself. McCone and Forrestal had reported that General Eisenhower favored much stronger action and was ready to urge putting U.S. troops into Laos. Since Kennedy regularly briefed the General and cultivated his support on foreign policy, he decided to meet his suggestions part way.[65]

The full retinue of White House advisors met on May 12. McNamara, just off the plane from Bangkok, announced his support for initial troop movements and for improvements in communications and supply lines to prepare for possible large-scale intervention in Laos. This tipped the balance in favor of sending troops. The meeting adjourned quickly so that detailed plans could be worked out. In the afternoon the President approved those plans.[66]

Several military plans competed for implementation. A year before the most carefully considered operation was SEATO Plan 5, which called for spearheads across the Mekong to hold the major towns in Laos. It required 25,000 troops initially, but with a projected ceiling of 40,000. All plans available in 1962 would have required three or four divisions if the operation were to be more than just a show of force. One of the most widely favored plans in the Pentagon was to occupy the southern panhandle of Laos right up to the North Vietnamese border. Although this territory was rough and difficult to hold, the military was ready to maintain its position there by starting the bombing of North Vietnam. This was a policy recommended by others (including Walt Rostow), who saw Hanoi as the main source of trouble in the region and who wanted to solve several problems at once.[67]

These plans, however, had been ruled out during the policy debates in front of the President. He did not want to provoke Chinese intervention, which intelligence reports said was likely if the United States tried to retake territory from the Pathet Lao. He wanted a political use of military forces, not the start of a regular military operation which might generate its own forward momentum, as in Korea. The plan which was implemented involved the use of only about 3,000 men. Their deployment was intended to signal that the United States was not about to take over Laos, but that an attack to the Mekong would result in a clash with American forces. These forces were not equipped for sustained operations without substantial additional equipment and men. Most of the President's civilian advisors thought that he was bluffing the Communists, but the military men knew that they could expand the task force if necessary.[68]

Continued diplomatic pressure on Phoumi accompanied the troop deployments. Phoumi was informed that the troops were being sent in for the benefit of Thailand rather than Laos. The Vientiane government cabled Souvanna Phouma, telling him that he could appoint his own followers to the key ministries of Defense and Interior. On May 25 Souvanna agreed to further negotiations, setting a dealine of June 15, at which time he had to return to Paris for his daughter's wedding. On June 7 the three princes began meeting at Khang Khay on the Plaine des Jarres.[69]

Four days later the princes signed a formal agreement on the composition of the government of national union. Souvanna was to be Prime Minister and Minister of Defense. Phoumi and Souphanouvong would be Deputy Premiers, each with a veto over cabinet decisions. The General was named Finance Minister, giving him control over aid and other funds, including those channeled through Souphanouvong, who returned to his former position in charge of planning. The cabinet itself was an amalgam of regional and political factions. Souvanna Phouma's neutralists held seven seats. Four went to the Pathet Lao. Four went to Phoumi's supporters, who came mainly from southern Laos. The remaining four seats went to the "Vientiane neutralists," right-wing politicians who had remained in Vientiane but had not committed themselves to

Phoumi. They came primarily from the Sananikone family, which had little reason to feel affinity for the General.[70]

The world applauded the settlement. The United States resumed its financial aid to Laos on June 14. The existing National Assembly formally approved the new government on the fifteenth. On June 23 the cabinet was presented to the King, then met for the first time. Its first action was to proclaim a ceasefire throughout Laos. Souvanna Phouma also declared that his new government would not recognize the protection of SEATO and would seek friendly relations with all nations, "primarily with neighboring countries." The cabinet also named a unified delegation to Geneva.[71]

Laos presented its declaration of neutrality to the conference on July 6. After three days of negotiations over wording, it was formally incorporated into the final conference document. On July 23 the foreign ministers of the fourteen nations at Geneva signed the "Declaration on the Neutrality of Laos," thus ending the conference and, to a large extent, the crisis of the preceding two years.[72] The traditional three-headed elephant which appears on the Laotian flag came to symbolize a new political coalition. Unfortunately, the chances for the survival of either creature were slim. Souvanna Phouma returned to Vientiane by way of Washington, where he pledged neutrality and said that Laos would never become Communist.[73]

The United States then began to regularize its dealings with Laos. It changed its system of giving economic aid by refusing to support the kip at an established level. Instead, it provided a fixed amount of assistance, with no additional help in case of a run on the currency. AID officials also insisted on tighter controls on imports, including U.S. customs inspectors to certify receipt of goods in Laos. This new program was not only expected to be corruption-proof, but also was planned to cost less than the old system. The Laotians tried to resist these controls for several months before agreeing to them.[74]

Most of the troops sent into Thailand were withdrawn during June. The others left sporadically during the next four months. The ICC counted the 666 American military men and 403 Filipino technicians as they left Laos. But only forty of the estimated 10,000 North Vietnamese in Laos left through ICC checkpoints. The U.S. government faced a decision on what to do in response to this clear violation of the Geneva agreements.[75]

Shortly before the October 7 deadline for troop withdrawal, the President convened his advisors. Harriman estimated that things were going "just about as unsatisfactorily as we expected." But he argued for strict observance of the agreements by the United States. Only in that way would the onus of violation fall upon the Communists. Keeping American forces in Laos would not change the outcome, but would give the North Vietnamese a clear pretext for their own violations. If the neutralists learned for themselves about the North Vietnamese actions, they might become more skeptical and independent of the Communists.[76]

American intelligence estimates at the time judged the risk of compliance with the agreements fairly small. They concluded that the North Vietnamese were determined to preserve their corridor into South Vietnam—the Ho Chi Minh trails—but would not overtly expand or improve their infiltration routes. Within Laos, U.S. experts thought that the Pathet Lao would try to maintain their de facto control, otherwise restricting their actions to political meneuvering. Since no events in Laos were likely to force a strategic policy change, the President's advisors were willing to accept the violations relatively quietly. The United States protested the North Vietnamese actions, of course, but took no immediate counteraction.[77]

Laos passed into the background. Attention shifted to Vietnam. There, it seemed, was a manageable mess.

CHAPTER SEVEN

Watching the wart on the hog (1962–1968)

After 1963 Laos was only the wart on the hog of Vietnam.
—DEAN RUSK[1]

The Geneva Agreements of 1962 pushed Laos off the front pages of newspapers and, consequently, away from public concern. Presidential and bureaucratic energies shifted increasingly to the worsening situation in Vietnam. The formulation of American policy toward Laos devolved upon the various components of the national security bureaucracy—the State and Defense Departments, AID, CIA—each of which tried to continue its existing programs and to preserve its role in Laos.

Coordination rarely went above the Assistant Secretary level in Washington. In the field, strong ambassadors kept their country teams generally united. Policy in both places emerged from a consensus that it was still important to preserve the government of Souvanna Phouma, if not for its own sake, then at least for the protection of American involvement in Vietnam.

Although the technical provisions of the agreements were violated, no major international crisis ensued. The basic patterns of restrained military activities and the façade of a coalition remained for some time. One American diplomat has made a useful distinction between the Geneva "agreements" and the Geneva "settlement."[2] The documents signed by the participants in the fourteen-nation conference, with their specific provisions, constituted the "agreements." The broader "settlement" ignored some of those technicalities and focused instead on the underlying consensus on a stabilization of the *status quo ante bellum.* In particular, this consensus meant, as viewed by the United States, that the Pathet Lao would not seek a major increase in the territory under their control and that they would especially avoid moving into the Mekong Valley. In return, the United States was obligated to uphold an avowedly neutralist regime in Vientiane and to refrain from threatening Pathet Lao control in its own zone. Although the agreements never got full compliance, the settlement was not seriously challenged until 1969.

The failure of the Geneva Agreements of 1962 ever to be fully implemented illustrates the importance of the process of implementation of foreign policy decisions. The words on the papers signed in July had to be turned into actions in the subsequent weeks. But insofar as the prescribed actions involved changing existing behavior, they were caught up in disputes over timing.

None of the Laotian factions wanted to give up any weapons, territory, or control first. Each side was jealously protective of its position. The Americans likewise were reluctant to reduce or halt support of their clients until their interests had been safeguarded. The same was true for the North Vietnamese. As a result, each party perceived the actions of its antagonists as proof of a rejection of the understandings reached at Geneva. Cautious adherence to the accords reenforced mutual suspicions. In less than a year the agreements had collapsed.

Perhaps the coalition never could have succeeded in Laos. The façade of cooperation which lasted from the summer of 1962 until April 1963 concealed profound antagonisms and probably irreconcilable disagreements. Left completely to themselves, the Laotians might well have learned to live peacefully together—or regionally separated. But Laos was a stake in the competition for influence and control in Asia. Other nations would not leave it alone.

American officials in Washington sincerely believed that they were adhering to both the letter and the spirit of Geneva, at least until the spring of 1963. President Kennedy reportedly decided to adopt the policy recommended by Averell Harriman and Roger Hilsman to keep the U.S. record absolutely clean. As Hilsman phrased it, "Our military advisors should be withdrawn promptly, and thereafter there should be no violation of any kind by the United States, neither 'black' reconnaissance flights to confirm whether the North Vietnamese had actually withdrawn nor cloak-and-dagger hanky-panky."[3] Another official intimately associated with policy toward Laos at this period said, "We were simon pure until 1964."[4] That view may have been the consensus in Washington, but the evidence in Laos was not so clear.

Aerial reconnaissance continued at least through August, gathering evidence of North Vietnamese military supply missions. The flights probably continued even after the October 7 troop withdrawal deadline, though at a higher altitude. Since the flights had begun in connection with contingency planning for possible troop deployments in Thailand, it seems likely that such flights would have been resumed, if ever suspended on the President's orders, at least by the time of the renewed fighting in April 1963, when troop deployments were again contemplated.[5]

Troops sent to Thailand were gradually withdrawn during the early summer of 1962, with all ground troops gone by November.[6] Americans assigned to the MAAG were also withdrawn, starting in mid-August and finishing on the October 7 deadline. William Sullivan, who visited Laos in September in order to confer with Souvanna Phouma, later testified that all military and quasi-military personnel were withdrawn.[7]

Military aid, however, continued at the request of Souvanna Phouma. The Prime Minister referred to "assurances of support" given by President Kennedy and other U.S. officials in July when he wrote his formal request for aid on September 10. He asked for supplies and repair parts to maintain U.S. equipment furnished earlier, training ammunition, and certain consumable supplies such as POL, cement, and clothing. Presumably at the same time he also requested continuation of supplies from the Soviet Union.[8]

The Americans speedily complied with this request and continued giving money and equipment to General Phoumi Nosavan and his 48,000 men. The Russians, however, gradually phased down their assistance. They worked through the North Vietnamese to supply the 19,000 Pathet Lao troops (and, presumably, also the 6,000 or so North Vietnamese troops estimated by American intelligence still to be in Laos). Kong-Le's 10,000 neutralist soldiers lost their direct pipeline from the Soviet Union when the airlift was ended in October.[9]

Channeling aid through Hanoi put the neutralist forces at the mercy of the Pathet Lao, who naturally preferred to control the additional troops. Although there is no available evidence of what the Pathet Lao demanded in return for the provision of aid, it is clear that they substantially reduced their support of Kong-Le's forces. In order to keep the neutralist army from being absorbed by the Pathet Lao, Souvanna asked the United States to provide supplies. The American Ambassador complied.[10]

Relief missions were also requested by Souvanna. An agreement was signed on October 7, providing an increase in assistance to refugees. This agreement was initialed and implemented by the rightist Secretary of State for Social Welfare, Keo Viphakone, despite the apparent objections of the Pathet Lao, who did not want Air America flights delivering supplies to opposition villages within their zone of control. Souvanna was unwilling or unable to repudiate the agreement.[11]

The relief and resupply missions were the key American contribution to the breakdown of the Geneva agreements. Since the Pathet Lao protested continuation of such aid even before the withdrawal deadline, they probably considered the aid a violation of the accords. The North Vietnamese, in turn, violated the agreements by withdrawing only about half of their forces in Laos.

Blame for breaking the Geneva Accords cannot be placed on only one group. There was no point in time when the agreed provisions were in effect, and after which there were violations. During the transition period from July 23 until October 7, all sides acted to protect themselves, thereby increasing suspicions and fears.

The Americans continued supplying the refugees and rightist forces and eventually received formal requests for such aid from the provisional government. The Russians continued their airlift but gradually turned supply operations over to the North Vietnamese, who improved their road links into Laos. The Pathet Lao sought to strengthen control in their areas by denying aid to neutralists and others in pockets of resistance. The rightists similarly tried to preserve their position, not only militarily, but especially politically. Caught in the middle was Souvanna Phouma. His only power base, Kong-Le's neutralist army, was threatened by internal dissension and decreasing Soviet aid. He had to turn to the Americans in order to bolster his position. But by tolerating U.S. insistence on continued relief operations, he earned the suspicion and hostility of the Pathet Lao.

U.S. economic aid still dominated the Laotian economy. In fact, at the very time that the contending factions moved cautiously toward implementation of the agreements, an American economic mission was in Vientiane, pressing for more stringent import controls.[12] In the absence of countervailing aid, the Lao were at the mercy of the Americans, both economically and militarily.

Whether or not the military and relief programs were separate, they were viewed by the Pathet Lao as an effort to violate and sabotage the Geneva Accords. Leftist forces fired on an American reconnaissance plane on August 13, 1962. They clashed with Meo units about a week later. On August 28, a Pathet Lao spokesman demanded an end to U.S. support of the Meo.[13]

Aid to the Meo tribes was a major and growing program for the Americans. After years of trying unsuccessfully to create a strong, Western-style army in the Mekong Valley, U.S. personnel began to organize, train, and advise the hill people, who had resisted the imposition of any government, either from Vientiane or Hanoi. One report claims that this activity was planned as early as 1959 and began in Laos in 1960.[14] Another report says that by the end of 1960 Vang Pao had drawn up plans to unify the Meo tribes in Xieng Khouang province and organize them into a guerrilla army.[15]

In any event, the White Star Teams dispatched to Laos

by President Eisenhower only a few weeks before he left office made a major effort to organize the Meo. These hardy, independent hill tribesmen proved themselves tough fighters. By 1962 the U.S. Special Forces soldiers had built up an armed strength of 11,000 men, whom they placed under the command of Meo Colonel Vang Pao. These men lived in mountain villages scattered throughout the territory under the general control of the Pathet Lao.[16]

When the Geneva accords were signed, the Americans felt compelled to withdraw their military advisors. Anticipating this action, Vang Pao had stockpiled arms and supplies at a CIA-built airstrip at Long Tieng. U.S. civilians remained with the Meo to coordinate relief supplies.[17]

One of these civilians was the now legendary Edgar "Pop" Buell, an Indiana farmer who has spent the past decade trying to help the Meo. His transformation from relief worker to guerrilla organizer, chronicled by Don Schanche, is analogous to the change which took place after Geneva in American policy. As Schanche writes of Buell:

> His job was fundamentally humanitarian, helping to keep alive a displaced and war-weary people. Yet to perform this compassionate task, he was finding it necessary to become a Meo guerrilla himself. He still thought of Vang Pao's irregular military activities and of his own civil relief activities as related but entirely separate operations. Yet the two inexorably had become so intertwined that there was no real separation. Neither activity could live without the other, and the continued freedom of the Meo, and thousands of Lao and Lao Thung refugees as well, depended coequally upon Vang Pao's guns and Edgar's rice.[18]

Other Americans, too, slid from relief operations back into military activities.

The AID program became a cover for CIA activities when the Requirements Office was established in October 1962. Staffed by retired military officers, this unit gathered information on Lao military needs and arranged for delivery from

Thailand. It also provided food, shelter, ammunition, and supplies to the Meo. The only differences between the Requirements Office and the former MAAG were that its personnel
were technically civilians, were not involved in field operations
advice, and did not run end-use checks of equipment.[19]

In subsequent months, other minor and major American
violations of the Geneva agreements took place.[20] Leftist opposition to the supply operations to the Meo and neutralists led to
the shooting down of U.S. planes in November 1962 and January 1963. The Americans were not deterred, however, for
they continued and defended their logistics missions. Knowing
of North Vietnamese violations of the accords, they saw no
reason for complete adherence on their own part. As one
official in Washington said, "We thought we were getting
something where there could be cheating, but within tolerable
limits."[21]

From the American viewpoint, relief and military assistance were quite legal under the Geneva agreements, especially since Article 6 permitted "such quantities of conventional
armaments as the Royal Government of Laos may consider
necessary for the national defense of Laos." The Pathet Lao,
however, pointed to the provisions requiring withdrawal of all
"foreign military personnel" and prohibiting their reintroduc-
tion. The crucial term was broadly defined to include: "members of foreign military missions, foreign military advisers,
experts, instructors, consultants, technicians, observers, and any
other foreign military persons, including those serving in any
armed forces in Laos, and foreign civilians connected with the
supply, maintenance, storing, and utilization of war materials."[22]
The only exception was the provision that the French, with the
approval of the Laotian government, could provide a strictly
limited number of instructors for the army. This they did, but
their instructors taught only nonlethal skills like communications and engineering.[23]

Covert operations continued despite the ostensible with-
drawal of all "foreign military personnel," as provided in the
Geneva agreements. Books by men who worked with the Green
Berets suggest that there was no major pause in activity because

of Geneva. Americans were reportedly put into guerrilla bases with warnings to avoid capture, lest the United States be caught violating the accords. The code name for this CIA effort was Operation Hardnose.[24]

To supplement its own activities, both open and clandestine, the United States hired third-country nationals. The Thais, many of whom were from the same ethnic stock as the Lao, could operate less visibly and without the language barrier. Having provided military units in 1961–62, they then turned to covert operations. The United States also used Thai and Filipino nationals for regular aid projects.[25]

What seems surprising in retrospect is that no one seemed to question the policy of aiding the Meo and neutralists. Souvanna needed supplies for his army, which the Americans could provide quite legally under Article 6 of the agreements, since it had been formally requested. Perhaps Soviet loss of interest in Laos made continued U.S. aid less troublesome.

Refugee relief also went unquestioned. Perhaps it was genuinely thought to be humanitarian and without political consequences. Or perhaps the Americans were hopeful enough that a truly integrated government would be established that they wanted leverage to keep the Pathet Lao from consolidating their control and thus partitioning the country. Whatever the reasons, U.S. aid sustained pockets of resistance to the Pathet Lao and consequently contributed to the ultimate collapse of the agreements.

North Vietnamese involvement in the breakdown is not clear. Although about 6,000 troops remained in Laos, these forces apparently did not engage in significant military operations until 1964. Political advisors may have encouraged the Pathet Lao to stimulate dissension among the neutralists, but the evidence is lacking.[26]

The three major Laotian factions never really came together. They formed a coalition cabinet, but not a coalition government. The armies were never integrated as provided by the Geneva Accords. Nor did Vientiane ever establish its authority in Pathet Lao areas. The cabinet splintered before any effective or lasting steps were taken toward reconciliation.

At first, the Government of National Union appeared to function well. It assumed administrative powers on August 27, 1962, and soon permitted the establishment of diplomatic relations with several Eastern European nations. The Soviet, Chinese, and North Vietnamese representatives, formerly accredited to Souvanna Phouma's government at Khang Khay, presented their credentials to the King, thereby prompting the Nationalist Chinese and South Vietnamese to recall their ambassadors from Vientiane.[27]

Diplomatic activities occupied most attention during September 1962. When the troop withdrawal deadline arrived, Souvanna arranged for the National Assembly to vote him full powers for a year. The Pathet Lao denounced this step because it considered that parliament, chosen in the rigged election of 1960, irrelevant to the new coalition.

Souvanna asserted his leadership in the National Assembly action and in requesting continued military and relief supplies. He was not able, however, to keep his neutralist army together.

Both the Americans and the Communists struggled for the allegiance of the neutralists, using aid and propaganda. Foreign Minister Quinim Pholsena, a left-leaning neutralist, reportedly developed a network of agents who worked to turn neutralist officers against Kong-Le. He succeeded with Colonel Deuan Siphaseuth, who had quarreled with Kong-Le and briefly defected from him just before the 1960 battle of Vientiane. In early November 1962, Deuan objected strongly to Kong-Le's acceptance of American aid. It was his battalion which shot down a U.S. cargo plane on the twenty-seventh as it tried to land supplies on the Plaine des Jarres.[28]

On the following day, the coalition government announced agreement on a unified national army of 30,000 men drawn equally from the three existing armies. The disagreements evident the previous day among the neutralists help to explain why the army was never unified. Tensions and intrigue increased between the Kong-Le neutralists and the Pathet Lao during December and January. Pathet Lao forces warned against further air drops and shot down another U.S. cargo plane on January 6.

Soldiers from both groups kept up their façade of mixed patrols in the Plaine des Jarres, but Kong-Le's men were no longer safe in the ostensibly "mixed zones" of Khang Khay and Xieng Khouang. On February 12, 1963, Colonel Ketsana Vongsavong was assassinated in his home in Phong Savan (on the Plaine), allegedly by Pathet Lao agents. Ketsana had long been close to both Kong-Le and Souvanna, but had reportedly also been working with the Americans and against the Pathet Lao. He had survived an attempt on his life the previous November.[29]

Kong-Le vowed revenge for the death of his friend. He ordered his men to stay away from Pathet Lao camps and forbade entry into his zones of Pathet Lao personnel and defectors to Colonel Deuan, thus formalizing the split between the two factions. Kong-Le also may well have been behind the transfer of one of Ketsana's soldiers to guard duty at the home of the Foreign Minister. Two days after the King and cabinet ended a lengthy tour of all countries which had signed the Geneva Agreements, that soldier shot and killed Quinim as the Foreign Minister was returning to his home. His escape was aided by a neutralist officer, who came by immediately after the assassination and drove him to the airport.[30]

By the end of March, Kong-Le had broken with the Pathet Lao, whom he denounced as "foreign lackeys" who were trying to make Laos "a new kind of colony of international communism." He blamed the North Vietnamese for subverting some of his soldiers with propaganda and for infiltrating men and equipment.[31] Fighting broke out the following day, March 13, between his men and Colonel Deuan's. Clashes grew more frequent during early April. Souvanna Phouma tried to engineer a cease-fire and, failing that, tried to authorize an ICC inspection of the area on April 8. That same day, Souphanouvong flew to Khang Khay, both because he objected to use of the ICC and because he no longer considered himself safe in Vientiane. He remembered his arrest in 1959. On April 12, the head of the

Vientiane police force, a man aligned to Quinim's faction, was assassinated. The second of four Pathet Lao cabinet ministers left Vientiane on April 19, 1963, thus marking the effective end of the coalition cabinet.[32]

There is no evidence that Americans were active in these final stages of the coalition. Although they had favored resistance to Pathet Lao demands, they had little reason to want renewed fighting or a clear break from the Geneva settlement. Soon afterward, however, they responded vigorously in supplying Kong-Le's forces.

Souvanna must have turned to the Americans reluctantly. He tried at first to get the ICC to investigate and act, but with only partial success. He negotiated a cease-fire on April 12, only to have fighting break out four hours later. Continued pressure on the neutralist army, his only power base, eventually forced him to ask the Americans for increased aid.

The tripartite International Commission for Supervision and Control in Laos (ICC), reconstituted by the 1962 accords, was as ineffective after 1962 as its predecessor had been between 1954 and 1958. Denied fixed inspection teams and rarely able to get unanimity for an investigation of alleged violations of the agreements, the ICC had no significant influence on the course of events in Laos. The United States made ritual defenses of the Commission, but did not devote much diplomatic energy to its reinvigoration.

Supervision and control were impossible without agreement and cooperation among the parties to the agreements, and the ICC could not compel such behavior. The only function served by the Commission was a propaganda one: to provide authoritative proof that the other side had broken the agreements. The inspection function, at least for the United States, was performed by aerial reconnaissance flights. At best, the existence of the ICC served only to mitigate flagrant violations of the agreements.[33]

The missing ingredient in the political struggle was the Soviet Union. Having stopped their airlift and rechanneled their aid through Hanoi, the Russians lacked close, daily involvement in Laos. Nor did they use their position as a Cochairman of the Geneva Conference to press for adherence to the accords.

Why the Russians lost interest in Laos is unclear. One plausible explanation is that they were preoccupied with much more important matters, for the autumn of 1962 saw the Cuban missile crisis and the Sino-Indian border war. Laos could have seemed insignificant by comparison.

What *was* obvious was the widening rift between the Soviet Union and China. The esoteric ideological debates had been going on since the mid-1950s. Khrushchev's denunciation of the Albanians at the Twenty-Second Party Congress in November 1961 brought the clash into the open. By early 1963, the Russians and Chinese were publishing inflammatory polemics, and other Communist parties were taking sides.

As late as February 1963, the North Vietnamese remained neutral, trying to play a mediating role. On March 13, however, Lao Dong Party Secretary-General Le Duan gave an important speech which generally supported the Chinese side in the dispute. Relations between the two countries were further strengthened by Chief of State Liu Shao-ch'i's visit to Hanoi in May. In the following months, Hanoi party publications stressed the Chinese argument that armed struggle was superior to peaceful revolution. When the nuclear test ban treaty was negotiated in Moscow in July, the North Vietnamese joined the Chinese in refusing to sign.[34]

By reducing its support in the continuing struggle against the Americans, the Soviet Union lost influence over the North Vietnamese and, consequently, over the Pathet Lao. Khrushchev no longer seemed interested in Laos when Averell Harriman, newly named Under Secretary of State, visited him in April 1963. Harriman had been sent by President Kennedy to remind the Soviet Union of its pledge to insure the compliance of the Communist nations with the Geneva Accords. The Soviet leader indicated that he no longer could restrain the pro-Communist forces in Laos, and would not try to do so. He gave Harriman only a general reaffirmation of Soviet support for the 1962 agreements.[35] Not until the ouster of Khrushchev and the American escalation of the war in Vietnam did the Soviet Union resume active involvement in Southeast Asia.

American officials were surprised and dismayed at the Soviet reluctance to play a major role in preserving the Laos settlement. President Kennedy seemed to consider the agreement as much a personal one between himself and the Soviet Premier as a formal international obligation. Secretary Rusk viewed Laos as a test of Communist willingness to keep agreements. The feeling was widespread in the State Department that, with the Laos problem pushed to a back burner, the United States could turn to what was considered the more important "manageable mess" in Vietnam.[36]

Laos was no longer central, one high-ranking official observed, because American action there required no strategic change in policy; nor could events there cause any such strategic change in policy. In other words, basic American policy had been decided and was expected to be maintained. Washington was inclined to let Leonard Unger, Ambassador 1962–64, take the lead in proposing policy actions.[37] One can discern, however, two phases in that policy before it became "the wart on the hog of Vietnam."

At first the emphasis of American policy makers was on the legal provisions of the Geneva Agreements and on the ICC as the instrument for enforcement. Although the men in Washington were assured of the presence of North Vietnamese cadres in Laos, U.S. diplomats were slow to call their presence a deliberate violation of the accords. In February 1963, Secretary Rusk put the point negatively: "we are not convinced that the agreements are being loyally supported by the Pathet Lao and the regime in Hanoi."[38] Only when fighting in April threatened Kong-Le's foothold on the Plaine des Jarres did the United States charge "a serious violation of the ceasefire" which endangered the implementation of the agreements. Even then, the United States called only for "prompt and effective action" by the cochairmen (U.K. and U.S.S.R.) and the ICC.[39]

President Kennedy sent Averell Harriman to Moscow, but he also sent the Seventh Fleet into the South China Sea and approved plans for 3,000 U.S. troops to take part in SEATO maneuvers in Thailand in May. The President's reluctance to risk deeper involvement contrasted sharply with the reaction of Thai officials, who expressed pessimism over any enduring settlements in Laos and feared an early Communist triumph there. White House sources consistently denied plans to send in ground forces and stressed instead the search for a new diplomatic approach to the Soviet Union. U.S. officials expressed pleasure when the fighting tapered off at the end of April and when the cochairmen issued a joint call for a cease-fire in May.[40]

Following this initial phase of relying on the ICC and external powers to preserve the settlement in Laos, the United States shifted its efforts to the forces within Laos. American planes increased their airdrops of weapons and supplies. In June the President decided to send six T-28 planes to Laos to replace the older T-6 aircraft supplied in 1961.[41]

This military assistance was given at the request of Souvanna Phouma. He must have asked both the Russians and Americans for help, because the Soviet Union turned over two transport planes to him in June, following the withdrawal of the last Soviet pilots and technicians at the end of May. Souvanna himself about this time seems to have become convinced—or persuaded—of North Vietnamese unwillingness to abide by the Geneva Agreements. He later said that he had made an agreement with Hanoi in 1962 not to reveal that North Vietnamese troops were operating in Laos, in return for a promise that they would be withdrawn after Geneva. By May 1963, the evidence of North Vietnamese involvement was substantial. Observers on the Plaine des Jarres overheard Vietnamese voices on field radios directing guns at neutralist positions. On June 6, Souvanna, for the first time, accused the Pathet Lao of using weapons and soldiers from North Vietnam. On June 24 he terminated military budget funds to the Pathet Lao.[42]

Monsoons had descended on Laos by then, as they did every year from May through October. Souvanna continued sporadic negotiations with Souphanouvong but reached no definite or lasting agreement. British, Soviet, and ICC representatives also shuttled between Vientiane and Khang Khay, the

Pathet Lao headquarters, in an elusive search for a settlement. Intermittent shelling continued during and after the monsoons, but neither side made a major drive to capture territory until January 1964, when pro-Communist forces launched a probe toward Thakhek in south central Laos. Fighting broke out throughout the country during the subsequent months.

Changed circumstances elsewhere brought Laos deeper into the Indochina war. On November 1, a coup in Saigon had ended the reign and the life of Ngo Dinh Diem. The new leaders, given their broader domestic popularity, seemed more likely to press the war against the Communists. In the short run, however, the situation in South Vietnam continued to deteriorate. Ambassador Henry Cabot Lodge returned to Washington for consultations. Because of another assassination, Lodge had to make his presentation to a man who had been President barely forty-eight hours.

Lyndon Johnson was new to his office and to the complexities of foreign affairs, but he had already formulated firm ideas on American policy toward Southeast Asia. President Kennedy had sent him on a journey there in the spring of 1961. He returned shocked by Thailand's criticism of America's half-hearted support of the anti-Communists in Laos. He concluded that Southeast Asia was a crucial battleground in the struggle against communism, and that the United States had to live up to its treaty commitments and stand by its friends or else risk seeing "the vast Pacific" become "a Red Sea." When Ambassador Lodge offered his pessimistic view of the situation and of the hard decisions ahead, the new President stated his attitude clearly: "I am not going to lose South Vietnam. I am not going to be the President who saw Southeast Asia go the way China went."[43]

The new militancy—or perhaps desperation—about Vietnam made American policy makers more receptive to suggestions for deeper involvement in Laos. Secretary McNamara reported in December 1963 that the situation was "very disturbing." The same month, someone proposed establishing a special air warfare unit in Thailand which would train the Royal Laotian Air Force in counterinsurgency tactics. The idea was approved by the State and Defense Departments and then suggested to Thailand. Following that nation's approval in February 1964, an American air commando training advisory team was deployed. The American training planes added to the pool of aircraft available for use in Laos.[44]

Already in March, the basis was being laid for more extensive military action. At the same time, General Phoumi Nosavan met with the South Vietnamese leader, General Khanh, and reportedly agreed to permit South Vietnamese troops to enter Laos in hot pursuit of enemy soldiers.[45]

Souvanna Phouma tried to maintain a relative peace. He journeyed to Hanoi and Peking, then theatened to resign unless the Geneva signatories fulfilled their obligations to preserve Laotian neutrality. In April he went to the Plaine des Jarres for another tripartite conference with General Phoumi and Souphanouvong. This turned out to be the last such meeting, and it ended in sharp dispute on plans for neutralization and demilitarization of Luang Prabang. Part of the difficulty also came from Phoumi's refusal to submit the plans to all of the rightists at once. The General's position was not as strong as in the past, for there had been rumors of plots against him by other rightists in recent months. In any event, the conference failed to reach an agreement. Souvanna flew back to Vientiane and announced, in tears, his intention to resign.[46]

The next day, April 19, 1964, Generals Kouprasith Abhay and Siho Lamphouthacoul arrested Souvanna and seized control of the government. Their action was apparently aimed less at Souvanna than at Phoumi Nosavan, whom they wanted to forestall from seizing power himself in the uncertainty likely to follow Souvanna's resignation. They were probably emboldened to move against Phoumi because the recent death of Marshal Sarit of Thailand had deprived him of close and attentive Thai support.[47]

The State Department learned of the coup and immediately issued a statement supporting Souvanna and the Government of National Union. To have supported the coup would have threatened to bring down the whole shaky structure established at Geneva.

The United States tied its policy to Souvanna Phouma primarily because of his seemingly indispensable qualities. Although he had a withering power base in the neutralist army, he was everyone's second choice as leader. He was the only prominent Laotian politician who had not totally alienated one of the major factions. He alone was held in high esteem by the French, Russians, and British—as well as by the Americans.

Key U.S. officials were also personally committed to Souvanna. President Kennedy had overridden protests from his military advisors in order to back the Laotian Prince. President Johnson lacked his predecessor's personal involvement with the Premier, but he took no steps to diminish U.S. support for him. Secretary Rusk was linked to Souvanna only through the Geneva accords. Under Secretary Harriman, however, had tied his prestige both to the Geneva settlement and to Souvanna as head of the government. The sense of commitment also extended throughout the Far Eastern Bureau of the State Department, by then largely void of holdovers from the inhospitable days of Robertson and Parsons, and throughout at least the political sections of the embassy in Vientiane. Pentagon officials were still cool to Souvanna, since they retained a fondness for Phoumi's politics in spite of doubts about his generalship.

Perhaps there was also a residual American hope that Souvanna could be the kind of strongman whom the United States seemed to favor in other Asian governments. That pattern was already clear: from Rhee to Park; from Diem to Minh to Khanh; from Phoui to Phoumi to Souvanna. A year before, U.S. officials reported urging the Prince to become more active and visible.[48]

The immediate American reaction to the coup, however, sprang from the belief that Souvanna was the only alternative to communism. In testimony which presumably reflected informed thinking within the State Department, the head of AID said on April 20: "If the civil war broke out again, it is certainly conceivable, perhaps it would be likely, that the Communists would just extend their domination over the whole country."[49]

Ambassador Leonard Unger, who had held that position

since July 1962, flew to Vientiane on the afternoon of April 19 and went at once to tell General Kouprasith of his opposition to the coup. Unger had been attending a meeting in Saigon with Secretary Rusk and Assistant Secretary William Bundy. President Johnson, on the same day, ordered Bundy to Laos to make U.S. support for Souvanna unmistakably clear. Bundy told congressmen two weeks later about his efforts:

> . . . we made it clear to the generals who had led the coup that we could sympathize with their frustrations about the failure of the International Control Commission to act effectively, and so on, but for them to upset the accords at this time was to take on a civil war which they could not handle. Frankly, it comes down to our introducing forces, if you talk in terms of a civil war, or else you lose territory in large doses to the Communists.[50]

This testimony suggests that the United States had shifted from reliance on the Geneva Agreements to reliance on Souvanna. It also shows that there was some sympathy in Washington, presumably in the Pentagon, for a right-wing government. Officials told Max Frankel of the *New York Times* on April 20 that Ambassador Unger would give the coup leaders an implied warning about American aid, but would use such threats cautiously because the right-wing forces offered "the only hope for sturdy resistance" in Laos.[51]

On April 23 the coup leaders announced that "in consideration of external policy" they were calling on Souvanna to reinstate his coalition government. They also demanded some enlargement and reorganization of the cabinet. In fact, the Generals delayed returning full power to the civilian authorities until Souvanna had placed about eighty junior officers in positions to implement their desired reforms, most of which strengthened their military faction vis-à-vis General Phoumi Nosavan.[52]

Souvanna then tried in vain to reestablish the coalition. Pressed by the military to make major changes, he announced on May 2 that he had merged the neutralist and rightist factions and would henceforth lead both. This change, as well as others which came in the wake of the coup, was unacceptable to the Pathet Lao. They had already anticipated the rightward trend in Vientiane and had launched a new offensive at the end of April. By May 16 they had succeeded in driving Kong-Le's forces off the Plaine des Jarres.

Men in the State Department believed that the Pathet Lao, assisted by the North Vietnamese, intended to break through the tacit lines of demarcation and destroy the neutralists. The American Ambassador to the United Nations, Adlai Stevenson, gave this assessment to the UN Security Council on May 21:

> These violations are obviously aimed at increasing the amount of Lao territory under Communist control . . . [and] must be seen as an outright attempt to destroy by violence what the whole structure of the Geneva Accords was intended to preserve.[53]

Despite this clear consensus in Washington, the evidence in Laos was much more ambiguous. Western sources said that the Pathet Lao already controlled two-thirds of the countryside, with North Vietnamese battalions stretched along the supply routes to South Vietnam. Since the neutralists had not initiated any major drive against the Pathet Lao, the Communists had little obvious incentive to attack them. South of the Plaine, however, rightist troops had for months been conducting operations aimed at severing some of the trails to the South. Meo tribesmen had also been harassing the North Vietnamese in the border areas. The initial Pathet Lao attacks at the end of April struck the Meo especially, driving thousands of refugees into rightist territory.[54]

Only in mid-May did the Pathet Lao begin their effort which drove Kong-Le's neutralist troops from the Plaine des Jarres. And the political events which had just occurred in Vientiane could certainly not have been viewed with equanimity in Khang Khay or Hanoi. On May 2, Souvanna Phouma announced that the neutralist and rightist factions had merged under his leadership. The following day he explained his political and administrative changes to Souphanouvong, who demanded a return to tripartite government.

Although Souvanna later emerged as the undisputed leader of the non-Communist factions, he was not so clearly in command in early May. The coup leaders still retained effective control over important policy. When the plans for merging the neutralist and Royal armies were announced on May 13, they appeared to presage the complete subordination of the neutralists. Kong-Le was not even included in the high command. Souvanna flew to the neutralist headquarters the next day in order to try to calm the army officers there. Nevertheless, several hundred neutralist troops defected to the Pathet Lao.[55]

Under these circumstances, it should not have been surprising that the Pathet Lao perceived the recent political events as evidence of a swing to the right. In fact, as seen by the Pathet Lao, the coalition was dead. Souvanna had lost his neutrality by merging with the right, as had the remnants of the neutralist army. To this day, Pathet Lao documents trace the collapse of the coalition to April 1964.

Before tracing the sequence of decisions by which the United States began its secret war in Laos, it may prove useful to have in mind the development of American policy in Vietnam which was taking place at the same time. In fact, the argument here is that by 1964 U.S. decisions relating to Laos were part and parcel of the emerging American strategy for preventing the collapse of South Vietnam.

President Johnson found his subordinates divided on what to do in Vietnam. During 1963, men in the Pentagon and CIA tended to favor increased conventional military activities, including low-level reconnaissance over Laos and various military pressures against North Vietnam. Some State Department officials, led by Assistant Secretary for the Far East Roger Hilsman, urged more vigorous counterinsurgency efforts and pressures on the Saigon regime for political reforms. Hilsman, who had replaced Harriman in April 1963, had an abrasive and aggressive personality. In January 1964 he was encouraged to resign.[56]

Secretary McNamara traveled to Vietnam in December 1963 and returned to tell the new President of the deteriorating military situation. Ruling out cross-border operations into Laos as politically unacceptable and probably militarily ineffective, the Defense Secretary urged instead high-altitude mapping of the border areas and expansion of the intelligence teams put into the corridor under Operation Hardnose.[57]

At about the same time, President Johnson named an interdepartmental committee to handle management of all Vietnam planning and activities at the working level. This move was designed specifically to bypass Hilsman and make a consensus easier to achieve. When Hilsman left, the committee was formally designated the Vietnam Working Group, and its reports rechanneled through the Far East Bureau. The Chairman was Harriman's protégé from the Geneva Conference, William Sullivan.[58]

While this Group conducted an intensive review of U.S. policy and strategy in Southeast Asia, pressure for quick action came from the military. Arguing the domino theory, the Joint Chiefs urged McNamara in January to remove restrictions and take bolder actions for victory. The President approved only increased harassment measures against North Vietnam, under what was called Operations Plan 34A, which began in February 1964.[59]

There was a consensus among officials that a Communist takeover in South Vietnam was still unacceptable. The only questions which really confronted top policy makers were the specific means to be used to forestall such a loss. Recommendations from the Sullivan Group came before the National Security Council on March 17. The President steered a middle course between overt military pressure on North Vietnam and any acceptance of neutralization for the country. He approved continued intelligence-gathering operations and preparations for launching border control actions within seventy-two hours of a decision. Preparation of plans for systematic, gradually increasing military pressures against North Vietnam within thirty days of a decision were also ordered.[60]

While these plans were being developed, the sense of urgency diminished. The President had delayed any major changes in Indochina policy pending some major military reversal in the field. That reversal came first in Laos rather than Vietnam, but it set the stage for the next escalation in U.S. involvement.

As discussed earlier, the collapse of the tripartite talks and April 19 coup attempt in Vientiane stimulated a major Pathet Lao attack on Kong-Le's forces. By May 17 Washington knew that Kong-Le had been driven from his headquarters at Muong Phanh. What had been a deliberate and cautious approach was set aside in order to prevent further deterioration of the situation.

The new crisis resembled the May crises of 1962 and 1963 in many aspects. Once again the President ordered a troop alert on Okinawa and preparations by the Seventh Fleet, already in the South China Sea, for military action. Some officials told newspaper reporters that the time for subtle hints and diplomatic maneuvers had passed, making some direct use of American force inevitable.[61]

Linkage of Laos with Vietnam was implicit in the thinking of policy makers and explicit in their plans for congressional action. The draft of a joint resolution, roughly similar to one proposed and adopted after the Gulf of Tonkin incident in August, declared the independence and integrity of both Laos and South Vietnam vital to the U.S. national interest and world peace. The draft went on to assert American willingness to use all measures upon the request of the governments in Saigon or Vientiane.[62]

Responding to the immediate pressures in Laos, the President approved a series of recommendations from Ambassador Unger for military support. Low-level reconnaissance began over southern Laos on May 19 and over the Plaine des Jarres and northern Laos two days later. Souvanna Phouma was consulted about the flights in advance and gave his approval. The President also decided to release bomb fuses to the Laotian Air Force in order to make operational bombs which had been delivered earlier. In addition, the United States began sending enough additional T-28s to triple the size of the air force.[63]

While these actions were soon made public, other air activities were not. So long as American planes were to be kept out of direct participation in combat, military planners thought it necessary to increase bombing by the T-28s. Since the supply of Laotian pilots was insufficient, civilians associated with Air America and Thai pilots were put into small planes, all of which carried Laotian Air Force markings, although only some actually belonged to the Royal Government. These planes intensified their air strikes as Kong-Le's forces fell back. Within a few weeks, U.S. planes joined the effort by conducting troop transport operations and nighttime reconnaissance in preparation for a counteroffensive.[64]

Reconnaissance jets, called Yankee Team, met with enemy ground fire. This prompted a request and a decision for "armed reconnaissance" flights, which included fighter escorts for the U.S. planes. The downing of jets on June 6 and 7 made the flights open knowledge in the United States and led to admitted retaliatory attacks against Pathet Lao gun positions. Flying in poor weather, the planes apparently hit the wrong target; another mission was sent to bomb the intended installation. Thus, two raids occurred in spite of the President's reported determination to hit only one gun emplacement in tit-for-tat retaliation.[65]

Souvanna Phouma threatened to resign if the flights did not cease, presumably because he was embarrassed over the disclosure of U.S. participation. He reportedly argued that if armed reconnaissance were necessary, the Laotian Air Force should provide it. On June 10 the United States announced the suspension of the flights for "at least two days." Ambassador Unger conferred with Souvanna and persuaded him to allow the flights to continue. One of Unger's strongest arguments, presumably, was a threat to reduce the U.S. assistance on which Laos now depended. Souvanna wanted help for his forces in the north and thus could not easily oppose U.S. demands for flights which assisted the fight in Vietnam. On June 11 the State Department announced that reconnaissance flights would continue "as necessary," but that operational aspects would not be discussed. In other words, the United States did not want to embarrass Souvanna by making the military actions public. For the next six years, all U.S. air operations in Laos would be officially described as reconnaissance flights, both to protect Souvanna and to keep from destroying the façade of American adherence to the Geneva Accords once and for all.[66]

Despite an American effort to keep a tight rein on the activities which threatened to undermine the 1962 settlement, control over military operations was far from complete. Not only had two raids been conducted after one had been authorized, but the announced suspension of flights was not coordinated with the Laotian Air Force. On June 11 Thai pilots bombed the Pathet Lao headquarters at Khang Khay, destroying the Chinese mission there and killing one civilian.[67] In early August 1964, some T-28s hit villages across the border in North Vietnam, contrary to orders. By the end of August, Secretary Rusk was concerned enough about the independent actions of the Lao Air Force that he cabled Vientiane his "impression" that the local pilots were "not really under any kind of firm control."[68]

Policy in Washington was tightly controlled and carefully orchestrated to arouse American public opinion and convey the U.S. government's sense of urgency about the situation in Indochina. By mid-June the consensus of U.S. policy makers seemed to be that the United States was on the brink of war with China and North Vietnam. Secretary Rusk told reporters that the American commitment to the security of Southeast Asia was now unlimited and comparable to the commitment to West Berlin. He said that the United States was prepared to act with or without its allies, if China and North Vietnam did not leave their neighbors alone. With regard to Laos, Rusk said that the United States wanted full compliance with the Geneva Accords, including a coalition government, an effective ICC, withdrawal of North Vietnamese troops, and an end to the use of a Laotian corridor to move supplies into South Vietnam. Indicating the linkage between the two conflicts, he said that Laos could no longer be handled separately.

Another unnamed official said in a background interview that the United States had adopted a "thus-far-and-no-farther" attitude in Laos and was determined to "rollback" the territorial gains made by the Pathet Lao in May.[69]

The basic consensus had been reached which led inexorably to further military escalation, first in Laos and later in Vietnam. The following months saw the further steps in escalation. Thailand became more deeply involved, providing both bases from which reconnaissance and rescue missions could be launched and pilots for the Laotian Air Force. War materials were stockpiled in Korat. Between March and August of 1964, the number of F-100s based at Takhli grew from six to eighteen. By the end of the year, seventy-five U.S. aircraft were based there to assist operations in Laos.[70]

Rules of engagement changed for the U.S. pilots. At first, they could fire only when fired upon. But by summer 1964, they were allowed to hit targets of opportunity. Americans also provided airlift of Laotian troops and supplies into combat areas, but the Air America planes were technically civilian-owned and under contract to AID.[71]

To help Souvanna and Kong-Le recoup some of their losses in May, Americans helped to plan and assist a ground operation to clear the junction of the road from the Plaine des Jarres with the road between Vientiane and Luang Prabang. Operation Triangle (or Three Arrows) was Lao-inspired but dependent on crucial American support. A handful of U.S. Army personnel were brought in to accompany and advise the Laotian regiments. Other Americans functioned as ground controllers for U.S. air strikes. The operation was successful, and many of the Americans were subsequently withdrawn.[72]

Action against the North Vietnamese supply effort through Laos into South Vietnam was repeatedly urged by U.S. military planners. They drew attention to the large supply center at Tchepone on Route 9 and complained about the "privileged sanctuary" accorded the place. They proposed either bombing Tchepone and Route 9 or putting U.S. troops into Laos to form a shield against the movement of supplies to the

South.* Failing that, they wanted at least increased aggressiveness on the part of the South Vietnamese, since they thought that the teams infiltrated into Laos were simply waiting a respectable amount of time before returning to their homeland.[73]

Ground operations were planned but not carried out. One reason for the planning was simply to boost the morale of the South Vietnamese, who had been pressing since spring for a march to the North.[74] Meanwhile, guerrilla teams were being infiltrated into North Vietnam and commando raids were launched along the coast. These activities probably provoked the North Vietnamese naval action in the Gulf of Tonkin on August 2.[75]

President Johnson seized the opportunity provided by the Tonkin incident to win rapid congressional approval of a far-reaching joint resolution approving "all measures necessary to repel any armed attack against the forces of the United States and to prevent further aggression."[76]

He ordered a halt to continued clandestine activities under Operations Plan 34A, as well as U-2 reconnaissance flights over North Vietnam, pending a reassessment of policy.[77]

Military men wanted a continuation and expansion of pressure against the North Vietnamese. The Joint Chiefs praised the military actions in Laos and North Vietnam and warned that a failure to continue them might be misinterpreted by the enemy as a lack of resolve by the United States. They urged, among other things, interdiction efforts in the Laotian panhandle.[78]

Diplomats in Washington and Saigon wanted to maintain freedom of action in the panhandle. They apparently feared that Souvanna, off to Paris for another try at talks with Souphanouvong, might reach a settlement which denied such discretion for the United States. Even a cease-fire in Laos was not considered compatible with U.S. interests.[79] Souvanna Phouma took a relatively hard line with his half-brother, so the talks got nowhere.

* This same plan was advanced regularly during subsequent years, until it was finally put into operation by South Vietnamese units with American air support in February 1971.

President Johnson gave the green light to the next stage of escalation of the war on September 10. Although pressed by his top advisors to approve limited South Vietnamese air and ground operations into the panhandle, he approved only discussion of such plans with the Laotian government, as well as a resumption of covert activities and naval patrols against North Vietnam. The memorandum recording Johnson's decision expressed doubt that ground operations would have more than a limited effect.[80]

Ambassador Unger came under strong pressure from all sides to agree to the South Vietnamese ground and air operations, but he resisted. He argued that Souvanna Phouma's position would be threatened by South Vietnamese air strikes and the whole Geneva settlement might be destroyed by ground operations. The American Ambassadors to Saigon, Vientiane, and Bangkok agreed on September 11 that success of such attacks would depend on authorization for U.S. advisors to accompany the invading troops. Subsequent to that meeting, Unger said that ground incursions by company-sized units up to twenty kilometers would be acceptable, but that Souvanna would not be told of them.[81]

In view of the Laotian opposition to actions by the Americans and South Vietnamese in the panhandle, the United States pressed Souvanna to let the T-28s do the job. A cable to this effect on October 6 specifically ruled out, for the time being, any suppressive fire attacks, although these were said to be anticipated later. The same cable reported that cross-border operations had not yet been authorized.[82]

Souvanna accepted the plan but pressed for and received combat air patrol missions to protect against MiGs and to raise the morale of the Laotian pilots. U.S. officials deny any quid pro quo for these cover flights, despite the obvious balancing of this panhandle bombing with increased efforts in northern Laos.[83]

Once the election was over, Lyndon Johnson turned his attention to the still-deteriorating situation in Indochina. Pressure was building for bombing of North Vietnam from almost all of his advisors. On December 1 the President approved plans for an aerial interdiction campaign in Laos and readiness for one in Vietnam. The Laotian bombing had not been very successful in strategic terms, principally because the Laotians could put only fifteen aircraft aloft for a mission, each with a maximum load of only 500 pounds. The pilots were semiskilled and capable of flying only by day. As a result, Americans in the field argued, the Communists had shifted their activities to nighttime. To overcome these obstacles, the Americans wanted to begin their own strikes.[84]

Souvanna agreed to the U.S. proposal on December 10. A National Security Council meeting two days later approved final details for what was called Operation Barrel Roll, including a determination that no public statements on operations would be made unless a plane was lost, in which case the United States would insist that its planes were merely escorting reconnaissance flights as requested by the Laotian government. The bombing began on December 14, first in northern Laos and a few weeks later along the Ho Chi Minh trails.[85]

Bombing in Laos may have seemed preferable to bombing the North directly, at least in 1964. Since an important argument for initiating the air strikes in May had been that they would demonstrate American determination to stand and fight in Asia, the risks could be minimized by making that demonstration in Laos, where public attention was much more limited. One writer quotes a State Department official deeply involved with Laos policy at that time:

> I think that the President was privately relieved that he could take such a momentous first step somewhere other than in Vietnam. . . . By late spring we had decided it would take some bullets and bombs, and not just words, to impress upon the North Vietnamese the fact that we weren't going to run. Since they had to be fired, Johnson thought it best that it be off in the woods where it would escape notice.[86]

Evidence available to the policy makers in Washington suggested that the bombing was a success. It had not stopped the flow of supplies, but that was blamed more on the primitive

Lao airplanes than on the efficacy of bombing in a jungle environment. More significantly, bombing had won some supporters from the ranks of previous opponents. Denis Warner quotes an unidentified source in Laos:

> I opposed the use of the T-28s. I thought they would aggravate rather than help. I was wrong. Especially in the region of Route 7 leading to the Plaine des Jarres, they have thrown complete confusion into the ranks of the Pathet Lao and Vietminh.[87]

The most important effect of the bombing was psychological. It lifted the spirits of the pro-American forces which had been driven from some of their former strongholds.[88] Although arguments citing the Laotian experience were not prominent in the debate prior to the commencement of bombing against North Vietnam, it is probably significant that the negative evidence on the technical efficacy of bombing was far outweighed by the positive psychological benefits. Boosting the morale of the South Vietnamese was a major purpose of the subsequent full-scale bombing of North Vietnam.[89]

Bombing had become an accepted tactic by the end of 1964. U.S. policy makers consequently found it reasonable to approve a shift from jungle trails to initial staging points in North Vietnam. Indeed, air force representatives pleaded for the chance to get at hard targets.[90] Administration officials had reached a consensus on the need for extending the war; only the right moment was left to be found.

These escalatory decisions appear to have been made without much disagreement in Washington. Military planners urged continued actions in Laos as well as new steps against North Vietnam. Diplomats tried to keep Laos a separate issue so that they could resist pressures to neutralize and therefore "lose" South Vietnam. The U.S. Embassy in Vientiane welcomed American military assistance but fought to keep it within limits. As the new and wider war flared in Vietnam, the war in Laos slipped into deliberate obscurity.

The secret war in Laos was William Sullivan's war. He

was Ambassador for over four years, from December 1964 until March 1969. During that time, he ran an efficient, closely controlled country team. "There wasn't a bag of rice dropped in Laos that he didn't know about," says Sullivan's superior in Washington, Assistant Secretary William Bundy.[91]

Sullivan tried to impose two crucial conditions on American actions in Laos during his tenure. One was that the war was to be carried out in relative secrecy so as to avoid embarrassing Souvanna Phouma or the Russians. The second was that no regular U.S. ground combat troops were to be allowed to operate in Laos. Intelligence patrols and some hot pursuits were permitted, but no U.S. Army units for sustained operations.

To an important extent, Sullivan succeeded in maintaining secrecy. Revelations about U.S. involvement shocked and surprised many members of Congress in 1969 and 1970. Senator J. W. Fulbright commented during the hearings on Laos, "I have never seen a country engage in so many devious undertakings as this."[92] But American ground troops did not move in and take over the war the way they had done in South Vietnam. Only a few thousand Americans, at most, contributed directly to the fighting in Laos.

Despite these achievements, the war was not as secret or as limited as U.S. officials might have hoped. A careful researcher could find ample, though uncorroborated, evidence of the size and scope of American involvement in the fighting. Now that many allegations have been confirmed, one can observe the completeness of the story which was available before the conscious revelations beginning in 1969.

To say, as U.S. officials have said repeatedly, "There are no American ground combat forces in Laos," is true, but misleading. As in every modern army, most soldiers do not fight the enemy directly. But they draw the plans, operate the radios, fuel the aircraft, direct the bombers, repair the equipment, move the supplies, and give advice (which may be tantamount to orders) to the men who do fight. American planes, with American pilots, drop bombs on roads, bridges, trucks, villages, and Pathet Lao and North Vietnamese troops. U.S.

planes and helicopters are shot at and shoot back. On the ground, American officers and civilians (many of whom were formerly in uniform in Vietnam) work with Laotian soldiers in their base camps. The Americans fight when attacked, and several dozen have admittedly been killed. For this work, they have received "hostile fire" pay supplements since January 1966. In the ordinary meaning of the term, they are at war.[93]

American participation has been limited in numbers but not in ferocity. Total bomb tonnage dropped on Laos reached staggering proportions, making that small country one of the most heavily bombed areas in history.[94] One Foreign Service Officer quietly expressed pride in what the conflict in Laos had demonstrated—a way of maintaining a level of violence so as to keep from losing, a model for future wars fully in keeping with the Nixon Doctrine and Vietnamization. "The Lao have shown us a new way of fighting a war," he said.[95]

This secret war was really four wars, administratively distinct and only partially coordinated. One was the conflict fought by the Royal Army (the FAR), which was generally limited to the areas surrounding the principal towns. Another was the vigorous, deadly war for survival by the Meos under the close supervision and support of the CIA. Third was the air war in northern Laos, under the code name of Barrel Roll, at first shared with the Laotian Air Force, but gradually dominated by the Americans. Fourth was the air war in the southern panhandle of Laos, under the code name of Steel Tiger, along the Ho Chi Minh trails to South Vietnam; this war was a direct adjunct to the struggle in that neighboring nation.

The Ambassador had access to information about these military operations and a veto over certain plans. Remembering the malcoordination of the late 1950s, Sullivan deliberately tried to achieve a unity of purpose in the country team. Each day he held a meeting of the chiefs of the component elements of the U.S. mission at which they could discuss their common problems and future plans. These meetings seem to have been generally successful in preventing the chaos and conflict of the past. When debates arose, the Ambassador made the final decision and made it stick.[96]

No one could end run Sullivan because of his peculiar strength in Washington. Having worked closely on Laos and Vietnam at the highest levels, he knew most of the key people in Washington—and they knew and trusted him. His subordinates in Laos knew that he was likely to have more influence with their bosses than they were, because of his established relationship with them. Thus Sullivan was able to exert strong and tight control over his country team.[97]

Ground warfare had a seasonal nature to it that made planning both possible and easy. Monsoons last from May through October, severely limiting ground mobility. Roads are usually dry by sometime in November. December is set aside for harvesting. The Pathet Lao make their greatest gains in dry-season offensives, when they have maximum mobility. Royalist forces, assisted by U.S. bombing and air mobility, have been most active during the rainy season.[98]

Each year the country team would draw upon intelligence sources to estimate the level and locus of forthcoming enemy activity during the dry season. They would also estimate the likely counterattack and the consequent need for airlift, air support, and refugee relief. These prognoses were claimed to be fairly accurate until early in 1968 during the prelude to the Tet offensive in South Vietnam.[99]

U.S. military attachés worked with the FAR. Although they would have liked to stimulate them to undertake more frequent operations, they found themselves hampered. They were not even allowed to train the Lao in-country. Instead, training was conducted across the border in Thailand or sometimes in the Philippines or the United States. Once trained, the soldiers were subject to their Lao commanders' lethargy. The Americans tried to encourage greater activity. When the Lao complied, one observer reports, it was in recognition of the truth: "no boom-boom, no rice."[100]

The FAR grew modestly, from about 48,000 in 1964 to about 60,000 in 1972. Units were said to be roughly equally distributed among the five military regions. The local commanders are reportedly jealous and extremely resistant to attempts at civilian interference with them. Each commander has powerful ties with a leading local family and its source of wealth. In effect, he is a modest warlord.[101]

Except in Military Region 2, commanded by General Vang Pao, the FAR units were under their own control. They did launch major operations in the years after 1964, but only with modest success.

The bulk of the fighting in recent years has been by the secret army of irregulars under Vang Pao's command and with CIA tutelage as well as U.S. logistical and air support. The Meo and other hill tribes were much more vigorous fighters than the lowland Lao since their own homelands were directly threatened and contested. From about 5,000 in 1961 and 11,000 in 1962, this secret army grew to 40,000 in 1969, of whom only about 15,000 were considered full-time soldiers. Heavy losses in recent years have cut the army to 30,000 but it has reportedly been augmented by up to 12,000 Thai troops.[102]

The war in the North was multi-faceted, with regular ground operations, guerrilla harassment, intelligence patrols, and refugee relief. In addition to air strips and refugee centers, the Americans also built special aerial navigation facilities for use over both Laos and North Vietnam. The most important of these, located on a mountain only seventeen miles from the North Vietnamese border, functioned from at least 1966 until its capture in March 1968.[103]

Center for the Meo-CIA operations was a base at Long Tieng (also spelled Long Cheng), southwest of the Plaine des Jarres. This base was supposedly secret and off-limits to outsiders. Virtually uninhabited in 1961, Long Tieng by the late 1960s had grown into the second largest city in Laos, with a population of 40,000. Journalists making an unannounced and unauthorized visit in 1970 discovered American transport planes, short-take-off and landing (STOL) planes, reconnaissance planes, and rescue helicopters in addition to Laotian T-28s. They clocked one American take-off or landing every minute during an hour's stay.[104]

Air operations over the North comprise the third war in Laos. As the Long Tieng installation suggests, however, this aspect of the fighting was closely coordinated with the Clandestine Army's ground war in the North. Within Laos, there were only reconnaissance, supply, and rescue aircraft under the immediate command of Americans. The Laotian Air Force was relatively free to use its small planes to bomb where it liked. Air support consequently had come from Thailand, particularly from the 7/13th Air Force based at Udorn.

Bringing another bureaucracy into the picture caused additional coordination problems. The 7/13th was under the command of the 7th Air Force in Saigon, where the priorities were set. Although the embassy in Vientiane made regular requests for certain sortie levels over Laos, the 7/13th could make no promises in advance. Tactical requirements in Vietnam might force diversions from the less important Laotian targets.[105]

The U.S. Air Force also ran the fourth war, along the Ho Chi Minh trails in the southern panhandle of Laos. Although the embassy imposed some restrictions on targets, much of the region was written off as enemy territory. Pilots were permitted to strike anything east of a certain line. Their missions were usually attacks on fixed choke points or armed route reconnaissance, a term for operations in search of trucks and troop formations.[106]

CIA personnel played the key operational role in Laos and were subject only to control by the Ambassador. Such control contrasted with earlier periods in Laos, but it did not significantly reduce their influence over the whole range of local events. In other countries, the CIA is largely confined to an intelligence-gathering role. In Laos, it not only gathered the information, but then recommended and implemented policies based on it. CIA personnel advised the Clandestine Army and helped decide on targeting for the air war in the North. They also had sole control of intelligence from enemy zones. Their involvement in the full spectrum of the Laotian government came from their role as the primary intermediaries between American and Laotian counterparts.[107]

Over time, CIA power grew with its operational responsibilities. The influence of the military attachés declined as civilians took over the planning of the war. The political section of the embassy lost power as military operations over-shadowed diplomatic ones. Even AID personnel saw much of their budget siphoned off by the CIA-run Requirements Office.

Ambassador Sullivan prevailed over the CIA in most disputes. There are reports, however, that he opposed the un-successful defense of Nam Bac in 1968 and that he later lost his check on bombing controls when some military personnel were transferred back to Thailand. On balance, Sullivan knew and controlled what happened in Laos. He is said to have ac-cepted CIA involvement as a compromise—the only way of forestalling an American ground troop presence. He also dis-counted the possibility of a military solution in Laos.[108]

Bombing was the most controversial U.S. activity in Laos. Although all operations were technically at the request of the Royal Government, such military operations clearly contravened the Geneva Accords. In an effort to minimize the political and physical damage done by the bombing, it was subjected to restraints and restrictions imposed by the Ambas-sador.

Working with the Lao, the CIA and U.S. Air Force developed targets. These were then brought to the embassy, where political criteria were applied. These criteria included the presence of civilians and nearness to sensitive areas such as China or the Chinese road-building crews. If the target was disapproved, there was no further appeal; if accepted, the re-quest would be transmitted to higher military authorities for execution.[109]

Disputes often arose over the presence of civilians. Under the rules of engagement, on which all Americans flying over Laos were tested, an active village was defined as any hut, village, or structure not validated for a strike. Validation re-quired confirming evidence that no one lived in the still-stand-ing buildings. The Ambassador's targeting officer frequently demanded recent aerial photos before validating a requested tar-get. Part of the difficulty came from the fact that villages nor-mally moved every five to seven years when they had exhausted one patch of land. Others fled from the nearby warfare. Al-though there were telltale signs when a place had been abandoned over one rainy season, only recent photographs could prove that no one had moved into a previously validated target area.

Besides outright rejection of a target, the embassy could also impose restrictions such as on the type of aircraft or the angle of attack. U.S. officials say that great pains were taken to avoid civilian casualties. They say that three-fourths of the sorties over northern Laos were in areas where there were no civilians and that most sorties were on route reconnaissance or against fixed choke points.[110] Critics of the bombing policy have cited widespread destruction of villages and surveys of refugees who witnessed and then fled from bombing of their villages.

The truth seems to be a mixture of the charges. Efforts to avoid civilian targets, however diligent or well-intentioned, ultimately were swamped by the increased level of U.S. bombing. Particularly since 1969, there has been a steady erosion of restraints and limitations. Larger areas have been designated for heavy B-52 attacks, making them, in effect, free-fire zones. The radius of the safety zone around civilian areas has reportedly been slashed from three kilometers in 1969 to two kilometers to only 500 yards by 1972.

Massive bomb tonnages and the predictable inaccuracies of bombing have produced widespread devastation and numerous civilian casualties. No mere handful of men could have been expected to doublecheck the escalating numbers of sortie requests. Nor were post attack reviews systematic or adequate, despite the increased controversy over civilian bombing.

One embassy official relied on his memory of coordinates to spot discrepancies between approved targets and those actually struck.

When errors and violations occurred, the offenders were rarely punished. The errors generally resulted from the difficulties involved in dropping bombs from high-speed aircraft on precisely the right mountain valley. Violations took place when eager pilots deliberately broke the rules of engagement or accepted validation from a Lao Forward Air Controller (FAC) contrary to instructions. The most severe punishment given was transfer out of Laos.

At first, air operations were few in number and often at the initial request of Laotian officials. The United States says that in 1964 there were only twenty strikes in northern Laos. In 1965 the figure was 4,568, which would average to only about fifteen per day. The following year the strikes totaled 7,316. Figures since then are still classified, but the trend line is known. In 1967 the level of bombing in the North was still comparatively light. It nearly doubled in 1968 and reached a peak in 1969 before dropping by about one-fourth in 1970.[111]

Once begun, air operations took on a life and momentum of their own. Propeller planes did most of the work until late in 1966. By then a major American base had been opened at Udorn, in north central Thailand south of Vientiane. The U.S. buildup throughout Thailand was substantial in 1966. Military construction was seven times the amount of the previous year, and by year's end the number of U.S. Air Force personnel had nearly tripled. Many of the additional men and aircraft saw service over Laos as well as Vietnam.[112]

The availability of additional planes, especially jets, led to a decision to introduce American Forward Air Controllers (FAC) in October 1966. Souvanna Phouma had not requested the FACs, only more assistance. Ambassador Sullivan later testified, "the form in which it was rendered, however, was a unilateral decision by the United States."[113] As U.S. air involvement increased, American needs took precedence over Laotian wishes.

Bombing was the main component of the fourth war in Laos, the one fought along the Ho Chi Minh trails into South Vietnam. By 1972 about 70 percent of all U.S. air strikes in Indochina were being flown against targets in Laos. Of these, over 80 percent were said to be in the region of the trails, including the bulk of B-52 flights. The number of sorties grew over time, from a daily average of fifty-five in 1965 to one hundred in 1967 and one hundred fifty in 1968. After the suspension of regular bombing of North Vietnam in November 1968, the strikes in Laos doubled. Despite these increases, the embassy retained and exercised targeting approval authority.[114]

Plans for an American ground invasion of southern

Laos were repeatedly drawn up and pushed forward. The American commander in Vietnam, General William Westmoreland, requested U.S. operations for reconnaissance and trail monitoring in September 1966 and for major ground action, primarily by the South Vietnamese. Despite the pressure for these operations and escalated bombing, Ambassador Sullivan kept saying no. As one U.S. official put it, "The biggest job Bill Sullivan had was to keep Westmoreland's paws off Laos."[115]

Sullivan feared the international ramifications of any overt repudiation of the Geneva Accords, particularly the reactions of China and Russia. Other Americans feared a coup against Souvanna, once he was no longer needed as a symbol of the 1962 coalition. The entire country team was in general agreement in opposing an invasion. They also had parochial concerns, such as a reluctance to see their own role diminished by having Laos operations directed from Saigon.[116]

In the wake of the Tet offensive in 1968, General Westmoreland proposed a more sophisticated invasion plan. Although it was rejected in Washington because of the additional manpower which would be required, U.S. officials in Vientiane saw the call for border raids into Laos and Cambodia as "the cutting edge of the axe."[117] That specific plan died with General Westmoreland's transfer to Washington and President Johnson's announcement of retirement.

The remainder of 1968 saw a shift in American military and diplomatic strategy. The partial bombing halt over North Vietnam led to increased bombing over Laos, just as bombing pauses had led to a shift of activity from North Vietnam to its neighbor. The additional sorties were welcome because enemy forces had advanced in various parts of the country and had surrounded the southern towns of Attopeu, Saravane, and Thakhek.

Debate in Washington continued over a total bombing halt over North Vietnam, which was Hanoi's prerequisite for full-scale peace talks. Some advocates of a total cessation of bombing argued that Laos provided better and safer places for stopping infiltration of men and supplies. General Abrams reportedly agreed on the basis of experience during the partial halt. On October 31, 1968, President Johnson announced an end to all bombing of North Vietnam. Simultaneously, it was reported that bombing would be shifted into Laos. Some observers say that this shift was part of a deal to win Abrams' approval, but other officials, including William Bundy, deny any such deal.[118]

The stage was set for a new administration. Laos had been linked even more closely to the war in Vietnam, both by American bombing and by increased infiltration by the North Vietnamese. Souvanna Phouma seemed to have written off any attempt to assert control over the area of the trails. There the fight was between the Americans and North Vietnamese.

Political events within Laos have been ignored to this point because they did not significantly affect American policy. Nothing much changed in Laotian politics after the events surrounding the April 1964 coup. That event marked the beginning of the downfall of Phoumi Nosavan, who had been getting rich and gaining enemies through his operation of gambling casinos and the import monopolies for gold, perfume, and alcohol. General Kouprasith used the occasion to get about eighty younger officers put in charge of ending corruption in the government and taking over Phoumi's monopolies. Souvanna also replaced Phoumi as operational head of the Ministry of Defense. There were additional coup scares in July, August, and December 1964, but government troops moved into the streets of the capital and forestalled any attempt to seize power. In January 1965, Souvanna reshuffled military commands to weaken further the power of officers loyal to Phoumi. When the rightist General failed in a coup attempt at the end of January, he was forced to flee to Thailand, where he still resides.[119]

U.S. military officers dropped their strong support for Phoumi when they saw him devoting most of his energies to making money rather than making war. Their attention was shifting to those groups, especially the mountain tribes, that were willing to fight. The Americans supported Souvanna as the best compromise. So long as the Royal Laotian Government was neutralist on paper and anti-Communist in practice—by not interfering with the U.S. war effort against the North Vietnamese—the Americans were content. In time, of course, Souvanna became openly committed to U.S. policies in Laos.

Souvanna called elections in July 1965, but reduced the suffrage to only about 20,000 people, mostly army officers, civil servants, teachers, and businessmen. There were 204 carefully screened candidates for the fifty-nine seats. The government opened polling stations in all provinces except Phong Saly, thanks to strenuous efforts by Air America to fly isolated voters to the polls. Newcomers to politics scored dramatic gains, while only fifteen old-time politicians won reelection. Although the Pathet Lao had boycotted the elections, Souvanna left some places in the Assembly and in the cabinet vacant pending their return to the coalition.[120]

These newcomers, perhaps encouraged as in earlier years by elements within the American Embassy, demanded more power and privileges for themselves. They wanted more of their own people in the cabinet, even if that meant abandoning the fiction of a coalition government. In September 1966 they provoked a cabinet crisis by defeating the budget in the National Assembly. Souvanna took the unprecedented step of getting the King to prorogue the assembly. The winners in the January 1967 elections were "mostly French-educated notables beholden to regional army leaders, prominent merchant families or local political chiefs."[121]

Dissension among Laotian military officers also increased during the autumn of 1966. Air Force General Thao Ma, moved to a desk job the previous May after he refused to provide transports for the opium trade, led a brief revolt in October. Planes from his old unit in southern Laos bombed the army headquarters near Vientiane. When loyal army troops occupied the airfield from which they had flown, General Ma led his men—one-third of the air force pilots—to asylum in Thailand. Kong-Le also fled to Thailand in October, charging that the Americans had supported his deputy in a power struggle. U.S. officers apparently sided with neutralist soldiers who wanted their army split up and placed under Royal Army regional commands.[122]

Although Souvanna Phouma's chief rivals for power had been eclipsed, the Prince emerged more dependent on rightist elements and the Americans than ever before. Together they provided support for his government in case of attempted coups or military attacks. The neutralists, never a strong political force, had even less influence as their army supporters merged with the rightists. The polarization of Laotian politics continued.[123]

American aid programs did little to strengthen the Royal Government. In practice, U.S. efforts bolstered regional and subordinate groups. Community Development Advisors, for example, frequently ignored the red tape in Vientiane and completed projects before they had been formally approved in the capital. In their eagerness to do something for the people in their village, they sometimes bypassed local officials, whose institutions withered under American neglect. The Laotians soon learned that to get things done they had to go to the Americans.[124]

The Vientiane bureaucracy was not only inefficient, it was also fundamentally out of touch with developments in the rest of Laos. On paper a parallel administration developed, with U.S. counterparts for the Lao down to the village level. In practice, the Americans ran the show. Several U.S. officials agreed with the conclusion by one, "The U.S. Embassy was the strongest part of the RLG's administrative structure in Laos."[125] An AID report in 1969 admitted the same problem: "The Lao government operates at relatively low effectiveness at both the national and local level."[126]

These results should not be surprising because the Americans provided money and quick actions. They could build the dam or produce the textbooks faster than the Lao. They were also impatient with delays, especially since people suffered in the interim.

Growing numbers of refugees added to these pressures for Americans to assume a greater role in providing for the citizens of Laos. The refugee population fluctuated only moderately from 1964 until mid-1968. These refugees imposed a budgetary and personnel burden on the aid program which it was slow to meet, particularly when increased fighting in 1969 led to an upsurge in the numbers of displaced persons. Among these refugees, the State Department admitted, "there is an attitude that the central government in Vientiane is far removed from pleas for assistance and protection. . . ."[127]

By the end of 1968, Americans were in charge of much that went on in Laos. They had supplanted the military and civil authorities in many functions and were responsive to their own government's needs and wishes. But the war was reaching a stage where it no longer could be kept secret.

CHAPTER EIGHT

Reaching the end of the mountains (1969–1971)

We must stay here. We must die here. There is no place to go. For many years my people have had a saying. They had it long before they left China. There is always another mountain, they said. My Father, there are no more mountains.
—VANG PAO[1]

A new administration took up the policy reins in Washington in January 1969. President Richard Nixon had long considered friendly regimes in Indochina vital to American interests. He was willing to urge American intervention in April 1954 to save the crumbling French empire; exactly ten years later he was advocating U.S. bombing of Communist base areas.[2] Subsequent events in no way lessened his determination to maintain the U.S. commitment to defend the area from Communist domination.

Laos was insignificant to Nixon and his advisors, at least compared to the diplomatic and military problems raised by Vietnam. The new foreign policy officials—Henry Kissinger at the White House, William Rogers at State, and Melvin Laird at Defense—had no reason to question or dispute policy toward Laos in their early months in office.

Still in his key post was William Bundy, who remained Assistant Secretary for East Asia and the Pacific until May. The new administration recalled Ambassador Sullivan and placed him in charge of Laotian (and Vietnamese) matters as a Deputy Assistant Secretary. His replacement as Ambassador, G. McMurtrie Godley, was transferred from a post in charge of Southeast Asia, excluding Vietnam. There were some fresh faces, but little new thought about Laos.

The military situation was deteriorating in the first half of 1969. Combined North Vietnamese and Pathet Lao forces attacked in both northern and southern Laos. They captured several airstrips in the north which were vital to the effort to resupply Meo troops. In response to these losses, the Laotians requested additional bombing. The number of strikes over the north more than doubled starting in March. Towns in the south were cut off from land transportation and had to be supplied by air starting in late April.[3]

These developments put pressure on the Americans for some kind of holding action. Yet they came at a time of transition, for Sullivan had left Vientiane on March 15 and Godley did not arrive until July 15. The Acting Ambassador for the interim was Robert Hurwitch, who had been Deputy Chief of Mission for three years.

Hurwitch had been close to Sullivan and thus knew what was happening. He accepted existing policy and made no efforts to depart from it during his four-month tenure. When the Pathet Lao made a new offer for peace talks in May, Hurwitch shared his embassy's analysis that there was nothing new in the proposal. Souvanna himself refused to ask for a bombing halt until the North Vietnamese began withdrawing their troops.[4]

The peace initiative seems in retrospect to have been more significant. The North Vietnamese Ambassador visited Vientiane for discussions with Souvanna for the first time in four years. The Soviet Union was also involved, for its Ambassador took a message from Souvanna to Souphanouvong and another Soviet official spoke to the Premier about a possible settlement.[5] The effort to get talks going, however, was more impressive than the actual negotiating positions of both sides. The Pathet Lao demand for a total bombing halt was unrealistic, for Souvanna knew that he could not force an end to U.S. bombing of the trails. Secretary Laird said as much publicly in March 1970.[6] Nor was Souvanna's demand for North Vietnamese withdrawal very realistic, given their need to use Laos to infiltrate South Vietnam and their desire for control over the border provinces. As the chances for peace faded, the war grew more severe.

For more than five years, U.S. officials had refused Laotian military requests to provide logistical and air support for an attack on the Plaine des Jarres. American bombing on or near the Plaine had been carefully restricted to military targets, sparing major towns and even forced labor squads of civilians carrying supplies. In an attempt to stop the deteriorating situation in the North by diverting military attention, U.S. planes attacked and leveled the town of Xieng Khouang in April 1969.[7]

Rebuffed by Souvanna and angered over the destruction of Xieng Khouang, the North Vietnamese broke their usual wet season lull and pushed toward the neutralist army headquarters at Muong Soui, just west of the Plaine. Muong Soui was not only symbolically important to Souvanna as his military headquarters, but was also strategically important as the largest airfield in the North.

Officials in Indochina and in Washington were distressed by the attack on Muong Soui. The deputy U.S. commander at the Udorn base later admitted, "When the situation got close to desperate in June in Laos, certain restrictions were removed and we were allowed to use airpower in a little freer manner."[8] Despite the increased bombing, Muong Soui fell on June 27. The losing forces suffered heavy casualties, perhaps as many as one-fourth. Desertions increased in the following weeks, as enemy forces moved westward and briefly held the junction with the road between Vientiane and Luang Prabang.[9] One American official, speaking the day after the event, called the fall of Muong Soui "the most important event in Laos in the past five years."[10]

Souvanna Phouma and Vang Pao were also distressed. They conferred in the capital and agreed that Vang Pao would launch an offensive to retake Muong Soui by cutting the road between Xieng Khouangville and the former neutralist headquarters. The Americans responded positively and began preparing for an offensive.[11]

The attacks were planned by the new Ambassador, who arrived in mid-July. George McMurtrie Godley was a man of action, a "field marshal" to both friends and nonadmirers. His reason for approving expanded military operations in Laos was quite simple: "I don't like to see the United States get beaten."[12] He had been a highly regarded Ambassador in the Congo during 1964–66. His military proclivities and ability to work well with secret operations were tested there and later put to work in Laos. Prior to moving to Vientiane, he had worked in Washington on Laotian matters.[13]

Once in Laos, Godley either found or added people who had previously served with him in the Congo. The Ambassador and his CIA station chief had been together in the Congo, as had the Deputy Chief of Mission and the head of the Political Section of the embassy. Their close associations were regarded by their subordinates as a "Congo Club."[14] Understandably, these men worked well together and shared a common view of how to fight the enemy.

Godley seemed fascinated with military operations and was decidedly sympathetic to military requests. Surrounded by people whom he trusted, he tended to ignore the suggestions or cautions of some of his other subordinates. These men consequently saw their influence over policy gradually decline.[15]

Before Vang Pao moved north in August 1969, U.S. planes subjected the area of the Plaine to extremely heavy bombing. The attacks turned the town of Xieng Khouang, already heavily hit, to "rubble" and Khang Khay to a "shell of houses," according to an American reporter visiting the scene in September.[16] That Khang Khay was deliberately bombed for the first time, despite its role as Pathet Lao headquarters and the site of a Chinese civilian mission, was a major symbolic escalation in the war; that the town was destroyed showed the American reluctance to put diplomatic restraints on military operations.

His path cleared by bombing, Vang Pao moved onto

the Plaine with amazing speed and facility. The Americans and
the Meo leader himself seemed surprised. Why the North
Vietnamese retreated is a mystery. One theory is that U.S. air
support was successful and Vang Pao's attack was a genuine
surprise. Another view is that the North Vietnamese overex-
tended themselves by going as far as Muong Soui and had
weakened their position with normal troop rotations. A third
hypothesis is that the troops were recalled home because of the
unsettled conditions in Hanoi immediately after the death of
Ho Chi Minh. Whatever the reason, the pro-American forces
suddenly found themselves in unexpected control of new territory.[17]

These military operations and the lessened restraints
on U.S. bombing created a dramatic rise in the number of
refugees, nearly a doubling between February and October
1969. Such large numbers had not been anticipated, thus requiring makeshift accommodations. Laos was becoming a land
of refugees, with perhaps one-fourth of the population rendered homeless by the decade of fighting. The staff report of
the Kennedy Subcommittee pointed out bitterly that six days
of heavy bombing (600 sorties) cost as much as the entire
refugee relief budget for a year.[18]

Public attention had been attracted to the situation in
Laos during 1969. Newspapers gave coverage to reports of the
Vang Pao offensive and the growing refugee problem. As revelations continued, the immediate public reaction was to demand
the whole truth.

Critics of the Vietnam War seized upon the growing
evidence of American involvement in Laos as the basis for
renewed public discussion of the war. They acted with several
motives. Some saw Laos as a surrogate for criticisms of the
larger war, a way to circumvent public indifference to what
seemed to be a war soon to end. Others saw an opportunity to
return the war-making power to the Congress. No longer were
lawmakers willing to approve blank-check resolutions for the
President, especially not after seeing their 1964 resolution on
Southeast Asia used as the functional equivalent of a declaration

of war. Some legislators reacted to the Laotian situation itself; they wanted to alert public opinion to the dangers of deeper involvement. Many could already see that, in Laos, alleged military necessity was the mother of intervention. First advisors, then team leaders, then airlift, then tactical support, then strategic bombing—it was Vietnam all over again.

Senator John Sherman Cooper of Kentucky had followed developments in Laos closely for two years. In December 1967 he had secured a letter from Secretary of State Rusk assuring him that U.S. policy was to respect the territorial integrity of Laos and Cambodia. Cooper raised the question with Rusk when one of his staff members learned that plans to invade Laos and Cambodia were under consideration. During 1968, opponents of the Vietnam War focused their energies on ending the bombing of North Vietnam. With that achieved, the new administration received only muted criticism as it pursued its own war policy.[19]

The deteriorating situation in Laos and the escalation of American involvement stirred the interest of Senators Cooper and Stuart Symington of Missouri. In mid-September Cooper offered an amendment to the Military Procurement Authorization Bill which sought to prohibit combat involvement by American forces in support of local forces in Laos or Thailand. After short debate, the amendment passed unanimously, 86–0. One stimulus for approval was a dispatch that day in the *New York Times* reporting U.S. air support for the Laotian drive toward the Plaine des Jarres. The Defense Department did little to reassure Congress when an official said that the amendment would "have no impact on the use of funds for support of U.S. forces in Laos or Thailand." Senator John C. Stennis of Mississippi, head of the Senate delegation to the Joint Conference Committee, later told Cooper of his doubts as to the legislative effect of the amendment and urged him to attach it instead to the Appropriations Bill. The amendment was dropped by the Conference Committee.[20]

Two days after the Senate action, Senator Symington announced that his Subcommittee on Security Agreements and Commitments Abroad would hold hearings on Laos in October.

Symington had become interested in the country and specifically directed his Subcommittee staff to visit Laos, which they
did in July 1969. The Missouri Senator was particularly concerned about the evolving U.S. commitment to defend Laos as
it had done in Vietnam. In announcing the hearings, he said,
"We have been at war in Laos for years, and it is time the
American people knew more of the facts."[21]

Hearings by the Symington Subcommittee were held a
month later, and with some reluctance on the part of the Nixon
Administration. Although the hearings were secret, they coincided with, and probably helped to stimulate, greater press and
public attention to Laos. The very fact of secrecy later produced several weeks of debate over the Administration's refusal to release an unclassified version of the testimony. Only
in April 1970, after the President's own statement on Laos,
was a heavily censored transcript made public.

Antiwar sentiment grew more voluble in the autumn
of 1969, prodded by the October Moratorium demonstrations,
the President's hard-line speech on November 3, and the subsequent huge march on Washington. An opinion poll at the time
found majority support (57 percent) for sending military advisors to Laos, but only 19 percent in favor of sending troops.
Over one-third of the people surveyed urged staying out altogether, even at the risk of a Communist takeover.[22]

These results may have aided the congressional efforts
to impose limits on U.S. involvement in Laos. Senator Cooper
planned to reintroduce his amendment but was called from the
capital by an illness in his family. Another such illness kept
Senator Symington from taking part in the legislative maneuvering. Senator J. W. Fulbright decided on the tactic of calling
the Senate into secret session in order to inform them of the
extent of U.S. involvement in Laos. This rare device—used
again to discuss Laos in June 1971—succeeded in focusing attention of both the public and the Senate on Laos. Fulbright also
saw the issue as a vehicle for setting outer limits on the Vietnam War for the first time.[23]

The Cooper Amendment was criticized as unclear and
as going too far. Some Senators interpreted it as forbidding all

U.S. bombing in Laos, thus halting what was considered the necessary operations against the Ho Chi Minh trails. A compromise, drafted by Senators Gordon Allott of Colorado, Frank Church of Idaho, and Jacob Javits of New York, was introduced and adopted, 73–17. It said directly that no funds were to be used "to finance the introduction of American ground combat troops into Laos or Thailand." The vote on final passage was 80–9.[24]

The chief effect of the amendment was to limit future action. As Senator Church said in the debate, "We are simply not undertaking to make any changes in the status quo. The limiting language is precise. And it does not undertake to repeal the past or roll back the present. It looks to the future."[25] This was in line with the strategy of Cooper and Fulbright, and other antiwar Senators, to set limits to the conflict.

Although the White House was preparing to oppose the amendment in conference, Senator Hugh Scott of Pennsylvania, the Minority Leader, reportedly persuaded the President to accept the language. Not only did the Church version have widespread bipartisan support and permit continuation of the bombing, but its less restrictive wording had also been opposed by Fulbright and other staunch critics of Administration policies. The following day, the White House took the surprising step of announcing that the amendment was "definitely in line with Administration policy" and should be seen as an endorsement of that policy rather than as a restriction.[26]

Policy makers in Washington and Vientiane claim that the congressional action had practically no effect on U.S. activities in Laos.[27] In retrospect, however, it seems that Senator Church was right—the amendment did inhibit future actions. Despite continued pressures for an American invasion of Laos, none occurred. What did take place, after congressional reaffirmation of the prohibition late in 1970, was a South Vietnamese invasion of the country with American ground combat troops specifically ruled out.

Left out of the amendment was reference to Cambodia, apparently on the grounds that it would be considered offensive to Prince Sihanouk. American officers had long desired to

attack enemy sanctuaries inside Cambodia but had been forbidden to do so on a sustained basis. Yet this legislative oversight
provided the opportunity for a widening of the war, when
military and diplomatic circumstances changed in the spring of
1970.

Shortly before that time, Laos was again in the spot-
light. Although Vang Pao had recaptured the Plaine des Jarres,
his American advisors were convinced that his forces could not
hold it in the face of the expected enemy assault during the dry
season. The Americans ordered what one reporter called a
"scorched earth policy" on the Plaine. They provided support
for the forcible evacuation of all merchants and artisans from
the towns and villages of the area in order to deny their taxes
and support to the Pathet Lao. Vang Pao's soldiers reportedly
burned homes, shot livestock, raped women, and impressed the
male Lao refugees into the army. In February 1970, when the
anticipated attacks came, the Americans provided air support
for the evacuation of the remaining civilians from the Plaine.[28]

Since the Americans had broadcast their intention not
to try to hold the Plaine, it is not surprising that the North
Vietnamese and Pathet Lao fought to recapture it. Nevertheless, American officials and news media treated the event as a
dangerous threat to the stability of Southeast Asia. Despite extremely heavy U.S. bombardment, including the first use of
B-52s in northern Laos, the pro-Communist forces rapidly
overran Van Pao's positions. The last important Royal Government stronghold, the Xieng Khouang air base, known by its
code name of Lima-Lima, fell in typical Laotian fashion. Vang
Pao had American and Laotian air support throughout the
battle. He also had 1,500 men in defensive positions and artillery in the hills overlooking the airstrip. Despite these advantages, his forces retreated under an attack by an estimated
400 enemy soldiers. The Laotian Army claims that 6,000 North
Vietnamese had attacked and prevailed only after bloody,
close-in fighting were disputed by U.S. advisors.[29]

This defeat was the most significant one suffered by
the forces loyal to the Vientiane government, but it was not
the only one. In fact, the Royal Government's writ did not run

very far in Laos. For years the Pathet Lao have had an extensive governmental organization in operation along the North
Vietnamese border. By early 1970, pro-Communist troops had
established a major base area in the southern corner of Laos
bordering Thailand and Cambodia. In western Laos, enemy
forces had infiltrated both sides of the Mekong beyond Luang
Prabang. Nor could Royalist forces maintain security in areas
near the Mekong in the panhandle region. A western reporter
concluded:

> All along the nominally government-held banks
> of the Mekong up to the Burmese border, the Royal
> Lao Government finds itself with its overland com-
> munications cut, its main towns isolated, and small
> parties of Communist troops able virtually at will to
> attack a wide variety of targets.[30]

In another time or another place, such circumstances
would probably have led to massive American military intervention. But things were different in Washington, in part because
of conscious administration policy to reduce public anxiety
over the war, in part because of clear congressional opposition
to any intervention. In order to correct "intense public speculation" about U.S. involvement in Laos, the President issued a
statement on March 6 which revealed more about that involvement than the U.S. government had admitted in the previous
eight years. While admitting combat air operations for the
first time, the President said that they had been "flown only
when requested by the Laotian government." He also declared
that there were no American ground combat troops in Laos
and that no American stationed in Laos had ever been killed in
ground combat operations.[31]

These revelations, intended to quiet public debate, only
sparked more interest in what was happening in Laos. Enterprising reporters soon widened what seemed to be a credibility
gap. One correspondent wrote that a U.S. Army captain had
been killed in 1969 while helping to coordinate ground units,
artillery, and air support. This story prompted the White
House to reveal that twenty-seven Americans had been killed

by "hostile action" on the ground in Laos, leaving the impression that the remaining 175 or so deaths since 1962 had been due to air action. Nevertheless, U.S. officials maintained, no American had been killed in ground combat operations. Apparently, the definition of such encounters was a situation where the Americans shot first. Another reporter told of the 1968 incident in which at least a dozen air force personnel were killed when their base near the North Vietnamese border was overrun. There was no further comment from the White House.[32]

The March 6 statement also included an appeal to the British and Soviet leaders for consultations to work for a restoration of the Geneva Agreements to Laos. The same day, the Pathet Lao announced a new five-point program for a peace settlement, including a cease-fire in place and a total, unconditional halt to American bombing. This latter demand was the sticking point. Although Souvanna was willing to end the bombing over the North, he knew that the Americans would never halt their bombing of the trails. He responded with the equally unacceptable demand that all North Vietnamese troops be withdrawn.[33]

Before the latest peace initiatives had a chance to fail through incompatibility, events in Cambodia diverted American attention and ultimately American policy. Provincial demonstrations against the Vietnamese Communists in Cambodia in early March were followed by the sacking of the North Vietnamese and Provisional Revolutionary Government (Viet Cong) embassies in Phnom Penh. Within a few days it was disclosed that South Vietnamese forces had supplied Cambodians with maps and radios so that artillery strikes along the border could be coordinated. On March 18 the Cambodian Parliament deposed the Chief of State, Prince Norodom Sihanouk, who was in Moscow at the time.[34]

American officers were surprised but pleased that anti-Communist generals had come to power. "I don't see how we can miss," one told an American reporter. "This is the sort of thing we've been waiting for."[35] The subsequent weeks showed what he meant. The new Cambodian rulers ended the trade and payments arrangements which had enabled the Vietnamese to purchase and transport supplies to their forces inside South Vietnam. With that supply line snapped, their logistical position was much more difficult. The American military then recommended the decisive action by which widening the war would shorten it.

On April 30, President Nixon announced the joint U.S.–South Vietnamese invasion of Cambodia. The same day pro-Communist forces captured Attopeu, a town generally surrounded for five years and supplied only by air for over one year. In the following weeks, while American attention was riveted on the new Indochina war and increased domestic opposition to it, the Pathet Lao and North Vietnamese captured other Royalist positions in southern Laos. In June the Americans began training Cambodians in southern Laos, only to shift the operation to Thailand when news of it leaked out.[36]

Seizing the towns near the Bolovens Plateau may have been symbolic retaliation for the Cambodian invasion. During the summer months, however, the North Vietnamese added extra forces to improve their supply lines through Laos and into Cambodia. The Americans saw this as a threat to the Phnom Penh government and responded with heavier bombing and even closer air support.

By midsummer 1970, the situation in Laos had deteriorated further. Politically, Souvanna Phouma was threatened by a rightist coup from generals who no longer saw any need to preserve the few remaining fictions of the 1962 accords. The Premier barely survived some confidence votes in the National Assembly early in the summer. One factor helping to save him was strong American support for him and firm opposition to any coup.[37]

Militarily, the situation was also worse. The increased North Vietnamese activity led U.S. military men to press for the invasion of the Laotian sanctuaries, which the President had contemplated but refused in April. Some minor raids apparently were conducted, for the South Vietnamese Foreign Minister admitted border raids on May 17. By August military planners in Saigon and Washington admitted that they were pressing for large-scale incursions. Although such an invasion was rejected on domestic and international political grounds, the Pathet Lao charged—and official sources acknowledged—operations by commando units.[38]

The Cambodian invasion shattered several assumptions and restraints on the war. No longer was it simply the Vietnam War; all of Indochina was a single theater of operations. A satisfactory solution in Vietnam, once thought sufficient for American prestige, now seemed dependent on similar results in Laos and Cambodia. If one sanctuary could be hit, why not all of them? Why not Laos as well? Why not a resumption of the bombing of North Vietnam? Having received approval for a plan long denied by Washington, the strategists in Saigon dusted off other proposals for the decisive blow.

Eight months after the Cambodian invasion, which at the time was said to have bought eight months for the processes of Vietnamization and U.S. troop withdrawal, another attack was launched into what had been North Vietnamese sanctuaries in Laos and Cambodia. The military logic was clear. The North Vietnamese, cut off from supplies through Cambodia, had expanded their logistical network in Laos and seemed to be building strength for what could have been a damaging offensive against the northern part of South Vietnam later in the dry season. A thrust at the "jugular," meaning the fifty-mile-wide Ho Chi Minh Trail network, was hoped to forestall the possible offensive and perhaps permanently cripple the North Vietnamese.

Political considerations had also changed to make the invasion acceptable. In particular, U.S. policy makers no longer feared a military reaction by China. Official spokesmen took great pains to emphasize that the operations posed no threat to China and that the United States still wished to improve relations with Peking.[39] Domestically, the attack was tolerable because the letter of the law on U.S. ground combat troops was to be upheld and troop withdrawals were to be continued. The usual critics muted their criticisms. Within the administration there was apparently little opposition to the policy.

Several plans for an invasion along Route 9 to Tchepone

had been proposed in the past by the Americans. But instead of sending 60,000 U.S. troops, the eventual decision was for 22,000 South Vietnamese. The legal prohibition on the use of American ground combat troops was ostensibly honored. The only Americans announced as going into Laos were helicopter crews, airlifting Vietnamese troops and supplies. When helicopters were shot down, however, the United States claimed the right to send in troops to protect the rescue missions.[40]

The invasion was announced on February 7, 1971, following a week of speculation about it. The State Department said that the operation would be limited, would not enlarge the war, and was "consistent with statutory requirements," since no U.S. ground combat forces or advisors would cross into Laos.[41] The Royal Lao Government criticized the action mildly, putting the primary responsibility on the North Vietnamese for having used the territory of Laos for violations of the Geneva Accords.

After only six weeks the last South Vietnamese soldiers were brought out of Laos, some clinging desperately to the skids of U.S. helicopters. The North Vietnamese had stood and fought, as President Nixon had said they must. Although the administration called the operation a success for the South Vietnamese, the consensus of journalists was quite the opposite.* Nevertheless, the invasion had wrought some damage on the North Vietnamese supply system, though the precise amount was in dispute. At least the invasion seemed to blunt any offensive prior to the October elections in South Vietnam.

One reporter got this assessment of the local effects of the invasion from a member of the Laotian general staff: "The Ho Chi Minh Trail is not cut and our neutralist status has been hurt. We are worse off than before."[42] Other officers were reportedly willing to oust Souvanna Phouma, and with him, the

---

* Many factors went into these conclusions, such as an intelligence failure in estimating North Vietnamese strength and likely strategy, poor air-ground coordination, bad weather, and the refusal of the South Vietnamese to commit more men to battle when they were in trouble. See *Los Angeles Times*, March 28, 1971, and *New York Times*, March 30 and April 1, 1971.

last traces of neutralism. American support once again carried the day for Souvanna.

The military picture in Laos had been bleak even before the invasion of the panhandle. In fact, the situation has been desperate but not serious for several years. Most observers believe that the Pathet Lao with North Vietnamese support could take any or all of the country at almost any time. As if to prove this point, pro-Communist forces threatened Luang Prabang in the North, Pakse in the South, and the CIA base at Long Tieng in the aftermath of the South Vietnamese invasion.

Renewed peace initiatives got nowhere. In their sporadic talks about having talks, the Pathet Lao and Royal Government representatives came to the verge of a compromise. The Royal Government agreed to consider the meeting one between princes, rather than between neutralist and leftist. The Pathet Lao reduced their demand for a total, unconditional halt to U.S. bombing in Laos to a cease-fire and bombing cessation in the province where the talks were to take place.[43] Then, suddenly, in January 1971, the talks were suspended. When they were renewed in May, the Pathet Lao had restored their demand for a total national bombing halt.

What had happened? The most plausible explanation is that the South Vietnamese invasion stiffened North Vietnamese resistance and increased the need for an unhindered supply trail to the South. But the American Embassy in Vientiane also had an important role in keeping the talks from making progress.

A dispute had been growing within the embassy between the Ambassador and his political section. Members of that section had been most critical of the bombing policy; they had also urged greater efforts to pursue peace talks.

One younger Foreign Service officer had resigned in 1970 after finding the embassy reluctant to work for a political settlement and unwilling to report the full story of Laotian developments to Washington. Ambassador Godley disagreed with the analysis of the political section and, by late summer 1970, was hardly talking to its members. In explanation, one U.S. diplomat told a reporter: "Laos is an operational post. We're fighting a war here. The political section doesn't understand this. They keep making such ridiculous suggestions as that we should accept a widespread bombing halt."[44]

The head of the political section continued to press his argument. He reportedly felt that the only way to guarantee the security of the important CIA base at Long Tieng, as well as the U.S. position along the Mekong, was to trade a bombing halt for informal guarantees of a cease-fire. Acting on his own, he urged a Royalist official to sound out the Pathet Lao about such a deal. He was told that that could be done only if it were a formal U.S. position. The soundings were never taken, but two weeks later the diplomat was abruptly transferred to the post of Economic Attaché in Liberia.[45] Only in March 1971 did Ambassador Godley give his first public support for the Laotian negotiations.

With the peace talks stalemated, the war continued, and with it the casualties. The Meo have been the hardest hit, both from direct involvement in combat and from the hardships which accompany refugees. A decade of fighting has killed at least one-fourth of the Meo population. Youngsters of twelve and thirteen are forming a larger part of the fighting force. In moments of despair, Vang Pao has wondered whether his people might not have reached the end of their mountains.[46]

Thai soldiers and other Laotian personnel have been brought in as replacements for the dwindling Meo forces. U.S. officials were reportedly hopeful that any congressional limitations could be circumvented by letting Thailand continue the struggle in the mountains.[47] The Americans seemed determined to avoid any lasting military defeat.

Reports from Laos have suggested growing war weariness among the people. "We are tired, so tired," a Laotian colonel admitted. The same officer also described his precarious military position as "like a cow in a barnyard waiting for the tiger."[48] Other Laotians, noting the casualties from the bombing and the shifting ground combat, cited the proverb: "When elephants fight, the grass gets trampled."

The many nations involved in Laos did not much care about whom they trampled. The North Vietnamese were determined to preserve their access to South Vietnam. When pushed westward by the February 1971 invasion, they extended and strengthened their hold in new areas. The Thai continued fighting in the mountains in order to avoid further conflict on their own soil. The Americans refused to halt the bombing which they claimed protected the lives of men being withdrawn from Vietnam.

Little disagreement was voiced on this policy either in the U.S. Embassy or among the top policy makers in Washington. Only in the Congress did critics press their opposition, which was aimed as much at the continued war in Vietnam as at the specific involvement in Laos. Several congressmen charged that the massive American bombing had been directed at civilian targets and population. Administration denials were coupled with refusals to make public the photographic evidence on villages which allegedly had been struck. The unavoidable conclusion from interviews with refugees, however, was that U.S. air attacks had devastated many villages, caused widespread casualties, and had driven large segments of the population from their traditional homes into caves or refugee camps.[49]

A special staff report for the Symington Subcommittee revealed for the first time details about CIA activities, Thai involvement, and the figures for military aid since 1963. Shock at the rising cost of U.S. activities prompted an overwhelming Senate vote for an amendment by Senator Symington to limit expenditures, except for U.S. bombing, to $350 million for 1972. Under Administration pressure, the Congress raised the ceiling for 1973 to $375 million.

During the 1971 rainy season, Royal Government forces made their usual counteroffensive and achieved symbolic but costly victories. A major effort was made in southern Laos in order to prevent the North Vietnamese from shifting their trails any farther westward.

Pathet Lao and North Vietnamese forces scored their biggest gains since 1962 in their dry season offensive as they seized the Plaine des Jarres and the southern town of Paksong in rapid succession in December 1971. At one point in January 1972 they briefly overran the former CIA stronghold at Long Tieng. These secret facilities were reportedly shifted first to

Ban Son and later to the neutralist army base at Vang Vieng. The communist advance was accompanied by the first significant involvement of North Vietnamese MiGs over Laos, a factor which disrupted the American tactics based on unhindered air superiority.

Newcomers favoring neutralism won the bulk of National Assembly seats in the January 1972 elections. Although they lacked the power to force a change in Souvanna Phouma's policies, they augured an important change of mood. Even Ambassador Godley had testified that "the Lao have been bled white by this war."[50]

Renewed exchanges between Souvanna and the Pathet Lao led to flurries of speculation and hope during 1972, but no concrete settlement has yet emerged. Meanwhile, the people of Laos remain the hostages and victims of the war in Vietnam.

Many contingencies could still bring down the shaky structure of the Royal Government—a determined North Vietnamese attack against the few remaining royalist towns, the death or overthrow of Souvanna Phouma, or a reduction in American support for the ongoing struggle. Fatalistically, the Laotians whom the United States has supported for nearly two decades faced their dilemma, which was expressed by a general early in 1971: "We don't want to be Communists, but we don't want to be dead. Whoever wins, Laos will remain Laos."[51]

Learning the lessons of Laos

This is the end of nowhere. We can do anything we want here because Washington doesn't seem to know it exists.
—An unnamed American official in Vientiane
in November 1960[1]

The story of American policy toward Laos since 1954, detailed in the preceding chapters, is not a happy one. Too much blood has been shed and too much money has been spent in a vain attempt to "save" Laos from Communist influence—an influence which is probably unavoidable, albeit minimizable, given Laos' proximity to Communist states and the entrenched power of the Pathet Lao in some regions.

The roots of the American sense of failure in Laos lie in the view of the world which exaggerated the strategic importance of that country and the obsessive anti-communism which prevented adjustments to its political realities. For too long the United States opposed and thwarted a coalition government with the Pathet Lao. For too short a time the United States accepted a policy of neutralization. American concern with preventing the "loss" of South Vietnam prompted the discard of that policy. Whenever the United States did intervene to try to influence the course of events in Laos, it tended to side with those most willing to use the rhetoric of anti-communism rather than those most likely to strengthen and make viable the fragile bonds of the Laotian political system. Although one might disagree with these explanations for the failure of U.S. policy because one agrees with an anti-communist strategy, no one can deny the extent to which that policy was inadequately controlled by the highest officials in Washington. Whatever actions are decided upon and carried

240

out, responsible government requires that men be held account-
able. In the case of Laos, the men ultimately responsible for
U.S. policy frequently did not know how their wishes were
being implemented; or, knowing, they did not keep them under
close control.

Laos has lessons for the students and practitioners of
foreign policy because it is not an isolated but rather a typical
case, because it illustrates the way many U.S. policy decisions are made, and because it raises important questions about
the control of policy at a distance and over time. These lessons
are the subject of this concluding chapter.

Most studies of foreign policy cases focus on acute
crises when the fate of the world seemed to hang in the balance
for a few days or when nations finally went over the brink to
war. These are not only the most interesting for other readers
but also the easiest to research. Policy makers remember what
happened in Europe in July 1914 or in Washington, Moscow,
and Havana in October 1962; they forget what happened, say,
three years ago in April.

Perhaps they should forget. One cannot remember
everything. But today's crisis and tomorrow's war were often
yesterday's business as usual. Studies of acute crises may lead to
better management of tensions, but they may overlook ways of
avoiding dangerous situations altogether.

The process of foreign policy-making in Washington
consists of answering cables, holding meetings, writing memos,
skimming reports, and so forth.[2] Top officials like the President
and Secretary of State are rarely called upon for decisions. They
concern themselves only with the most urgent questions and
those which affect their political interests. The Congress and
the public at large are brought into the policy process even less
frequently. Most of the decisions and actions taken involve only
the career bureaucrats directly concerned with a subject.
Higher level officials may be informed or consulted, but they
have to decide for their subordinates only occasionally. Although this delegation of responsibility is inevitable, given
limitations of time, it has its costs. One high-level official in the

Eisenhower Administration complained: "The problem of policy in government is that low-priced help writes the policy and high-priced help just proofreads it. Hence, ideas get set in concrete as they move up."[3]

One can distinguish four magnitudes of foreign policy problems, depending on which levels of the U.S. government are most deeply involved in the decision-making.* These categories cannot be sharply differentiated some of the time because policy questions can easily and quickly slip up or down the scale. And like the magnitude of stars, these rankings suggest only a distance from a central vantage point—here, the President—and not the intensity of light or heat at the origin.

First-magnitude problems are those which absorb the full attention of the President and his top advisors for an extended period of time, such as the first week of the Korean War or the two weeks of the Cuban Missile crisis. Second-magnitude problems deeply involve the President and his advisors, but only for a short time and rarely to the exclusion of other matters. Often in response to external events—for example, the imposition of the Berlin blockade or war crises in the Middle East—leading policy makers will immerse themselves in a question until they feel safe in returning immediate responsibility to their subordinates. Third-magnitude problems are those primarily involving men at the middle levels of the bureaucracy—the regional and country desk officers, perhaps with meetings chaired by an Assistant Secretary. The bulk of perceived problems are handled at this level. Routine decisions, in the absence of any sense of urgency or threat, account for the rest of foreign policy, and will be labeled fourth-magnitude problems.

Laos was usually a third-magnitude problem in the instances of decision-making discussed in this study. There is little evidence of the strictly routine (fourth-magnitude) functioning of the policy machine. It would be buried in the cables

---

* At which level a problem is handled depends upon its perceived importance. This is usually in terms of threat, surprise, and time available for a decision. What determines these perceptions is a mystery locked in the cognitive processes and personal stakes of the policy makers concerned with the matter.

and internal files which are still classified. Second-magnitude consideration of Laos by the President and his primary advisors occurred only occasionally, when the use of military force was seriously contemplated. This has been discussed in several first-hand accounts. In these instances, the existing literature on decision-making in crises is relevant and useful in explanation. That literature is inadequate, however, to explain third-magnitude problems.

Third-magnitude problems are handled differently from first- and second-magnitude ones because the people and the environment are fundamentally changed. When the President is involved, by contrast, a great many other people may be in attendance—personal advisors, congressional leaders, influential cabinet members, and representatives of the foreign policy establishment. These men bring their own personal stakes and political responsibilities to the decisions. They are more sensitive to factors like public and congressional opinion than are career bureaucrats. If they have organizational roles, they cannot be indifferent to policy outcomes because they are in continual struggles with other men and agencies for money, influence, or prestige. As Theodore Sorensen has written: "Politics pervades the White House without seeming to prevail."[4]

When the setting is a closed arena with participation limited to career officials, politics is a distant, secondary concern. This conclusion, based on the evidence of Laos, relates only to foreign policy. The role of politics in domestic agencies may well be different. Discussion of partisan advantages or electoral effects is taboo. The men involved in these third-magnitude problems know that they will have to work with each other in the future and that they all will be judged on the success of the policies which they suggest to their superiors. They, thus, have a special incentive to work for consensus and to avoid choices which seriously aggrieve or threaten other participants in the decision. As a result, they tend to seek agreements on sets of words which will enable each agency to do what it wants with minimum interference or conflict. Words and papers are the weapons of combat and the end product of policy. These career men operate in a relatively closed system: as they are generally free from political pressures from the Congress and the society (except with regard to budgets), so also are they unable to mobilize those outside forces to support their own positions in the bargaining over policy.

Wherever decisions are made, policy results from a bargaining process. Since different groups can affect decisions, policy makers must bargain with those who share power over outcomes.[5] Without proper coordination, one agency might undermine or obviate another's policy. Even with such coordination, as the case of Laos illustrates so frequently, they may act at cross-purposes. This is most striking in the way different American groups supported different Laotian factions in the late 1950s, but it is true today of the conflicts between those who favor bombing for military objectives and those who find that such bombing hampers their efforts at refugee relief or at achieving a negotiated settlement among the political factions in Laos. Although bargaining may not always resolve these conflicts, it is necessary if there is to be any coordination.

Since this is a case study of the evolution of American policy toward Laos since 1954, it seeks to reconstruct the series of decisions and actions which made up that policy. In so doing, it may be useful in providing a more detailed picture of how policy choices are made and implemented.*

The foregoing analysis of events has been guided by a conscious conceptual framework of the organizational and political processes by which the U.S. government operates. The focal concept is policy as a series of outcomes; that is, the consequences of decisions and actions on a given subject. This definition of policy is special since it excludes some of the common notions of that term. To many people, policy is the set of statements and justifications by government officials; it can be "looked up" like the population of Denver or the ingredients

---

* One case, of course, cannot prove a theory of foreign policy-making, but it can help to confirm or disprove general propositions derived from research into other cases. The conclusions offered here are tentative and restricted to certain circumstances. They are probably not unique, however, and are, hopefully, suggestive of further investigation.

of a Hollandaise sauce. More rigorous analysts read between the lines of such declarations of policy, looking for intentions, implicit assumptions, and principles which give consistency. They infer policy from statements and actions, just as they might infer a recipe from the taste and appearance of the sauce.* The framework for analysis used here avoids such inferences, since policy as announced is not always the same as policy as decided, nor is either necessarily the same as policy as implemented. What is important is what is actually said and done. These are the realities for other nations, not what might have been intended by some officials. Intentions are relevant for evaluation of policy but not for changing or understanding its results.† Policy should be studied as the outcomes of organizations acting according to established procedures and under the direction of men in positions who have a tendency to seek to maximize their own control and minimize interference by others over their own actions.‡

---

* Graham T. Allison, "Conceptual Models and the Cuban Missile Crisis," *American Political Science Review*, Vol. 63 (September 1969), shows that this is the most frequent type of foreign policy analysis. The present study draws heavily upon, and is greatly indebted to, that work; but it endeavors to add detail to the bargaining and implementation processes in such a way as to blur Allison's distinction between analytical models two (organizational process) and three (bureaucratic politics). His distinction is heuristically useful but not always necessary because men sometimes control their organizations and sometimes are controlled by them. There is no hard and fast rule for which will occur in given circumstances, for bureaucratic and political processes form a continuum from blind organizational momentum to highly idiosyncratic decisions.

† Although evaluation cannot be avoided, it plays a secondary role in this work to explanation of the decision process. Intentions are crucially important to evaluations, since one must compare express or implicit goals with the actions and choices adopted as means to those ends. On this earth, perhaps in contrast to heaven, men are judged at least as much by their works as by their faith.

‡ One need not assume that all men in policy-making positions seek to maximize their own power, as Gordon Tullock does in *The Politics of Bureaucracy* (Washington, D.C.: Public Affairs Press, 1965). It is sufficient to note that such men do participate in a bargaining process over outcomes and rarely surrender influence on those outcomes entirely

The policy-making process has two major phases: decision and implementation. They are not always separate, since a decision to do nothing now is immediately effected. Moreover, any major decision may require hundreds of subsequent choices while being carried out. But the distinction is useful for studying the way organizations operate along their chains of command. Frequently, in the case of Laos, the decisions made at one level of the bureaucracy were not implemented as anticipated further down. "Decision" may be a misleading term since it connotes deliberation and intention—much too conscious a process. Such decisions were rare in the case of Laos, where bargaining produced varied, often mutually contradictory outcomes. "Choice" avoids the connotation of intention and calculation, but it implies an act at a single point in time.[6] It, therefore, makes difficult an analysis of choices at different levels over time. As long as one realizes that decisions are not always conscious or deliberate, that term is useful because it also connotes a conclusion or a settlement, as of a bargaining interaction. In studying Laos or other objects of American foreign policy, one can see occasional decision points, where the trendline of policy moved in a different direction and out of a smooth curve. This study tries to explain the smoothness of that trendline as well as when and why it diverged.

Each group involved in the bargaining over Laos policy brought to those discussions its own perspective on the situation and each reacted to external events in terms of it. These attitudes were fairly consistent and very important for understanding why policy changed so little and so slowly.

The State Department was primarily interested in avoiding increased Communist influence in Laos and in maintaining good relations with the established government. Although some high-level officials in the department were more aggressively anti-Communist than others, all shared a fear that any involvement of the Pathet Lao in the Royal Government would be very

---

to their peers. If they are not completely passive, they are trying to influence decisions and actions; that is, they are trying to get or maintain some control on the outcome.

dangerous. The career foreign service officers had an additional interest in not rocking the policy boat. They had what James C. Thomson, Jr., has called a "curator mentality" which venerated existing policy and cautiously avoided any change in it.[7]

Foreign aid officials, whether for ICA or AID, were interested mainly in getting a sound currency and economy in Laos. They could not really plan for economic development since their resources and those of the target country were both quite limited. But they did seek to minimize inflation and build up some of the infrastructure which Laos desperately needed.

Pentagon officers saw Laos in strategic terms. Although they were slow to accept the military importance of the area, they became committed to the financing of a large, well-paid Laotian Army. Throughout subsequent years, the Pentagon consistently opposed any efforts to restrict the political or military freedom of the army. In the 1960s, military men also considered Laos an important area for flanking operations against North Vietnam.

The Central Intelligence Agency shared the anticommunism of other U.S. officials and saw its task as that of building a viable non-French, anti-Communist political system. Its operations attempted to manipulate various political groups in order to keep pro-Americans on top. Gradually the Agency took over planning and coordination of daily warfare, thus creating a tension between its traditional political role and its new military one.

Each group perceived developments in Laos according to its own major tasks and concerns and used policies which preserved its own primary interests. For example, when Souvanna Phouma took two Pathet Lao assemblymen into his cabinet in 1957, the State Department was frightened, seeing its whole anti-Communist policy at stake. Officials looked for some way to turn back the clock, either by defeating the Pathet Lao in new elections or by withholding aid to weaken the government. The Pentagon was not deeply involved in that policy debate because its operations in Laos were still minor and low priority. As long as the Laotian Army was not affected, U.S. officers were content. The CIA, however, considered the coalition as proof that new political groups had to be established to replace the old, insufficiently anti-Communist ones. The foreign aid agency (ICA) seized upon U.S. dissatisfaction by pressing for reforms in the aid program in order to eliminate abuses which threatened its entire aid budget. The resulting policy combined the interests of the major participants: financial aid was suspended but the army continued to be supplied and paid; reforms were demanded and ultimately conceded; new political groups received U.S. support; when leftists won the elections, the Americans engineered the replacement of Souvanna Phouma and his coalition by solid, anti-Communist and pro-American politicians.

When Kong-Le seized power in August 1960, the same constellation of bureaucratic interests determined policy. State Department officials differed on their recommendations, but all accepted the general principle of restoring a government which would oppose both a coalition with the Pathet Lao and aid from the Soviet Union and China. The Pentagon and CIA worked together in supporting the army and, in particular, General Phoumi Nosavan; they insisted that he be given a major role in any government. ICA saved itself embarrassment by suspending its aid until the situation was clarified. Prodded by the embassy in Vientiane, the State Department temporized, resisting pressures from the Pentagon and CIA to oust Souvanna's government immediately. State dropped its resistance when Souvanna welcomed assistance from the Soviet Union.

These positions were unchanged in the early weeks of the Kennedy Administration. But many of the new officials, especially the President, became convinced that Laos was a military quagmire and was not worth a further deterioration in Soviet-American relations. These new people were able to prevail over entrenched positions only because the Joint Chiefs were divided on the question of actual (instead of threatened) intervention and because the new men could bypass the hardliners in the State Department by entrusting the negotiations to Averell Harriman.

In the first two years after the Geneva settlement in

1962, State Department officials placed a high value on compliance with the agreements and, thus, on support for Souvanna Phouma. The Pentagon accepted compliance because it was still permitted to support the Laotian Army and fly reconnaissance missions. The CIA continued to support its clients, the Meo tribesmen, although that support was provocative to the Communists and probably a violation of the Geneva Accords. AID had a new and expanded program for Laos, which it eagerly pushed forward, sometimes to the point of undermining native institutions. Each U.S. group was satisfied as long as it was able to run its own show.

During the years since 1964, bureaucratic positions changed somewhat in response to increased opportunities for action in Laos. As the CIA budget and personnel contingent in Laos grew larger, the Agency became a stronger advocate of counterinsurgency operations and particularly of its major client, the Meo army. But as the air war expanded, especially after 1968, there were reports of friction between the CIA and Air Force, which still viewed Laos as a tactical theater of the war in Vietnam and which resisted efforts to impose restrictions on its operations.

Except for these recent modifications, there has been a basic continuity in the attitudes and actions of the agencies involved in U.S. foreign policy. When external events or internal demands forced new decisions, each group brought its own perspectives and interests to the bargaining table. Not all decisions gave green lights to all agencies to continue as before. Some decisions imposed detours and red lights. But the process of decision brought the concerned groups together to resolve their differences by bargaining.

The actual process of bargaining took place in two phases: preliminary posturing and direct negotiations. In the first phase, the participants in policy-making carried on as before, acting to safeguard their interests in the changing circumstances in Washington and Vientiane. Each group tried to convince others of its interpretation of events by argument and by manipulation of the decision environment.* When the policy makers met for direct negotiations, they used their positional advantages and bargaining skills to influence the outcome.

Manipulation of the decision environment was done in different ways. One of the most effective means was the press, which was always ready to run scare headlines about alleged Communist invasions.[8] The Lao were even more adept at stirring up crises than the Americans, for they did it successfully in 1955, 1958, 1959, 1960, 1961, 1962, 1964, 1969, and 1970. U.S. officials must have been complicit with these wars by press releases since their denials or minimization of the threat would have led most reporters to disregard the handouts from the information ministry. These alarms changed the perceived threat to Laos and, hence, the definition of the situation to which policy had to respond.†

Another object of manipulation is the face of the issue under immediate consideration.‡ By raising the possibility of a

---

* Bargaining takes many forms in addition to negotiations and various efforts to manipulate the decision situation (tacit bargaining), but these two terms are intended to cover that range of techniques. Other forms of bargaining include persuasion, threats, adaptation, and creating and discharging obligations. See Charles Lindblom, *Policy-Making Process*, pp. 93–98.

† The definition of the situation is the combination of threat perception, amount of time available for decision, and the extent of prior warning. The components of this concept are taken from Charles F. Hermann, "International Crisis as a Situational Variable," in James N. Rosenau (ed.), *International Politics and Foreign Policy* (Revised Edition. New York: The Free Press, 1969). Discussion of the concept as a psychological response rather than as an organizational one can be found in Dean G. Pruitt, "Definition of the Situation as a Determinant of International Action," in Herbert C. Kelman (ed.), *International Behavior* (New York: Holt, Rinehart and Winston, 1965). Different definitions call forth different procedures and involve different decision makers and, consequently, bring varying personal and political interests to bear on the decision.

‡ The face of the issue depends upon the agency which first raises an issue for decision and the particular kind of issue that is raised. The face of the issue establishes a context and a criterion of relevance for the ensuing policy debate. For example, budgetary decisions are usually treated in terms of costs and are weighed against other costs; political

United Nations debate on American support of Phoumi No-savan's rebel army in November 1960, for example, State Department officials changed the context in which aid to that army was discussed. Since Phoumi's forces were well-supplied and already on the march against Vientiane, a demand for aid suspension in order to prevent UN condemnation was much more acceptable to policy makers. Similarly, in 1962, the decision to continue assistance to the Meo guerrillas behind the Pathet Lao lines wore a humanitarian face rather than that of a counterinsurgency strategy in possible violation of the Geneva Agreements.

Another change in the face of the issue took place in 1964 when advocates of increased military pressure against North Vietnam succeeded in linking actions in Laos to their preferred policy. Until that time, Laotian questions had been considered on their own merits and in the context of neutralization, usually without much influence from the Pentagon. Even the initial armed reconnaissance missions in May 1964 were designed to rescue the neutralist government rather than to expand the Vietnam War. But the agencies doing the bombing placed more importance on the fight against North Vietnam and soon won others to that view of the bombing issue.

Direct bargaining over decisions usually took place in the closed arena described earlier. Some of the outcomes may have been strongly influenced by factors of personality or the group dynamics of the meeting, but the evidence available is insufficient to test any of the propositions of small group psychology.[9] There are some generalizations, however, which one

---

consequences may be ignored, as they were in the case of Skybolt. (See Richard E. Neustadt, *Alliance Politics* [New York: Columbia University Press, 1970].) In the case of Laos, one of the best examples of the difference the face of the issue made was in 1954. When the Joint Chiefs of Staff supported the State Department's desire to replace the French and build strong, pro-American governments in Indochina, they considered only questions of political strategy. When they refused to recommend force levels for the Laotian Army a few months later, they acted in response to a budgetary question in which the trade-offs were not between American firmness and Communist expansion but, rather, between small weapons for a foreign army and large ones for U.S. forces.

can make about the bargaining process with regard to Laos.

Each agency involved in Laos fought to win policy debates by getting its views and proposals incorporated into decisions. That was only natural, since officials knew that those groups and individuals which lose repeatedly develop a kind of bureaucratic leprosy, in which the official or agency is shunned by others and soon loses some organizational appendages. Horace Smith, Ambassador 1958–60, suffered from that trouble. He was unable to control his subordinates and, consequently, to win the confidence of his superiors, who proceeded to ignore and bypass him. Assistant Secretary of State Walter McConaughy (April–November 1961) argued for a hard-line anti-Communist stance in Laos which was incompatible with the consensus higher in the State Department and in the White House. He was replaced by Averell Harriman, who had been in effective control of Laos policy since the start of the Geneva Conference in May 1961. Similarly in the embassy, political officers lost influence as they pushed for reduced bombing in 1969 and 1970, when higher officials were convinced of the need for escalated force.

Each group used arguments in the policy debates which reflected its own perspective and which emphasized its administrative or budgetary stake in the outcome.* The Pentagon and CIA were consistently vigorous advocates of support for their clients and strong opponents of any reductions in that support. The foreign aid agency succeeded in winning support for suspensions in assistance only when it could argue that its entire budget was jeopardized by the lack of reforms in Laos or when

---

* The whole process of bargaining, at least at the middle levels of government, seems to be one of argumentation and debate. Policy must take the form of words arranged into analyses, prescriptions, and orders. Debate over those words lets each participant try to persuade the others to think about the problem in the same way. Since there is rarely consensus on what the "given problem" is, each organization will define it according to its own perspectives and concerns. Even analysis is partisan and is clearly subordinated to the play of the bargaining game, as Charles Lindblom argues in *The Policy-Making Process,* pp. 19, 33, 34. Prescriptions and orders are also partisan because they are selected for their persuasibility in comprehending, expressing, or justifying policy.

it cut only economic aid and permitted a continuation in military deliveries.

Policy debates over which faction to support were usually settled by the compromise of letting each agency continue its programs to its own favorites. When two groups clashed, as in Phoumi's coup against Phoui Sananikone in December 1959, the American supporters of the army won. They had not only the biggest budgetary stake but also the powerful argument that the army was the only effective arm of the Laotian government in much of the country.

No agency was forced to implement a policy which it opposed. In other words, each group had a veto power on matters which were its primary responsibility. This is most evident in the case of Laos in the U.S. Army's continued and successful opposition to the introduction of American ground troops into Laos.

Two possible exceptions point up the limits of this rule. In the one instance that equipment deliveries were halted (in November 1960), U.S. military opposition had delayed that decision until it could no longer prevent Phoumi from taking Vientiane. There is even some doubt that the aid was ever fully suspended, since U.S. advisors marched north with the rightist forces and the Ambassador did not inform the Premier until a week after the cut-off was supposed to have been made. Another instance of a policy adopted over strong opposition was President Kennedy's decision early in his term to try to neutralize Laos by international agreement. This was opposed by the military chiefs, many State Department holdovers from the previous administration, and possibly even the new Secretary of State. The Pentagon had its chance to try to win short of intervention, but the Royal Army did not perform as expected. The new administration had a special antipathy to "Walter Robertson's boys" and was not likely to heed them when it had an Ambassador in Vientiane who was recommending neutralization. Secretary Rusk kept his counsel guarded and was able to turn over the burden of reaching an acceptable agreement to another man. Thus, the opponents of the policy were not themselves required to implement it.

These conclusions should not be surprising. Since Laos was never an issue of vital concern to any agency, one on which its fundamental objectives or its bureaucratic survival rested, officials could concede points on Laos in return for support on other questions. Advocates of an extensive counter-insurgency effort in South Vietnam, for example, won the support of those policy makers who saw futility in Laos yet were concerned with containing communism in Asia. To most men in Washington, Laos was a minor issue in which acquiescence to the views of those most intensely concerned and deeply involved was as good a rule for agreement as any. The veto power given to those directly responsible for implementation was rooted not only in the reluctance of officials to deny others the reciprocity they themselves would expect but, also, in the practical realization that such decisions could easily be twisted or sabotaged. At the middle levels of government, reciprocity, compromise, and consensus are acceptable and at times necessary practices, especially on third-magnitude problems like Laos.[10]

Decisions in Washington were not consistent, value-maximizing choices, but, rather, ad hoc responses to discrete situations. Policy directives were the outcome of a process of tacit and direct bargaining among the groups and representatives involved in Laos matters. These observations confirm the literature on decision-making, which stresses bargaining and incrementalism in the way policy changes. Although much of this literature is based upon studies of first and second magnitude problems, it is applicable to cases like Laos if one discounts the influence of personal factors and idiosyncracies. Career policy makers are still men, but they derive their influence more from their bureaucratic roles than do political appointees, who often can speak for constituencies outside the Executive Branch.[11]

Perhaps the most striking aspect of the history of American policy toward Laos is how decisions in Washington were turned into actions in Laos. The foregoing chapters have revealed numerous instances of conflicts among agencies in the field and of actions at cross-purposes and contrary to expectations. The remainder of this chapter will try to explain why these conflicts and deviations occurred.

Decisions are rarely self-executing. Even when the President is directly involved, giving unambiguous orders to respectful subordinates with the capability for carrying them out, the results may not be as anticipated.[12] When lesser officials, dependent on others for coordination and action, try to implement decisions, the chances for deviation are even greater.

Most foreign policy studies stop at the point of decision and assume implementation.[13] They generally fail to consider what happens after officials choose to start the war, move the troops, make the speech, send the warning, provide the support, cut off the aid, and so forth. But what happens is important, since it is to happenings and perceived events that other nations respond. People must choose and then execute plans. Implementation is not automatic, but, rather, is subject to strong centrifugal tendencies which can overcome the centripetal forces for compliance and control.

Especially in third-magnitude problems like Laos, one should not assume implementation as anticipated by top policy makers. The men in Washington were too busy with many urgent matters to exercise close supervision over Laos and the men in the field had their own priorities, which often differed from what their superiors would have wished. The USOM members in 1955, for example, were too busy helping to establish credit and trade institutions in Vientiane to pay much attention to how the Royal Army used its cash grants. The urgency of getting visible aid projects going before the 1958 elections made the Ambassador less sensitive to the consequences of some of those projects in strengthening factions which opposed the traditional political leadership. The many other duties of the Ambassador's bombing control officer in the late 1960s and early 1970s prevented him from exercising the closeness of supervision expected in Washington, where officials confidentially denied violations of the rules of engagement and the bombing of villages.

Time and space create difficulties for control. On low

priority matters, or where calm seems to prevail, the time between major foreign policy decisions is long. The subordinates
are, thus, free to act according to their old mandate, whether
or not those actions are consistent. Space inhibits control because information and directives must travel a long chain of
command, in which each link has an opportunity to impose its
own perspective and judgment. Messages get distorted.[14] When
the center, out of ignorance of the details of local conditions,
defers to the opinion at the periphery, the men in the field
gain even greater freedom from control.

Laos was separated from Washington in time and space.
The occasional decisions by higher officials gave considerable
leeway to middle level bureaucrats much of the time. The U.S.
capital's dependence on the men in the field for information
gave those men opportunities to do as they wished with relative impunity, as noted in the statement at the start of this
chapter.

The standard methods of achieving central control over
the actions of subordinates are coercion, norms, and incentives.[15]
Coercion is a rare and drastic step, however, and, in Laos,
evidently was used only when there seemed to be especially
strong evidence of flagrant and conscious disobedience. The
most obvious examples of coercion in this case were four personnel transfers: in 1959, the CIA Station Chief; in 1961, John
Steeves from the Geneva Delegation; in 1962, the CIA man
attached to Phoumi Nosavan; and, in 1971, the head of the
political section of the embassy.

Norms were a poor guide to action, and, hence, control, because they were too ambiguous. The general American
consensus on anticommunism did not extend to the question of
which faction to support in Laos. New norms, like neutralization, conflicted with the earlier anticommunism, so there was
no gain in clarity. The more deeply rooted principle of supporting one's pro-American friends—in this case, the clients of
the various agencies—only made central control more difficult.

Incentives were an uncertain method of control since
some produced compliance and others encouraged deviation.
Career advancement is considered the most important objective

of men in a bureaucracy, leading them to do what is rewarded and refrain from that which is punished.[16] But rewards and punishments are given within a single agency and, thus, for compliance with its goals and directives rather than with what might be the conflicting orders of central decision makers. To advance his career, a military officer in Laos had to support his organization's preference for Phoumi and the army over the established politicians. A foreign service officer, similarly, had a career incentive to oppose any coalition with the Pathet Lao, whatever he might have thought was best for peace and stability in Laos.

Not all compliance is good. Although central decision-makers want their orders obeyed, they also want responsible criticisms and suggestions for change. Since the line between persistent dissent and disobedience is not always clear, many officials err on the side of caution. Just as there were some men who sacrificed their policy convictions in order to protect their careers (for example, the younger diplomats who opposed the anti-French stance of the embassy or who preferred the CDNI Lao to the older, seemingly corrupt politicians but followed the dictates of the Ambassador), there were also some, like Ambassador Brown, who risked their careers in order to protect what they saw as sound policy. If a man believes strongly enough in the wisdom of his preferred policy and the inefficacy of the established ones, he may be proved "right" by history, or at least by the next administration.

Resistance to control is so pervasive in bureaucracies that one scholar has called the phenomenon a law of behavior. "The greater the effort made by a sovereign or top-level official to control the behavior of subordinate officials, the greater the efforts made by those subordinates to evade or counteract such control."[17] The bureaucracies which made policy toward Laos were not immune to this "law." In fact, the men in the field consistently fought any restrictions on their freedom of action in support of their clients.

Even in Washington, subordinates handling Laotian matters tried to keep decisions in their own hands rather than shifting them upward for decision. One member of various

State Department working groups on Laos between 1959 and 1961 freely admitted this practice.

> If there was going to be a higher level confer-
> ence because of some disagreement, the papers would
> be prepared differently depending on whether we (the
> subordinates) would be present at the conference or
> not. If we were to be there, the papers would include
> controversial matters. If not, we would not submit
> papers that produced a head-on clash. We disliked this
> because we feared that something might be put over on
> our boss by his counterpart (from another agency) if
> we were not there to defend him and backstop him. We
> often joked, "These things are too important to be de-
> cided at higher levels."[18]

Effective control requires supervision and feedback to evaluate the operation of the incentives and norms intended to insure compliance. The trouble in Laos was that there was little supervision and only limited channels for feedback from the field.

Since Laos was not a high priority matter for top-level policy makers, the task of supervision devolved on officials who were happiest when nothing was apparently wrong or in need of change. In fact, this reluctance to change policy is common to most bureaucrats. Anthony Downs says that there are strong pressures for most officials to become "conservers" in the long run; that is, to seek to maximize their security and convenience and to be biased against any change in the status quo.[19]

Lacking the time to oversee every directive, Washington officials focused their attention on the course of policy in Laos only when issues crossed some threshold of significance, usually by becoming a matter of public controversy. The embassy in Vientiane, for example, was able to get effective action on its requests for reforms in the aid programs only when Laos was being more closely watched because of its coalition government including the Pathet Lao and when reporters were writing stories of corruption and abuses in those aid programs.

Similarly the Congress pried information from the Executive Branch only when numerous press reports in 1969 made further secrecy extremely difficult.

Feedback to Washington from Laos was generally inadequate. One Ambassador surprised and pleased the State Department by sending more cables than almost all of the rest of the Far East posts combined.[20] This occurred, however, during a period when Washington was particularly interested in conditions in Laos. At other times, to be sure, there were extensive reports and numerous cables, but apparently not enough to give an adequate picture of the events there. The complaint cited earlier of one man involved with Laos during the chaotic autumn of 1960 was true for many at other times: "I couldn't get good information from *anybody*."[21] Nor did the Washington officials have a good background or perspective for evaluating them.

No one in Laos seemed to report troubles unless he wanted more money or had a suggested plan for alleviating the problem. This is understandable, since officials do not like others to believe that they are somehow failing at their assigned tasks. They like to tell their superiors what they expect to hear.[22] Criticism affects careers; self-criticism can be suicide. This abhorrence of bad reports led to a deemphasis on the corrupting effects of the aid program and a persistent reluctance to admit the poor fighting qualities of the Laotian Army.*

Washington officials were sensitive primarily to anticommunism. Other factors in reports were probably dismissed as less significant. Because of their own concerns, Americans tended to see the struggle against Communist influence as the major issue in Lao politics, while, in fact, the deeper reality was the nonideological factionalism among the ruling elites.

---

* Tullock, *op. cit.*, pp. 137–141, says that such distortion is inevitable since reports have to be culled, summarized, condensed, and otherwise distorted. The same phenomenon emerged recently in the minimization of the extent of the atrocities committed at My Lai 4 hamlet in March 1968 as reports of the incident moved through successively higher levels of the military chain of command. See *New York Times*, March 27, 1970.

This perspective distorted much of the feedback available from Laos.

In the absence of tighter controls, the people and groups in the embassy in Vientiane were relatively free to act in ways which undermined, vitiated, and stultified decisions from Washington. The causes are numerous and understandable; the effects, however, were frightening.

Weakness and, in some cases, the impossibility of control are evident throughout the history of American policy toward Laos. Some types of decisions in Washington gave free rein to the men in the field. Individuals and agencies in Laos became committed to the protection of their own clients, often to the disregard of overall policy guidelines. The bureaucratic structures which implemented policy were slow to adjust to new directives from higher officials or to new circumstances in Laos. Sometimes there was even outright sabotage of policy by the men in the field. These examples are probably the most important, but they were not the only ones.

Decisions in Washington always give some unintended freedom to the men in the field. Except when an official approves a detailed plan or scenario (which itself is usually drafted by the people responsible for implementation), policy decisions are only guidelines for action. These can never be specific enough to eliminate subsequent judgment and discretion. Nor should top officials demand rigid adherence to plans.* What they should favor is a judicious combination of unambiguous guidelines, discretionary flexibility, and adequate supervision. In a perfect world, such combinations are abundant and easy.

* Robert Anthony criticizes the bulk of the literature on management for asserting that the aim of control is to assure that operations conform as closely as possible to plans. Such rigidity is bad, he argues, because circumstances are always changing and plans are always outdated. Anthony says that superiors should rather let their middle level managers adjust to unforeseen events and then judge them by their efficiency and effectiveness in carrying out specific tasks. Robert N. Anthony, *Planning and Control Systems: A Framework for Analysis* (Boston: Division of Research, Graduate School of Business Administration, Harvard University, 1965), pp. 28, 29, 68, 69.

Usually, decisions are ambiguous compromises. The many divergencies over Laos policy strengthened that tendency. As the product of bargaining among powerful governmental factions, policy papers frequently carried one agency's proviso, another's caveat, and whatever remained of the initial group's draft proposal. Ambassador Brown took advantage of these sometimes conflicting instructions by going ahead with what he preferred and asking for clarification on the remaining paragraphs. This ploy has presumably been repeated by officials in Laos and elsewhere for years, if not centuries.

Subordinates can pick and choose their orders from compromise decisions, especially ones that temporize in a fluid situation. The different U.S. agencies supporting different factions in the political struggles during the summer of 1958 each had a license from Washington to do something like what it actually did. The same was true after the Geneva Conference in 1962. Yet, in both cases, as well as during the aftermath of the Kong-Le coup, the lack of a clearcut decision in Washington gave the men in the field a hunting license[23] to fight for their own preferred policies and to poach almost at will on the bureaucratic territory of other groups.

One great stimulus to such internecine struggles was the tendency and the frequent strategy for decisions to be minimal and incremental.[24] So long as they were not expressly prohibited from supporting their clients, the CIA continued to strengthen the CDNI in 1958 and the military advisors continued to encourage Phoumi Nosavan to hold out for a more powerful role in any government established by the Geneva Conference in 1961–62. When Washington itself was divided over the response to the Kong-Le coup, policy decisions mirrored that division and left subordinates fighting for control over future decisions, each trying to create faits accomplis or a better decisional environment for its proposals.

The desire by higher level officials to preserve a wide range of possible options for future decisions, when the facts might be clearer and the sense of consensus greater, encouraged minimal decisions in the present. Thus, President Eisenhower alerted military forces for possible action in 1959 and 1960, as did President Kennedy in 1961 and 1962. In the several weeks immediately after the Kong-Le coup, Washington officials also acted to preserve their options by neither endorsing nor condemning Phoumi's self-proclaimed revolutionary committee and by giving aid to both sides and control to neither. The trouble in this latter case was that no one in Washington knew when the freedom *not* to choose would eventually vanish and certain lines of policy would be foreclosed. Choices averted become choices by inadvertence as time and circumstances change. In this instance, the U.S. denial of Souvanna's requests for assistance (to mitigate the effects of the Thai blockade and to provide some leverage over Phoumi) thrust the Premier toward the Soviet Union and prevented the realization of the primary American objective in Laos: limiting all Communist influence.

Another case of inadequate control developed in the relations between U.S. officials in Laos and their host-country clients and counterparts. Close work with them led the Americans to adopt some of their perspectives and to defend their interests in policy debates.

The arrangement was quite natural and predictable. The diplomats had frequent contact with the leading politicians; the various U.S. Ambassadors met socially and hunted and rode with the Premiers during their tours of duty. When there was a conflict between these elite politicians and younger aspiring rulers, the diplomats sided with the older men whom they knew well. In the same conflict, CIA operatives who had helped to build the CDNI supported their proteges, as did the Agency men who later gave advice and assistance to Phoumi Nosavan and still later to the Meo tribesmen. CIA officials had good reasons for considering these groups as more effective political and military forces, and certainly as more pro-American, than the existing groups within Laos. Military advisors, first in the PEO and later in the MAAG, were advocates of continued reliance on the army and apologists for the army's failings. The U.S. officers were often close personal friends of the Laotian military leaders.*

* The evidence on the relations between foreign aid personnel and their counterparts is insufficient for a similar comparison. Much of

One consequence of these close relations was the increased susceptibility of the Americans to manipulation by the Lao. Twice the army commanders engineered military pay raises in spite of objections by some Americans. U.S. officials believed and repeated to Washington many allegations of North Vietnamese or Chinese intervention in Laos which turned out to be false or grossly exaggerated. As they accepted Laotian military claims, so also did they agree with the army officers' analysis of domestic politics—especially the need for a strong military voice in the government.

Another consequence was the bitter-end support of their clients by U.S. officials. Military advisors stuck by Phoumi Nosavan from 1958 until his fall from grace in 1964; by then, they had found new favorites in the Lao Army. The CIA has persisted for nearly a decade in its support of the Meo tribesmen, despite the protests of Royal Army officers that only the Meo got new weapons and equipment and that Vang Pao might try to establish a separate Meo nation. The diplomats in Vientiane have remained committed to governments by the ruling elites, preferring vigorous anti-Communists such as Katay Don Sasorith, Phoui Sananikone, or Boun Oum to the soft neutralism of Souvanna Phouma. When the United States set about to evacuate the Plaine des Jarres early in 1970, the first to be airlifted were the leading merchants and artisans. The Americans could not turn their backs on their clients because they had faith in them and they had risked resources to promote them. To support another faction would be to discredit their own judgment and activities.

When policies or circumstances changed in Laos, the various U.S. agencies were slow to adjust. Aid officials resisted some changes in their programs, in particular devaluation and

---

the effort in the early years was handled through United States contractors, though perhaps some of the men who oversaw import licensing were more tolerant of abuses than those not familiar with the elaborate procedures. There are no examples either way. In recent years the aid programs have been greatly expanded, but again with unclear consequences for United States/client relations.

a shift from cash grants to commodity imports, despite the clear
and mounting evidence of abuses. They were relatively tolerant
of petty corruption because they saw that Laos was being saved
from communism. Before the Geneva Conference in 1962, the
economic aid programs were primarily concerned with building infrastructure beneficial to military operations. There was
no integrated effort to give Laos a self-sustaining economy or
to strengthen nonmilitary political institutions. After 1962, the
aid program reflected the new counterinsurgency doctrines
being tried in South Vietnam.

Military assistance likewise took the form of plans applied elsewhere. The Laotian Army was given a conventional
war capability dependent on adequate ground transportation,
although the monsoons rendered even some of the so-called
all-weather roads impassable at times. Only in recent years have
these problems been lessened by the provision of U.S. helicopter support for greatly increased mobility.

Some U.S. officials were also slow to accept changes
dictated by Washington. The idea of neutralization, for example, had been anathema during the Dulles years and continued to be so for many officials in Laos and in the Far East
Bureau in Washington even after President Kennedy made clear
his support of that policy goal. Americans who had encouraged
their Lao friends to resist a coalition found it hard to change.

Bureaucratic momentum in some programs decreased
Washington's ability to control policy by making changes hard
to effect. Frequently U.S. officials pursued their directives so
zealously that they vitiated higher level plans. Instead of cooperating with French advisors working with the Lao government, U.S. diplomats consciously avoided them and opposed any
politicians, like Souvanna Phouma, who seemed pro-French.
Hostility between the French and Americans in Laos reached
such a level that one of the primary objectives of Ambassador
Smith on his arrival in 1958 was an improvement in those relations.

Overzealousness weakened the effects of the 1958 Operation Booster Shot as well. Instead of letting the Laotian politicians take credit for the village aid projects and special air lifts

of commodities, many U.S. officials flaunted the American role in the effort and, consequently, added to the credibility of Pathet Lao charges that the established politicians were U.S. lackeys.

Several interventions in internal affairs were also heavy-handed. The CIA's manipulation of Souvanna's ouster in 1958 was not well concealed; nor was its help in rigging the 1960 elections. The partiality shown in aid suspensions was undeniable. After the Kong-Le coup, for example, military aid continued to pour into the supply depots in southern Laos but no effort was made to channel it northward, as promised.

In recent years, enthusiasm for concrete results led many U.S. aid officials to bypass the red tape and legitimizing procedures which delayed their projects. An important result of this has been to weaken local governments at a time when the major reason for extending development projects to the village level was to strengthen those political structures as an alternative to the Pathet Lao.

Bombing developed a momentum of its own. The air war over Laos grew during pauses in the bombing of North Vietnam not because of any strategic urgency but rather because the planes were available and would otherwise sit idle. Rigid rules of engagement were laid down, only to be violated by pilots used to greater freedom and initiative. The Americans built large, modern facilities and took over more control of operations in order to impose their own procedures.

None of these events should have been particularly surprising. Bureaucracies, by their nature, reduce administration to rules. And rules, once set, are hard to change. Routines develop; new members of the organization are trained in the routines and socialized in the norms of the office. In order to do any work at all, new problems must be treated as if they were the old ones, or at least similar enough to be dealt with by the established routines. This rigidity by itself can lead to a displacement of goals, so that changing goals without changing procedures may produce no change at all because of bureaucratic momentum.[25] Thus, the consequence of inflexibility is a weakening of central control.

The lack of close supervision and the reluctance of officials to punish their subordinates for overzealousness permitted outright sabotage of policy. Ambassador Smith was weak and his subordinates were skilled at making end runs around him. Their work with the CDNI undermined his support for Phoui Sananikone and the older politicians. Apparently the only principle Washington officials could agree on was free market political competition among anti-Communists, for they neither supported Smith nor ordered him to side with the Young Ones.

CIA operatives continued to aid the army financially despite aid suspensions in 1958 and 1960, thereby stultifying the impact of those policies. It is not clear that Washington even knew of these actions, for in an earlier aid suspension, officers at CINCPAC channeled their aid through a "transportation" contract. The CIA men in Laos had more latitude than their military colleagues and, thus, could more easily have acted without authority from higher levels.

During the autumn of 1960, Washington really lost effective control over policy in Laos. Each agency was either permitted or took free rein. Ambassador Brown resisted orders to get rid of Souvanna Phouma and Kong-Le while he tried to engineer a coalition of neutralists and rightists, excluding the Pathet Lao. He also promised Souvanna that the U.S. aid channeled to Phoumi would not be used against the Royal Government. But the Americans stationed with Phoumi encouraged him to oppose that coalition government and did not discourage him from using American arms to march against Vientiane. The one attempt to punish Phoumi and his advisors—the suspension of aid at the end of November—was too late to be effective, perhaps deliberately so.

Incidents of policy sabotage since 1962 are much harder to find, probably because there has been a general consensus on U.S. actions in Laos among the policy makers. Continued secrecy also helps, of course, to hide criticisms and deviations. Each U.S. agency has been relatively free to run its own show, and all have been vigorously anti-Communist. Only in the 1970 effort by the head of the political section to query the Pathet Lao about guarantees in return for a bombing halt and the deliberate disregard of rules of engagement by overzealous pilots seem to come close to examples of policy sabotage. If orders are ever given to end or even drastically change the U.S. involvement in Laos, additional examples can be expected.

What could have been done differently in the past? What can and should be done in the future? These questions have not been addressed directly because the main purpose of this book is to explain and understand the policy-making process rather than to evaluate or criticize the results of that process. Inevitably such an analysis is deterministic, stressing why the outcomes had to be as they were.

But things could have been different. The United States did not have to involve itself in a last-ditch stand to preserve its influence in Laos, first by political manipulation and later by warfare. Americans need not have imposed their own values and interests on Laos while being insensitive to the problems they were creating. Better decisions and better control of implementation were possible, though difficult, if policy makers had greater awareness of what those processes entailed.

Knowledge of these bureaucratic processes can lead to better control over them. If bargaining skill rather than good judgment determines who prevails in a policy dispute, one would do well to develop that skill. An official who is aware of the consequences of the ambiguity in his guidelines or of his effort to preserve his options may be more effective in preventing or coping with those consequences. Recognition that bureaucracies are inflexible and dependent on routines might force more attention to small details which have significant long-term effects.

Dilemmas and limitations abound in the search for closer supervision and control. The standard remedies are clear, acceptable norms; continual, high-level attention to details; and multiple feedback channels. But norms and guidelines always leave room for judgment, and they cannot be accepted too rigidly or they will prevent necessary flexibility and change. Only lower-echelon officials have the time to pay close attention to details in a generally low-priority matter like Laos. Yet these are the very men whose career incentives are to be cautious and uncritical. Distortion and concealment are frequent if there is only one information channel. But too many channels overload the supervisor with data and lead to a selectivity which may be even worse.

Is better control worth the effort? The answer is not necessarily affirmative. Firm control over bad policy is at least as bad as inadequate control over good policy. Rigid application of Washington's perspective and judgment, which is necessarily general and for many circumstances, might destroy the chances for flexible adaptation to local conditions. Men in policy posts in the United States are more susceptible, for example, to the obsessions with anticommunism and pro-Americanism than the people in the field, who can view the political system on its own terms and not solely with categories concerned with foreign policy.

Maybe there is no solution to the control problem. That issue has been stressed here because U.S. policy toward Laos was significantly affected by the process of implementation. Yet in the broader complexities of foreign policy, control is only one problem among many.

There is no mechanical solution, no magic organization chart, which can dispel bureaucratic tendencies. Builders of policy machines should remember the warning of computer experts: garbage in, garbage out. Precisely because bureaucracies see selectively, think narrowly, and act rigidly, the men within them must act to counteract those inherent tendencies. And officials at the highest levels of government must try hardest of all.

Instead of trying to change our policy machinery we should try to change our minds. If U.S. officials had been more sensitive to ethnic and generational cleavages within Laos and more willing to accept Pathet Lao participation in the government, they might have been able to avoid the kind of warfare which is today devastating Laos. If the Americans had been less concerned with containing anything called communism, they might have been able to live with the natural divisions among the Pathet Lao, North Vietnamese, Chinese, and Russians. By insisting on a whole loaf, the United States may wind up with only a charred crust.

The obsession with anticommunism and the consequent opposition to a coalition government were deeply rooted in the minds of policy makers in the 1950s and 1960s. This continued fear of any loss of territory to Communist control, or even to substantially increased Communist influence, has been the driving force of American foreign policy for a quarter of a century. Unfortunately, this obsession is still prevalent now and is likely to continue until the old generation of cold warriors fades away.

Although there are potential threats to U.S. security which should be anticipated and resisted, none involve the nation of Laos. American interests would be protected and the cause of freedom advanced if Laos were neutral or simply at peace. Control over territory is less important than intellectual and commercial access to others. The prevailing chessboard view of world politics is demeaning and ultimately dehumanizing to the world's people.

Looked at now, U.S. policy toward Laos since 1954 cannot be called stupid or irrational, no matter how much one may dissent from that policy. Honest, sincere, and intelligent men provided careful, sensible plans to achieve the policy goals they were given. The real problem is in these objectives.

Why should it have been assumed that the United States could intervene actively in Laotian affairs and yet not be as suspect of colonialism as the French? Why were coalition governments and neutralization so often rejected out of hand? Why was military force considered an appropriate means of coping with the internecine struggles in Laos?

To have altered Laos policy, one would have had to raise those questions and then give very unpopular answers. That few men did so explains why U.S. policy took the course it did. And if one wishes to change policy in the future, similar questions must be raised and given very different answers.

Reversals in U.S. policy toward Laos—that is, significant deviations from the trendline of current actions—have occurred when serious questions were raised about existing policy. These questions were usually not raised internally, where they would be disruptive, but externally by the press and Congress. The aid scandals of 1958 and 1959 and the special congressional investigations of 1969 are such examples, as was the Kennedy Administration's review of policy in 1961. In all such cases, the bright lights of public interest and awareness focused, if only briefly, on Laos.

Normally, as this study has shown, Laos has been a third-magnitude policy problem, confined to a closed system of career-minded officials. The most questionable decisions made within this system have been the ones most subject to secrecy. Since political intervention and covert military involvement did not have to survive public scrutiny, these measures were not challenged by independent outsiders. Once secrecy was made official policy, it was used to cover a multitude of other actions which seemed acceptable because nobody ever had to know about them.

Openness will not necessarily guarantee good judgment, of course, since outside forces may react more to symbols, catch phrases, and supposed precedents than to the facts. But ultimately American foreign policy must have public approval, if only to secure budget requests and to avoid political defeat. Even in the short run, a policy that depends on secrecy is difficult and dangerous to pursue—difficult because a dissenter may leak the knowledge to the press and dangerous because secrecy often becomes its own justification.

Unless foreign policy is open to public scrutiny, the important questions and values may never be considered. Regardless of the difficulties or embarrassments of government officials in the face of the truth, they are not likely to be worse than the consequences of misleading or deceiving the public if and when those best-laid plans go astray. The basic argument for the public's right to know is simply that, in a democracy at least, the people are the bosses of the diplomats and soldiers.

Because of the secrecy surrounding it and the bureaucratic problems discussed in this book, Laos may well be an all too typical case of U.S. foreign policy-making. Others will have to study additional cases to see whether the kinds of problems noted here were common or extraordinary. It may help us to realize, however, that most foreign policy matters coast along day to day, subjected to analysis only in a relatively closed bureaucratic system. Officials build up their own prejudices; organizations develop their own momentum; policies take a certain direction. Crises may bring these tendencies into view and force close attention by top policy makers, but their choices are still likely to be limited by the options perceived by their subordinates. If we are to avoid repeating the events chonicled here, we must remember that Laos is not synonymous with chaos, but with everyday policy.

Postscript on the Pentagon Papers

The 7,800 pages of the Defense Department study on "United States–Vietnam Relations, 1945–1967" are the richest documentary lode ever made available to students of American foreign policy at a single time. The Pentagon Papers will be mined for years; these brief comments regarding new information about Laos come from only a quick sluicing.

Laos was a peripheral matter to the writers of the study, both in their analyses and in the documents which they included. Nevertheless, there is some hard evidence against which to test the interviews which are central to this book. At several crucial periods—especially 1954, early 1961, and 1964—Laos and Vietnam were closely related policy issues, and the information is abundant.

In the Pentagon Papers one can see the working papers as well as the decision documents, both the anguished cables and the action orders. The only drawback to the analysis is that the writers could not weigh their interpretations of the written documents against the testimony of key participants.

On the basis of this new information, I would make some modifications in my interpretations, point to several confirmations of my analysis, and offer some additional insights into the policy-making process.

My emphasis on President Kennedy's preference for negotiations over military involvement should be modified. Although Kennedy did nothing to hinder negotiations, neither did he ever eliminate the option of using force in Laos. He also showed surprising willingness to permit extensive covert operations in Indochina. The deep disagreements evident during the confused meetings of late April and early May 1961 were resolved only by permitting detailed contingency planning for

272

military operations and by agreeing to stand firm against communist advances in Vietnam. The National Security Council Action Memorandum (NSAM) 52 of May 11 reported the President's approval of covert operations to infiltrate intelligence and even assault teams into Laos regardless of a cease-fire.[1] These particular plans, however, were aimed solely at communist bases and lines of communication affecting South Vietnam.

As late as August 29, 1961, when officials said that the basic decision to support Souvanna Phouma and negotiated neutralization had already been made, NSAM 80 reveals that that support was conditional on his agreement to some earlier proposals. At the same time the President authorized conversations on enlarging the SEATO Plan 5 for military operations and immediate action to increase mobile training teams with U.S. advisors down to the company levels.[2] On September 20, the JCS sent the President a plan for intervention in Laos which was deleted from the official version of the Pentagon Papers and was not available to Senator Gravel.[3] Thus, the military track was far from being abandoned.

Another modification which should now be made is in the portrayal of Souvanna Phouma as a beleaguered man in the middle, nearly as reluctant to receive U.S. assistance as he was to permit Pathet Lao gains. By 1964, at least, he had cast his lot with the Americans and may even have been pressing Washington to increase its military support to him. One possible explanation is that he shared the optimism of many Americans that Operation Triangle had turned back the tide of Pathet Lao advances. On December 10, 1964, newly arrived Ambassador

    1. *The Senator Gravel Edition—The Pentagon Papers* (Boston: Beacon Press, 4 vols., 1971), II:641, 643 (Documents 98 and 99).
    2. *United States–Vietnam Relations, 1945–1967*, study prepared by the Department of Defense (Washington: U.S. Government Printing Office, 12 vols., 1971), 11:247 (Document 27). [The Department of Defense edition does not bear consecutive page numbers; therefore the references to that edition are cited by volume number (arabic) and the page numbers that appear therein.]
    3. DoD 11:vi (Document 28).

Sullivan cabled that Souvanna "Fully supports the U.S. pressures program and is prepared to cooperate in full."[4] The sensitivity of this question of Souvanna's role can be seen in the fact that several deletions from the official version of the study, including the Sullivan cable, involve the Premier's requests or support for U.S. military action.

The Polish proposals in 1964 for an international conference on Laos were apparently much more important to policy makers at the time than they subsequently remembered in interviews. This discrepancy probably springs from the fact that the conference never occurred, in part because of U.S. delaying tactics so as to avoid negotiations which might also involve Vietnam and thus hinder U.S. freedom of action there. The Americans may also have prompted Souvanna to demand prior conditions which the Pathet Lao found unacceptable.[5]

Pressures on the Embassy in Vientiane to permit U.S. and South Vietnamese military operations in Laos were at least as strong in 1964 as in subsequent years. And Ambassador Unger resisted them just as vehemently then as Ambassador Sullivan did later. In late summer and early autumn 1964 Unger repeatedly cautioned against ground operations and even flights which might damage Souvanna's position. He also insisted on advance clearance of any cross-border operations if they should be authorized.[6] There is no evidence from later years, however, that Vientiane's opposition had a significant effect on U.S. military proposals for operations in the sanctuary areas.

The assertion that the Joint Chiefs, and especially the Army, were reluctant to intervene in Laos should be changed to a question mark. The Pentagon Papers reveal a readiness to deploy forces which may or may not be the same as eagerness for such operations, particularly during 1961. What is clear is that the military planners wanted to be free to escalate if necessary in order to win. Further study will be required in order to distinguish "can do" from "want to do," and to dis-

---

4. Gravel III:253.
5. DoD 4:IV.C.2.(b), pp. 16–18; Gravel III:197–8.
6. Gravel III:515–17, 566–68, 584–85.

cern when actions in Laos were urged primarily so as to make proposals for Vietnam more acceptable. The new documents are more confusing on this issue than the later memory of officers.

Confirmed by the Pentagon Papers is the strongly anti-communist orientation of the American government, extending back at least as far as the Czech coup. A 1948 policy statement declared U.S. objectives in Indochina to be: eliminating communist influence, fostering cooperation with the west, raising the standard of living, and preventing undue Chinese penetration.[7] The strategic importance of Southeast Asia was a well-established part of the basic consensus among U.S. policy makers even prior to 1954.

The domino theory also was widely held. In February 1950 the National Security Council concluded that communists planned to seize all of Southeast Asia. If they dominated a government in Indochina, Thailand and Burma were expected to fall to communism. "The balance of Southeast Asia would then be in grave hazard."[8] As late as 1964, the theory was still espoused by the Joint Chiefs, despite State Department reluctance to accept such a rigid formulation. The Chiefs held that the theory was "the most realistic estimate for Cambodia and Thailand, probably Burma, possibly Malaysia."[9] Although there are no documents from President Johnson himself, his 1961 report on his Asian trip, printed in full for the first time, shows his belief at that time that failure to oppose communism in Southeast Asia would force the United States to "surrender the Pacific and take up our defenses on our own shores."[10]

Despite the fear of communist advances throughout the years after 1954, the Pentagon Papers reveal little direct involvement in Laos by outside forces. An agreed National Intelligence Estimate (NIE) in July 1955 concluded that the

7. DoD 8:144 (Document 91).
8. NSC 64, February 27, 1950, in DoD 8:282–85; also Gravel I:361–2.
9. Gravel III:626.
10. DoD 11:182 (Document 18).

North Vietnamese would infiltrate armed units into Laos only
if the Royal Government took military action which seriously
threatened the Pathet Lao position in the two northern provinces.[11] The study says that the North Vietnamese left some
cadres in Laos after 1954, both as advisors and administrators.
Some of these were withdrawn by early 1957, and during 1958
and early 1959 North Vietnamese activities were "evidently
attenuated." Only when the Royal Government tried to "dis-
establish" the two remaining Pathet Lao battalions in May 1959
did they increase their aid and military involvement.[12]

Soviet aid greatly worried American policy makers,
though in retrospect the amount seems small. Between December 1960 and early 1962, the U.S.S.R. airlifted somewhat more
than 3,000 tons of supplies to the Pathet Lao and neutralist
forces—an amount which the 17,800 men of a typical U.S. Army
infantry division would consume in less than four days.[13] Truck
convoys of supplies were also detected at some stages during
this period. Although this aid was undoubtedly quite helpful
to the opposition forces, the available intelligence estimates
suggest that the United States had little fear of direct intervention by Soviet or Chinese forces. A study in October 1961
predicted that even a direct SEATO intervention in South
Vietnam would lead only to increased communist political
activities in Laos, once a neutralization agreement had been
signed.[14]

The anti-French orientation of American policy in
Indochina is also quite clear in the Pentagon Papers. The first
post-Geneva NSC policy paper, issued on August 20, 1954,
specifically called for the U.S. to work through the French
"only insofar as necessary" and instead deal directly with the
local governments in Indochina.[15] By 1958, however, the basic
policy paper added an objective of developing "greater mutual

11. DoD 10:995 (Document 260).
12. DoD 8:IV.A.5 Tab 3, pp. 60–61.
13. *Ibid.*
14. DoD 11:318 (Document 34).
15. DoD 10:737 (Document 201).

understanding and cooperation with the French."[16] Although the French subsequently agreed to let Americans take a greater role in training the Laotian army, U.S. policy makers believed that the French disagreed on the nature of the communist threat and on the need for Americans to participate in the training.[17]

Documents regarding U.S. aid show a continuing concern over corruption and ineffectiveness. By November 1956 NSC policy papers for both Laos and Cambodia said that the United States should terminate its aid if the local government "ceases to demonstrate a will to resist internal Communist subversion and to carry out a policy of maintaining its independence."[18] There is no mention, however, of any decision to suspend aid because of the coalition with the Pathet Lao. In fact, the documents reveal that the Americans agreed to defer pressures for monetary reform until after the 1958 elections. Aid throughout the region was criticized for premature commitments and then extraordinary delays in delivery.[19]

Reports during the 1959 crisis confirm the lack of hard evidence on which to blame outside communists for aggression. An OCB report on August 12 said that it was reasonable to assume North Vietnamese involvement, but "there is no conclusive evidence as to the exact composition and objectives of the attacking forces."[20] The same report noted "a disappointing lack of capacity to control a small scale internal security problem" on the part of the Royal Army the previous May when it permitted a Pathet Lao battalion to escape custody.

An agreed Special National Intelligence Estimate (SNIE) on September 18 attributed the renewed guerrilla war to "a reaction to a stronger anti-Communist posture by the Laotian Government and to recent US initiatives in support

16. DoD 10:1130 (Document 281).
17. See OCB Report, 7 January 1959, DoD 10:1165 (Document 284).
18. NSC 5612/1, DoD 10:1092.
19. OCB Report, May 28, 1958, DoD 10:1138, 1142.
20. DoD 10:1238–39.

of Laos."[21] There was some dissent from the conclusion that U.S. military intervention would increase the likelihood of an open communist invasion. While the number of guerrillas was admitted to be small (1,500–2,000 at most), they were said to have "considerable additional potential strength." An intelligence estimate in December 1958 had concluded that the political front for the Pathet Lao, the Neo Lao Hak Xat, was "making strong gains in almost every sector of Laotian society."[22]

Instead of being content with the anti-communism which they had urged on the Royal Government, American officials by February 1960 admitted that their "immediate operational problem has been to persuade the Lao leadership from taking too drastic actions" which might provoke a North Vietnamese response.[23] Although the NSC papers do not acknowledge conflicts among U.S. agencies in Laos at that time, they do admit the need for greater cohesion among anticommunist elements.

Documents from the period of maximum division and confusion in official policy—August–December 1960—have generally been deleted from the official study. Part of the conflict among U.S. officials was legitimized by an addition to the basic NSC paper on Laos, which was revised on August 24, 1960, when Souvanna and Phoumi were still negotiating a settlement to the Kong-Le coup. Besides providing military aid against communist subversion, the paper added the words "or other elements hostile to U.S. interests."[24] This proviso made the CIA's payments to Phoumi Nosavan (also admitted in a December 20 document)[25] harder to oppose. A SNIE on December 6 concluded that the present situation was one of "confusion, drift, and disintegration. . . . Laos is heading toward civil war."[26] One further indication of the split among U.S. policy makers

21. DoD 10:1242.
22. DoD 10:1172.
23. DoD 10:1250.
24. DoD 10:1292–93.
25. DoD 10:1347.
26. DoD 10:LII (Document 311).

was the State Department's lone dissent on December 20 that the new Boun Oum government was too narrowly based to be popular.[27]

The American government's efforts to preserve the secrecy of its actions in Laos after 1962 are abundantly clear in the Pentagon Papers. Particularly during 1964, this secrecy was also demanded by the Royal Laotian Government. It is important to realize, however, that efforts to circumvent the provision of the 1954 Geneva Accords regarding Vietnam had also been made secretly and with little opposition or sense of guilt. The basic NSC policy paper on Indochina of August 20, 1954, called for "covert operations on a large and effective scale."[28] Not only did the United States encourage the Diem government to resist unified elections, but it also got around the limitation on the number of U.S. military advisors to South Vietnam by adding 350 men on what was called a Temporary Equipment Recovery Mission (TERM). The study calls this action, which parallels the establishment of the PEO in Laos, "a convenient cover for a larger intelligence effort."[29] Paper agreements were thus not allowed to stand in the way of preferred military activities.

The Pentagon Papers also provide additional examples of some of the problems discussed in the Conclusions. Control of American operatives and their clients was never easy. In light of the recent controversy over bombing operations, one is struck by the concerned State Department cable to Vientiane on August 26, 1964, which complained about Thai and Lao pilots and observed: "We have impression latter not really under any kind of firm control."[30]

Hunting licenses provided by Washington's compromises are clear in the August 1960 NSC paper approving aid to oppose elements hostile to the United States and in President Kennedy's dual-track policy of preserving the option of military intervention. As early as 1956, official policy also sanctioned

27. DoD 10:1347.
28. DoD 10:731.
29. Gravel II:433.
30. Gravel III:553 (Document 184).

support for clients: "individuals and groups in Laos who oppose dealing with the Communist bloc."[31] These earlier decisions thus paved the way for many subsequent troubles.

Bureaucratic momentum shows up in the development of MAAG missions to both Laos and South Vietnam. The Pentagon Papers include the documents in which the Joint Chiefs of Staff resisted the idea of a MAAG in Laos until Secretary Dulles persuaded them that political considerations were overriding. They also reveal that the military advisors sent to Vietnam created a force which was the mirror image of U.S. forces, and thus not well suited to the guerrilla warfare which they encountered.[32]

The tendency to put the best possible face on developments is illustrated by the analyses after the 1957 coalition government and the 1958 electoral victories by the Pathet Lao. At the time, NSC reports were cautiously optimistic about these setbacks, seeing in them opportunities for strengthening anticommunists. When those forces had united by 1960, official documents said that the fate of Laos earlier had been "very cloudy indeed."[33]

Reading the documents on Vietnam, one is struck by the many parallels to developments regarding Laos. In both countries the United States conducted large-scale covert operations and was deeply involved in encouraging or thwarting coups. Aid was seen as a lever, but policy makers could never bring themselves to risk "losing" the country by stopping aid in order to force desired changes. Further study would probably expand this list of parallels.

The Pentagon Papers reveal American policy makers as tough pragmatists. They circumvented the various Geneva Agreements without any words of chagrin. They approved devious and deadly covert operations with little regard for the consequences of publicity and with no regard for the ethical problems of such operations. They tried to manipulate internal

31. DoD 10:1092.
32. Gravel II:408; DoD 10:756; 3:IV.B.3, p. i.
33. DoD 10:1252, 1142.

politics without seeing any contradiction between such actions and America's declared abhorrence of such interference. They repeatedly opposed international negotiations which might threaten U.S. control over events.

For both Laos and Vietnam, the study illustrates the same decisionmaking process described in this book. Policy makers operated in a relatively closed system. Many of the key documents emerged from middle-level working groups, where the debates and apparent bargaining took place over words. Particularly in the many papers from the 1964 policy debates one can read impassioned debates over the phrasing of analyses as well as objectives, thus showing that the papers were taken seriously. Men kept pushing for their own preferred outline of a paper or agenda and for the adoption of their categories and labels as well as their action recommendations.

These men were generally isolated from domestic political pressures, as this analysis would predict. The taboo on mentioning domestic factors was evident even in the election year of 1964—at least in the documents which have survived. Instead, policy makers made only vague references to informing the Congress and preparing public opinion for escalation. And all this seems based on the assumption that these forces could easily be manipulated and were hardly a constraint on policy. The need to sell policy to uninformed people resulted in a frightening preoccupation with the appearances of actions rather than the actual consequences in furthering U.S. policy goals.

President Johnson's resistance to the apparent consensus for action against North Vietnam which had formed by September 1964 confirms the different assessment of domestic factors by a man not caught in the closed system of foreign policy makers. The tragedy for America—and Indochina—came when he spurned his instincts and agreed to the elaborate, reasonably argued "solutions" presented by his advisors.

In Laos as well as in Vietnam, "the system worked."[34] Minimal decisions proved irreversible; commitments took on

---

34. See Leslie H. Gelb, "Vietnam: The System Worked," *Foreign Policy*, No. 3, Summer 1971, pp. 140–167.

lives of their own; new programs arose, like Phoenix, from the ashes of dashed hopes. If we learn nothing else from the Pentagon Papers and the experience which they describe, we must learn how our policy-making system does work—particularly its assumptions and its operation largely divorced from public opinion. With such knowledge, we may be able to act to avoid future tragedies in places which now appear to be the end of nowhere.

C. A. S.

October 1971

Notes

INTRODUCTION

1. Interview.
2. "Laos: April 1971," Staff Report, Committee on Foreign Relations, U.S. Senate, August 3, 1971, 92nd Cong., 1st sess., p. 6 (hereafter the Moose-Lowenstein Report). "Thailand, Laos, and Cambodia: January 1972," May 8, 1972, 92nd Cong., 2nd sess., pp. 20–22 (1972 Moose-Lowenstein Report); Raphael Littauer and Norman Uphoff (eds.), *The Air War in Indochina*, revised edition (Boston: Beacon Press, 1972), pp. 9, 281 (hereafter the Cornell Air War Study).
3. See the article by Jacques Decornoy, "Life in the Pathet Lao Liberated Zone," reprinted in Nina S. Adams and Alfred W. McCoy (eds.), *Laos: War and Revolution* (New York: Harper Colophon Books, 1970), pp. 411–423; Georges Chapelier and Josyane Van Malderghem, "Plain of Jars, Social Changes Under Five Years of Pathet Lao Administration," *Asia Quarterly*, vol. 1, no. 1 (1971), pp. 61–89.
4. These figures come from several sources: the Agency for International Development; Arthur J. Dommen, *Conflict in Laos: The Politics of Neutralization* (New York: Frederick A. Praeger, 1965), p. 104; United States, Senate, Committee on Foreign Relations, *United States Security Agreements and Commitments Abroad: Kingdom of Laos, Hearings* before the Subcommittee on U.S. Security Agreements and Commitments Abroad of the Committee on Foreign Relations, part 2, 91st Cong., 1st sess., 1970 (hereafter called the *Laos Hearings*), p. 556; the Moose-Lowenstein Report, p. 13; and 1972 Moose-Lowenstein, pp. 34–35; Cornell Air War Study, p. 101.
5. The (Washington) *Evening Star*, January 8, 1971.
6. Washington admits U.S. air operations and even the use of forward air guides on the ground, but it denies any ground combat role for its 643 men admittedly involved in military training, advice, or supply. Reporters claim, however, that they have seen Americans give direct orders to Laotian soldiers, that they knew Americans killed in combat, and that they have learned of guerrilla operations led by U.S. personnel. See *New York Times*, March 7 and 12, 1970, March 12 and May 22, 1971; The (Washington) *Star*, October 28, 1970, February 19 and June 10, 1971. Also 1972 Moose-Lowenstein, p. 19.
7. See the *New York Times* and *Washington Post*, May 19, 1970, and the subsequent charges by antiwar veterans that Americans had participated in a two-week invasion of Laos in February 1969 in the *New York Times*, April 24, 1971. Much confirming evidence of U.S. policy actions since 1964 can be found in the *New York Times* reports on a 1968

283

Defense Department study of the history of the Vietnam War, June 13–15, 1971 (henceforth cited as *"New York Times Documents"*).

8. *New York Times*, March 12 and June 12, 1971; (Washington) *Star*, October 28, 1970.

9. Background on Air America can be found in Peter Dale Scott, "Air America: Flying the U.S. into Laos," *Ramparts*, February 1970, and *New York Times*, April 4, 1970. See also *New York Times*, January 20, 1971, and (Washington) *Star*, October 23, 1970.

10. State Department figures plus *New York Times*, June 16, 1971.

11. United States, Senate, Committee on Foreign Relations, "Security Agreements and Commitments Abroad," *Report* by the Subcommittee on Security Agreements and Commitments Abroad, December 21, 1970, p. 1 (henceforth cited as *Symington Report*).

12. United States, Senate, Committee on Appropriations, *Mutual Security Appropriations for 1955, Hearings* on H.R. 10051, an act making appropriations for Mutual Security for the Fiscal Year ending June 30, 1955, and for other purposes, 83rd Cong., 2nd sess., 1954, p. 306.

13. United States, Department of State, *The Situation in Laos*, September 1959, p. i.

14. See President Kennedy's March 23, 1961, statement, noting especially the argument that the ". . . security of all Southeast Asia will be endangered if Laos loses its neutral independence. Its own safety runs with the safety of us all. . . ." (*New York Times*, March 24, 1961).

15. News conference, text in *New York Times*, April 26, 1964.

16. Paul, *loc. cit.*, p. 541.

17. Statement of March 6, 1970.

18. Bernard B. Fall, *Anatomy of a Crisis: The Laotian Crisis of 1960–1961* (Garden City, New York: Doubleday and Company, 1969), p. 23.

19. Joel Halpern and Peter Kunstadter, "Laos: Introduction," in Peter Kunstadter (ed.), *Southeast Asian Tribes, Minorities, and Nations*, vol. I (Princeton: Princeton University Press, 1967), p. 240.

20. Confidential Source.

21. Dommen, *op. cit.*, p. 115.

22. 1972 Moose-Lowenstein, pp. 18, 21.

23. Bernard B. Fall, "The Pathet Lao: A 'Liberation' Party," in Robert A. Scalapino (ed.), *The Communist Revolution in Asia* (Englewood Cliffs, New Jersey: Prentice-Hall, Inc., 1965), p. 183; Fall, *op. cit.*, p. 121; Joel M. Halpern, *Government, Politics, and Social Structure in Laos*, Monograph Series No. 4, Southeast Asia Studies, Yale University, 1964, p. 81.

24. Joel M. Halpern, *Economy and Society of Laos*, Monograph Series No. 5, Southeast Asia Studies, Yale University, 1964, Table 9, pp. 5–6, 10–11; Frank M. LeBar and Adrienne Suddard (eds.), *Laos* (New Haven: HRAF Press, 1960), p. 240; Dommen, op. cit., pp. 3, 5.

25. LeBar and Suddard, *op. cit*, pp. 74–76; Halpern, *Government, Politics*, pp. 8, 18, 42.

26. T. D. Roberts, Mary Elizabeth Carroll, Irving Kaplan, Jan M. Matthews, David S. McMorris, Charles Townsend (coauthors), *Area Handbook for Laos*, DA Pam. No. 550-58 (Washington, D.C.: Govern-

ment Printing Office, June, 1967), p. 58; Halpern and Kunstadter, *loc. cit.*, pp. 243, 245; Halpern, *Government, Politics*, p. 85.

27. Robert Shaplen, *The Lost Revolution* (New York: Harper and Row, 1965), p. 362; United States, Congress, Senate, Special Committee to study the Foreign Aid Program, *Foreign Aid Program: Compilation of Studies and Surveys*, S. Doc. 52, 85th Cong., 1st sess., 1957, "Southeast Asia: Report on United States Foreign Assistance Programs," by Clement Johnston, survey no. 7, p. 11; Halpern, *Government, Politics*, pp. 43–45.

28. Paul F. Langer and Joseph J. Zasloff, *North Vietnam and the Pathet Lao* (Cambridge, Mass.: Harvard University Press, 1970), p. 90.

29. Roberts, *et al., Handbook*, p. 302.

30. Confidential Source; Halpern, *Government, Politics*, pp. 102–103.

31. Halpern, *Government, Politics*, pp. 97–99; LeBar and Suddard, *op. cit.*, p. 105.

CHAPTER ONE

1. Quoted in Emmet John Hughes, *The Ordeal of Power: A Political Memoir of the Eisenhower Years* (New York: Dell Publishing Company, Inc., 1964), p. 182, from a 1956 conversation.

2. Knowland quotation from the *New York Times*, July 22, 1954; Eisenhower in *Public Papers of the President, 1954*, pp. 642, 647 (July 21 news conference); Dulles in United States, Congress, Senate, Committee on Appropriations, *Mutual Security Appropriations for 1955, Hearings* on H.R. 10051, an act making appropriations for Mutual Security for the Fiscal Year Ending June 30, 1955, and for other purposes, 83rd Cong., 2nd sess., 1954, p. 305; Wilson in *New York Times*, July 21, 1954.

3. See Dean Acheson, *Present at the Creation* (New York: W. W. Norton and Company, 1969), Chapter 70, for background.

4. Robert McClintock, *The Meaning of Limited War* (Boston: Houghton Mifflin Company, 1967), p. 175.

5. Dwight D. Eisenhower, *Mandate for Change, 1953–1956* (Garden City, New York: Doubleday and Company, Inc., 1965), p. 373.

6. *Public Papers of the Presidents of the United States, Dwight D. Eisenhower, 1954* (Washington, D.C.: Office of the Federal Register, National Archives and Records Service, 1960), p. 341 (March 24 news conference) and pp. 382–383 (April 7 news conference). These basic assumptions were rarely enunciated because there was little, if any, disagreement with them.

7. Eisenhower, *Mandate*, pp. 352–353; Melvin Gurtov, *The First Vietnam Crisis* (New York: Columbia University Press, 1967), pp. 24–25. See Gurtov for the most complete picture of the fight over intervention in April 1954.

The following summary of Dulles' actions and beliefs during 1954 draws heavily on the persuasive arguments by Victor Bator, *Vietnam: A Diplomatic Tragedy* (Dobbs Ferry, N.Y.: Oceana Publications, Inc., 1965). Although all previous writings had suggested that Dulles argued and fought for direct United States military intervention in Indochina on several occasions before the end of the Geneva Conference only to be overruled by the more peaceful Eisenhower, Bator contends that these proposals were always contingent upon and subordinate to actions which would implement his deterrent theory and establish a strong security system in Southeast Asia. See especially pp. 34-40, on the April intervention crisis.

8. Eisenhower wrote in *Waging Peace, 1956–1961* (Garden City, N.Y.: Doubleday and Company, Inc., 1965), p. 364, that Dulles believed in making clear American intentions as early as possible in a crisis. This is an excellent example of Thomas Schelling's point that the first person to commit himself to a course of action is likely to prevail. (See his *The Strategy of Conflict* [Cambridge: Harvard University Press, 1960], ch. 2.)

9. This set of beliefs is identified from content analysis of Dulles' public statements and is elaborated in Ole R. Holsti, "Comparative 'Operational Codes' of Recent U.S. Secretaries of State: John Foster Dulles," paper prepared for the 65th annual meeting of the American Political Science Association, 1969 (mimeo.), p. 7. See also David J. Finlay, Richard R. Fagen, and Ole R. Holsti, *Enemies in Politics* (Chicago: Rand McNally, 1967).

10. Anthony Eden (Lord Avon), *Full Circle* (Boston: Houghton Mifflin Company, 1960), pp. 149, 161.

11. Philippe Devillers and Jean Lacouture, *End of a War: Indochina, 1954* (New York: Frederick A. Praeger, 1969), p. 322.

12. *Department of State Bulletin*, August 24, 1954, 31:260, 263; see also Robertson's obituary in *New York Times*, January 20, 1970.

13. Interview with Robert Bowie.

14. Acheson, *op. cit.*, pp. 674–676; Gustov, *op. cit.*, pp. 24 25; Samuel P. Huntington, *The Common Defense* (New York: Columbia University Press, 1961), pp. 64–84, 279–283.

15. United States, Congress, Senate, Committee on Appropriations, *Mutual Security Appropriations for 1955, Hearings* on H.R. 10051, an act making appropriations for Mutual Security for the Fiscal Year ending June 30, 1955, and for other purposes, 83rd Cong., 2nd sess., 1954, pp. 171–173, 307.

16. United Press Dispatch in *New York Times*, July 25, 1954.

17. *Ibid.*, August 19, 1954.

18. Louis L. Gerson, *John Foster Dulles* (vol. XVII in The American Secretaries of State and their Diplomacy, Robert H. Ferrell, ed., New York: Cooper Square Publishers, Inc., 1967), pp. 144–146, 195–197.

19. *New York Times*, July 23, 1954, *op. cit.*, pp. 161–162.

20. Dulles quoted in Gerson, *op. cit.*, pp. 196–197; *New York Times*, August 13, 1954. See text of treaty and official exegesis by Dulles in United States, Congress, Senate, Committee on Foreign Relations, *The Southeast Asia Collective Defense Treaty, Hearings on Executive K*, 83rd Cong., 2nd sess., 1954, part 1, pp. 2–9.

21. *Public Papers of the Presidents, 1954*, p. 277; Eisenhower, *Mandate*, pp. 336, 352. For an excellent discussion of the Eisenhower and Dulles views on colonialism, see Bator, *op. cit.*, ch. 16.

22. Gerson, *op. cit.*, pp. 189–190; Senate Foreign Relations Committee, *Mutual Security Act of 1954, Hearings*, p. 19; Senate Appropriations Committee, *Hearings*, p. 305.

23. Devillers and Lacouture, *op. cit.*, p. 218; *New York Times*, July 21, 1954.

24. Interviews with Confidential Source and Walter Robertson.

25. McClintock, *op. cit.*, p. 170; Devillers and Lacouture, *op. cit.*, p. 195; Eisenhower, *Mandate*, p. 361; Bator, *op. cit.*, p. 91; United States, Congress, Senate, Committee on Foreign Relations, Mutual Security Act of 1954, *Hearings on the Mutual Security Program for Fiscal Year 1955*, 83rd Cong., 2nd sess., 1954, p. 126.

26. McClintock, *op. cit.*, pp. 175 177.

27. Devillers and Lacouture, *op. cit.*, p. 357n.

28. *Ibid.*, pp. 340–347. The official communiqué is State Department Press Release 542, September 29, 1954. See also *New York Times*, September 25, and *Washington Post*, September 28 and 30, 1954.

29. Devillers and Lacouture, *op. cit.*, pp. 369 373.

30. State Department Press Release 245; Gurtov, *op. cit.*, p. 121.

31. Devillers and Lacouture, *op. cit.*, pp. 290–300.

32. *Ibid.*, pp. 301–310. The Declaration by the Royal Government of Laos, July 21, 1954, is reprinted in Dommen, *op. cit.*, p. 310.

33. Confidential Source; General J. Lawton Collins, January 1966, Dulles Oral History Project.

34. Interview with Admiral Arthur Radford; Dommen, *op. cit.*, pp. 98–99, which draws upon United States, Congress, House, Committee on Government Operations, U.S. Aid Operations in Laos; Seventh Report by the Committee, H.R. 546, 86th Cong., 1st sess., 1959, pp. 2, 8 (henceforth cited as *Porter Hardy Report*). Also Confidential Source.

35. Dommen, *op. cit.*, pp. 98–99; *Porter Hardy Report*, pp. 2, 8; *Porter Hardy Hearings*, p. 6.

36. Confidential Sources; *Porter Hardy Report*, p. 9.

37. Letter to author, November 6, 1969.

CHAPTER TWO

1. In United States, Congress, House, Committee on Foreign Affairs, *Mutual Security Act of 1959*, *Hearings* before the Committee on Foreign Affairs, 86th Cong., 1st sess., 1959, p. 1129.

2. Oden Meeker, *The Little World of Laos* (New York: Charles Scribner's Sons, 1959), pp. 214, 215–216.

3. Figures on the size of the American mission in Laos come from Mike Mansfield (Senator), *Viet Nam, Cambodia, and Laos*, Committee Print for Senate Committee on Foreign Relations, 84th Cong., 1st sess., October 6, 1955, p. 19; Meeker, *op. cit.*, p. 39; Allen J. Ellender (Senator) *Report on Overseas Operations of the United States Government*, Committee Print for Senate Committee on Appropriations, 85th Cong., 1st sess., 1957, p. 380; and House Foreign Affairs Committee, *Hearings, Mutual Security Act of 1958*, p. 68. Sessions Report is excerpted in *Porter Hardy Hearings*, pp. 52–53; interviews with Joseph Anderson and a Confidential Source.

4. United States, Congress, House, Committee on Government Operations, *United States Aid Operations in Laos, Hearings* before a Sub-

committee of the Committee on Government Operations, 86th Cong., 1st sess., 1959, pp. 184–185. In subsequent references, these hearings will be cited as *Porter Hardy Hearings*, after the Subcommittee Chairman.

5. *New York Herald-Tribune*, January 8, 1955.

6. Hugh Toye, *Laos: Buffer State or Battleground* (London: Oxford University Press, 1968), pp. 106–107.

7. Although the argument was not made at the time, the Polish representative on the ICC later (April 1955) pointed out an ambiguity in Article 19 of the cease-fire agreement, which declared that the military forces of each party "shall respect the territory under the military control" of the other. The original French text referred to "le territoire *placé* sous le controle militaire." (Emphasis supplied.) The Polish representative argued that the whole provinces had been placed under Pathet Lao control. See D. R. SarDesai, *Indian Foreign Policy in Cambodia, Laos, and Vietnam, 1947–1964* (Berkeley: University of California Press, 1968), p. 169.

8. For an excellent summary of the role of the ICC, see SarDesai, *op. cit.*, ch. VI, especially pp. 157, 160, 169, 177; Anita Lauve Nutt, *Troika on Trial, Control or Compromise* (Rand Corporation SD-220, 3 vols., 1967), vol. I, pp. iii, 154, 203. Text of agreements can be found in Mike Mansfield (Senator), *Report on Indochina*, Committee Print for Senate Committee on Foreign Relations, 83rd Cong., 2nd sess., October 15, 1954.

9. Quotations from Dulles, Non-attributable news conference, Manila, March 2, 1955. Joint State-USIA message, in Dulles Papers, Box 478; Interview with a Confidential Source; Robert McClintock, *The Meaning of Limited War* (Boston: Houghton Mifflin Company, 1967), p. 174.

10. Confidential Sources.

11. Bernard B. Fall, *Anatomy of a Crisis: The Laotian Crisis of 1960–1961* (Garden City, New York: Doubleday and Company, 1969), p. 168. Anti-French feelings have been confirmed by J. Graham Parsons and a Confidential Source.

12. *Bangkok Post*, September 23, 1954; Toye, *op. cit.*, pp. 100–101; *New York Times*, November 18, 1954.

13. Confidential Source.

14. Nutt, *op. cit.*, vol. I, p. 200; Confidential Source.

15. Confidential Sources; *Porter Hardy Hearings*, p. 142; *Porter Hardy Report*, pp. 9, 10.

16. Confidential Source.

17. Interview with Walter S. Robertson, June 30, 1969; Confidential Source; *New York Times*, February 28, 1955. Notice the early reliance on the royal family rather than on Vientiane politicians. It is not clear whether this was a conscious policy decision, but the Crown Prince had been reported as being much closer to the U.S. position than Katay, who was negotiating with the Pathet Lao in January–April 1955. Savang reportedly opposed a coalition government and integration of the Pathet Lao fighting units with the Royal Army. (See *New York Times*, January 8, 1955.) Robertson said in 1959 that the Lao government threatened "a number of times" to retake the provinces by force, but were discouraged by the French and British each time on the grounds that the ICC should handle the matter and that they didn't want to provoke a North Vietnam-

ese invasion which would mean another war. *Porter Hardy Hearings*, p. 189.

18. *New York Times*, February 28, March 2, and November 15, 1955.

19. *New York Times*, July 9, 16, and 18, 1955.

20. *Porter Hardy Hearings*, p. 182.

21. United States, Congress, Senate, "Report of Proceedings, Hearing Held before the Committee on Foreign Relations, Nomination of J. Graham Parsons of New York to be Assistant Secretary of State for Far Eastern Affairs," May 26, 1959 (Washington: Ward and Paul—duplicated), p. 15.

22. Breakdown of projects by type is in Report of Director of U.S. Operations Mission to Laos (Daly C. LaVergne), "American Aid to Laos—A vital link in the chain of Mutual Security," July 1, 1959 (mimeo., unclassified), p. 79 (henceforth, LaVergne Report). Population information comes from Joel M. Halpern, *Economy and Society of Laos* (Yale University, Southeast Asia Studies, Monograph Series No. 5, 1964), p. 16.

23. United States, Congress, House, Committee on Appropriations, *Mutual Security Appropriations for 1956, Hearings* before the Subcommittee of the Committee on Appropriations, 84th Cong., 1st sess., 1955, pp. 376, 546; United States, Congress, Senate, Committee on Foreign Relations, *Mutual Security Act of 1955, Hearings* before the Committee on Foreign Relations, 84th Cong., 1st sess., 1955, p. 180.

24. Aid figures from Dommen, *op. cit.*, p. 104, LaVergne Report, p. 79, and United States, Congress, House, Committee on Foreign Affairs, *Mutual Security Program in Laos, Hearings* before the Subcommittee on the Far East and the Pacific, 85th Cong., 2nd sess., 1958, p. 3. Information on the CIA from Confidential Sources.

25. The trends appear in both the Dommen and the LaVergne Report figures.

26. Testimony by Parsons, in United States, Congress, House, Committee on Appropriations, *Mutual Security Appropriations for 1959, Hearings* before the Subcommittee of the Committee on Appropriations, 85th Cong., 2nd sess., 1958, p. 972.

27. Interview with Joseph Anderson, July 1, 1969; *Porter Hardy Hearings*, p. 47.

28. House Appropriations Committee *Hearings, Mutual Security Appropriations for 1959*, p. 354. See p. 599 for a denial of a MAAG presence.

29. Interviews with William M. Leffingwell, May 12, 1969, and a Confidential Source.

30. Roger M. Smith, "Laos," in George McTurnan Kahin (ed.), *Government and Politics of Southeast Asia* (Ithaca, New York: Cornell University Press, second edition 1964), pp. 540–541; Dommen, *op. cit.*, p. 82.

31. Program put forward by Souvanna Phouma on February 28, 1956, quoted in Great Britain, Parliament, Laos No. 1 (1957), *Third Interim Report of the International Commission for Supervision and Control in Laos, July 1, 1955–May 16, 1957* (Cmnd. 314), p. 53. For subsequent negotiation, see pp. 54–57.

32. Interviews with Parsons and Confidential Sources.

33. Details of trip are in Fall, *op. cit.*, pp. 69–70, 72–74, and Sisouk na Champassak, *Storm Over Laos* (New York: Frederick A. Praeger, 1961), pp. 41–50.

34. Confidential Source.

35. *Porter Hardy Hearings*, p. 191. It is interesting that almost all persons interviewed on the question of policy toward a coalition government volunteered the Czech analogy. Despite the other examples of successful and unsuccessful Communist domination of coalition governments, these policy makers seemed fixated on Czechoslovakia. The coup there in 1948 must have been the traumatic event which confirmed their anticommunism. Interviews with Robert Amory, Robert Bowie, Arleigh Burke, Kenneth Landon, Robert Murphy, Arthur Radford, Walter Robertson, Kenneth Young, and Confidential Sources.

36. Interview with Kenneth Young, February 13, 1969; *New York Times*, September 14, 1955; "Comments by the Department of State and ICA on the Report of the House Committee on Government Operations 'United States Aid Operations in Laos,'" pp. 32–33.

37. Interview with Parsons.

38. Third Interim *Report*, p. 61.

39. House Foreign Affairs Committee, *Hearings, Mutual Security Program in Laos*, pp. 60–61; House Appropriations Committee, *Hearings, Mutual Security Appropriations for 1959*, p. 951; Senate Appropriations Committee, *Hearings, Mutual Security Appropriations for 1959*, pp. 299–300.

40. Interview.

41. Confidential Sources.

42. Interview with Don Ropa.

43. *Ibid.;* Fall, *op. cit.*, pp. 76–78; Wilfred G. Burchett, *Mekong Upstream: A Visit to Laos and Cambodia* (Berlin: Seven Seas Publishers, 1959), pp. 280–282; Sisouk na Champassak, *op. cit.*, pp. 52–55.

44. *New York Times*, April 25, 1957.

45. Fall, *op. cit.*, pp. 76–78; Sisouk, *op. cit.*, pp. 55–58. There is no clear evidence of what, besides implied threats, the United States did during the crisis to bolster Katay.

46. This reaction, printed in the *New York Times*, August 26, 1957, as an AP dispatch from Hong Kong, presumably was written on the basis of information supplied from Vientiane and, thus, reflects American Embassy opinion there.

47. Interview with Parsons.

48. Compare the August 5, 10, October 31, November 2, December 24 and 28 agreements between the Royal Government and the Pathet Lao in 1956 with those of November 2, 1957. These are printed in the *Third Interim Report*, pp. 54–67 and the *Fourth Interim Report* (Great Britain, Parliament, Laos No. 1 (1958), *Fourth Interim Report of the International Commission for Supervision and Control in Laos, May 17, 1957–May 31, 1958* [Cmnd. 541]), pp. 57–67.

49. *New York Times*, November 21, 1957; also quoted in Sisouk, *op. cit.*, p. 60.

50. *New York Times*, January 20, 1958.

51. *Porter Hardy Hearings,* pp. 186, 221, 229; Interviews with Rufus Phillips, Don Ropa, and a Confidential Source.

52. Confidential Source.

53. *Porter Hardy Report,* p. 46; Fall, *op. cit.,* p. 85.

54. *Porter Hardy Report,* p. 46.

55. Interviews with Parsons and Phillips.

56. Article by Igor Oganesoff, *Wall Street Journal,* April 9, 1958.

57. *Mansfield Report,* 1955, pp. 18, 19.

58. Clement Johnson, "Southeast Asia: Report on United States Foreign Assistance Programs," survey no. 7 for United States, Congress, Senate, Special Committee to study the Foreign Aid Program, in *Foreign Aid Program: Compilation of Studies and Surveys,* S. Doc. 52, 85th Cong., 1st sess., 1957, pp. 27–29.

59. *Porter Hardy Report,* pp. 15–16; *Porter Hardy Hearings,* pp. 970–974.

60. *Ibid.;* Interview with Parsons.

61. House Foreign Affairs Committee, *Mutual Security Program In Laos,* p. 19; House Appropriations Committee, *Mutual Security Appropriations for 1959,* pp. 519–520, 554–555.

62. United States, Congress, Senate, Committee on Appropriations, *Mutual Security Appropriations for 1959, Hearings* before the Committee on Appropriations, 85th Cong., 2nd sess., 1958, p. 308.

63. For some of the criticism, see *Wall Street Journal,* April 9, 1958, and Haynes Miller, "A Bulwark Built on Sand," *The Reporter,* November 13, 1958, pp. 11–16. For some of the defenses, see Dommen, *op. cit.,* pp. 104–105 and "Comments by the Department of State and ICA on the Report of the House Committee on Government Operations 'United States Aid Operations In Laos,'" June 15, 1959 (typewritten).

64. Senate Appropriations Committee, *Mutual Security Appropriations for 1959, Hearings,* p. 308; *Porter Hardy Hearings,* p. 803.

65. House Foreign Affairs Committee, *Mutual Security Program in Laos,* pp. 3, 38–39.

66. *Porter Hardy Hearings,* p. 807.

67. United States, Congress, House, Committee on Foreign Affairs, *Mutual Security Act of 1958, Hearings* before the Committee on Foreign Affairs, 85th Cong., 2nd sess., 1958, p. 1810.

68. United States Department of Commerce, "Basic Data on the Economy of Laos," *Economic Reports, World Trade Information Service,* part 1, no. 58–59, September 1958, p. 6; House Foreign Affairs Committee, *Hearings, Mutual Security Act of 1958,* pp. 548–549, 567; Confidential Source.

69. *Porter Hardy Report,* pp. 2–3.

70. State and ICA, "Comments," p. 19; Interview with Parsons.

71. "State Department Answers to Questions from the House Foreign Affairs Committee on March 12, 1958," in the Committee's *Hearings, Mutual Security Act of 1958,* p. 568.

72. Confidential Sources.

73. House Appropriations Committee, *Hearings, Mutual Security Appropriations for 1959,* p. 986; *Porter Hardy Hearings,* p. 215.

74. The following discussion of events leading to the currency

reforms draws principally on information obtained from interviews with Ambassador Parsons; J. V. Mladek (May 12, 1969), an IMF official who was hired by the U.S. government to study and recommend reforms in 1957–58; Robert Cleveland (January 14, 1969), who dealt with Laos economic matters during 1958–62; and other Confidential Sources who participated in the decisions.

75. House Appropriations Committee, *Hearings, Mutual Security Appropriations for 1959*, p. 952; Senate Appropriations Committee, *Hearings, Mutual Security Appropriations for 1959*, p. 319.

76. Interview with J. V. Mladek.

77. Toye, *op. cit.*, p. 114; House Foreign Affairs Committee, *Mutual Security Program in Laos*, p. 34.

78. Senate Appropriations Committee, *Hearings, Mutual Security Appropriations for 1959*, p. 319. Toye (p. 118) and Dommen (p. 110) both argue that the cutoff of aid was a pretext to oust Souvanna Phouma. Fall does not mention the suspension. The line of argument presented here is supported by the interviews with J. V. Mladek, Don Ropa, and a Confidential Source.

79. House Foreign Affairs Committee, *Hearings, Mutual Security Act of 1959*, p. 1108; House Appropriations Committee, *Hearings, Mutual Security Appropriations for 1959*, p. 985; Confidential Sources.

80. *Porter Hardy Hearings*, p. 719.

81. The following paragraphs are based on interviews with people who were in Washington, Vientiane, or CINCPAC headquarters during this period: Robert Amory, Richard Bissell, Rufus Phillips, Admiral Herbert Riley, Walter Robertson, Don Ropa, and five Confidential Sources.

82. The following analysis of the divisions within Laos and the American Embassy is based on interviews with several people in the embassy and some in Washington, including several CIA personnel. Interviews with Robert Amory, Lyman Kirkpatrick, J. G. Parsons, Rufus Phillips, Don Ropa, and three Confidential Sources. There is also some evidence in a very discreet chapter by Sisouk, *op. cit.*, pp. 61–66.

83. Wilfred G. Burchett, *The Furtive War: The United States in Vietnam and Laos* (New York: International Publishers, 1963), p. 172.

84. Confidential Source.

85. Dommen, *op. cit.*, pp. 110–111.

86. Both men quoted in Fall, *op. cit.*, p. 94.

87. Souvanna Phouma (Prince), "Laos: le fond du problème," *France-Asie*, XVII (Mars–Avril 1961), p. 1825.

88. Fall, *op. cit.*, p. 94.

89. *Porter Hardy Hearings*, pp. 48–49.

90. Confidential Sources; aid figures from Dommen, *op. cit.*, p. 104.

91. Interviews with Rufus Phillips and Vice-Admiral Herbert D. Riley (April 3, 1969). For Phoumi Nosavan's early career, see Toye, *op. cit.*, pp. 121, 145–146.

92. Interviews with Robert Amory and three Confidential Sources.

93. Toye, *op. cit.*, pp. 120–122. A British journalist in Laos at the time called the border clashes the first of the "phantom offensives"

claimed by the Lao government. Michael Field, *The Prevailing Wind: Witness in Indo-China* (London: Methuen and Company, Ltd., 1965), p. 57. The Rand report by A. M. Halpern and H. B. Fredman (*Communist Strategy in Laos* [Santa Monica, California: Rand Corporation Research Memorandum RM-2561, 1960], p. 23) also blames the Royal Government for initiating the troubles.

94. Sisouk, *op. cit.*, pp. 68–69; Fall, *op. cit.*, p. 96.

95. *Porter Hardy Hearings*, pp. 713–721, 739–740.

96. Sisouk, *op. cit.*, p. 67; Burchett, *Furtive War*, pp. 172–173.

97. The most extensive description of these events is in Fall, *op. cit.*, pp. 99–106. See also Toye, *op. cit.*, pp. 124–25 and Sisouk, *op. cit.*, pp. 75–84.

98. Toye, *op. cit.*, p. 126; Fall, *op. cit.*, pp. 120–121. The only available source for this May 29 statement quoted by Fall is the *Bangkok Post*, May 30, 1959.

CHAPTER THREE

1. United States, Congress, House, Committee on Foreign Affairs, *Mutual Security Act of 1960, Hearings* before the Committee on Foreign Affairs, 86th Cong., 2nd sess., 1960, p. 553.

2. Interview with Joseph Anderson.

3. Bernard B. Fall, "The Pathet Lao," in Robert A. Scalapino (ed.), *The Communist Revolution in Asia* (Englewood Cliffs, N.J.: Prentice-Hall, Inc., 1965), p. 183.

4. United States Department of State, *The Situation in Laos*, September 1959.

5. Bernard B. Fall, *Anatomy of a Crisis: The Story of the Laotian Crisis of 1960–1961* (Garden City, N.Y.: Doubleday and Company, Inc., 1969), p. 121; A. M. Halpern and H. B. Fredman, *Communist Strategy in Laos* (Santa Monica, California: Rand Corporation, Research Memorandum RM-2561, 1960), p. 51.

6. Confidential Sources; interview with Amory; *New York Times*, August 10 and 26, 1959; United States, Department of State, *The Situation in Laos*, September 1959, p. 23.

7. Confidential Source.

8. Interview with Parsons; Fall, *op. cit.*, p. 122.

9. *Department of State Bulletin*, August 24, 1959, 41:278–279.

10. *New York Times*, August 6, 1959 (UPI dispatch); Fall, *op. cit.*, pp. 122–127; Confidential Source.

11. *New York Times*, August 6 and 12, 1959.

12. Fall, *op. cit.*, ch. VII, "The Laos Fraud."

13. William J. Lederer, *A Nation of Sheep* (New York: W. W. Norton and Company, Inc., 1961), pp. 25, 27; *New York Times*, August 10, 1959.

14. *New York Times*, August 13, 1959.

15. *Department of State Bulletin*, September 7, 1959, 41:344.

16. Secretary Herter admitted this to SEATO representatives at the end of September. *New York Times*, September 29, 1959; *Public Papers of the Presidents of the United States, Dwight D. Eisenhower,*

1959 (Washington, D.C.: Office of the Federal Register, National Archives and Records Service, 1960), p. 580 (August 12 news conference).

17. *Public Papers of the Presidents, 1959*, pp. 595, 597 (August 25 news conference).

18. Fall, *op. cit.*, ch. VII.

19. *Ibid.*, pp. 130–131.

20. Statement reprinted in *Department of State Bulletin*, September 14, 1959, 41:374; see also *New York Times*, August 27 and September 1, 1959. Reuters was more generous than the *New York Times*, for it reported on August 31 that 4,320 pairs of canvas jungle shoes had been delivered. *Washington Post*, September 1, 1959.

21. Sisouk na Champassak, *Storm Over Laos* (New York: Frederick A. Praeger, 1961), p. 95; Fall, *op. cit.*, p. 135.

22. Dwight D. Eisenhower, *Waging Peace, 1956–1961* (Garden City, New York: Doubleday and Company, Inc., 1965), p. 421. This strange reluctance by the President to call the Pathet Lao Communists suggests uncertainty as to the extent of external Communist support to the movement, a view further confirmed by a footnote on p. 431.

23. Interviews with J. Graham Parsons and Confidential Source. Another Confidential Source disputes the contention that Herter saw Laos as a place for cooperation with France. Whatever the truth, Herter's thinking about these events remains obscure.

24. Interview with Parsons.

25. Interview with Richard Bissell and a Confidential Source. For more background on Air America, see Peter Dale Scott, "Air America: Flying the U.S. into Laos," *Ramparts*, February 1970, especially p. 42.

26. *New York Times*, August 18 and 22, September 5, 1959.

27. Interviews with Admirals Burke and Riley and a Confidential Source.

28. Interviews with a Confidential Source and General Donald M. Weller (USMC, ret.), who was on the staff of Task Force 116 from 1959–62 and commander 1960–61.

29. Interview with a Confidential Source and Fall, *op. cit.*, pp. 155–156 (where he quotes Joseph Alsop).

30. *Department of State Bulletin*, September 21, 1959, 41:414; see also *New York Times*, September 5, 1959.

31. United Nations, Security Council, *Report of the Security Council Sub-Committee under Resolution of 7 September 1959*, S/4236, November 5, 1959, New York: Security Council, especially paragraph 98.

32. Sisouk, *op. cit.*, pp. 125, 131; Michael Field, *The Prevailing Wind: Witness in Indo-China* (London: Methuen and Company, Ltd., 1965), pp. 62–63; Interview with a Confidential Source.

33. Sisouk, *op. cit.*, pp. 125–127; *New York Times*, October 25, 1959.

34. Accounts of the coup are in basic agreement, although some sources put more emphasis on the constitutional question of continuing the mandate of the National Assembly beyond its expiration in December until the elections the following April. Sisouk (p. 129) admits that this was only a "façade." See Sisouk, *op. cit.*, pp. 128–138; Hugh Toye, *Laos: Buffer State or Battleground* (London: Oxford University Press, 1968), p.

132; Fall, *op. cit.*, pp. 175–176; and Stuart Simmonds, "Independence and Political Rivalry in Laos 1945–61," in Saul Rose (ed.), *Politics in Southern Asia* (London: St. Martin's Press, 1963), pp. 187–188.

35. In addition to the sources cited in note 34, information on the CIA comes from three Confidential Sources.

36. The following analysis of the divisions within the United States Embassy has been derived from interviews with three Confidential Sources.

37. Quoted in an article, the first of three, written by Jim G. Lucas for the Scripps-Howard newspapers and released January 18, 1960.

38. Confidential Sources.

39. Interviews with Roy Wehle and three Confidential Sources.

40. Sisouk, *op. cit.*, pp. 136–138; Fall, *op. cit.*, p. 176.

41. Sisouk, *op. cit.*, pp. 139–140.

42. Quoted in Simmonds, *loc cit.*, p. 189. See also Arthur J. Dommen, *Conflict in Laos: The Politics of Neutralization* (New York: Frederick A. Praeger, 1965), pp. 132–133. Interviews with two Confidential Sources.

43. Fall, *op. cit.*, p. 180; Sisouk, *op. cit.*, pp. 145–46; Reuters dispatch in *New York Times*, June 3, 1960.

44. House Foreign Affairs Committee, *Hearings, Mutual Security Act of 1960*, p. 1009.

45. Fall, *op. cit.*, p. 119n.

46. Jim Lucas, in articles cited in note 37.

47. *Ibid.;* Fall, *op. cit.*, p. 117; House Foreign Affairs Committee, *Hearings, Mutual Security Pact of 1960*, p. 553.

48. Interview with Joseph Anderson, author of the report. The articles were those by Lucas in the Scripps-Howard papers.

49. Interview with Anderson.

50. Interviews with Kenneth Landon and Robert Myers.

CHAPTER FOUR

1. Quoted in Arthur M. Schlesinger, Jr., *A Thousand Days: John F. Kennedy in the White House* (Boston: Houghton Mifflin Company, 1965), p. 327.

2. Quoted in Bernard B. Fall, *Anatomy of a Crisis: The Laotian Crisis of 1960–1961* (Garden City, N.Y.: Doubleday and Company, Inc., 1969), p. 187.

3. Interview with Winthrop Brown.

4. Interview with Confidential Source. At that time Phoumi Nosavan requested $1 million immediately and $1 million later. This request was not processed before the coup.

5. Interview with Brown.

6. Hugh Toye, *Laos: Buffer State or Battleground* (London: Oxford University Press, 1968), p. 142.

7. Interviews with Robert Amory, Richard Bissell, and Confidential Source.

8. Arthur J. Dommen, *Conflict in Laos: The Politics of Neutralization* (New York: Frederick A. Praeger, 1965), p. 157.

9. Sisouk na Champassak, *Storm Over Laos* (New York: Frederick A. Praeger, 1961), p. 157; Fall, *op. cit.*, p. 188; Toye, *op. cit.*, p. 144; Michael Field, *The Prevailing Wind: Witness in Indo-China* (London: Methuen and Company, Ltd., 1965), p. 72.

10. These descriptions come mainly from eyewitnesses to these events. Field, *op. cit.*, pp. 73–75; Dommen, *op. cit.*, pp. 146–147; Toye, *op. cit.*, p. 144; and Sisouk, *op. cit.*, pp. 158, 162–163.

11. Toye, *op. cit.*, p. 145; Dommen, *op. cit.*, p. 148.

12. Field, *op. cit.*, p. 86.

13. Toye, *op. cit.*, p. 147.

14. Quoted by Field, *op. cit.*, p. 79; Confidential Source; Toye, *op. cit.*, p. 147.

15. Interviews with Brown, Charles T. Cross, and Confidential Source.

16. Interview with Kenneth Landon.

17. Confidential Source; Field, *op. cit.*, pp. 81–82.

18. Quoted in Toye, *op. cit.*, p. 147.

19. Interview with Brown; Fall, *op. cit.*, p. 190.

20. Toye, *op. cit.*, pp. 148–149; Fall, *op. cit.*, p. 190; Field, *op. cit.*, p. 87; interview with Brown.

21. Confidential Sources.

22. Quoted in *The Economist*, September 3, 1960, p. 911.

23. Toye, *op. cit.*, p. 149.

24. Quoted in *Public Papers of the Presidents of the United States, Dwight D. Eisenhower, 1960–61* (Washington, D.C.: Office of the Federal Register, National Archives and Records Service, 1961), pp. 626, 641.

25. Press Release 527, September 10, 1960, printed in *Department of State Bulletin*, September 26, 1960, 43:499.

26. Confidential Sources.

27. Interviews with Brown and Confidential Source.

28. Interview with Parson.

29. Confidential Sources, and interview with Cross.

30. Interview with Burke.

31. Interviews with Burke and Decker and Confidential Sources.

32. Confidential Source.

33. Confidential Source.

34. Interviews with Myers and Bissell.

35. Interviews with Bissell and Confidential Sources; David Wise and Thomas B. Ross, *The Invisible Government* (New York: Bantam Books, 1965), pp. 157–160.

36. Interviews with Cross and Confidential Source.

37. Interview with Brown.

38. Confidential Sources.

39. Quoted in an interview in *New York Times*, January 20, 1961. See other criticism in Schlesinger, *op. cit.*, pp. 327–328 and Field, *op. cit.*, p. 96.

40. Confidential Source; Dommen, *op. cit.*, p. 154.

41. Fall, *op. cit.*, p. 191.

42. *New York Times*, September 15, 1960.

43. Interview with Admiral Riley.

44. *New York Times,* September 24, 1960; Confidential Source.

45. *New York Times,* September 26, 1960 (AP dispatch), and October 1, 1960.

46. Interviews with William M. Leffingwell and Confidential Sources.

47. AP File, September 30, October 4 and 5, 1960, cited in Estelle Holt (untitled: chronology of events in Laos through May, 1964, typewritten). Henceforth cited as Holt Chronology.

48. Interviews with Parsons and Confidential Sources.

49. Interviews with Parsons, Irwin, and Riley.

50. Confidential Source.

51. *Ibid.*

52. Interview with Amory.

53. Dommen, *op. cit.,* p. 159; Fall, *op. cit.,* p. 194.

54. Quoted in Roger M. Smith, "Laos," in George McT. Kahin (ed.), *Governments and Politics in Southeast Asia* (2d ed., Ithaca, N.Y.: Cornell University Press, 1964), p. 555.

55. Interviews with Brown and Parsons.

56. Interview with Brown.

57. Interview with Parsons. (Admiral Riley's description of this report contrasts sharply with Parsons'. Riley says that the report concluded that Souvanna was capable of leading the government and that there was no use in making a last stand to keep the Communists out. Parsons denies that he ever favored a coalition with the Pathet Lao. Since the text of the report is not available, one cannot resolve these differences in recollections.)

58. Interview with Riley.

59. Interviews with Riley and Confidential Source.

60. Keyes Beech, "How Uncle Sam Fumbled in Laos," *Saturday Evening Post,* April 22, 1961, p. 89; Averell Harriman (interview) used the same words.

61. Confidential Source.

62. Dommen, *op. cit.,* pp. 154, 161; Interview with Parsons.

63. Public sources for the extent of U.S. involvement in the rebellion and among the tribes include *New York Times,* October 21, 1960, and Peter Dale Scott, "Air America: Flying the U.S. into Laos," *Ramparts,* February 1970, p. 52. These are partially confirmed by reliable notes on a secret congressional hearing on November 14, 1960, to which the author has had access.

64. Fall, *op. cit.,* p. 195; *New York Times,* November 7, 1960.

65. Confidential Source.

66. Schlesinger, *op. cit.,* p. 328.

67. Confidential Source.

68. From reliable note on that hearing, to which the author has had access.

69. *New York Times,* November 16, 1960.

70. *Ibid.,* November 19 and 20, 1960.

71. *New York Times,* November 17 (AP dispatch), 18, and 19, 1960; Dommen, *op. cit.,* p. 164.

72. Interview with Bissell.

73. *New York Times,* November 20, 1960 (UPI dispatch); Fall,

op. cit., p. 197; *Christian Science Monitor*, December 7, 1960 (Reuters dispatch); and Confidential Sources.

74. Confidential Source.

75. Interviews with Admiral Burke and Confidential Source.

76. Interviews with Burke, Brown, and Confidential Sources.

77. Interview with Brown.

78. Confidential Source.

79. *New York Times*, December 16, 1960; Dommen, *op. cit.*, pp. 168–170; Fall, *op. cit.*, p. 198.

80. For a more detailed analysis of Soviet policy during this period, see Dommen, *op. cit.*, pp. 179–181.

81. Text in *Department of State Bulletin, January* 2, 1961, 44:16–17.

82. *Ibid.*, pp. 15–16.

83. Interviews with Bissell and Confidential Source; Schlesinger, *op. cit.*, p. 331; *Department of State Bulletin*, January 23, 1961, 44:114.

84. Confidential Source; *Dwight D. Eisenhower, Waging Peace, 1956–1961* (Garden City, N.Y.: Doubleday and Company, Inc., 1965), p. 609.

85. Dommen, *op. cit.*, pp. 177–179; Toye, *op. cit.*, p. 162.

86. *New York Times*, January 27, 1961; Toye, *op. cit.*, pp. 164–165.

87. Eisenhower, *Waging Peace*, pp. 609–610; Interview with Gordon Gray.

88. Interview with John Steeves; Fall, *op. cit.*, pp. 213–214.

89. D. R. SarDesai, *Indian Foreign Policy in Cambodia, Laos, and Vietnam, 1947–1964* (Berkeley, Calif.: University of California Press, 1968), pp. 225–226; Fall, *op. cit.*, pp. 210–211.

90. Confidential Source; *New York Times*, December 31, 1960; *New York Herald-Tribune*, December 24, 1960; SarDesai, *op. cit.*, pp. 226–227, 229.

91. SarDesai, *op. cit.*, p. 227; Eisenhower, *Waging Peace*, pp. 610, 717; Interview with Brown; Dommen, *op. cit.*, pp. 173–175.

92. Donald E. Nuechterlein, *Thailand and the Struggle for Southeast Asia* (Ithaca, N.Y.: Cornell University Press, 1965), pp. 179, 185; Norman Harper, "Australia and the United States," in Gordon Greenwood and Norman Harper (eds.), *Australia in World Affairs 1956–1960* (issued under the auspices of the Australian Institute of International Affairs, Publications Centre, The University of British Columbia, Vancouver, Canada, 1963), pp. 201–202; Interview with Admiral Felix Stump, October, 1964, Dulles Oral History Project.

93. Interview with Charles Cross; *New York Times*, December 28, 1960.

94. Confidential Source; Eisenhower, *Waging Peace*, pp. 610–611.

95. Eisenhower, *Waging Peace*, p. 610.

96. Clark M. Clifford, "A Viet Nam Reappraisal," *Foreign Affairs*, July, 1969, 47:604.

97. Confidential Sources.

98. Interviews with Bissell, Irwin, and two Confidential Sources. The CIA pointed to Chinese Defense Minister Lin Piao's December 21 declaration that China would do everything possible to "put a stop to

U.S. imperialism's intervention and aggression in Laos." (Quoted in Holt Chronology.)

99. Interviews with Burke, Decker, and Irwin.

100. Interview with Bissell; Eisenhower, *Waging Peace*, p. 611.

101. Dommen, *op. cit.*, pp. 183–184; Interview with General Weller; *New York Herald-Tribune*, January 3, 1961.

102. See *New York Herald-Tribune*, January 3 and 4, 1961, both articles by Marguerite Higgins.

103. Marguerite Higgins in *New York Herald-Tribune*, January 6, 1961.

104. *New York Times*, January 4 and 5, 1961; Nuechterlein, *op. cit.*, p. 187.

105. Text in *Department of State Bulletin*, January 23, 1961, 44:115–117; See also *New York Herald-Tribune*, January 8, 10, 12, and 14. 1961.

106. Theodore C. Sorenson, *Kennedy* (New York: Harper and Row, 1965), p. 640; Clifford, *loc. cit.*, p. 604.

CHAPTER FIVE

1. Quoted in Theodore Sorensen, *Kennedy* (New York: Harper and Row, 1965), p. 644.

2. See John F. Kennedy's speeches (United States, Congress, Senate, Final Report of the Committee on Commerce, *Freedom of Communications*, Rept. 994, 87th Cong., 1st sess., September 13, 1961, parts I (Kennedy), II (Nixon), and III (Joint Appearances), especially pp. I:94, 528, and 630). Richard Nixon made only one reference to Laos in his entire campaign (p. II:29), admitting that setbacks such as in Laos made some people want to return to isolationism.

3. Henry A. Kissinger has pointed out ("Domestic Structure and Foreign Policy," *Daedalus*, vol. 95, no. 2 [Spring, 1966], p. 518) the danger inherent in this situation: that the policy maker will overlook the background historical factors and will believe that the problem arose the first day he had to deal with it.

4. Interviews with Paul Nitze and Confidential Source.

5. *New York Times*, January 22, 1961.

6. Interview with J. Graham Parsons; Sorensen, *op. cit.*, p. 652. This linkage was even more apparent in the decisions of May 1961, according to documents in *New York Times*, July 1, 1971.

7. Keith C. Clark and Laurence J. Legere (eds.), *The President and the Management of National Security: A report by the Institute for Defense Analyses* (New York: Frederick A. Praeger, 1969), p. 77. This book, based on interviews with State, Defense, CIA, and NSC officials, has the most complete explanation yet available of how the national security decision process operates in practice.

8. Interview with Parsons.

9. Interview with John Steeves.

10. Confidential Sources.

11. *Public Papers of the Presidents of the United States, John F.*

Kennedy, 1961 (Washington, D.C.: Office of the Federal Register, National Archives and Records Service, 1962), p. 16.

12. *Christian Science Monitor,* January 23, 1961.

13. Interview with Ambassador Winthrop Brown.

14. *Washington Post,* February 2, 1961.

15. Text in United States, Department of State, *American Foreign Policy: Current Documents, 1961,* Department of State Publication 7808 (Released June, 1965), pp. 991–992; interview with Parsons.

16. *New York Times,* February 22, 1961.

17. Major General C. V. Clifton, "Hail to the Chief," *Army* (January, 1964), 14:32.

18. General Howell M. Estes, Jr., "The Revolution in Airlift," *Aviation Report* (March/April, 1966), 17:6.

19. Text in *Department of State Bulletin,* February 13, 1961, 44:211.

20. Interviews with General George H. Decker and Paul Nitze.

21. Interviews with Admiral Burke, General Decker, and Confidential Source.

22. Interviews with Brown and Bissell.

23. Sorensen notes (p. 306) the same reluctance to appear "soft" in the early discussions on the Bay of Pigs invasion.

24. *New York Times,* February 9, 1961. President Kennedy met with the formal NSC much less frequently than President Eisenhower and usually only to give a formal hearing to plans already worked out among the leading participants. Whenever a large-scale foreign policy meeting was held, it shall be called an "NSC meeting" as a shorthand phrase, unless clear evidence to the contrary is available. The two statutory members of the NSC most often not in attendance were the Vice President and the Director of the Office of Emergency Planning.

25. *New York Times,* February 24 and 25, March 4, 1961; Arthur J. Dommen, *Conflict in Laos: The Politics of Neutralization* (New York: Frederick A. Praeger, 1965), p. 186.

26. *New York Times,* March 11, 1961; Holt Chronology. Accounts of Souvanna Phouma's visit to the Pathet Lao areas were written by the two Western newsmen accompanying him, Michael Field (*The Prevailing Wind: Witness in Indo-China* (London: Methuen and Company, Ltd., 1965), pp. 115–123) and James Wilde, *New York Times,* March 3, 1961.

27. *New York Times,* March 3, 1961.

28. *Christian Science Monitor,* March 4, 1961 and *New York Herald-Tribune,* March 5, 1961. Also interview with Parsons.

29. Sorensen, *op. cit.,* p. 642; *New York Herald-Tribune,* March 5, 1961; *Washington Post,* March 11, 1961.

30. Confidential Source.

31. *Ibid.*

32. Interview with Joseph Neubert.

33. Interview with Steeves.

34. Quoted in Roger Hilsman, *To Move a Nation: The Politics of Foreign Policy in the Administration of John F. Kennedy* (Garden City, N.Y.: Doubleday and Company, Inc., 1967), p. 130.

35. Dommen, *op. cit.,* pp. 187–188.

36. Hugh Sidey, *John F. Kennedy, President* (New York: Fawcett World Library, 1964), pp. 77–78; *New York Times*, March 18, 1961; *Washington Post*, March 22, 1961.

37. *New York Times*, March 20, 1961.

38. Arthur M. Schlesinger, Jr., *A Thousand Days: John F. Kennedy in the White House* (Boston: Houghton Mifflin Company, 1965), p. 332.

39. Confidential Source and Paul Nitze.

40. *New York Times*, March 21 and 22, 1961.

41. Confidential Sources; *The Times* (London), March 30, 1961; John Kenneth Galbraith, *Ambassador's Journal* (Boston: Houghton Mifflin Company, 1969), p. 50.

42. *New York Times*, March 23, 1961.

43. *Washington Post*, March 23, 1961.

44. Joseph Alsop in *Washington Post*, March 27, 1961; Sidey, *op. cit.*, pp. 79, 81.

45. *Public Papers of the Presidents, 1961*, pp. 213–215.

46. Interview with General Donald M. Weller; *New York Herald-Tribune*, March 24, 1961.

47. Joseph Alsop in *Washington Post*, March 31, 1961; Interviews with Confidential Source and Christian Chapman.

48. Sidey, *op. cit.*, pp. 83–84; *New York Times*, March 28, 1961; Schlesinger, *op. cit.*, p. 334.

49. Richard H. Rovere, "Letter From Washington," *The New Yorker*, April 15, 1961, pp. 156–160. One suspects that the official was Bundy since he quoted Henry Stimson, whose autobiography Bundy had helped to write.

50. Text in *Department of State Bulletin*, April 17, 1961, 44:549; Schlesinger, *op. cit.*, p. 334; *New York Times*, March 30, 1961.

51. Texts in *Department of State Bulletin*, April 17, 1961, 44:544–546.

52. Quoted in Sidey, *op. cit.*, p. 86.

53. Dommen, *op. cit.*, pp. 193–196.

54. Holt Chronology.

55. *Ibid.*

56. *Ibid.*

57. Interview with Averell Harriman.

58. Interview with Kenneth Young; Hilsman, *op. cit.*, p. 134; Arthur Krock, *Memoirs* (New York: Popular Library, 1968), p. 345.

59. See this argument in United States, Congress, House, Committee on Appropriations, *Foreign Operations Appropriations for 1962, Hearings* before the Subcommittee of the Committee on Appropriations, 87th Cong., 1st sess., 1961, pp. 91, 590–591; *New York Times*, April 21, 1961 (AP dispatch); Confidential Source.

60. Quotations and some other information from Schlesinger, *op. cit.*, pp. 337–338; also interviews with Averell Harriman and Robert Amory. The Chiefs of Staff were not really worried about war with China. Their plans in case of Chinese intervention, however, were quite frightening. These called for seizure of Hainan Island, which was defended by three Chinese divisions, deployment of 250,000 U.S. troops to South Vietnam, followed by operations across North Vietnam into Laos

to block Chinese intrusions. If these U.S. forces were in danger of being overrun, the Chiefs expected to use nuclear weapons. (Confidential Source)

61. Interview with Admiral Burke.

62. Interview with Nitze; JCS views are discussed in *New York Times*, July 1, 1971.

63. Quoted in Schlesinger, *op. cit.*, p. 338.

64. Sorensen, *op. cit.*, pp. 644–645.

65. Pentagon documents discussed in *Boston Globe*, June 22, 1971, and *New York Times*, July 1, 1971, especially JCS memo of 10 May 1961.

66. Confidential Source.

67. Interviews with Harriman, Nitze, and Confidential Source.

68. Interview with General Weller.

69. Text in *Department of State Bulletin*, June 26, 1961, 44:999.

70. Reports of the meeting are in Sorensen (*op. cit.*), pp. 548–549 and Schlesinger (*op. cit.*), pp. 363–368.

71. Interview with Harriman.

CHAPTER SIX

1. Related by William Sullivan in interview, June 28, 1969.

2. In testimony before the Senate Committee on Foreign Relations, *Hearing before the Senate Committee on Foreign Relations on the Nomination of W. Averell Harriman to be Under Secretary of State for Political Affairs*, April 2, 1963 (Washington: Ward and Paul, duplicated, n.d.), p. 11.

3. Quoted in Arthur J. Dommen, *Conflict in Laos: The Politics of Neutralization* (New York: Frederick A. Praeger, 1965), p. 204; Arthur M. Schlesinger, Jr., *A Thousand Days: John F. Kennedy in the White House* (Boston: Houghton Mifflin Company, 1965), p. 335.

4. Interview with Averell Harriman.

5. *Ibid.*

6. Interviews with Harriman, John Steeves, and Confidential Source. The specific incident which forced Harriman to remove Steeves was the latter's polemical speech on July 4, while Harriman was briefly away from Geneva. In contrast to Harriman's firm but not belligerent phrasing, Steeves attacked the Communists for an "elaborate charade" and suggested that they did not really want peace. Disturbed at the tone of the speech, the Russians asked (through the British delegation) whether there had been a change in U.S. policy. Harriman replied in the negative and acted to remove Steeves from the conference platform. (Interview with Harriman; for speech summary, see George Modelski, *International Conference on the Settlement of the Laotian Question 1961–62*, Working Paper no. 2, Department of International Relations, Research School of Pacific Studies, The Australian National University [Canberra: 1962], p. 88.)

7. Interview with Charles Cross.

8. Quoted in Schlesinger, *op. cit.*, p. 515.

9. Confidential Sources.

10. Dommen, *op. cit.*, pp. 205–209.

11. Text in Bernard Fall, *Anatomy of a Crisis* (Garden City, N.Y.: Doubleday and Company, Inc., 1969), pp. 250–252.

12. Confidential Source.

13. Confidential Source.

14. Hugh Toye, *Laos: Buffer State or Battleground* (London: Oxford University Press, 1968), p. 179; interviews with Robert Amory, Admiral Burke, and General Decker.

15. Interviews with Burke and two Confidential Sources.

16. Warren Unna in *Washington Post*, July 1, 1961.

17. Interview with Ambassador Brown.

18. The details of the Geneva Conference have already been extensively covered by others. See especially John J. Czyzak and Carl F. Salans, "The International Conference on the Settlement of the Laotian Question and the Geneva Agreements of 1962," *American Journal of International Law*, vol. 57 (April, 1963), pp. 300–317; Modelski, *op. cit.*; and Arthur Lall, *How Communist China Negotiates* (New York: Columbia University Press, 1968). This section merely tries to summarize the course of the conference with reference to United States policy.

19. Lall, *op. cit.*, p. 83; Czyzak and Salans, *loc. cit.*, p. 303.

20. Quoted in Lall, *op. cit.*, p. 69.

21. *Ibid.*, pp. 69–70; Dommen, *op. cit.*, pp. 207–208.

22. Czyzak and Salans, *loc. cit.*, pp. 303–304; Lall, *op. cit.*, pp. 130–131; Interview with Harriman. This experience at Geneva suggests why the Paris negotiations on Vietnam have not, as of this writing (Sept. 1972), moved very close to a settlement. There is not yet any congruence on the broad outlines of a settlement. The sessions are a forum for posturing and emphasizing differences rather than working toward agreement.

23. Interview with Charles Cross.

24. Interview with Harriman.

25. Czyzak and Salans, *loc. cit.*, p. 308.

26. *Ibid.*, pp. 310–311.

27. Interview with Abram Chayes.

28. Interview with a Confidential Source.

29. Czyzak and Salans, *loc. cit.*, pp. 312–314.

30. *Ibid.*, pp. 308–309.

31. Interview with Harriman; Pierre Salinger, *With Kennedy* (New York: Doubleday, 1966), p. 194. Khrushchev admitted having difficulties getting the three princes together and an agreement worked out. C. L. Sulzberger, *New York Times*, September 8, 1961.

32. *New York Times*, August 3 and 19, 1961.

33. Interview with Harriman.

34. Michael Field, *The Prevailing Wind: Witness in Indo-China* (London: Methuen and Company, Ltd., 1965), p. 138.

35. *New York Times*, October 10, 1961.

36. Quoted in Toye, *op. cit.*, p. 185; Dommen, *op. cit.*, p. 211. The JCS at the same time were calling for "concentration" on Laos. See Gravel II:74.

37. Confidential Source.

38. Toye, *op. cit.*, pp. 179–180.

39. Interview with Harriman and Robert Cleveland; *New York*

304 THE END OF NOWHERE

Times, November 29, 1961. Evidence of the intransigence of U. Alexis
Johnson and Walter McConaughy is in John Kenneth Galbraith's *Ambassador's Journal* (Boston: Houghton Mifflin Company, 1969), pp. 242–243.

40. Text in *American Foreign Policy: Current Documents, 1961*, Department of State Publication 7808 (Released June, 1965), p. 1026.

41. Quoted from Holt Chronology.

42. *Ibid.*, and *New York Times*, January 5 and 10, 1962.

43. The *New York Times* and *New York Herald-Tribune*, both January 20, 1962, disagree over Boun Oum's position in this matter.

44. The contrasting judgments are evident in Dommen, *op. cit.*, pp. 213–214 and Toye, *op. cit.*, pp. 180, 195.

45. Toye, *op. cit.*, pp. 182, 180; Hilsman, *op. cit.*, p. 140; Confidential Source.

46. *The Times* (London), May 24, 1962; Interviews with Harriman and a Confidential Source. *The Times'* report on CIA activities was denied by a State Department spokesman but reasserted by its Washington correspondent. See *The Times* (London), May 25 and 31, 1962.

47. Interview with a Confidential Source; Goldwater speech reported in the *New York Times*, January 20, 1962.

48. Holt Chronology.

49. Quoted in D. Insor, *Thailand: A Political, Social, and Economic Analysis* (London: George Allen and Unwin, Ltd., 1963), p. 131.

50. Interview with Kenneth Young.

51. Donald E. Nuechterlein, *Thailand and the Struggle for Southeast Asia* (Ithaca, N.Y.: Cornell University Press, 1965), p. 228.

52. Text in *Department of State Bulletin*, March 26, 1962, 46:498–99; also interviews with Cleveland and a Confidential Source. This explicit U.S. commitment may also have been in response to the deepening (though secret) Thai involvement in Laos. Already in 1961 the Thais were providing pilots and special advisory teams called Police Aerial Resupply Units (PARU) to the Meo. Gravel II:645–646.

53. Holt Chronology; *Christian Science Monitor*, March 30, 1962.

54. Interview with Michael Forrestal; Holt Chronology.

55. Dommen, *op. cit.*, p. 218; Schlesinger, *op. cit.*, pp. 515–516.

56. Quoted in Nuechterlein, *op. cit.*, p. 234; Holt Chronology.

57. Hilsman, *op. cit.*, pp. 140–141; *New York Times*, April 15, 21, and 24, 1962.

58. Nuechterlein, *op. cit.*, pp. 237–238; Holt Chronology; Interview with Cross.

59. Quoted by a Confidential Source; the report may be apocryphal, but it is consistent with the performance of the Royal Army; Hilsman, *op. cit.*, p. 141, and Dommen, *op. cit.*, pp. 217–218 stress the idea of a Pathet Lao attack even though there was no assault on Nam Tha. Toye (*op. cit.*, p. 182) here, as elsewhere, gives a much more realistic picture of the military situation.

60. Confidential Source; Dommen, *op. cit.*, p. 218.

61. Hilsman, *op. cit.*, pp. 141–143; Nuechterlein, *op. cit.*, p. 239. The contrast between the realistic and symbolic reactions to Nam Tha was well illustrated in statements by unnamed United States officials, presumably in the State Department, and by the President. The officials, Max Frankel reported in the *New York Times*, May 7, 1962, said that the

Pathet Lao forces had provoked the attack and, therefore, it was not a clearcut violation of the cease-fire. The President, however, called it a "clear breach of the cease-fire" at his May 9 news conference. (*Public Papers of the Presidents of the United States, John F. Kennedy, 1962* [Washington, D.C.: Office of the Federal Register, National Archives and Records Service, 1963], p. 378.)

62. Hilsman, *op. cit.*, pp. 142–143; *Public Papers of the Presidents, 1962*, pp. 377–378; Schlesinger, *op. cit.*, p. 516.

63. Hilsman, *op. cit.*, p. 143; interview with General Decker.

64. Hilsman, *op. cit.*, p. 144.

65. *Ibid.*

66. *Ibid.*, pp. 145–146.

67. *Ibid.*, p. 147; interviews with Amory, Weller, and a Confidential Source.

68. Interviews with Hilsman and Weller.

69. Hilsman, *op. cit.*, p. 150; Dommen, *op. cit.*, p. 219; Confidential Source.

70. Toye, *op. cit.*, p. 186; Dommen, *op. cit.*, p. 220.

71. Holt Chronology.

72. Text in Fall and Dommen.

73. *New York Times*, July 31, 1962.

74. Interviews with James Fowler and Roy Wehrle.

75. Interview with Weller; Toye, *op. cit.*, p. 187; Dommen, *op. cit.*, p. 240.

76. Hilsman, *op. cit.*, pp. 151–153; also interview with Harriman.

77. Interviews with Confidential Sources; Hilsman, *op. cit.*, pp. 151–152. In spite of Walt Rostow's claim (in interview with *New York Times*, January 5, 1969) that this was a crucial, hotly contested decision, none of the participants interviewed by the author remembers much debate at the time.

CHAPTER SEVEN

1. Interview, May 17, 1969.

2. Interview with Charles T. Cross.

3. Roger Hilsman, *To Move a Nation* (Garden City, N.Y.: Doubleday and Company, 1967), p. 152.

4. Confidential Source.

5. Arthur Dommen, who traveled throughout Southeast Asia during this period, writes that reconnaissance was made public in May 1964, thereby clearly implying that it had continued until that date. See his *Conflict in Laos: The Politics of Neutralization* (New York: Frederick A. Praeger, 1965), p. 238. The *New York Times* analysis of the Defense Department's history of the Vietnam War confirms high altitude flights in early 1964. See June 13–15, 1971, editions.

6. Interview with General Donald Weller; U.S. Senate, Committee on Foreign Relations, *United States Security Agreements and Commitments Abroad: Kingdom of Thailand, Hearings* before the Sub-Committee on United States Security Agreements and Commitments

Abroad of the Committee on Foreign Relations, part 3, 91st Cong., 1st sess., 1970 (hereafter the *Thai Hearings*), p. 615.

7. U.S. Senate, Committee on Foreign Relations, *United States Security Agreements and Commitments Abroad: Kingdom of Laos, Hearings* before the Sub-Committee on United States Security Agreements and Commitments Abroad of the Committee on Foreign Relations, part 2, 91st Cong., 1st sess., 1970 (hereafter the *Laos Hearings*), p. 423.

8. The letters are reprinted in the *Laos Hearings*, pp. 441–443.

9. Dommen, *op. cit.*, pp. 234–235, 242, 244; *Laos Hearings*, pp. 443, 444.

10. Dommen, *op. cit.*, p. 235.

11. The formal U.S. explanation was given in *Department of State Bulletin*, April 15, 1963, pp. 567, 571; Dommen, *op. cit.*, p. 244.

12. Interview with Roy Wehrle.

13. Estelle Holt (untitled, undated, typewritten chronology of events in Laos, 1939–May 31, 1964; henceforth cited as Holt Chronology). The Americans later contended that relief programs were totally legal and open for inspection. A statement issued in January 1963 claimed that no armaments were being given in violation of the 1962 accords. This careful phrasing probably meant that all military aid was legal since it had been requested by Souvanna Phouma.

14. D. Gareth Porter, "After Geneva: Subverting Laotian Neutrality," in Nina S. Adams and Alfred W. McCoy (eds.), *Laos: War and Revolution* (New York: Harper Colophon Books, 1970), p. 183.

15. Don A. Schanche, *Mister Pop* (New York: David McKay Company, Inc.: 1970), p. 64.

16. Hugh Toye, *Laos: Buffer State or Battleground* (London: Oxford University Press, 1968), p. 179; *New York Times*, October 26, 1969. This newspaper article, the most complete account of United States support to this clandestine guerrilla force, says that after the Geneva settlement, "The Central Intelligence Agency then took over the functions [of organizing, training, and equipping the Meo], sometimes using officers who had resigned from the Army so they could continue their tasks."

17. Schanche, *op. cit.*, pp. 64, 80, 131–132, 134, 154; *Thai Hearings*, pp. 722–723.

18. Schanche, *op. cit.*, p. 159.

19. *Laos Hearings*, p. 473. AID Administrator John A. Hannah admitted the CIA cover on June 7, 1970. See Adams and McCoy, *op. cit.*, p. 408.

20. One instance, cited by Arthur Dommen (*op. cit.*, p. 260), was the use of Air America helicopters to ferry neutralist troops in the spring of 1963.

21. Confidential Source.

22. Article 1(a) of the Protocol to the Declaration on the Neutrality of Laos, reprinted in Dommen, *op. cit.*, p. 315. The Pathet Lao pointed to that last phrase about "foreign civilians" when they protested clandestine operations and even the Air America flights to resupply the Meos.

23. *New York Times*, August 2, 1966.

24. Joseph C. Goulden, *Truth is the First Casualty: The Gulf of Tonkin Affair—Illusion and Reality* (Chicago: A James B. Adler, Inc.,

Book published in association with Rand McNally and Company, 1969), pp. 85–86, citing Robin Moore's book, *The Green Berets* (New York: Crown, 1965), pp. 164–165; Donald Duncan, *The New Legions* (New York: Pocket Books, 1967), p. 180. This operation was considered a success by late 1964, according to the *New York Times Documents*.

25. Confidential Source. The best analysis of Thai activities can be found in T. D. Allman *(Far Eastern Economic Review [FEER],* October 9, 1969). One early discussion of the use of third-country nationals is in House Appropriations Committee, *Foreign Operations Appropriations for 1964,* part 3, pp. 610–611.

26. Paul F. Langer and Joseph J. Zasloff, *North Vietnam and the Pathet Lao* (Cambridge, Mass.: Harvard University Press, 1970), pp. 87–88, argue that North Vietnamese control has become much greater since 1963, but they admit that there is no evidence of direct aid in the fight against Kong-Le before the spring of 1964.

27. Dommen, *op. cit.* pp. 226–227; Holt Chronology.

28. Hilsman, *op. cit.,* p. 153; Holt Chronology.

29. Holt Chronology; *Keesing's Contemporary Archives,* August 24–31, 1963, p. 19593.

30. Holt Chronology.

31. *New York Times,* April 6, 1963.

32. Dommen, *op. cit.,* pp. 246–247.

33. The unhappy history of the ICC after Geneva is recounted by Dommen, *op. cit.,* pp. 224–226, 239–241, 246–250; 253–256. The most optimistic U.S. statements about the ICC were made in testimony requesting authorization to pay the American share of ICC expenses. See United States, Congress, House, Committee on Foreign Affairs, *International Commission for Supervision and Control in Laos, Hearing* before the Subcommittee on the Far East and the Pacific, Committee on Foreign Affairs, 88th Cong., 1st sess., September 24, 1963.

34. William E. Griffith, *The Sino-Soviet Rift* (Cambridge: The M.I.T. Press, 1964), pp. 128–130; Donald S. Zagoria, *Vietnam Triangle: Moscow, Peking, Hanoi* (New York: Pegasus, 1967), pp. 108–110; P. J. Honey, *Communism in North Vietnam* (Cambridge: The M.I.T. Press, 1963), p. 196.

35. Interview with Averell Harriman; *New York Times,* April 28, 1963. The Soviet pledge was given by chief delegate Georgi Pushkin in return for a British promise to keep the Western signatories faithful to the agreements. The British, who did not relish that assignment, never formally verified the "Pushkin Agreement" with Moscow. By the time of the Harriman visit, Pushkin was dead and his pledge unredeemable. (Interview with Harriman.)

36. Confidential Sources.

37. Confidential Source; John C. Ausland and Colonel Hugh F. Richardson, "Crisis Management: Berlin, Cyprus, Laos," *Foreign Affairs* (January 1966), 44:295.

38. *Department of State Bulletin* (March 4, 1963), 48:312.

39. April 8, 1963 statement, published in *Department of State Bulletin* (April 24, 1963), 48:646.

40. *New York Times,* April 20, 22, 28, May 1, 30, 1963; *Washington Post,* April 15, 1963.

41. House Appropriations Committee, *Foreign Operations Appropriations for 1965*, part 1, p. 466; *Department of State Bulletin* (September 30, 1963), 49:500; Dommen, *op. cit.*, p. 249.

42. Holt Chronology; *New York Times*, June 25, 1963 and June 16, 1968.

43. Tom Wicker, *JFK and LBJ: The Influence of Personality on Politics* (New York: William Morrow and Company, Inc., 1968), pp. 200, 201, 205.

44. *Laos Hearings*, pp. 457, 369, and McNamara report of December 21, 1963, in Gravel III:495.

45. Dommen, *op. cit.*, p. 255; *New York Times*, April 21, 1964.

46. *New York Times*, February 16 and April 12, 1964; Holt Chronology; Confidential Source.

47. Confidential Source; Robert Shaplen, *The New Yorker*, January 16, 1965, pp. 105–106.

48. *New York Times*, March 1, 1963.

49. David Bell before House Appropriations Committee, *Foreign Operations Appropriations for 1965*, part 2, p. 172.

50. *Ibid.*, part 2, p. 415.

51. *New York Times*, April 20, 1964. William Bundy (interview) says that the Geneva Agreements and Souvanna "were essentially inseparable."

52. Holt Chronology; *New York Times*, April 24, 1964; Robert Shaplen, *The New Yorker*, January 16, 1965, p. 106.

53. *Department of State Bulletin* (June 8, 1964), 50:910; confirmed in interview with William Bundy.

54. Holt Chronology.

55. *Ibid.*

56. Hilsman, *op. cit.*, pp. 526–528; Edward Weintal and Charles Bartlett, *Facing the Brink: An Intimate Study of Crisis Diplomacy* (New York: Charles Scribner's Sons, 1967), pp. 80–81; Confidential Source.

57. McNamara Report of December 21, 1963, in Gravel III:495.

58. Hilsman, *op. cit.*, p. 534; Confidential Source.

59. JCS Memo to McNamara of January 22, 1964, Gravel III:498.

60. McNamara to Johnson of March 16, 1964, and NSAM 288 of March 17, 1964, Gravel III:503, 509, 50, 51, 56. Before these documents were published, a less detailed account was available in Goulden, *op. cit.*, p. 91.

61. *New York Times*, May 18, 19, 20, 21, 1964.

62. Draft Resolution of May 23, 1964. DoD 4:IV.C.2(b), p. 43.

63. Laos Hearings, p. 370: Interview with William Bundy; *New York Times*, May 22 and 28, 1964. Bundy confirms the actions but cannot verify from memory the dates given in the newspapers.

64. Gravel III:514, 538, 543, 552–553, 578–579, and 608–610.

65. *New York Times*, June 7, 8, 10, 18, 1964. Although Washington officials claimed that armed reconnaissance raids began only on June 7, Goulden says that the flights began in mid-May, following complaints from pilots about the risks involved. The President reportedly approved the armed reconnaissance subject to the provision that no U.S.

bombing would occur until and unless American planes were damaged. See *Laos Hearings*, pp. 370 and 476; Goulden, *op. cit.*, pp. 97–98. Sullivan's strangely worded testimony—". . . with the Prime Minister's approval, armed escorts had been added to the flights"—suggests that they had indeed flown earlier than June 7. The *New York Times Documents*, however, say that the escorts were added after the shootings of June 6 and 7.

66. *Department of State Bulletin* (June 29, 1964), 50:995; *New York Times*, June 10, 11, 12, 1964; Goulden, *op. cit.*, p. 98. These reasons for secrecy were admitted by Unger in *Thai Hearings*, p. 791. They were also confirmed in the Rusk cables of August 7 and 26, 1964, Gravel III: 518–519, 552–553.

67. *Washington Post*, June 18, 1964. The U.S. involvement in this highly provocative attack is uncertain, but American officers were working closely with the Lao Army and Air Force throughout this period.

68. Rusk cable of August 26, 1964, Gravel III:553.

69. *Washington Post*, June 18 and 20, 1964; *New York Times*, June 18 and 20, 1964. The July 2 *New York Times* revealed Rusk as the source for the June 20 stories.

70. *Laos Hearings*, p. 369; *Thai Hearings*, p .615; *New York Times*, June 3, 1964. One result of this effort to secure proxies was the secret 1965 contingency plan with Thailand which contained provisions for using U.S. troops, some nominally under Thai command, to fight Communist forces in Laos. *New York Times*, August 16, 1969.

71. *Laos Hearings*, pp. 476, 477.

72. *Ibid.*, pp. 479, 457; *New York Times*, July 9, 1964; Goulden, *op. cit.*, p. 98; Lieutenant Colonel Edgar W. Duskin, USA, "Laos," *Military Review* (March, 1968), 48:7.

73. *U.S. News and World Report*, July 20, 1964, vol. 57, pp. 46–48; Duncan, *op. cit.*, p. 18n.

74. William Bundy memo of August 11, 1964, Gravel III:526.

75. *New York Times Documents*. The Tonkin Gulf Incident is a very complicated matter. The best analysis prior to the publication of the Pentagon study is Goulden, *op. cit.*

76. Public Law 88-408, approved August 10, 1964.

77. The Saigon mission cable of August 18, 1964, urged resumption of such efforts. See Gravel III:547.

78. JCS Memo to McNamara of August 26, 1964, in Gravel III: 550.

79. Analysis and William Bundy Memo of August 11, 1964, and Saigon mission cable of August 18, 1964, in Gravel III:525–529.

80. NSAM 314 of September 10, 1964 following the consensus memo of September 8, in Gravel III:565.

81. Analysis and Taylor cable of September 19, 1964, in Gravel III:566–568.

82. State/Defense Cable to Vientiane of October 6, 1964, in Gravel III:576–577.

83. Analysis in *New York Times Documents; Laos Hearings*, pp. 476, 481–482.

84. *New York Times*, November 18 and December 22, 1964, plus analysis in *New York Times Documents*.

85. *Laos Hearings*, pp. 476, 481, 370–371; *Thai Hearings*, pp. 667, 669; *New York Times Documents*.

86. Goulden, *op. cit.*, p. 98.

87. Denis Warner, *Reporting South-East Asia* (Sydney: Angus and Robertson, 1966), p. 200. (Reprinting article in April 22, 1965, issue of *The Reporter*.)

88. Interview with William Bundy; *Washington Post*, January 15, 1965.

89. Wicker, *op. cit.*, pp. 258–259; Philip Geyelin, *Lyndon B. Johnson and the World* (New York: Frederick A. Praeger, 1966), pp. 215–216.

90. Confidential Source.

91. Interview with William Bundy.

92. *Laos Hearings*, p. 535.

93. There are numerous public sources for this information. Perhaps the most extensive are *New York Times*, October 26, 27, and 28, 1969; *Washington Post*, March 11 and 16, 1970; *Bangkok Post*, September 24 and 25, 1969; and the *Far Eastern Economic Review*, January 1, 1970. Earlier evaluations of the extent of United States involvement appeared in the *New York Times*, August 14, 1965 and *Atlas*, January 1968.

94. The Cornell Air War Study estimates (p. 281) that the United States dropped 1,544,000 tons of munitions in Laos during 1965–71 —or about one-fourth of the total tonnage in the Indochina War during those years.

95. Confidential Source.

96. *Laos Hearings*, p. 518; Confidential Sources.

97. Confidential Source.

98. Confidential Source.

99. Confidential Source.

100. Quoted by Fred Branfman, "Presidential War in Laos, 1964–1970," in Adams and McCoy (eds.), *op. cit.*, p. 250; interviews with Confidential Sources; *Laos Hearings*, p. 529.

101. Dommen, *op. cit.*, p. 275; Branfman, *loc. cit.*, pp. 223–225.

102. Schanche, *op. cit.*, p. 127; *New York Times*, October 26, 1969.

103. Schanche (*op. cit.*, pp. 297–298) says that the Meo had controlled the mountain, Phou Pha Thi, since 1963, but he makes no mention of the CIA installation. Official testimony in *Laos Hearings*, p. 489, says that radar was installed in 1966. T. D. Allman cites reliable American sources as saying that construction at Phou Pha Thi began in late 1964, *Washington Post*, March 16, 1970.

104. Schanche, *op. cit.*, p. 263; *New York Times*, March 6, 1970.

105. Confidential Source; *Laos Hearings*, pp. 463, 468.

106. Interviews with Confidential Sources.

107. Interview with Fred Branfman with some confirming hints from Confidential Sources.

108. Interviews with Confidential Sources.

109. *Laos Hearings*, pp. 459, 468; This and subsequent paragraphs on bombing are based on interviews with U.S. officials closely involved in the targeting procedures.

110. This bombing controversy has been dealt with most exten-

sively in hearings before Senator Edward Kennedy's Subcommittee on Refugees in April 1971. See also the administration's defense, reported in the (Washington) *Star*, April 25, 1971.

111. *Thai Hearings*, p. 712; Statement by Congressman Paul Mc-Closkey before Kennedy Subcommittee, 1971.

112. *Thai Hearings*, pp. 615, 621, 622; Branfman, *loc. cit.*, p. 233 generally confirmed by testimony of Ambassador Sullivan to Kennedy Subcommittee.

113. *Laos Hearings*, pp. 437, 439.

114. *Washington Post*, November 5, 1968; *Thai Hearings*, p. 777; Confidential Source; Sullivan testimony before Kennedy Subcommittee, 1971. Cornell Air War Study, chs. 5 and 6; 1972 Moose-Lowenstein, pp. 34-35.

115. Interviews with Confidential Sources. Also Gravel IV:337, 443.

116. Interviews with Confidential Sources.

117. Interview with Confidential Source; *Baltimore Sun*, February 10, 1971.

118. Interviews with William Bundy and Les Gelb; *New York Times*, November 2, 1968.

119. Shaplen, *The New Yorker*, January 16, 1965, pp. 105-106; Warner, *op. cit.*, p. 196; Holt Chronology; *New York Times*, January 17, 1965, February 2, 6, 7, 1965.

120. Denis Warner, "A Cautionary Report on Laos," *The Reporter*, December 2, 1965, p. 37; *New York Times*, July 19, 1965.

121. *New York Times*, January 8, 1967; Donald Kirk, "An Election to Test Laotian Stability," *The Reporter*, December 29, 1966, p. 27.

122. *New York Times*, October 21, 24, 28, November 22, 1966.

123. E. H. S. Simmonds, "The Evolution of Foreign Policy in Laos Since Independence," *Modern Asian Studies*, II, 1 (1968), p. 25; *Washington Post*, November 2, 1969.

124. Interview with Thomas Stanton.

125. Interviews with Confidential Sources.

126. A more elaborate discussion of the weakness of the Laotian government can be found in Branfman, *loc. cit.*, pp. 256-264; also *Laos Hearings*, p. 569.

127. U.S., Senate, Committee on the Judiciary, *Refugee and Civilian War Casualty Problems in Laos and Cambodia, Hearings*, the Subcommittee to Investigate Problems Connected with Refugees and Escapees, 91st Cong., 2d sess., May 7, 1970 (hereafter *Kennedy Subcommittee Hearings, 1970*), pp. 41, 63; the Subcommittee's *Staff Report* of September 28, 1970, entitled *Refugee and Civilian War Casualty Problems in Indochina* (hereafter *Kennedy Subcommittee Report*), see pp. 71, 20.

CHAPTER EIGHT

1. Quoted in Don A. Schanche, *Mister Pop* (New York: David McKay Company, Inc., 1970), p. 304.

2. *New York Times*, April 17, 1964.

3. U.S. Senate, Committee on Foreign Relations, *United States Security Agreements and Commitments Abroad; Kingdom of Laos, Hear-*

ings before the Sub-Committee on United States Security Agreements and Commitments Abroad of the Committee on Foreign Relations, part 2, 91st Cong., 1st sess., 1970 (hereafter called *Laos Hearings*), p. 502; *Bangkok Post*, September 24 and 25, 1969; *Keesing's Contemporary Archives*, pp. 24090–1.

4. Interviews with Confidential Sources.

5. *Washington Post*, May 19 and 20 (Chalmers Roberts' column) and July 20, 1969; *New York Times*, May 21, 1969.

6. *New York Times*, March 19, 1970.

7. *Bangkok Post*, September 24 and 25, 1969. Reports conflict on whether the town was bombed before or after its seizure by Meo forces. A substantial cave network was discovered beneath the town, however, which suggests some fear of bombing. These caves were systematically destroyed.

8. U.S. Senate, Committee on Foreign Relations, *United States Security Agreements and Commitments Abroad: Kingdom of Thailand, Hearings* before the Subcommittee on United States Security Agreements and Commitments Abroad of the Committee on Foreign Relations, part 3, 91st Cong., 1st sess., 1970 (hereafter called *Thai Hearings*), p. 784.

9. *Keesing's Contemporary Archives*, p. 24091.

10. Confidential Source; *New York Times*, June 29, 1969.

11. Interview with Confidential Source.

12. Quoted in the *Los Angeles Times*, April 1, 1971.

13. Interviews with Confidential Sources; *New York Times*, March 23, 1971.

14. Interviews with Confidential Sources.

15. Interviews with Confidential Source and Fred Branfman.

16. Robert Shaplen, "Our Involvement in Laos," *Foreign Affairs* (April 1970), 48:489. U.S. planes have been forbidden, however, to conduct operations along a road being built by the Chinese in northern Laos. *New York Times*, March 3, 1970.

17. Arnold Abrams in *Far Eastern Economic Review (FEER)*, January 1, 1970; *Laos Hearings*, p. 504.

18. U.S. Senate, Committee on the Judiciary, *Staff Report* on *Refugee and Civilian War Casualty Problems in Indochina*, from the Subcommittee to Investigate Problems Connected with Refugees and Escapees, 91st Cong., 2d sess., September 28, 1970 (hereafter called *Kennedy Subcommittee Report*), pp. 43, 20; *Hearings* before the Subcommittee, *Refugee and Civilian War Casualty Problems in Laos and Cambodia*, 91st Cong, 2d sess., May 7, 1970 (hereafter called *Kennedy Subcommittee Hearings, 1970*), p. 41; New York Times, October 1, 1969.

19. Interview with William Miller.

20. *Ibid.*; *New York Times*, September 17, 18, 19, 1969; *Congressional Record* (daily ed.), December 15, 1969, p. S16755 and January 21, 1970, p. E160.

21. *New York Times*, September 20, 1969.

22. Louis Harris Survey printed in *Boston Globe*, November 24, 1969.

23. Interview with William Miller and Walter Pincus.

24. *Congressional Record* (daily ed.), December 15, 1969, pp. S16752–65 and January 21, 1970, pp. E151–166.

25. *Congressional Record*, December 15, 1969, p. S16761.

26. *New York Times*, December 17 and 21, 1969; interview with Walter Pincus.

27. Interviews with Confidential Sources.

28. Jack Foisie in *Washington Post*, March 2, 1970; interview with Confidential Source.

29. *Washington Post*, February 22, 1970.

30. T. D. Allman in *FEER*, January 1, 1970.

31. See reprint of Statement and stories in *New York Times* and *Washington Post*, March 7, 1970.

32. See *New York Times*, March 9, 1970, and *Washington Post*, March 16, 1970.

33. *New York Times*, March 7, 1970; Arthur J. Dommen, "Laos in the Second Indochina War," *Current History*, December 1970, p. 331.

34. *New York Times*, March 18, 1970.

35. Henry Kamm, in *New York Times*, March 22, 1970.

36. *New York Times*, October 23, 1970; Interview with Confidential Source.

37. Dommen, *loc. cit.*, p. 332.

38. *Washington Post*, May 18, August 19 and 20, 1970; *Christian Science Monitor*, August 3, 1970.

39. *Washington Post*, February 13, 1971.

40. No announcements were made of such "protective encirclement" missions. Official sources did deny an ABC television report that the body of an American wearing a South Vietnamese uniform had been brought back from Laos. *Washington Post*, February 27, 1971; (Washington) *Star*, February 12, 1971; earlier plans were discussed in Arthur Schlesinger's account of the Kennedy years, p. 332, the *New York Times*, December 17, 1965, and in interview with Robert Amory.

41. *New York Times*, February 9, 1971.

42. (Washington) *Star*, March 25, 1971.

43. *New York Times*, October 30, 1970; *Washington Post*, November 28, 1970.

44. Interviews with Fred Branfman and Confidential Sources.

45. Interviews with Fred Branfman and Confidential Source.

46. *Baltimore Sun*, February 21, 1971 and *Washington Post*, October 18, 1970.

47. (Washington) *Star*, June 15, 1971.

48. *Wall Street Journal*, March 18, 1971.

49. The debate took place before the Kennedy Subcommittee in April 1971.

50. Testimony July 22, 1971, in Hearings before the Senate Armed Services Committee, *Fiscal Year 1972 Authorization for Military Procurement, Research and Development, Constructions and Real Estate Acquisition for the Safeguard ABM, and Reserve Strengths*, 92nd Cong., 1st sess., p. 4271.

51. *New York Times*, February 6, 1971.

CONCLUSIONS

1. Quoted by Saville R. Davis in the *Christian Science Monitor*, November 26, 1960.

2. One can find an excellent picture of the minutiae of the policy-making environment in Charles Ogburn, Jr.'s "The Flow of Policy Making in the Department of State," reprinted as Appendix A of Burton M. Sapin, *The Making of United States Foreign Policy* (New York: Frederick A. Praeger for the Brookings Institution, 1966).

3. Confidential Source.

4. Theodore C. Sorensen, *Decision-Making in the White House* (New York: Columbia University Press, 1963), p. 44.

5. For a seminal discussion of bargaining, see Thomas C. Schelling, *The Strategy of Conflict* (Cambridge: Harvard University Press, 1960), especially chs. 1 and 2. For an application of bargaining concepts to policy-making, see Charles E. Lindblom, *The Policy-Making Process* (Englewood Cliffs, New Jersey: Prentice-Hall, 1968) and *The Intelligence of Democracy* (New York: The Free Press, 1965). For a synthesis of this literature and an application of it to U.S. foreign policy, see Graham T. Allison, "Conceptual Models and the Cuban Missile Crisis," *American Political Science Review*, vol. 63 (September 1969), pp. 689–718.

6. Although I have persisted in using "decision" rather than "choice," I am grateful to Tom Karas for pointing out the distinction and directing my attention to Kenneth H. Sayre, "Choice, Decision, and the Origin of Information," in Frederick J. Crosson and Kenneth M. Sayre (eds.), *Philosophy and Cybernetics* (Notre Dame: University of Notre Dame Press, 1967).

7. James C. Thomson, Jr., "How Could Vietnam Happen?", *The Atlantic*, April 1968, p. 50.

8. For an extended analysis of use of the press to influence policy, see Leon V. Sigal, "Reporters and Officials: The Organization and Politics of Press-Government Relations," Harvard University doctoral dissertation, forthcoming. For a factual discussion of how this manipulation was carried on in Laos, see Bernard B. Fall, *Anatomy of a Crisis: The Laotian Crisis of 1960–1961* (Garden City, N.Y.: Doubleday and Company, Inc., 1969), ch. 7.

9. This is an expanding area of inquiry, but the results so far have been relatively meager compared to other methods of analysis. See, for example, Joseph deRivera, *The Psychological Dimension of Foreign Policy* (Columbus, Ohio: Charles E. Merrill Publishing Company, 1968) and John Steinbruner, "Memorandum to the Public Policy Program," (typewritten) September 29, 1969. For a fictional treatment of the dynamics of policy meetings, see John Kenneth Galbraith, *The Triumph* (New York: Signet Books, 1968).

10. Emphasis on reciprocity can be found in Lindblom, *Policy-Making Process*, pp. 94–95.

11. This study has tried consciously to employ the conceptual models of organizational processes and political bargaining developed by Graham Allison. (See his *APSR* article, *loc. cit.*; his Rand Paper P-3919 (August 1968); and his forthcoming book, *Bureaucracy and Policy: Con-*

ceptual Models and the Cuban Missile Crisis.) Allison summarizes much of the literature on decision-making. Other summaries of the literature can be found in James A. Robinson and R. Roger Majak, "The Theory of Decision-Making" and James N. Rosenau, "The Premises and Promises of Decision-Making Analysis," both in James C. Charlesworth (ed.), *Contemporary Political Analysis* (New York: The Free Press, 1967).

12. These characteristics of self-executing orders come from Richard E. Neustadt, *Presidential Power* (New York: John Wiley and Sons, Inc., Science Editions, 1962), p. 19. This book also discusses why even such orders are not always implemented as expected. Even Allison (*APSR*, p. 706) has evidence of inadequtae control over implementation in his case of very close supervision.

13. Allison does discuss implementation, but only briefly. See *APSR*, pp. 702–703.

14. See Anthony Downs, *Inside Bureaucracy* (Boston: Little, Brown and Company, 1967), ch. X, which draws heavily upon Gordon Tullock, *The Politics of Bureaucracy* (Washington: Public Affairs Press, 1965), pp. 137–141.

15. Amitai Etzioni, *Complex Organizations* (New York: The Free Press of Glencoe, Inc., 1961), especially Introduction and chs. 1–3.

16. Tullock, *op. cit.*, pp. 51, 66, 73.

17. Downs, *op. cit.*, p. 147.

18. Interview with Richard Usher. Downs, *op. cit.*, p. 148 makes the theoretical case for the same phenomenon.

19. Downs, *op. cit.*, pp. 96–97.

20. Confidential Source.

21. Confidential Source.

22. Tullock, *op. cit.*, p. 69.

23. The phrase is Richard Neustadt's.

24. See Lindblom, *Intelligence of Democracy*, for an extended discussion of incrementalism. An earlier, briefer article made the same point: "The Science of 'Muddling Through'," reprinted in Raymond E. Wolfinger (ed.), *Readings in American Political Behavior* (Englewood Cliffs, New Jersey: Prentice-Hall, 1966), pp. 211–226.

25. Max Weber, in H. H. Gerth and C. Wright Mills, *From Max Weber: Essays in Sociology* (New York: Oxford University Press, A Galaxy Book, 1959), pp. 196–198; Robert K. Merton in Merton *et al.*, *Reader in Bureaucracy* (New York: The Free Press, 1952), pp. 364–365.

Bibliography

INTERVIEWS

The following people were interviewed by the author on the dates given and were willing to have their remarks, in whole or in part, attributed by name. Other subjects were interviewed but wished to remain Confidential Sources.

AMORY, ROBERT, JR.—March 10 and April 1, 1969 (CIA, 1952–62, rising to post of Deputy Director for Intelligence).

ANDERSON, JOSEPH (Colonel, USA, Ret.)—July 1, 1969 (Head of budgetary mission to Laos, January–March, 1960).

BISSELL, RICHARD M.—June 23, 1969 (CIA, Deputy Director for Plans, 1959–62).

BOWIE, ROBERT R.—March 19, 1969 (Head of State Department Policy Planning Staff, 1953–57).

BROWN, WINTHROP—January 13 and July 1, 1969 (Ambassador to Laos, 1960–62).

BRANFMAN, FRED—April 17, 1971 (In Laos for IVS and as journalist, 1967–71).

BUNDY, WILLIAM P.—May 12, 1969, and January 20, 1970 (CIA in 1950s; Deputy and later Assistant Secretary for International Security Affairs (ISA) in Department of Defense, 1961–64; Assistant Secretary of State for East Asian and Pacific Affairs, 1964–69).

BURKE, ADMIRAL ARLEIGH (USN, Ret.)—May 12, 1969 (Chief of Naval Operations, 1955–61).

CHAPMAN, CHRISTIAN—January 15, 1969 (Desk Officer for Laos, August 1959–August 1961).

CHAYES, ABRAM—March 18, 1969 (Legal advisor to State Department during Geneva Conference).

CLEVELAND, ROBERT—January 14, 1969 (Deputy Director, Office for Southeast Asia, State Department, 1958–62).

COOPER, CHESTER—May 13, 1969 (At Geneva, 1961–62; on NSC Staff dealing with Asia after 1962).

CORCORAN, THOMAS—January 14, 1969, and May 13, 1971 (Desk Officer for Laos, August 1958–August 1959 and since 1968.

CROSS, CHARLES T.—March 15, 1969 (Desk Officer for Laos, April 1961–June 1963).

CUTLER, ROBERT—June 3, 1969 (Special Assistant to the President for National Security Affairs, 1953–55, 1957–58).

316

DECKER, GENERAL GEORGE H. (USA, Ret.)—April 3, 1969 (Chief of Staff of the Army, 1959–62).

DUSKIN, COLONEL EDGAR W.—April 5, 1971 (Military attaché, 1964–66, 1968–70).

FORRESTAL, MICHAEL—February 14, 1969 (NSA Staff for Asia, 1962–65).

FOWLER, JAMES—May 15, 1969 (Assistant Regional Director for AID, 1961–63).

GELB, LES—May 10, 1971 (DOD, Director of Policy Planning Staff, 1966–69).

GENTRY, COLONEL CHARLES—May 12, 1969, and April 27, 1971 (Attaché to PEO, 1956–61).

GRAY, GORDON—May 14, 1969 (Assistant Secretary of Defense [ISA], 1955–57; Special Assistant to the President for National Security Affairs, 1959–61).

GULLION, EDMUND—May 1, 1969 (Chargé to Associated States, 1950–53).

HARRIMAN, AVERELL—May 13 and 16 and June 4, 1969 (Chief U.S. negotiator at 1961–62 Geneva Conference; Ambassador at Large, January–November, 1961; Assistant Secretary for the Far East, November 1961–April 1963; Under Secretary of State for Political Affairs, 1963–65).

HILSMAN, ROGER—February 14, 1969 (Assistant Secretary of State for Intelligence and Research, 1961–63; Assistant Secretary for the Far East, April 1963–March 1964).

IRWIN, JOHN—February 13, 1969 (Assistant Secretary of Defense, ISA, April 1957–January 1961).

KIRKPATRICK, LYMAN B., JR.—February 20, 1969 (Inspector General of CIA, 1950s–1962).

LANDON, KENNETH—May 14, 1969 (Member, Staff of Operations Coordinating Board of NSC, 1956–60).

LEFFINGWELL, WILLIAM M.—May 12, 1969 (Deputy Director, Military Assistance Program, 1950s–1967).

LOWENSTEIN, JAMES—May 12, 1971 (Staff of Senate Foreign Relations Committee).

MC CLINTOCK, ROBERT—April 1, 1969 (Ambassador to Cambodia, 1954–56).

MERCHANT, LIVINGSTON—August 12, 1969 (Deputy Assistant Secretary for the Far East, 1949–51; Assistant Secretary for Europe, 1954–56; Deputy Under Secretary of State, August–December 1959; Under Secretary, December 1959–January 1961).

MILLER, WILLIAM—May 4, 1971 (Aide to Senator J. S. Cooper).

MLADEK, J. V.—May 12, 1969 (IMF economist, sent on study missions to Laos, 1957–58).

MOOSE, RICHARD—April 2, 1971 (NSC Staff, 1966–68; Staff of Senate Foreign Relations Committee, 1970–71).

MURPHY, ROBERT—June 25, 1969 (Deputy and then Under Secretary of State, 1953–59).

MYERS, ROBERT—March 31, 1969 (With CIA, trips to Laos, 1960–64).

NEUBERT, JOSEPH—April 2, 1969 (Researcher on Sino-Soviet area, 1960–62; Special Assistant to Hilsman, 1962–63).

NITZE, PAUL—April 2, 1969 (Assistant Secretary of Defense [ISA], 1961–63).

PARSONS, J. GRAHAM—January 13, February 7, and December 4, 1969 (Ambassador to Laos, 1956–58; Deputy and then Assistant Secretary of State for the Far East, April 1958–April 1961).

PHILLIPS, RUFUS—May 15, 1969 (CIA, in Laos, 1957–August 1959).

PINCUS, WALTER—April 30, 1971 (Staff of Symington Subcommittee).

RADFORD, ADMIRAL ARTHUR (USN, Ret.)—May 12, 1969 (Chairman, JCS, 1952–57).

RILEY, ADMIRAL HERBERT D. (USN, Ret.)—April 3, 1969 (CINCPAC Staff Director, February 1958–April 1961; Head of Joint Staff, 1962–63).

ROBERTSON, WALTER S.—June 30, 1969 (Assistant Secretary of State for the Far East, March 1953–June 1959).

ROPA, DON—May 15, 1969 (CIA, in Laos, November 1956–January 1959).

SHOUP, GENERAL DAVID (USMC, Ret.)—March 28, 1969 (Commandant, Marine Corps, 1960–63).

STANTON, THOMAS—January 13, 1970 (AID Official in Southern Laos, summer 1966).

STEEVES, JOHN—January 10, 1969 (Deputy Assistant Secretary for the Far East, 1959–61).

SULLIVAN, WILLIAM H.—June 28, 1969, and May 8, 1971 (Aide to Harriman, 1961–62; Ambassador to Laos, 1964–69, Deputy Assistant Secretary of State, 1969–71).

THOMSON, JAMES C., JR.—January 21, 1969 (Work on Asia in State Department and NSC, 1961–66).

TINKER, JERRY—April 7, 1971 (Staff of Refugee Subcommittee).

USHER, RICHARD—January 10, 1969 (Deputy Director, Office of Southeast Asian Affairs, State Department, September 1959–September 1961).

WELLER, GENERAL DONALD M. (USMC, Ret.)—May 12, 1969 (On staff of Task Force 116, 1959–60; Commander until March 1961; Chief of Staff through 1962).

WEHRLE, ROY—March 17, 1969 (In Laos as economist, 1959–61; head of economic reform mission, 1962).

YOUNG, KENNETH—February 13, 1969 (Director, Office of Southeast Asia, 1954–58; Ambassador to Thailand, 1961–63).

LETTERS

Several other sources submitted letters in response to questions from the author. The following were willing to be cited by name for all or part of their comments.

HEINTGES, GENERAL JOHN A. (USA)—June 17, 1969 (Chief of PEO in Laos, October 1958–February 1961).

MC CREA, WILLIAM S.—June 11, 1969 (Laos Desk Officer, ISA, in early 1960s).

PRICE, C. HOYT—June 6, 1969 (In Saigon, 1953–55; aid work on Southeast Asia through 1958).

RIDGWAY, GENERAL MATTHEW B. (USA, Ret.)—May 29, 1969 (Chief of Staff of the Army, 1953–55).

MEMOIRS AND FIRSTHAND ACCOUNTS: LAOS

DOMMEN, ARTHUR J. *Conflict in Laos: The Politics of Neutralization.* New York: Frederick A. Praeger, 1965.

FALL, BERNARD B. *Anatomy of a Crisis: The Laotian Crisis of 1960–1961.* Garden City, New York: Doubleday and Company, Inc., 1969.

FIELD, MICHAEL. *The Prevailing Wind: Witness in Indo-China.* London: Methuen and Company, Ltd., 1965.

MEEKER, ODEN. *The Little World of Laos.* New York: Charles Schribner's Sons, 1959.

SISOUK NA CHAMPASSAK. *Storm Over Laos.* New York: Frederick A. Praeger, 1961.

MEMOIRS AND FIRSTHAND ACCOUNTS: UNITED STATES

ACHESON, DEAN. *Present at the Creation.* New York: W. W. Norton and Company, Inc., 1969.

ADAMS, SHERMAN. *Firsthand Report.* New York: Popular Library, 1962.

EDEN, ANTHONY (Lord Avon). *Full Circle.* Boston: Houghton Mifflin Company, 1960.

EISENHOWER, DWIGHT D. *Mandate for Change, 1955–1956.* Garden City, New York: Doubleday and Company, Inc., 1963.

———. *Waging Peace, 1956–1961.* Garden City, New York: Doubleday and Company, Inc., 1965.

GALBRAITH, JOHN KENNETH. *Ambassador's Journal.* Boston: Houghton Mifflin Company, 1969.

HILSMAN, ROGER. *To Move a Nation: The Politics of Foreign Policy in the Administration of John F. Kennedy.* Garden City, New York: Doubleday and Company, Inc., 1967.

HUGHES, EMMET JOHN. *The Ordeal of Power: A Political Memoir of the Eisenhower Years.* New York: Dell Publishing Company, Inc., 1964.

KROCK, ARTHUR. *Memoirs: Sixty Years on the Firing Line.* New York: Popular Library, 1968.

RIDGWAY, MATTHEW B. *Soldier: The Memoirs of Matthew B. Ridgway.* New York: Harper and Brothers, 1956.

SALINGER, PIERRE. *With Kennedy*. Garden City, New York: Doubleday and Company, Inc., 1966.

SCHLESINGER, ARTHUR M., JR. *A Thousand Days: John F. Kennedy in the White House*. Boston: Houghton Mifflin Company, 1965.

SORENSEN, THEODORE C. *Kennedy*. New York: Harper and Row, 1965.

OTHER BOOKS ON LAOS AND SOUTHEAST ASIA

ADAMS, NINA S. and MC COY, ALFRED W. (eds.) *Laos: War and Revolution*, New York: Harper Colophon Books, 1970.

BURCHETT, WILFRED G. *The Furtive War: The United States in Vietnam and Laos*. New York: International Publishers, 1963.

————. *Mekong Upstream: A Visit to Laos and Cambodia*. Berlin: Seven Seas Publishers, 1959.

DUNCAN, DONALD. *The New Legions*. New York: Pocket Books, 1967.

FALL, BERNARD B. "The Pathet Lao: A 'Liberation' Party," in Robert A. Scalapino (ed.), *The Communist Revolution in Asia*. Englewood Cliffs, New Jersey: Prentice-Hall, Inc., 1965.

GRIFFITH, WILLIAM E. *The Sino-Soviet Rift*. Cambridge: The M.I.T. Press, 1964.

HALPERN, A. M. and FREDMAN, H. B. *Communist Strategy in Laos*. Santa Monica, Calif.: Rand Corporation, 1960, Research Memorandum RM-2561.

HALPERN, JOEL M. *Government, Politics, and Social Structure in Laos*. Monograph Series No. 4, Southeast Asia Studies, Yale University, 1964.

————. *Economy and Society of Laos*. Monograph Series No. 5, Southeast Asia Studies, Yale University, 1964.

HONEY, P. J. *Communism in North Vietnam*. Cambridge: The M.I.T. Press, 1963.

INSOR, D. *Thailand: A Political, Social, and Economic Analysis*. London: George Allen and Unwin, Ltd., 1963.

KUNSTADTER, PETER (ed.). *Southeast Asian Tribes, Minorities, and Nations*. Princeton: Princeton University Press, 2 vols., 1967.

LALL, ARTHUR. *How Communist China Negotiates*. New York: Columbia University Press, 1968.

LANGER, PAUL F. and ZASLOFF, JOSEPH J. *North Vietnam and the Pathet Lao*. Cambridge, Mass.: Harvard University Press, 1970.

LEBAR, FRANK M., and SUDDARD, ADRIENNE (eds.). *Laos*. New Haven: HRAF Press, 1960.

LEDERER, WILLIAM J. *A Nation of Sheep*. New York: W. W. Norton and Company, Inc., 1961.

NUECHTERLEIN, DONALD E. *Thailand and the Struggle for Southeast Asia*. Ithaca, New York: Cornell University Press, 1965.

NUTT, ANITA LAUVE. *Troika on Trial, Control or Compromise*. Rand Corporation SD-220, 1967, 3 vols.

ROBERTS, T. D.; CARROLL, MARY ELIZABETH; KAPLAN, IRVING; MATTHEWS, JAN
M.; MC MORRIS, DAVID S.; TOWNSEND, CHARLES (coauthors). *Area
Handbook for Laos*, DA Pam. No. 550-58. Washington, D.C.:
Government Printing Office, June, 1967.

ROBINSON, DONALD (ed.). *The Dirty Wars*. New York: Delacorte Press,
1968.

SAR DESAI, D. R. *Indian Foreign Policy in Cambodia, Laos, and Vietnam,
1947-1964*. Berkeley: University of California Press, 1968.

SCHANCHE, DON A. *Mister Pop*. New York: David McKay Company, Inc.,
1970.

SHAPLEN, ROBERT. *The Lost Revolution*. New York: Harper and Row,
1965.

————. *Time Out of Hand: Revolution and Reaction in Southeast Asia*.
New York: Harper and Row, 1969.

SIMMONDS, STUART. "Independence and Political Rivalry in Laos, 1945–
61," in Saul Rose (ed.), *Politics in Southern Asia*. London: St.
Martin's Press, 1963.

SMITH, ROGER M. "Laos," in George McTurnan Kahin (ed.), *Governments
and Politics of Southeast Asia*. Ithaca, New York: Cornell University Press, second edition, 1964.

TOYE, HUGH. *Laos: Buffer State or Battleground*. London: Oxford University Press, 1968.

ZAGORIA, DONALD S. *Vietnam Triangle: Moscow, Peking, Hanoi*. New York:
Pegasus, 1967.

OTHER BOOKS ON U.S. FOREIGN POLICY

BARNET, RICHARD J. *Intervention and Revolution: America's Confrontation
With Insurgent Movements Around the World*. Cleveland:
Meridian Books, The World Publishing Company, 1968.

BATOR, VICTOR. *Vietnam: A Diplomatic Tragedy*. Dobbs Ferry, New York:
Oceana Publications, Inc., 1965.

CLARK, KEITH C., and LAURENCE J. LEGERE (eds.). *The President and the
Management of National Security: A Report by the Institute
for Defense Analyses*. New York: Frederick A. Praeger, 1969.

DEVILLERS, PHILIPPE, and LACOUTURE, JEAN. *End of a War: Indochina, 1954*.
New York: Frederick A. Praeger, 1969.

DULLES, ELEANOR LANSING. *John Foster Dulles: The Last Year*. New York:
Harcourt, Brace and World, Inc., 1963.

FINLAY, DAVID J.; HOLSTI, OLE R.; and FAGAN, RICHARD R. *Enemies in Politics*.
Chicago: Rand McNally and Company, 1967.

GALBRAITH, JOHN KENNETH. *The Triumph*. New York: Signet Books, 1968.

GERSON, LOUIS L. *John Foster Dulles*, vol. XVII, in The American Secretaries of State and Their Diplomacy, Robert H. Ferrell, ed.
New York: Cooper Square Publishers, Inc., 1967.

GEYELIN, PHILIP. *Lyndon B. Johnson and the World*. New York: Frederick A. Praeger, 1966.

GOOLD-ADAMS, RICHARD. *The Time of Power: A Reappraisal of John Foster Dulles*. London: Weidenfeld and Nicolson, 1962.

GOULDEN, JOSEPH C. *Truth is the First Casualty: The Gulf of Tonkin Affair—Illusion and Reality*. Chicago: A James B. Adler, Inc., Book published in association with Rand McNally and Company, 1969.

GURTOV, MELVIN. *The First Vietnam Crisis*. New York: Columbia University Press, 1967.

HARPER, NORMAN. "Australia and the United States," in Gordon Greenwood and Norman Harper (eds.), *Australia in World Affairs, 1956–1960*, issued under the auspices of the Australian Institute of International Affairs, Publications Centre, The University of British Columbia, Vancouver, Canada, 1963.

KISSINGER, HENRY A. *American Foreign Policy: Three Essays*. New York: W. W. Norton and Company, Inc., 1969.

MC CLINTOCK, ROBERT. *The Meaning of Limited War*. Boston: Houghton Mifflin Company, 1967.

MODELSKI, GEORGE (ed.). *SEATO: Six Studies*. Melbourne: F. W. Cheshire for the Australian National University, 1962.

ROPER, ELMO. *You and Your Leaders*. New York: William A. Morrow, 1957.

SAPIN, BURTON M. *The Making of United States Foreign Policy*. New York: Frederick A. Praeger for the Brookings Institution, 1966.

SIDNEY, HUGH. *John F. Kennedy, President*. New York: Fawcett World Library, 1964.

WEINTAL, EDWARD and CHARLES BARTLETT. *Facing the Brink: An Intimate Study of Crisis Diplomacy*. New York: Charles Scribner's Sons, 1967.

WICKER, TOM. *JFK and LBJ: The Influence of Personality on Politics*. New York: William Morrow and Company, Inc., 1968.

WISE, DAVID, and THOMAS B. ROSS. *The Invisible Government*. New York: Random House, 1964.

WORKS ON DECISION-MAKING

ALLISON, GRAHAM T. "Conceptual Models and the Cuban Missile Crisis: Rational Policy, Organization Process, and Bureaucratic Politics," Rand Paper P-3919, August 1968.

ANTHONY, ROBERT N. *Planning and Control System: A Framework For Analysis*. Division of Research, Graduate School of Business Administration, Harvard University, Boston, 1965.

BLAU, PETER M., and SCOTT, W. RICHARD. *Formal Organizations*. San Francisco: Chandler Publishing Company, 1962.

CHARLESWORTH, JAMES C. (ed.). *Contemporary Political Analysis*. New York: The Free Press, 1967.

CROZIER, MICHEL. *The Bureaucratic Phenomenon*. Chicago: The University of Chicago Press, 1964.

DOWNS, ANTHONY. *Inside Bureaucracy*. Boston: Little, Brown and Company, 1967.

ETZIONI, AMITAI. *Complex Organizations*. New York: The Free Press of Glencoe, Inc., 1961.

GERTH, H. H., and MILLS, C. WRIGHT. *From Max Weber: Essays in Sociology*. New York: Oxford University Press, A Galaxy Book, 1959.

HERMANN, CHARLES F. "International Crisis as a Situational Variable," in James N. Rosenau (ed.), *International Politics and Foreign Policy*, Revised Edition. New York: The Free Press, 1969.

KELMAN, HERBERT C. (ed.). *International Behavior*. New York: Holt, Rinehart and Winston, 1965.

LINDBLOM, CHARLES E. *The Intelligence of Democracy*. New York: Free Press, 1965.

————. *The Policy-Making Process*. Englewood Cliffs, New Jersey: Prentice Hall, Inc., 1968.

MARCH, JAMES G., and SIMON, HERBERT A. *Organizations*. New York: John Wiley and Sons, Inc., 1961.

MERTON, ROBERT, *et al. Reader in Bureaucracy*. New York: The Free Press, 1952.

NEUSTADT, RICHARD E. *Presidential Power*. New York: John Wiley and Sons, Inc., Science Editions, 1962.

SCHELLING, THOMAS C. *The Strategy of Conflict*. Cambridge: Harvard University Press, 1960.

SORENSEN, THEODORE C. *Decision-Making in the White House*. New York: Columbia University Press, 1963.

STEINBRUNER, JOHN. "Memorandum to the Public Policy Program" (typewritten), September 29, 1969.

TULLOCK, GORDON. *The Politics of Bureaucracy*. Washington: Public Affairs Press, 1965.

MAGAZINE AND JOURNAL ARTICLES

ABRAMS, ARNOLD. "Washington's Dilemma," *Far Eastern Economic Review (FEER)*, January 1, 1970.

ALLISON, GRAHAM T. "Conceptual Models and the Cuban Missile Crisis," *American Political Science Review*, vol. 63 (September 1969), pp. 689–718.

ALLMAN, T. D. "Big Brother is Watching," *FEER*, October 9, 1969.

————. "One Year Worse," *FEER*, January 1, 1970.

AUSLAND, JOHN C. and RICHARDSON, COLONEL HUGH F. "Crisis Management: Berlin, Cyprus, Laos," *Foreign Affairs*, January 1966, vol. 44.

BEECH, KEYES. "How Uncle Sam Fumbled in Laos," *Saturday Evening Post*, April 22, 1961.

CLIFFORD, CLARK M. "A Viet Nam Reappraisal," *Foreign Affairs*, July 1969.

CLIFTON, MAJOR GENERAL C. V. "Hail to the Chief," *Army* (January 1964) 14:28–33.

CORRADI, EGISTO. "This is Laos—A Vietnam in the Making," *Atlas*, January 1968 (15:28ff.), reprinted and translated from *Corriere della Sera* (Milan), October 12, 1967.

CZYZAK, JOHN J., and SALANS, CARL F. "The Internal Conference on the Settlement of the Laotian Question and the Geneva Agreements of 1962," *American Journal of International Law*, vol. 57 (April 1963), pp. 300–317.

DOMMEN, ARTHUR J. "Laos in the Second Indochina War," *Current History*, December, 1970, pp. 326–332.

DUSKIN, LIEUTENANT COLONEL EDGAR W., USA. "Laos," *Military Review* (March 1968), 48:3–10. (Note: Duskin was with the MAAG in Laos, later an Army Attaché.)

ESTES, GENERAL HOWELL M., JR. "The Revolution in Airlift," *Aviation Report*, vol. 17 (March/April 1966), p. 6.

Gallup Opinion Index, October 1969, report 52.

JOEL, CLARK. "The Foreign Exchange Operations Fund for Laos: An Interesting Experiment in Monetary Stabilization," *Asian Survey*, 6:134–149 (March 1966). (Note: Joel was an economist in Laos with AID, September 1963–September 1965.)

KALES, DAVID. "Enemy Below," *FEER*, January 22, 1970.

KIRK, DONALD. "An Election to Test Laotian Stability," *The Reporter*, December 29, 1966.

MILLER, HAYNES. "A Bulwark Built On Sand," *The Reporter*, November 13, 1958.

PACE, ERIC. "Laos: Continuing Crisis," *Foreign Affairs*, 43:64–74 (October, 1964).

PAUL, ROLAND A. "Laos: Anatomy of an American Involvement," *Foreign Affairs*, vol. 49 (April 1971), pp. 533–547.

ROBERTS, CHALMERS M. "The Day We Didn't Go to War," in Marcus G. Raskin and Bernard B. Fall (eds.), *The Vietnam Reader* (Revised Edition. New York: Vintage Books, 1967), reprinted from *The Reporter*, September 14, 1954.

ROVERE, RICHARD H. "Letter From Washington," *The New Yorker*, April 15, 1961.

SANDERS, SOL W. "For U.S.: It's War With One Arm," *U.S. News and World Report*, July 20, 1964.

SCOTT, PETER DALE. "Air America: Flying the U.S. into Laos," *Ramparts*, February 1970.

———. "Tonkin Bay: Was There a Conspiracy?" (a review of Joseph

C. Goulden's book, *Truth is the First Casualty*), *New York Review of Books*, January 29, 1970.

SHAPLEN, ROBERT. "Our Involvement in Laos," *Foreign Affairs*, vol. 48 (April 1970), pp. 478–493.

———. *The New Yorker*, January 16, 1965.

SIMMONDS, E. H. S. "The Evolution of Foreign Policy in Laos Since Independence," *Modern Asian Studies*, II, 1 (1968), pp. 1–30.

SOUVANNAPHOUMA (PRINCE). "Laos: le fond du problème," *France-Asie*, XVII (Mars–Avril 1961), pp. 1824–1826.

STANTON, THOMAS H. "Conflict in Laos: The Village Point of View," *Asian Survey*, 8:887-900 (November 1968).

THOMSON, JAMES C., JR. "How Could Vietnam Happen?", *The Atlantic*, April 1968.

WARNER, DENIS. "A Cautionary Report on Laos," *The Reporter*, December 2, 1965.

———. "The Secret War," *Reporting South-East Asia* (Sydney: Angus and Robertson, 1966), reprinted from April 22, 1965, issue of *The Reporter*.

OFFICIAL DOCUMENTS

Great Britain:

Parliament. Laos No. 1 (1955), *First Interim Report of the International Commission for Supervision and Control in Laos, August 11–December 31, 1954* (Cmd. 9445).

———. Laos No. 2 (1955), *Second Interim Report of the International Commission for Supervision and Control in Laos, January 1–June 30, 1955* (Cmd. 9630).

———. Laos No. 1 (1957), *Third Interim Report of the International Commission for Supervision and Control in Laos, July 1, 1955–May 16, 1957* (Cmnd. 314).

———. Laos No. 1 (1958), *Fourth Interim Report of the International Commission for Supervision and Control in Laos, May 17, 1957–May 31, 1958* (Cmnd. 541).

British Information Services. *Laos.* (R.5489/70) June 1970.

United Nations:

Security Council. *Report of the Security Council Sub-Committee Under Resolution of 7 September 1959*, S/4236, November 5, 1959, New York: Security Council.

United States: (See *Congress*, following.)

Congress:

The most useful and comprehensive documents on Laos in the 1950s are the 1959 hearings and report by the Subcommittee chaired by Congressman Porter Hardy of Virginia. They are cited throughout the text by the shorthand phrase *Porter Hardy Hearings* or *Porter Hardy Report*. For the period since 1962 the *Symington Hearings* are the basic reference. Additional listings include primarily the hearings on each year's foreign aid program which provided some information used in the text.

Porter Hardy Hearings

House, Committee on Government Operations, *United States Aid Operations in Laos, Hearings* before a Subcommittee of the Committee on Government Operations, 86th Cong., 1st sess., 1959.

Porter Hardy Report

House, Committee on Government Operations, *US. Aid Operations in Laos: Seventh Report by the Committee*, House Rept. 546, 86th Cong., 1st sess., 1959.

Symington Hearings

Senate, Committee on Foreign Relations, *United States Security Agreements and Commitments Abroad: Kingdom of Laos, Hearings* before the Subcommittee on United States Security Agreements and Commitments Abroad of the Committee on Foreign Relations, part 2, 91st Cong., 1st sess., 1970 (cited as *Laos Hearings*).

————. *United States Security Agreements and Commitments Abroad: Kingdom of Thailand, Hearings* before the Subcommittee on United States Security Agreements and Commitments Abroad of the Committee on Foreign Relations, part 3, 91st Cong., 1st sess., 1970 (cited as *Thai Hearings*).

————. "Security Agreements and Commitments Abroad," *Report* to the Committee on Foreign Relations by the Subcommittee on Security Agreements and Commitments Abroad, 91st Cong., 2d sess., December 21, 1970 (cited as *Symington Report*).

Moose-Lowenstein Report

Senate, Committee on Foreign Relations, "Laos: April 1971," a Staff Report prepared for the use of the Subcommittee on U.S. Security Agreements and Commitments Abroad, 92nd Cong., 1st sess., August 3, 1971.

Kennedy Subcommittee

Senate, Committee on the Judiciary. *Refugee and Civilian War Casualty Problems in Laos and Cambodia, Hearing* before the Subcommittee to Investigate Problems Connected with Refugees and Escapees of the Committee on the Judiciary, 91st Cong., 2d. sess., May 7, 1970 (cited as *Kennedy Subcommittee Hearings, 1970*).

————. "Refugee and Civilian War Casualty Problems in Indochina," *Staff Report* prepared for the use of the Subcommittee to Investigate Problems Connected with Refugees and Escapees of the Committee on the Judiciary, 91st Cong., 2d. sess., September 28, 1970 (cited as *Kennedy Subcommittee Report*).

————. *War-Related Civilian Problems—In Indochina, Hearings* before the Subcommittee on Refugees and Escapees (typewritten) April 22 and 23, 1971. (cited as *Kennedy Subcommittee Hearings, 1971*).

Debates

The most extensive and informative congressional debates on Laos took place in the Senate on December 15, 1969. See *Congressional Record* (Daily Edition), vol. 115, no. 208 (December 15, 1969), pp. S16751–65 and vol. 116, no. 3 (January 21, 1970), pp. E151–166. Further debate took place in a secret session on June 7, 1971, a censored version of which appeared on August 3, 1971, vol. 117, no. 124, pp. S12930–66.

Other Hearings and Reports

ELLENDER, ALLEN J. (SENATOR). *Report on Overseas Operations of the United States Government*, Committee Print for Senate Committee on Appropriations (85th Cong., 1st sess.), 1957.

House Appropriations

House, Committee on Appropriations. *Mutual Security Appropriations for 1956, Hearings* before the Subcommittee of the Committee on Appropriations, 84th Cong., 1st sess., 1955.

————. *Mutual Security Appropriations for 1957, Hearings* before the Subcommittee of the Committee on Appropriations, 84th Cong., 2d sess., 1956.

————. *Mutual Security Appropriations for 1958, Hearings* before the Subcommittee of the Committee on Appropriations, 85th Cong., 1st sess., 1957.

————. *Mutual Security Appropriations for 1959, Hearings* before the Subcommittee of the Committee on Appropriations, 85th Cong., 2d sess., 1958.

————. *Mutual Security Appropriations for 1960 (And Related Agencies), Hearings* before the Subcommittee of the Committee on Appropriations, 86th Cong., 1st sess., 1959.

————. *Foreign Operations Appropriations for 1962, Hearings* before the Subcommittee of the Committee on Appropriations, 87th Cong., 1st sess., 1961.

————. *Foreign Operations Appropriations for 1964, Hearings* before a Subcommittee of the Committee on Appropriations, 88th Cong., 1st sess., 1963 (in 3 parts).

————. *Foreign Operations Appropriations for 1965, Hearings* before a Subcommittee of the Committee on Appropriations, 88th Cong., 2d sess., 1964 (in 2 parts).

House Foreign Affairs

House, Committee on Foreign Affairs. *Mutual Security Act of 1955,*

Hearings before the Committee on Foreign Affairs, 84th Cong., 1st sess., 1955.

————. *Mutual Security Act of 1956, Hearings* before the Committee on Foreign Affairs, 84th Cong., 2d sess., 1956.

————. *Mutual Security Act of 1958, Hearings* before the Committee on Foreign Affairs, 85th Cong., 2d sess., 1958.

————. *Mutual Security Program in Laos, Hearings* before the Subcommittee on the Far East and the Pacific, 85th Cong., 2d sess., 1958.

————. *Mutual Security Act of 1959, Hearings* before the Committee on Foreign Affairs, 86th Cong., 1st sess., 1959.

————. *Mutual Security Act of 1960, Hearings* before the Committee on Foreign Affairs, 86th Cong., 2d sess., 1960.

————. *International Commission for Supervision and Control in Laos, Hearing* before the Subcommittee on the Far East and the Pacific, Committee on Foreign Affairs, 88th Cong., 1st sess., September 24, 1963.

————. *Foreign Assistance Act of 1967, Hearings* before the Committee on Foreign Affairs, 90th Cong., 1st sess., 1967.

MANSFIELD, MIKE (SENATOR). *Report on Indochina.* Committee Print for Senate Committee on Foreign Relations, 83rd Cong., 2d sess., October 15, 1954.

————. *Viet Nam, Cambodia, and Laos.* Committee Print for Senate Committee on Foreign Relations, 84th Cong., 1st sess., October 6, 1955.

Senate—Appropriations

Senate, Committee on Appropriations. *Mutual Appropriations for 1955, Hearings* on H.R. 10051, an act making appropriations for Mutual Security for the Fiscal Year ending June 30, 1955, and for other purposes, 83rd Cong., 2d sess., 1954.

————. *Mutual Security Appropriations for 1957, Hearings* before the Committee on Appropriations, 84th Cong., 2d sess., 1956.

————. *Mutual Security Appropriations for 1958, Hearings* before the Committee on Appropriations, 85th Cong., 1st sess., 1957.

————. *Mutual Security Appropriations for 1959, Hearings* before the Committee on Appropriations, 85th Cong., 2d sess., 1958.

————. *Mutual Security Appropriations for 1960 (And Related Agencies), Hearings* before the Committee on Appropriations, 86th Cong., 1st sess., 1959.

Senate—Foreign Relations

Senate, Committee on Foreign Relations. *Mutual Security Act of 1954, Hearings* on the Mutual Security Program for Fiscal Year 1955, 83rd Cong., 2d sess., 1954.

————. *The Southeast Asia Collective Defense Treaty, Hearing* on Executive K, 83rd Cong., 2d sess., 1954, part 1.

————. *Mutual Security Act of 1955, Hearings* before the Committee on Foreign Relations, 84th Cong., 1st sess., 1955.

————. *Mutual Security Act of 1956, Hearings* before the Committee on Foreign Relations, 84th Cong., 2d sess., 1956.

————. *Mutual Security Act of 1957, Hearings* before the Committee on Foreign Relations, 85th Cong., 1st sess., 1957.

————. *Review of Foreign Policy, 1958, Hearings* before the Committee on Foreign Relations, 85th Cong., 2d sess., 1958.

————. *Mutual Security Act of 1958, Hearings* before the Committee on Foreign Relations, 85th Cong., 2d sess., 1958.

————. *Mutual Security Act of 1959, Hearings* before the Committee on Foreign Relations, 86th Cong., 1st sess., 1959.

————. Report of Proceedings, Hearing Held before the Committee on Foreign Relations, Nomination of J. Graham Parsons of New York to be Assistant Secretary of State for Far Eastern Affairs, May 26, 1959 (Washington: Ward and Paul—duplicated).

————. Hearing before the Senate Committee on Foreign Relations on the Nomination of W. Averell Harriman to be Under-Secretary of State for Political Affairs, April 2, 1963 (Washington: Ward and Paul—duplicated).

————. Special Committee to Study the Foreign Aid Program, *The Foreign Aid Program, Hearings* before the Special Committee to Study the Foreign Aid Program, 85th Cong., 1st sess., 1957.

————. Special Committee to Study the Foreign Aid Program, *Foreign Aid Program: Compilation of Studies and Surveys*, S. Doc. 52, 85th Cong., 1st sess., 1957, "Southeast Asia: Report on United States Foreign Assistance Programs," by Clement Johnston, survey no. 7.

Executive Branch:

President

See *Public Papers of the Presidents of the United States*, annual volumes for Dwight D. Eisenhower, John F. Kennedy, and Lyndon B. Johnson, Washington, D.C.: Office of the Federal Register, National Archives and Records Service.

Commerce, Department of

————. "Basic Data on the Economy of Laos," Economic Reports, *World Trade Information Service*, part 1, no. 58–69, September 1958.

State, Department of

————. "American Aid to Laos—A Vital Link in the Chain of Mutual Security," Report of Director of U.S. Operations Mission to Laos, July 1, 1959 (typewritten).

————. *American Foreign Policy: Current Documents, 1961*, Department of State Publication 7808 (Released June 1965).

————. "Background Notes: Laos" (typewritten, 1969).

————. "Comments by the Department of State and ICA on the Report of the House Committee on Government Operations, 'United States Aid Operations in Laos'," (typewritten), June 15, 1959.

————. *Department of State Bulletin*, 1954–71.

————. *The Situation in Laos*, September 1959.

————. Office of Program and Economic Affairs, USAID/Laos, "Fact Sheet," (typewritten), October 1, 1967.

————. Agency for International Development, *Project Budget Submission FY 1971: Laos* (unclassified, September 1969).

————. Edwin T. McKeithen, "The Role of North Vietnamese Cadres in Pathet Lao Administration of Xieng Khouang Province," (typewritten) April 1970.

————. McKeithen, "Life Under the P.L. in the Xieng Khouang Ville Area," (typewritten) July 10, 1969.

NEWSPAPERS

The following newspapers were consulted, either by using a published index (in the case of the *New York Times* and *Wall Street Journal*) or by referring to issues at the time of major events. Additional newspaper references were obtained from the press clippings files of the Council on Foreign Relations in New York.

Bangkok Post, 1954–1971.
New York Herald-Tribune, 1954–1961.
New York Times, 1954–1971.
Wall Street Journal, 1955–1971.
Washington Post, 1954–1971.
Washington *Star*, 1969–1971.

MISCELLANEOUS SOURCES

Although the John Foster Dulles Papers at Princeton University have little information on Laos, they are the only source for texts of news conferences during 1953–1956. Some quotations have been taken from these texts. The Dulles Oral History Project has many transcripts of interviews with officials who worked with Dulles. The interviews used here, with the permission of the subjects, were the ones conducted with Robert R. Bowie and General Nathan F. Twining.

Estelle Holt, a journalist in Laos during the 1960s, has compiled a chronology of events from 1955 through May 1964. This undated, untitled, typewritten document, cited as the "Holt Chronology," draws upon newspapers, personal diaries, and Associated Press Files of the period.

Former Ambassador J. G. Parsons has made available some of his personal (but unclassified) papers dealing with his service in Laos and Washington.

The Scripps-Howard newspapers have supplied a copy of the articles by Jim G. Lucas, "Our Stake in Laos," which were released for publication on January 18, 1960.

Revelations about Laos also came from the Defense Department Study, *United States–Vietnam Relations, 1945–67,* which has been published in censored form by the U.S. Government Printing Office (12 vols., 1971) and by Beacon Press (4 vols., 1971). References in the text were to the documents and analyses printed in the *New York Times,* June 13–15, 1971, and have been cited as *New York Times Documents.*

Appendix

CHRONOLOGY OF MAJOR EVENTS RELATING TO LAOS, 1954–1971

The following chronology is designed to provide quick reference to the sequence and juxtaposition of events in Laos and Washington. Several possibly unfamiliar abbreviations have been used. These are:

DRV = Democratic Republic of Vietnam; that is, North Vietnam;

PL = Pathet Lao;

PM = Prime Minister;

PN = Phoumi Nosavan;

RLG = Royal Laotian Government;

RLP = Rally of the Laotian People;

RVN = Republic of Vietnam; that is, South Vietnam; and

SP = Souvanna Phouma.

Date	In Laos	In Washington and Elsewhere
1954		
Apr. 26– July 21		Geneva Conference
Aug.–		Decision to support Laos, give more aid
18	Yost named to head Legation	

332

Sept. 6		SEATO Pact signed at Manila, Laos a protocol state
18	Defense Min. Kou Voravong, strong for reconciliation with Pathet Lao (PL), assassinated in Vientiane	
Oct. 20	Souvanna Phouma (SP) resigns as PM	
Nov. 25	Katay Don Sasorith made PM (until 2/13/56)—southerner, for close ties with Thailand	
Oct.—		JCS recommends no force levels for Laos; State raises political considerations

1955

Jan.—	USOM begins operations; Embassy asks increase of army to 23,600	Defense agrees to State's military force proposals
—	Army pay increased	
·3	Katay begins talks with PL, broken off in April	
Feb. 27	Dulles visits Laos, supports offensive against PL	
Apr. 23		At Bandung, China and DRV pledge non-interference in Laos
June 6	PL demands new talks, delay of elections, end	

Date	In Laos	In Washington and Elsewhere
	of RLG troop movements	
July—	New RLG-PL talks	Increase in military aid, new economic aid agreement
5–20	Armed clashes reported; Thailand concerned	
Sept. 4	RLG-PL talks suspended	
Oct. 11	Katay and Souphanouvong meet in Rangoon, agree on Sam Neua cease-fire	
Nov. 4	RLG-PL talks again broken off	
Dec. 25	Elections held without PL participation in 10 provinces; none of 4 parties gets majority	
1956		
Jan.—	PEO established	State gets Defense agreement to increase army to 25,000
6	Neo Lao Hak Xat formed, urges united front	
Feb. 13	Katay resigns as PM	
Mar. 21	SP made PM (until 7/23/58) pledging reconciliation	
July—	Parsons arrives as Ambassador (until 3/58)	
Aug. 1	New talks between SP and Souphanouvong; mixed committees set up	US opposes coalition government

Aug. 19– *30*	RLG delegation visits Peking, Hanoi	
Dec.–	Discovery of import irregularities	US withholds aid to pressure administrative reforms
28	Agreement in principle on coalition government and supplementary elections	

1957

Jan.– Mar.	Katay, back from US, leads agitation against PL	
Mar.–	SP adjourns talks with PL	
Apr. 24		US, UK, France support RLG against PL
May 11	SP resigns after qualified vote of confidence	US increases aid
May– Aug.	Katay and leftist Bong Souvannavong fail to form govts; SP remains PM	US sees SP return as setback for West
Sept. 16	Talks with PL resumed	
Oct. 16	SP and Souphanouvong reach agreement	
Nov. 2	Agreements signed, 2 PL in cabinet	
18	Symbolic return of 2 provinces to King	US expresses concern about new govt.
Dec.–	Embassy recommends Booster Shot to aid rural areas	Decision for preelection crash program

1958

Jan. 12– 17		SP visits US, currency main issue

Date	In Laos	In Washington and Elsewhere
Feb. 18	Formal integration of 1,500 PL troops into RLG Army	
Mar. 5	ICC reports complete PL integration	
26	Smith arrives as Ambassador (until 7/60)	
May 4	Elections; PL and allies win 13 of 21 seats, get 32% of vote	US shocked and disturbed
7–8		Congressional hearings on aid
June 29	CDNI est. with CIA encouragement	
July 1		US suspends normal monthly aid payments (resumed 10/58)
20	SP gets ICC to adjourn sine die	
23	SP resigns after losing vote in Assembly	CIA gets State to press for inclusion of CDNI in cabinet
Aug. 18	Phoui Sananikone made PM (until 12/30/59) with 4 CDNI cabinet members	
Sept.–	Est. of relations with RVN and Taiwan	
Oct. 10	Kip devalued, other monetary reforms	Aid resumed
Dec. 15– 30	Border clashes with DRV	
1959		
Jan.–		New US aid granted

11	Phoui charges PL insurrection; Souphanouvong asks return of ICC	
15	Phoui gets 1-yr. emergency powers	
Mar.–	Hammarskjøld visit	US supports Phoui, sends Filipino military technicians
Mar.– Apr.		Congressional hearings on aid scandals
Apr.	RLG agrees to integrate PL officers	
May 11	PL, suspicious and angered, refuses	
17	One PL battalion accepts, other flees	
25	RLG calls this open rebellion, favors military solution	
June 15		House Committee report critical of aid
July–		Task Force 116 est. on Okinawa, ready for possible intervention in Asia
18–31	RLG reports attacks in Sam Neua	US decides on 100 more PEO technicians, increase in army to 29,-000
Aug. 4	State of emergency declared, message to UN	
6		US implicates USSR in fighting
23	Bridge washed out; PL advance feared	
24		Decision to increase aid

Date	In Laos	In Washington and Elsewhere
26– Sept. 7		Eisenhower trip to Europe
28		Emergency airlift of military supplies begun to Laos
30– Sept. 15	Heavy attacks reported in Sam Neua	
Sept. 4	RLG requests UN forces to meet Viet Minh attacks	US supports request, blames Communists
8		Security Council sends investigating group
7		Eisenhower returns from Europe, announces increased aid, rejects pressure for US intervention
15	UN group arrives, finds no evidence of DRV troops, much exaggeration of battle reports	Khrushchev visits US, Laos not discussed
Oct. 29	King Sisavang Vong dies	
Dec.—	Phoui announces intention to reshuffle cabinet, oust CDNI men	
17	Assembly votes to continue mandate past Dec. 25 expiration until April elections	
25	Phoumi Nosavan (PN) calls for Phoui's resignation, cordons his house with troops	CIA supports PN move
29	Katay dies of embolism, great blow to Phoui	

30	Phoui resigns	
31	Army takes over, claims rule until new government formed	

1960

Jan. 4	US, UK and French Ambassadors persuade King not to name PN as PM	
6	Kou Abhay named PM until elections	
Apr. 24	Elections held, rigged to bar PL and minimize RLP membership	CIA aids PN in rigging election
May 24	Souphanouvong escapes prison, fearing trial by PN	
June 2	Somsanith made PM (until Aug. 14)	
July 7	Brown arrives as Ambassador (until 7/62)	
Aug. 9	Cabinet in Luang Prabang; Kong-Le coup	State urges quick removal of Kong-Le, aid delayed
13	Assembly, surrounded by mob, votes out Somsanith	
14	Somsanith resigns; SP made PM	
15	PN forms counter-coup committee	
17	PN keeps investiture papers from King; SP takes power	
23	SP meets PN, agrees to further talks in Luang Prabang	

Date	In Laos	In Washington and Elsewhere
Aug. 30–31	In Luang Prabang, assembly approves new SP govt., PN as Vice Premier and Min. of Interior	
31	Kong-Le protests until persuaded by SP	
Sept.—	Air America support to PN increased; only aid to PN let through Thai blockade	US govt. temporizes, divided over which faction to support
Sept. 1	PN, told by US of plot against him, flies to Savannakhet, not Vientiane	
5	PN confers with Sarit, reestablishes counter-coup committee	
10	PN names Boun Oum head of new govt.	
18		Thai blockade begun
Oct. 1	SP says he will let USSR est. embassy	
7		US aid suspended (resumed Oct. 17)
12	Parsons and Irwin in Laos, demand SP and talks with PL, resume talks with PN, move govt. to Luang Prabang	
13	USSR Ambassador arrives	
17	SP agrees to let US arm PN	Aid resumed (but military aid still channeled

		through PM in Savan-nakhet)
28	USSR-Laos agree in principle on aid	
Nov. *10*		State and Defense agree SP must go, disagree on means
11	Luang Prabang troops switch to PN	
18	SP and Souphannouvong agree on coalition without PN	
23	PN starts move toward Vientiane; Brown requests aid to PN be stopped	
Dec. *4*	Start of USSR airlift	Defense says aid halted on Nov. 30 (resumed Dec. 19)
8	Abortive coup against Kong-Le	
9	PN nears Vientiane; SP flies to Phnom Penh	
10	Quinim Pholsena goes to Hanoi, gets Kong-Le–PL alliance and runs	
11	Some deputies in Savan-nakhet vote no confidence in SP govt.	
14	PN takes Vientiane after bloody fight	India asks return of ICC; US considers use of air force
15	Boun Oum named PM	US and Thailand extend immediate recognition
17		State blames USSR for Lao war
19		Aid to PN resumed
20–22		UK and USSR support return of ICC

Date	In Laos	In Washington and Elsewhere
28	USSR fires on US plane	Western allies reportedly split on policy
31	New govt. charges DRV invasion (later admitted as propaganda)	US considers deployment of various forces; carrier task force sent to Gulf of Siam

1961

Jan. 1	Sihanouk calls for 14-nation conference	
2		US increases readiness and airlift capability
3	SEATO finds no evidence of Communist intervention	US White Paper blames USSR but urges independent Laos
4	National Assembly in Vientiane approves Boun Oum govt.	
10–12		Herter confers with Amb. Menshikov
11		400 Special Forces troops sent from Okinawa; 6 AT-6s sent to PN
23		JFK sets up Laos Task Force
Feb. 19	US gets King to ask neighbors to visit Laos, confirm its neutrality	
20	SP meets his cabinet and Kong-Le on Plaine des Jarres	
Mar. 9		Task Force recommends increased military assistance

10	SP and PN meet in Phnom Penh, declare against foreign interference	
20–21		NSC meets, approves preliminary military moves
23		JFK news conference stresses importance of Laos; UK calls for Geneva Conference
26		JFK meets Macmillan, gets reluctant agreement for limited intervention
29	SEATO in Bangkok approves talks, not fighting	Harriman tells JFK of meeting with SP
Apr. 1		USSR accepts UK proposal for Geneva Conference
4		Soviet broadcast hints cease-fire
Apr. 10	SP agrees to visit US Apr. 19 (later cancels in huff), then visits Moscow, Peking, and Hanoi	
19		PEO formally changed to MAAG
24	Harriman in Laos for King's cremation	Invitations sent for May 12 Geneva Conference
27		Bitterly divided NSC meeting on intervention
May 3	Cease-fire proclaimed	
11	ICC confirms cease-fire; 3-sided military talks	US doubts cease-fire, delays Geneva Confer-

Date	In Laos	In Washington and Elsewhere
	on ceasefire begin at Ban Namone	ence; JFK authorizes covert teams in southeast Laos
16	LBJ reassures Thailand on cease-fire begin at on visit	Conference opens at Geneva
17	Agreement at Ban Namone on provisional coalition govt. to prepare elections	
19	Ceasefire violations and political discussions	
June 4		JFK-Khrushchev meet, agree on Laos
22	3 princes meet in Zurich, agree in principle on coalition govt.	
29–30		PN visits Washington; US decides to support SP
July—	PN forces increased to 60,000; US advisors to company level; also 18,000 Meo guerrillas	Restricted and informal meetings begin in Geneva
Sept.—	Ban Namone talks end, little accomplished	
—	Harriman meets SP in Rangoon, then PN, Boun Oum, and King; urges coalition	
26		JFK thru Salinger demands USSR good faith on Laos
Oct. 8	Princes agree on SP as head of coalition govt.	

21	PN meets US military men, gets encouragement, suspects US govt. divided	
27	New PN probe	

1962

Jan.—	PN claims Chinese and Soviet troops in Laos; Siege begins on Nam Tha; PN sends reinforcements, contrary to US advice	UN suspends cash grant to PN; Geneva talks suspended (resumed in June)
12		JFK warns Adzhubei of strong action if PL attacks continue
Feb.—		Harriman gets transfer of CIA man with PN
—		US again withholds cash grants at Harriman's insistence
13	Thailand moves troops to border	
16–19	SP confers with King and PN	
Mar. 6		Rusk-Thanat agreement reassures Thailand
24	Harriman meets PN and Sarit, presses coalition	
May 6	Fall of Nam Tha	
10		NSC meeting approves limited military moves
12		Another NSC meeting; announce 7th fleet readiness
15		Troops to Thailand as show of force

Date	In Laos	In Washington and Elsewhere
26	SP sets June 15 deadline for coalition	
June 11	Agreement on division of powers in coalition	
14		US resumes aid, recognizes SP govt.
July 3	Unger arrives as Ambassador (until 11/64)	
23		Geneva Conference approves neutralization declaration
26		SP visits Washington
30	US completes withdrawal of special troops from Thailand	
Aug.—		US begins aerial reconnaissance flights
Sept. 10	SP requests military supplies from US	
Oct. 7		US announces withdrawal of its forces from Laos, decides not to press DRV violation
Nov.—	Open quarreling among neutralist military factions	JFK warns Gromyko on DRV infiltration of Laos
8	US approves SP aid request	
Dec.—		US and USSR both give SP planes for airlift
1963		
Jan. 11		US defends relief flights
Feb. 11	Ketsana killed by leftist neutralist	

Mar. 30	New PL attacks on Kong-Le forces (cont'd until June)	US resumes arms aid to Kong-Le, first since 1960
		Vang Pao active in Kieng Khouang
Apr. 1	Quinim assassinated by rightists	
8	SP requests ICC; Souphanouvong leaves Vientiane, marking end of coalition	US urges SP condemn PL
14		Harriman says US won't get involved in the conflict
16	ICC tries to inspect, turned back by PL	
20		US presses USSR to restrain PL
22		NSC approves 7th fleet show of force
26		Harriman and Khrushchev agree on support for Geneva Accords
June–	SP denounces PL dependence on DRV for arms	US decides to supply T-28s
–	USSR ends airlift	
Aug.–		SP visits Moscow
Dec.–	Another assassination prompts more leftist departures from Vientiane	
21		McNamara report rules out cross-border operations, but plans expansion of "Hardnose" intelligence teams

Date	In Laos	In Washington and Elsewhere
1964		
Jan.–	New PN probe turned back	
Mar. 5		JCS order USAF air commando training advisory team to Thailand to train Lao pilots (had been proposed in December 1963)
10	NLHS conference produces 10-point program	
14	PN and Khanh agree to let RVN troops enter Laos in hot pursuit	
17		LBJ approves preparation of plans for bombing of DRV and for border raids in Laos
Apr. 17	SP confers with PN and Souphanouvong on demilitarization and neutralization of Luang Prabang	
19	Kouprasith attempts coup; Unger supports SP	US condemns coup
23	SP resumes limited control of government	
May 16	Kong-Le driven off Plaine des Jarres	
19	US begins recon flights over southern Laos	

21	US begins flights over northern Laos	
22	Thailand mobilizes border provinces	
–		Thais agree to use of bases by US for recon, search & rescue, and air attacks
June 1–2		High-level US conference in Honolulu decides against intervention, for use of US "civilian" and Thai air support
4	6 Ambassadors meet in prelude to int'l conf.	
6	US recon plane shot down	US decides to hit PL positions
9	SP asks halt in US flights	US suspends flights "at least 2 days"
14		US resumes retaliation on PL; pilots could hit targets of opportunity
19		US warns Asian Communists to leave neighbors alone or face war with US
July–		US plans ground and air assaults with RVN; ground controllers brought into Laos
–	Operation Triangle clears Vientiane–Luang Prabang road	
Aug. 1	Thai planes hit DRV villages	

Date	In Laos	In Washington and Elsewhere
28		SP cancels conference in Paris, says Souphanouvong's views too divergent
Sept. 10		LBJ approves discussing RVN air and ground operations with Laos
Oct. 14	US begins flying "cover missions" for Laos aircraft, which bomb trails at US request	
Nov. 25	Sullivan arrives as Ambassador (until 4/69)	
Dec. 1		LBJ approves first phase of air war—US strikes in Laos
—		SEACORD meetings begun
14		Systematic bombing of northern Laos begun
1965		
Jan. 31	Army officers attempt coup	US supports SP, promises no aid to PN
Mar. 20		Bombing of trails in southern Laos begun
6	PN flees to Thailand	
July 18	Elections held, restricted suffrage, boycotted by PL	
1966		
Jan.–June	RLG forces lose Sam Neua, recapture parts in June	

July– *Aug.*	RLG captures Nam Bac region north of LP for first time in several years
Sept. 17	Budget fails to pass assembly; new elections called
Oct.–	US Forward Air Controllers put into Laos
—	Bombing policy changes: more US aircraft participate; enemy-held villages bombed
21	AF Gen. Thao Ma bombs army HQ; attempted coup fails; several pilots and planes flee to Thailand
Nov.	Kong-Le resignation announced
—	US advisors in the field with Lao

1967

Jan. 1	Elections held, SP slate wins	
Jan.–Dec.	No heavy military action	
Oct. 16		Kittikachorn says Thailand is prepared to send troops to Laos if requested
Oct. 31	PL claim Thai troops enter Laos	
Dec. 26	SP charges "general offensive" by DRV; most fighting in south	

Date	In Laos	In Washington and Elsewhere
1968		
Jan. 14	Nam Bac lost with heavy casualties	
–		Close support missions approved
Feb. 23– 25		MACV recommends invasion of Laos to disrupt trails
Mar. 11	Phou Pha Thi falls	
–	Enemy forces surround Saravane, Thakhek, and Attopeu	
31		Partial bombing halt over North Vietnam; planes shifted to regular bombing over Laos; US planes outnumber Laotian for first time
Sept.–	Chinese road-building crews move into northern Laos	
Oct. 31		US bombing halt over all DRV, shifted to trails in Laos
Nov. 1	PL announce new program, keeping monarchy	
1969		
Jan. 28		USSR condemns bombing raids
Feb. 4	Soviet Ambassador carries SP letter to Souphanouvong	

Mar.–	PL and DRV troops capture key airstrips in north	
10		Laird admits some border crossings
Apr.–	RLG offensive against Plaine des Jarres; Xieng Khouang bombed; rte 13 to south cut, cities supplied by air	US increases bombing in north; refugee numbers soar
May–	Soviet and DRV Ambassadors offer peace talks on condition of halt in US bombing of trails; SP refuses under US pressure	
June 27	PL and DRV offensive captures Muong Soui for first time since 1964	
July 15	Godley arrives as Ambassador	US approves first air strikes and logistical support for RLG attack on Plaine des Jarres
Aug.– *Sept.*	Meo soldiers, with Thais and US support, capture Plaine for first time since 1964; also capture PL HQ in south at Muong Phine	Further increases in US bombing; fewer restrictions on pilots
Oct.–		Symington Subcommittee hearings
Dec.–		Congress approves amendment prohibiting funds for US ground combat opera-

Date	In Laos	In Washington and Elsewhere
		tions in Laos and Thailand
1970		
Jan.—	Evacuation of Plaine des Jarres	
Feb. 17		US sends first B-52 raid against Plaine
21	Fall of last RLG position on Plaine	
Mar. 6	PL offer 5-point plan for settlement	Nixon statement on Laos
16		USSR rejects US call for consultations
18	Sam Thong falls, recaptured March 30	Generals replace Sihanouk in Cambodia
Apr. 28	Fall of Attopeu	Nixon approves US invasion of Cambodia
June 9	Fall of Saravane	
6		Hannah admits AID runs cover for CIA in Laos
—	US begins training Cambodian forces in southern Laos	
Aug.—		JCS presses for invasion of Laos; clandestine operations approved instead
19	PL charge US units sent into Laos	US admits clandestine forays
Oct. 29	RLG accepts PL formula for peace talks	
Nov.—	PL/DRV dry season offensive captures several RLG bases	US again weighs invasion

	throughout the country	
21		Large scale strikes on North Vietnam; Son Tay raid
Dec.	Chances for talks collapse	Heavier bombing of trails
1971		
Jan.–	Thailand reportedly sends several battalions into southern panhandle	
19		US admits helicopter gunships give direct support to RLG ground troops
Feb. 7	RVN troops enter Laos with US air and logistical support; SP issues mild protest, puts primary blame on DRV	
12	RLG declares state of emergency	
Mar. 23	RVN troops withdraw from Laos	
May 16	PL/DRV forces capture Bolovens Plateau	
June 7		Secret Senate session on Laos.
July–Sept.	RLG forces recapture Plaine des Jarres and some areas in south	

Aug. 9	State Department admits US support for Thai troops, says US can "withhold compliance" with 1962 accords because of DRV violations
Oct. 4	Senate approves Symington amendment limiting US expenditures in Laos to $350 million in 1972
Nov.–	MiGs from DRV begin operations over Laos
Dec. 20	Plaine des Jarres falls to PL/DRV forces
28	Paksong falls to PL/DRV

1972

Jan. 2	Elections won by newcomers, favoring neutralism

Index